The Emergence of Roman Catholic Medical Ethics in North America

An Historical—Methodological—Bibliographical Study

David F. Kelly

The Edwin Mellen Press
New York and Toronto

Texts and Studies in Religion, Volume Three

Library of Congress Cataloging Number 79-66372

ISBN 0-88946-878-8

Texts and Studies in Religion ISBN 0-88946-976-8

Printed in the United States of America

To

Louis Janssens

PREFACE

This preface is not an introduction to the subject matter of our study. The introduction follows in a few pages. The purpose of the preface is to offer some suggestions to the reader as to how she or he might best make use of the book, according to her or his reasons for reading it.

The book will be of interest both to those who seek a detailed knowledge of the development of Roman Catholic North American medical ethics and to those whose focus is solely, or especially, on one or another of its aspects. For the former reader, the normal reading process will provide the detail sought. For the latter reader, it may be helpful to know that this work is designed to permit selective use. The table of contents and the introduction will point out the relevant sections. The background, definitional, and methodological sections form somewhat independent essays. There are specific analyses of individual works; there is also a synthetic systematic analysis of these works in the conclusion sections of chapter two, in chapter three, and in the first parts of chapters four and five. This synthetic analysis, while based on the individual works described elsewhere, can be read by itself.

Some readers may be interested in only one or a few specific works which the book considers, or in works of a specific period. For them a set of bibliographical apparatuses has been added. There is a chronological listing of the primary bibliography on pages 7-12, and a series of lists and indices at the end of the book. Together these should enable the reader to locate by type, by author, or by date the places in the text where works are discussed.

Among the many who have been of help in the preparation of this study, I would like to mention some specifically. Professor Herbert Richardson has advised me in this
project from its first conception to its final completion.
He has been especially helpful in clarifying difficult questions, in making organizational suggestions, and in pointing
out relationships which I otherwise would have missed.

Among my many other teachers, I want to acknowledge
particularly Professor Louis Janssens of the Catholic University of Louvain. His approach to moral theology, and the
sparkle in his eye, have been the inspiration for much of
the thematic approach in this study. His work is exact, ex-
citing, and humane.

Others have contributed to the ideas and to the process. At St. Michael's College in Toronto, discussions with
Professors Gregory Baum, Joanne Dewart, John Gallagher,
Arthur Gibson, and Joseph O'Connell have given me opportunity to study and debate the questions discussed in this book.
Professor Walter Principe helped with bibliographical suggestions.

A work of this sort involves much library research and
an inordinate number of requests to librarians for strange
and out-of-print books. Mrs. Margaret McGrath, reference
librarian at St. Michael's, has been of immense help in
tracking these down. She and Mrs. Agnes Breen, former cir-
culation librarian, who died recently, have also been of
help in allowing a flexible library loan policy during my
research. Similarly, Sister Ellen Waddell of St. Thomas
Seminary library in Kenmore, Washington, let me take un-
needed books for years, and arranged the sale to me of some
duplicate holdings. Sister Marie Michael of St. Augustine's
Seminary library in Toronto and Dorothy Adams at St. Vincent's School of Nursing in Worcester, Massachusetts, also
extended long-term borrowing privileges, permitting me to

keep books not in demand at the library for lengths of time exceeding the normal loan period, often for years. Without this flexibility my work simply could not have been done.

I am especially grateful to Mrs. Una Crist, who not only laid out and typed this manuscript, but who has also maintained interest in the project and offered helpful suggestions.

Finally, and most importantly, I thank my friends who supported me while I wrote it.

David F. Kelly
Rochester, New York

August 1979

CONTENTS

    5. Gerald Kelly and the "Ethical and
        Religious Directives"......................... 170
    6. Some Manuals of the Early 1950's.............. 181
    7. Jules Paquin: An Exception.................... 193
    8. Five Works in 1956............................ 200
    9. Other Works of the Late 1950's and
        Early 1960's.................................. 212

    Conclusion... 219

CHAPTER THREE   INTRODUCTION TO THE THEOLOGICAL
METHODOLOGY OF THE DISCIPLINE......................... 229

    1. Two Dominant Modalities: Physicalism
        and Ecclesiastical Positivism................. 230
    2. Sovereignty and Suffering: Two
        Subordinate Principles........................ 232
    3. The Use of Scripture.......................... 235
    4. Theology and Natural Ethics................... 236

CHAPTER FOUR   EARLY WORKS (1897-1940): THE
DEVELOPMENT OF PHYSICALISM........................... 244

    Part One   Physicalism in the Double Effect
    Framework.. 244
    1. The Double Effect Principle and
        Physicalism................................... 247
    2. Double Effect as General Framework............ 259
    3. Examples of Double Effect Physicalism
        in Medical Ethics............................. 264

    Part Two   The Literature of the Early Period...... 274
    1. Coppens and Klarmann: Developing
        Physicalist Categories........................ 279
    2. Austin O'Malley: Physicalism and
        Ecclesiastical Positivism..................... 291
    3. Burke and Finney: Strict Physicalism.......... 299
    4. T. Lincoln Bouscaren: An Important
        Physicalist Specification..................... 305

CHAPTER FIVE   LATER WORKS (1940-1960): THE
SHIFT TOWARDS ECCLESIASTICAL POSITIVISM.............. 311

    Part One   Ecclesiastical Positivism.............. 311

    Part Two   The Literature of the Later Period...... 321
    1. Alphonsus Bonnar: The Importance of
        Church Authority.............................. 321
    2. Some Works of the Early 1940's................ 324
    3. Bert Cunningham: An Early Challenge to
        Physicalism................................... 332
    4. Physicalism and Positivism in Charles
        McFadden...................................... 341

INTRODUCTION

The past ten years have witnessed a widespread increased interest in medico-moral topics in North America.
The literature which has appeared during this decade is truly vast. A number of research centers for investigating the
ethical dilemmas of biology and medicine have been founded,
courses in bioethics are popular on college campuses, and
medical schools are searching for new ways to integrate such
courses into their basic curricula. It has been estimated
that in the period from 1969 to 1973 the number of persons
teaching medical ethics in the United States increased from
a mere handful to over 300, and the number is rapidly growing.[1]

The rapidly developing field of contemporary bioethics
has not coalesced into any easily defineable discipline.
The topics which it investigates are many, and its limits
are hard to determine. Its formal definition and purpose
are not clearly established. No one methodology has emerged
to be predominant.

The recently developed "new" medical ethics is not without ancestry, however. Its principle precursor is the highly developed and explicitly self-conscious discipline of
medical ethics within Roman Catholic moral theology. Though
the new bioethics of the seventies does not speak precisely
the same language, investigate exactly the same topics, em-
ploy the same methodology, or arrive at the same conclusions,

---

[1]Callahan, *Recent Activities; 1973,* p. 3. (Data not
given in the footnotes, such as the author's full name, complete title and subtitle, and publication data, are found in
the general bibliography. Items are listed there alphabetically. The footnote form always gives the correct alphabetical word first--generally the author's last name.)

it is cognizant of the role that Roman Catholic medical
ethics has played in its development.[2]

---

[2]Other precursors could also be suggested. One is
Protestant medical ethics. With a few exceptions, however,
there was almost no Protestant contribution to the field
prior to the last decade. When Joseph Fletcher wrote his
pioneering work *Morals and Medicine* in 1954, he said that
"there is already a well tuned one [theology of medicine],
both explicit and implicit, in Catholic moral theology under
the headings of the Fifth, Sixth, and Ninth Commandments.
To my knowledge nothing of this kind has been undertaken by
non-Catholics as yet" (Fletcher, *Morals and Medicine,* p.
xix). And again he states: "Very probably the most important observation to make here is that Catholic literature on
the morals of medical care is both extensive and painstaking
in its technical detail, while Protestant and Jewish literature is practically non-existent. . . . Perhaps there is
even genuine hope in Catholic circles that others may take
these matters seriously" (*Ibid.*, pp. 16-17).
     Some Protestant works before the last ten or so years
can be cited. The most important is Joseph Fletcher's
Morals and Medicine (1954). John Oliver's *Psychiatry and
Mental Health* (1932) includes some medical ethical analysis.
Willard Sperry's *The Ethical Basis of Medical Practice* (1950)
is more an extended essay congratulating the medical profession on its high standards than a study of ethical issues.
A collection of essays edited by Edmunds and Scorer first
appeared in 1958 entitled *Ideals in Medicine: A Christian
Approach to Medical Practice*. With the exception of Fletcher's work, no Protestant work attempted any real medical
ethical study prior to the recent renewal of interest. Over
the past decade, however, Protestant authors writing from
specifically Protestant perspectives have contributed widely
and significantly to medical ethical discussion.
     Contributions from non-Christian religious sources are
also sparse, at least in their direct effect on the main
body of literature. Jewish medical ethics is described in
Jakobovits, *Jewish Medical Ethics*, and in Feldman, *Birth
Control in Jewish Law*. A brief discussion of Islamic medical ethics is found in Levey, *Medical Ethics of Medieval
Islam*. Some contributions of the Vedic literature are
studied in Singhal and Gaur, *Surgical Ethics in the Āyurveda*.
For a brief overview of medicine in various Eastern and
Western religions, including some ethics, see Barton, *Religious Doctrine and Medical Practice*.
     With the exception of the codes of the medical associa-
tions and the related literature, to be discussed in part
three of chapter one, contributions from non-religious
(philosophical ethics) sources are lacking, though one vast

The present study is an investigation of the emergence
of Roman Catholic medical ethics in North America as a developed and self-conscious discipline. Our purpose is to
present a detailed and complete compilation of the literature which comprised the field and to describe and evaluate
its definition and theological methodology. We will concentrate on works written during the period from the beginning
of the twentieth century to the Second Vatican Council
(1962-1965), the period during which Roman Catholic medical
ethics in North America evolved to establish itself as a
highly sophisticated discipline with a clearly defined definition and methodology. We shall also trace the discipline's
roots from earlier periods in the history of moral theology
and medical ethics, and offer a brief critique based on recent (post-Vatican II) developments in the field.

Our study will be a "special" rather than a "general"
history of the field.[3] The latter would require an investigation of North American Catholic medical ethics wherever it
occurred, even incidentally. It would demand a thorough
study of all works concerned with the relationship of medicine and theology, demonology, parapsychology, ascetical
theology, faith-healing, religion and mental health, and so
on. A "special" history of the field, on the other hand,
will limit itself to those works which are explicitly designed as works in medical ethics (though perhaps a different word might be used). It will limit itself to works
which are intended to treat of moral problems connected with
medicine. That our study is a "special" history in the
above sense does not mean, however, that it is a study of

European work can be cited: Moll, *Ärztliche Ethik*. Secular
philosophical contributions to contemporary bioethics have
been numerous.

[3]The distinction is made by Albert Niedermeyer in his
Allgemeine Pastoralmedizin, II, 42 ff.

any one particular medical ethical issue. Ours is a generic
study in that its purpose is to analyze the basic trends in
the developing definition and theological methodology of the
discipline. We will thus emphasize works which present
themselves as general texts or manuals more than works which
treat of one or another particular topic within the field.
The latter are not excluded, of course, and will be examined
in detail when they are found to be significant for the general development of the discipline.

In chapter one we will locate and survey the roots of
Roman Catholic medical ethics in North America. By means of
a brief overview of the general tradition of Catholic moral
theology and of the relationship between religion and medicine from the beginning of the Christian era to the twentieth century, together with a description of the codes of
ethics of the medical profession, we shall provide the background necessary for describing the development of our discipline during its period of emergence from 1900 to 1960.

In chapter two we will gather together the literature
which comprises the emergent phase of North American Roman
Catholic medical ethics, that is, the works written from the
beginning of the present century to the Second Vatican Council. A list of these works is given at the end of this introduction. They constitute the body of literature which is
the chief subject matter of our study. Our purpose here
will be twofold: first, we wish to compile the bibliography
of the discipline, a task which has not yet been accomplished in any detail; second, we propose to describe the
process whereby the discipline evolved to have a generally
accepted name and definition. Though many of the works are
quite similar, it is our purpose to offer here a complete
compilation together with a description of their formal and
material definition in order to catalogue the basic bibliography and to list the topics which constituted the field.

We will describe how the purpose of medical ethics evolved
and how authors came to include some topics and eliminate
others. We will find that the rubric for the field came to
be *Medical Ethics*, and that the discipline came to define
itself rather precisely as the moral theological investigation of the actual daily professional practice of medical
personnel.

In chapters three, four, and five we will turn our attention to the theological methodology operative in the
discipline. We are interested here in describing the general patterns according to which theological principles were
applied to medical ethical issues. We will demonstrate the
significance of two general modalities of application of
theological principles: physicalism and ecclesiastical positivism. We will analyze each of these in detail, and show
how they came to determine the methodology of Catholic medical ethics. In chapter three we will present an introduction to the basic theoretical questions involved. Chapter
four will describe the modality of physicalism, and trace
its development during the early period of the discipline
from 1900 to 1940, the period during which this approach
was dominant. In chapter five we will turn to the later
period, 1940-1960, where we will discover the growing importance of the role played by ecclesiastical authority. We
will describe the modality of ecclesiastical positivism and
show its application to medical ethical topics.

Our study of the emergent period of Catholic medical
ethics will reveal the influence of modern secular medicine
on both the definition and methodology of the field. We
will see how Catholic medical moralists applied scientific
ethical criteria to medical procedures in a manner which
enabled them to arrive at universally applicable conclusions based on cause-and-effect analysis.

The final chapter will offer a brief critique of the

discipline in its emergent, pre-Vatican II phase, by noting
some recent developments in the field. Here we will attempt
to set the definition and methodology of the discipline into
the perspective of current thinking in bio-medical ethics.

No history of Roman Catholic medical ethics in North
America has been written. The Second Vatican Council and
the radical definitional and methodological critique which
accompanied it led to significant changes in the discipline.
This development provides an historical and critical perspective from which to view the field in its emergent phase.
A critical historical survey of this important body of literature will offer today's ethicists a perspective from
which to analyze their own approaches to medical ethics.

Chronological List of Basic Works

The following list includes North American Roman Catholic works in medical ethics written during the emergent phase of the discipline from the turn of the century to the Second Vatican Council. They constitute the body of literature which is the chief subject matter of our study. The list includes the various editions of each work and length in pages. Several non-North American works of major influence are included, and noted by an asterisk. Full publication data can be found in the general bibliography.

1878 *Carl Capellmann. *Pastoral Medicine.* 262pp.

1897 Charles Coppens. *Moral Principles and Medical Practice: The Basis of Medical Jurisprudence.* 1st, 2nd, 3rd eds. 222pp.

1904 Alexander E. Sanford. *Pastoral Medicine: A Handbook for Catholic Clergy.* 234pp.

1905 Andrew Klarmann. *The Crux of Pastoral Medicine: The Perils of Embryonic Man.* 1st ed., approx. 160pp.; 2nd ed., rev., 221pp.

   Coppens. *Moral Principles.* 4th ed., rev. 227pp.

   Sanford. *Pastoral Medicine.* 2nd ed., rev. Walter M. Drum. 332pp.

1906 Austin O'Malley and James J. Walsh. *Essays in Pastoral Medicine.* 363pp.

1907 Klarmann. *The Crux of Pastoral Medicine.* 3rd ed., same as 2nd. 221pp.

1912 Klarmann. *The Crux of Pastoral Medicine.* 4th ed., rev. 282pp.

1915 Klarmann. *The Crux of Pastoral Medicine.* 5th ed., rev. 299pp.

1919 Austin O'Malley. *The Ethics of Medical Homicide and Mutilation.* 273pp.

1920   Henry S. Spalding. *Talks to Nurses: The Ethics of
       Nursing.* 197pp.

1921   Michael P. Bourke. *Some Medical Ethical Problems
       Solved.* 24pp.

       Charles Coppens and Henry S. Spalding. *Moral Princi-
       ples and Medical Practice.* New ed., rev. 320pp.

1922   Edward F. Burke. *Acute Cases in Moral Medicine.*
       136pp.

       Patrick A. Finney. *Moral Problems in Hospital Prac-
       tice: A Practical Handbook.* 208pp. Numerous
       "editions" and reprints over succeeding years are
       virtually identical.

       O'Malley. *The Ethics of Medical Homicide and Mutil-
       ation.* 2nd ed. ("3rd printing"), rev. 285pp.

1926   Medicus (pseud.). *Medical Essays: Compiled from Var-
       ious Sources.* 666pp.

       Hervé Trudel. *Éléments de morale médicale.* Approx.
       60pp.

1928   Medicus. *Medical Essays.* 2nd ed., rev. 683pp.

       Trudel. *Éléments de morale médicale.* 2nd ed., rev.
       60pp.

1929   Edward Francis Garesché. *Ethics and the Art of Con-
       duct for Nurses.* 341pp.

1931   Medicus. *Medical Essays.* 3rd ed., rev. 822pp.

1932   Trudel. *Éléments de morale médicale.* 3rd ed., same
       2nd. 60pp.

1933   T. Lincoln Bouscaren. *Ethics of Ectopic Operations.*
       191pp.

1935   Thomas Verner Moore. *Principles of Ethics.* 381pp.

1937   *Alphonsus Bonnar. *The Catholic Doctor.* 181pp.

       Moore. *Principles of Ethics.* 2nd ed., rev. 387pp.

1938   Leo Gregory Fink, ed. *Graduate Nurses: Symposium of
       Ethical Inspiration.* 306pp.

1939 *Bonnar. *The Catholic Doctor.* 2nd ed., rev. 184pp.

      Moore. *Principles of Ethics.* 3rd ed., same as 2nd.
      387pp.

1940 S. A. La Rochelle and C. T. Fink. *Précis de morale
      médicale pour infirmières, médecins et prêtres.*
      314pp.

      Hervé Trudel and Armand Perrier. *Éléments de morale
      médicale.* 4th ed., rev. 98pp.

1941 S. A. La Rochelle and C. T. Fink. *Handbook of Medical
      Ethics for Nurses, Physicians, and Priests.* Trans.
      M. E. Poupore. 363pp. Numerous "editions" and re-
      prints over succeeding years are virtually identical.

1943 Moore. *Principles of Ethics.* 4th ed., rev. 405pp.

1944 Bert Joseph Cunningham. *The Morality of Organic
      Transplantation.* 120pp.

      Josaphat-Zéphirin Dufort. *Application de l'éthique
      professionnelle.* 330pp.

      Bouscaren. *Ethics of Ectopic Operations.* 2nd ed.,
      rev. 179pp.

      Garesché. *Ethics and the Art of Conduct for Nurses.*
      2nd ed., rev. 358pp.

1946 Charles J. McFadden. *Medical Ethics for Nurses.*
      356pp.

1947 Joseph B. McAllister. *Ethics: With Special Applica-
      tion to the Nursing Profession.* 442pp.

1948 William Kevin Glover. *Artificial Insemination among
      Human Beings: Medical, Legal, and Moral Aspects.*
      175pp.

1949 Gerald Kelly. *Medico-Moral Problems.* Part I. 56pp.

      Timothy P. O'Connell. *Morality in Medicine.* 52pp.

      Catholic Hospital Association of the United States and
      Canada. *Ethical and Religious Directives for Catho-
      lic Hospitals, 1949.* 11pp.

      McFadden. *Medical Ethics.* 2nd ed., rev. (title
      changed from *Medical Ethics for Nurses* to *Medical
      Ethics*). 438pp.

Charles J. McFadden. *Reference Manual for Medical
Ethics.* 88pp.

1950 Kelly. *Medico-Moral Problems.* Part II. 45pp.

1951 Bernard J. Ficarra. *Newer Ethical Problems in Medicine and Surgery.* 168pp.

Frederick L. Good and Otis F. Kelly. *Marriage, Morals
and Medical Ethics.* 202pp.

Kelly. *Medico-Moral Problems.* Part III. 45pp.

1952 John P. Kenny. *Principles of Medical Ethics.* 208pp.

Kelly. *Medico-Moral Problems.* Part IV. 52pp.

1953 *Peter Flood, ed. *New Problems in Medical Ethics.*
Vol. I. 259pp.

McFadden. *Medical Ethics.* 3rd ed., rev. 465pp.

O'Connell. *Morality in Medicine.* 2nd ed., same as
1st. 52pp.

1954 Catholic Hospital Association of Canada. *A Workshop
on Medico-Moral Problems.* 178pp.

*Flood, ed. *New Problems in Medical Ethics.* Vol. II.
303pp.

Kelly. *Medico-Moral Problems.* Part V. 51pp.

1955 Jules Paquin. *Morale et médecine.* 489pp.

Alvin Werth and Clement S. Mihanovich. *Papal Pronouncements on Marriage and the Family.* 189pp.

Catholic Hospital Association of Canada. *Moral Code.*
17pp.

Catholic Hospital Association of the United States and
Canada. *Ethical and Religious Directives.* 2nd ed.,
rev. 18pp.

McAllister. *Ethics: With Special Application to the
Nursing Profession.* 2nd ed., rev. 423pp.

1956 Patrick A. Finney and Patrick O'Brien. *Moral Problems
in Hospital Practice: A Practical Handbook.* 321pp.

Edward J. Hayes, Paul J. Hayes, and Dorothy Ellen Kelly. *Moral Handbook of Nursing.* 180pp.

Edwin F. Healy. *Medical Ethics.* 440pp.

Nicholas Lohkamp. *The Morality of Hysterectomy Operations.* 206pp.

Thomas J. O'Donnell. *Morals in Medicine.* 281pp.

*Flood, ed. *New Problems in Medical Ethics.* Vol. III. 299pp.

McFadden. *Medical Ethics.* 4th ed., rev. 491pp.

1957 Edgar Godin and J. P. E. O'Hanley. *Hospital Ethics: A Commentary on the Moral Code of Catholic Hospitals.* 204pp.

Paquin. *Morale et médecine.* 2nd ed., rev. 504pp.

1958 John Joseph Shinners. *The Morality of Medical Experimentation on Living Human Subjects in the Light of Recent Papal Pronouncements.* 109pp.

Kelly. *Medico-Moral Problems.* Revised one volume edition. 375pp.

1959 Thomas Verner Moore and Gregory Stevens. *Principles of Ethics.* 5th ed., rev. 282pp.

O'Connell. *Morality in Medicine.* 3rd ed., rev. 53pp.

O'Donnell. *Morals in Medicine.* 2nd ed., rev. 398pp.

1960 *John Marshall. *Medicine and Morals.* 140pp.

Papal Teachings: The Human Body. 394pp.

*Flood, ed. *New Problems in Medical Ethics.* Vol. IV. 225pp.

Paquin. *Morale et médecine.* 3rd ed., rev. 510pp.

1961 *Albert Niedermeyer. *Compendium of Pastoral Medicine* (1953). Trans. Fulgence Buonanno. 492pp.

McFadden. *Medical Ethics.* 5th ed., rev. 441pp.

1962 William L. Wolkovich. *Norms of Conduct for Pharmacists.* 159pp.

Kenny. *Principles of Medical Ethics.* 2nd ed., rev.
274pp.

1963 *Papal Teachings: Matrimony.* 617pp.

CHAPTER ONE

HISTORICAL BACKGROUND TO THE DISCIPLINE

North American Roman Catholic medical ethics finds its immediate roots in the general moral theological tradition of Catholic moralists and in the discipline known as pastoral medicine, the field studying the medical, moral, and pastoral dimensions of the interface of medicine and theology. Two other fields of study also enter into its emergence. These are medical jurisprudence, the study of the legal aspects of medical practice, and "medical ethics" in the intra-professional sense of that rubric, the promulgation and explanation of professional codes of conduct and etiquette for medical personnel. It is the task of this chapter to locate and survey these roots.

The chapter is divided into three sections. The first is an overview of the history of Roman Catholic moral theology, not to write a new history of the field, but in order to discover in the general tradition the larger groupings of medical-moral issues.

The second section is a study of pastoral medicine, the most important of the sources for our discipline. The third is a brief description of the professional codes of ethics of the medical associations ("medical ethics"), and of medical jurisprudence.

Part One

The General Tradition of Moral Theology

Roman Catholic medical ethics emerged as a specialized subdivision of the general tradition of Catholic moral the-

ology. In this and the following chapters we will have occasion to note how the discipline gradually coalesced in response to the developing professionalization of medicine.
As the science of medicine became more and more self-de-
fining, topics of medical ethical significance which had
previously been scattered here and there in the literature
of moral theology were gathered together. In this section
we shall locate those topics in the general moral theological literature, and, in so doing, demonstrate the emergence
of various organizational rubrics for selecting and grouping
medical ethical topics within the general tradition. We
will note especially the creation of a special section in
the manuals of moral theology concerned with the duties and
obligations of physicians. This section, which treats of
medical ethical issues, emerges along with the professionalization of medicine, and signals the advent of the specific
area of moral theology which is today known generally as
Medical Ethics.

Historians of moral theology usually divide the history
of the discipline into three general periods: 1) the pre-
scholastic period, ending around the eleventh or twelfth
century; 2) the scholastic period, ending with the Council
of Trent (1545-1563); and 3) the modern period, from Trent
to the present.[1] Recent historians may subdivide this last,

---

[1]See, e.g., Prümmer, *Manuale,* I, 9; Iorio, *Theologia
moralis,* who calls the first period the "aetas infantiae,"
the second the "aetas adolescentiae," and the third the
"aetas perfecta" (I, 3); Murphy, Vereecke, and Farraher,
"Moral Theology, History of"; Ziegler, "Moraltheologie,
Geschichte"; Slater, *A Short History;* Zalba, *Theologiae
moralis summa,* I, 17-29 (Zalba's divisions are somewhat different, using the *Decretals* of Gratian [1139] and the end
of the 17th century as dividing points); Merkelbach, *Summa,*
I, 16-18; Aertnys-Damen, *Theologia moralis,* I, xvix-xxxvii
(the authors call the periods "patristica positiva,"
"scholastica-systematica," and "casuistica"); Koch-Preuss,
Handbook, I, 41-73; Lanza, *Theologia moralis,* I, 25-38;
Tanquerey, *Synopsis,* II, 11-35.

adding a fourth, or contemporary period.[2] Since it is our
purpose here to investigate the *roots* of twentieth century
medical ethics, it will not be necessary to discuss the contemporary period. The traditional triple division will be
adequate for us. Nor is it our purpose to enter into a discussion concerning the various periods, or to investigate in
detail the reciprocal influences of the individual schools
or "systems" of moral theology. For such a study one may
consult the various histories of moral theology.[3]

---

[2] Dublanchy, "Morale"; Häring, *Law of Christ,* I, 3-33.
(Häring uses nine divisions, which correspond to subdivisions of the original three.)

[3] No truly adequate history of the discipline has yet
been written, perhaps because of the enormity of the task.
There are studies of individual periods. There are historical overviews written as introductions to many of the moral
manuals. The encyclopedia articles cited in the preceding footnotes are generally inadequate. The *DTC* article
suffers from the author's desire to accentuate certain specific issues rather than present a general history
(Dublanchy, "Morale"). The *NCE* articles are better, and do
give a general overview, but are of insufficient detail
(Murphy, Vereecke, and Farraher, "Moral Theology"). Häring's
survey in his *Law of Christ* (I, 3-33) is good, but lacks any
detail or critical apparatus. Slater's *Short History* is
both short and apologetic, but does accentuate some of the
important moments in the development of the tradition.
George Regan's 1971 work includes an historical survey which,
though also short, is not apologetic and highlights the
principal movements and moments in the discipline's history
(*New Trends,* pp. 17-35). Among the overviews in the manuals,
that of Koch-Preuss is among the better ones: it contains an
adequate listing of primary sources and is written in English (Koch-Preuss, *Handbook*). Prümmer's synopsis is inadequate, among other reasons because it emphasizes the Dominicans and neglects the Jesuits, whose influence on the moral
manual tradition is of great importance. But Prümmer does
give a remarkably extensive list of moralists and canonists
over the centuries with a few words about each (Prümmer,
Manuale, I, xii-xl). A similar list is found in Ferreres,
who designates the authors according to the moral "system"
(probabilism, tutiorism, etc.) that each adhered to
(Ferreres, *Compendium,* I, xx-li). A history of the discipline is available in German, written by Rudolph Hofmann in
his *Moraltheologische Erkenntnis- und Methodenlehre,* pp.

In this section we will describe how the moral topics later included in pastoral medicine and Catholic medical ethics are selected and organized within the general tradition according to certain organizational rubrics. As the discipline of moral theology develops, certain topics come to form its content. Here we are interested in finding out how and why certain issues relevant to medical ethics are included. In later sections we will see that the very structure of the moral treatises of the various periods in the history of the general tradition plays an important role in pre-selecting and grouping topics for discussion in works of pastoral medicine and medical ethics.

In the pre-scholastic period (up to the twelfth century) the selecting rubric is pastoral application. At first there is no attempt at organization. Later the topics are organized in a primitive fashion in the *libri penitentiales* for pastoral application to the penitent. These early moralists are not so much interested in the ideas themselves, or in discussing or questioning their rightness or wrongness, as they are in solving practical confessional problems and in urging Christians to lead moral lives.

The scholastic period (from the twelfth century to the mid-sixteenth) begins the process of systematization. In discussing this period we will describe how moral works begin to be organized according to the commandments and virtues, the sacraments, and the obligations of various states in life. We will see that special recognition is given in some moral treatises to the ethical dilemmas of the physician. We will show how these rubrics come to be the gathering points for the content of medical ethical discussion.

14-53. His work is concerned, however, more with specifically methodological and epistemological questions than with historical ones, and his historical section is sparse.

The modern period (from Trent to the present) continues and establishes the organizational methods begun in the
scholastic era. The commandments, virtues, sacraments, and
states of life come more and more to determine the selection
of topics for moral discourse, and to determine their grouping, and hence their inclusion within subdisciplines of the
general tradition, such as pastoral medicine and medical
ethics. We will note during this time the growing importance given to specific moral problems of the physician as
such, treated under a rubric appearing late in the scholastic period: the moral obligations of medical personnel.
This recognition of the medical profession as an explicit
locus of moral investigation is expanded during the modern
period, both in the general tradition and in the specifically medical-theological discipline of pastoral medicine, one
of the cognate pre-disciplines to contemporary medical
ethics. This expansion parallels the growth of modern medicine as a self-defined profession.

1.   The Pre-Scholastic Period (To the twelfth century)

The process of systematization of a specifically moral
species of theology did not begin until the twelfth century.
Before the twelfth century works in Christian ethics were
topical, written not to develop a science of moral investigation, but to urge Christians to live a life worthy of
their vocation in Christ by exhorting them to certain forms
of behavior and by applying salutary penalties to those who
failed.

The Christian Scriptures themselves provide examples of
this kind of moral exhortation. Recent scholarship suggests
that the moral teachings of the New Testament are in the
form of parenesis rather than moral discourse.[4] Concerning

---

[4]McCormick, "Notes," 1975, pp. 83-85.

medical ethical topics the Christian Scriptures are largely silent. There is a possible allusion to abortion in Gal.
5:20, where Paul lists *pharmakeia* among other vices, but
the meaning of the term is disputed, and it might refer to
an abortifacient medicine or to something quite different.[5]
Later in our study we will discover that the emerging disciplines of pastoral medicine and medical ethics often include
issues of sexual behavior among their topics. The Christian
Scriptures clearly include exhortations and condemnations of
various sexual activities and attitudes.[6]

The writers of the patristic period continue this pare-
netic approach to moral teaching.[7] There is a greater vari-
iety of topics, as the fathers begin to apply what they consider to be the ethical ramifications of Christ's revelation
to all of life's situations. Strictly medical ethical issues appear, as various practices are urged or condemned.
Condemnation of contraception and abortion is found as early

---

[5]Callahan, *Abortion,* p. 410.

[6]Recent scholarship concerning the moral teaching of
the New Testament has partially filled the void which was
noted two decades ago (Lottin, *Morale fondamentale,* p. 15).
Examples include Schnackenburg, *The Moral Teaching of the
New Testament*; C. Spicq, *Théologie morale du Nouveau Testament* (Paris: Gabalda, 1965); Curran, *Catholic Moral Theology
in Dialogue,* pp. 24-64. A number of articles deal with
various sexual issues from a Scriptural perspective. The
reader is referred to the various works recently published
concerning divorce and indissolubility, homosexuality, and
celibacy, among others.

[7]Here, too, recent writers have partially filled the
void noted by Lottin. Francis X. Murphy's work studies the
ethical teachings of the earliest writers through Irenaeus
in a critical attempt to study their morality "as the individuals they were" rather than to "line [them] up . . . in
systematic analysis" (Murphy, *Moral Teaching,* p. vii).
Studies of individual moral issues include research into
the patristic period. The general histories we have already noted include cursory overviews.

as the Didache, though the exact meaning is not totally clear.[8] These practices are consistently forbidden by the Church fathers, and by the time of the first codes of canons the official teaching concerning them is more or less established.[9] Exhortation in matters of sexual behavior is also common among the writers and preachers of the early Church. Among them Augustine, whose treatises have had great impact on later moralists and canonists, is of primary importance.[10]

The first attempts at a systematization of moral issues, though by no means a systematization of moral theology as such, came as a result of the spread of frequent confession under the missionary impact of Celtic monks in the sixth and seventh centuries. Previously the penitential rite had been a public liturgical ceremony, usually limited to one reception by each penitent. Now the priest became confessor to individual penitents in private, and the sacrament could be repeated. The confessor was required to judge the rightness and wrongness of acts, to assess their magnitude, and to impose fitting penalties. To aid him in this the *libri penitentiales* were written. They were simply lists of sinful actions with their fitting tariffs, written by holy men, and without official canonical sanction. Originally written for Celts, their influence spread when St. Columbanus and his comrades introduced them to the main-

---

[8]Noonan, *Contraception,* p. 120; Grisez, *Abortion,* p. 138; Callahan, *Abortion,* p. 410; Noonan, "An Almost Absolute Value," p. 10.

[9]Noonan, *Contraception*, pp. 78-175; Grisez, *Abortion,* pp. 137-150.

[10]Noonan, *Contraception,* p. 637; David F. Kelly, "Sexual Concupiscence in Augustine's Anti-Pelagian Treatises," 1973, unpublished.

land.[11]

Medical ethical issues were included among the sinful
actions penalized. Again abortion and contraception are
specifically mentioned, and the penalties are severe.[12] An
act of oral intercourse could be punished by a lifetime of
fasting on bread and water. Even dorsal intercourse was
penalized by up to seven years of fasting, presumably since
it was deemed contraceptive. Abortion was punished by up to
ten years of fasting, distinction being made in some of the
penitentials according to the age of the fetus. Commuta-
tions of the penalties were provided by reducing them to
shorter periods of more severe penance, such as praying the
psalms with arms outstretched, or sleeping in water or on
nutshells.

Sexual behaviors were among those penalized. Adultery,
homosexuality, masturbation, incest, sodomy, fornication,
and sins against celibacy, all behaviors which will become
topics for some later medical ethical literature, are included among the lists of sins.[13]

We can see, then, that in this early period of Christian ethical teaching there is no specific attempt at a systematic grouping of moral topics in general or of medical-
moral topics in particular. There are only lists of actions
required or proscribed in light of salvation. The *libri
penitentiales* do tend to list like sins together, but there
is little real organizational format,[14] nor is there any

---

[11]Houssiau, "Penance," pp. 46 ff.; Bieler, "Penitentials," pp. 87-88.

[12]Noonan, *Contraception,* pp. 190-210, esp. p. 204;
Grisez, *Abortion,* pp. 151-152; McNeill and Gamer, *Medieval
Handbooks.*

[13]McNeill and Gamer, *Medieval Handbooks,* index.

[14]Some of the penitentials list sins under various

formal recognition of the physician or of sins peculiar to
his vocation.[15] These developments begin in the scholastic
period.

2. The Scholastic Period (The twelfth to the mid-sixteenth
        centuries)

      In his treatise *De virtutibus et de vitiis et de donis
Spiritus Sancti,* written about 1160, Alan of Lille begins
by dividing theology into two subdisciplines, one rational
and the other moral.[16] Beginning in the twelfth century
moral theology progressively distinguished itself as an explicit and separate discipline. The great theologians of
the High Middle Ages included moral issues in their general
theological works. On the more immediately practical level
the *libri penitentiales* of the sixth through eleventh centuries were replaced by the *summae* for confessors, practical
guides for confessors whose task now included lifting ecclesiastical censures and counselling penitents. They were
casuistic manuals of canon law for the easy use of the

---

vices. An example is the *Old Irish Penitential* (c. 800),
which includes these headings: gluttony, lust, avarice,
envy, anger, and dejection (McNeill and Gamer, pp. 155-168).
The *Penitential of Theodore* (668-690) includes the heading
"Matters Relating to Marriage," but there is no attempt at
completeness (McNeill and Gamer, pp. 208-211).

      [15]The physician may be mentioned in passing. In the
course of its condemnation of sorcery as a medical technique,
the *Penitential of Bartholomew Iscanus* (1161-1184) mentions
that the approved techniques are "godly prayer [and] the
liberal art of medicine" (McNeill and Gamer, p. 350).

      [16]"Theologie due sunt species: una rationalis que
celestium scientiam pollicetur; alia moralis que circa mores
sive informationes hominum vertitur" (Hofmann, *Moraltheologische Erkenntnis- und Methodenlehre,* p. 26, n. 42; see also
p. 10). This may have been the first time the term "moral
theology" was used (Vereecke, "Moral Theology, History,"
p. 1120).

priest-confessor.[17]

It is during the scholastic period that the rubrics
for selecting and organizing the topics of moral discourse
were first developed. Two general approaches appeared.
The first was based on the moral virtues, and often included, in addition to virtues, a section on the sacraments
and a section on the obligations of various specific vocations or states of life. The second used the decalogue as
its central organizational rubric, and also included sections based on the sacraments and on certain specific vocations. As we will discover, medical ethical issues will
often be grouped according to these organizational divisions. Thus a brief overview of their early development is
in order here.

Moral theological works which organize topics according to the virtues enumerate the three theological and the
four cardinal moral virtues.[18] Alan of Lille organizes his
1160 treatise along these lines.[19] In the *Sentences,*

---

[17]Häring, *Law of Christ,* I, 16; Étienne, "Fundamental
Moral," p. 41. The first written was the *Liber peniten-
tialis* of Alan of Lille (12th century). The thirteenth century *Summa de casibus penitentiae* of Raymond of Peñafort, a
canonist who depended heavily on the *Decretum* of Gratian,
and who himself gathered the decrees of Pope Gregory IX, and
the works of Antoninus of Florence (15th century), whose
Summa theologica is more extensive than the others and prefigures the later *institutiones morales,* are the most significant. For a description of individual *summae,* see
Michaud-Quantin, *Sommes de casuistique.*

[18]The three "theological virtues" come from Paul (1
Thess. 1:1, 1 Cor. 13:13, and elsewhere), and are a common
theme in the writings of the fathers. The four "cardinal"
moral virtues are listed in the Book of Wisdom, 8:7, whose
author took them from Platonic philosophy (Van Der Marck,
Toward a Christian Ethic, p. 144). Augustine discusses
them. It is Ambrose who first called them "cardinal" or
"hinge" virtues (*Ibid.*; Tanquerey, *Synopsis,* II, 424).

[19]"Constituamus ergo virtutem tanquam genus generaliss-

Lombard treats certain questions surrounding the moral virtues as an incidental part of his discussion of virtue in
Christ.[20]   The *Secunda Secundae* of Thomas Aquinas' *Summa* is
explicitly organized according to the three theological and
the four cardinal moral virtues, to which he adds a section
on the obligations of various states of life, largely limited to those of clerics and religious.   In the *Tertia Pars*
he treats of moral questions concerning the sacraments.[21]

Organization of moral discourse according to the commandments of the decalogue also begins in the scholastic
period.   Though many of the confessors' manuals of the period are merely alphabetical manuals of canon law, some of
the more influential ones are organized in methodic fashion.[22]   The *Summa Astesana,* a thirteenth century manual by
Astesanus of Asti, combines the virtue system with a com-
mandment-based organization, ordering cases according to
the commandments, virtues and vices, especially the virtue
of justice, and the sacraments.[23]   The *Summa de casibus
penitentiae* (1222-1229) of Raymond of Peñafort speaks of
sins against God, sins against neighbor, and various ecclesiastical impediments and penalties.[24]   The influential

---

imum in predicamento moralis theologiae" (Hofmann, *Moraltheologische Erkenntnis- und Methodenlehre,* pp. 26-27).

[20]Dublanchy, "Morale," p. 2241.

[21]Thomas Aquinas, *Summa;* see also Dublanchy, "Morale,"
p. 2242.

[22]Étienne, "Fundamental Moral," p. 41; Häring, *Law of
Christ,* I, 16.

[23]Michaud-Quantin, *Sommes de casuistique,* pp. 57-58.

[24]Raymond of Peñafort, *Summa.*   Raymond's original work
consisted of three volumes.   In 1235 he added a fourth, on
matrimony, largely copied from the *De matrimonio* of Vincent Tancred (Stenger, "Raymond of Peñafort," p. 105).

Summa theologica or *Summa moralis* of Antoninus of Florence
(1477) prefigures the *institutiones morales* of the post-
Tridentine period.[25]   Antoninus does not use the decalogue
as his major organizational rubric but he does include
short sections on each of the commandments as part of his
section on law. He speaks of the obligations of various
states of life, including that of physician.[26]   The confessors' manual of Martin of Azpilcueta (1573) is similarly
organized, with the decalogue gaining greater prominence as
a central principle of organization.[27]

In our study of the modern period we will speak at
length about the groupings of medical-moral topics in the
manuals of moral theology. We will investigate four major
locations: the fifth commandment ("Thou shalt not kill.") or
the virtue of justice; the sixth and ninth commandments
("Thou shalt not commit adultery," and "Thou shalt not covet thy neighbor's wife.") or the virtue of chastity; the
sacrament of matrimony; and the special section concerned
with the obligations of medical personnel. We have now
discovered that these rubrics are first developed in the
speculative works of the scholastic theologians and in the
practical confessors' *summae* of the scholastic period.

Though a detailed listing of the topics included under
these rubrics can await the next section, it is in order for
us to speak at some length here about the special section on
the obligations of physicians which appears in some of the
confessors' manuals of the fifteenth and sixteenth centuries. We have noted that Thomas Aquinas includes a discussion of the duties of states of life in the *Secunda Secundae,*

---

[25]Étienne, "Fundamental Moral," p. 41.

[26]Antoninus of Florence, *Repertorium.* See also Walker,
"Antoninus, St.," pp. 646-647.

[27]Azpilcueta, *Enchiridion.*

but that this is limited almost exclusively to questions of
clerics and religious. The explicit mention of the moral
obligations of the physician *qua* physician in the confessors' manuals is of great importance. Its appearance in
the moral literature coincides with the growing de-clericalization and professionalization of medicine.[28] It is true
that in this early period the physician is one among others,
including the clergy, religious, judges, rulers, soldiers,
merchants, teachers, and more. First importance is given
to the obligations and privileges of the clergy and religious, and second importance to those of judges and lawyers.
Nonetheless, this choice of the physician marks the explicit
recognition of the medical profession as a special case, as
one of a number of vocations selected for special consideration in the general moral treatises.

An exceptionally detailed and developed section on the
obligations of physicians is found in the *Summa moralis* of
Antoninus of Florence (1477).[29] He includes it as Title
Seven of Book Three, which is devoted to the obligations of
various states of life.[30] It is divided into two sections:

---

[28]We will discuss this development when we study the
pre-history of pastoral medicine in part two of this chapter.

[29]While it is impossible to say that this is the very
first appearance of such a section (some of the *libri penitentiales* and some earlier *summae* may never have been published, or may be unavailable, or passed over in the secondary literature), it is surely among the earliest examples of
such a section in the important literature of practical
moral theology. I have not been able to locate an earlier
one. The detailed histories of pastoral medicine (see part
two of this chapter) make no mention either of Antoninus or
of any earlier work containing such a section. In any case,
this work is outstanding in the attention paid both to the
heights and the depths, the honors and the shames of the
medical vocation.

[30]Antoninus of Florence, *Repertorium*, III, 7 (pp. 44B-
46B in the edition cited).

the honors due the physician and the vices and sins which
beset him.

Antoninus begins by praising the exalted vocation of
the physician. He quotes the Scriptures as honoring doctors.
He gives a brief history of medicine, mentioning Apollo,
Asclepius, Hippocrates, Galen, and Avicenna, as well as Luke
the Evangelist. There then follows a rather lengthy discussion of the honors of precedence due physicians. Antoninus compares the doctor's vocation to Christ's.

Then the author goes on to list ignorance, negligence,
and malice as the three possible sources of immoral behavior
in a physician. The doctor is urged to be knowledgeable in
his field, to apply the best therapies, and to prefer com-
mending the patient to God rather than harming him with
doubtful remedies. He must visit the patient in person.

The doctor sins gravely if he advises his patient to do
anything against God's law, such as having sex with a woman
outside of marriage, getting drunk, or ignoring the fast
laws. He must not procure an abortion or advise the patient
to do so in order to hide a woman's sin. Antoninus cites
the opinion of other scholars that the physician is required
to perform an abortion in order to save a woman's life as
long as he is sure that the fetus is still without a rational soul, and argues that this opinion, while disputed, may
be licitly followed. If the fetus is animated with a rational soul, or if there is doubt, then he must not abort.[31]
He must charge a just fee, must not drag out an illness in
order to increase his fee, and must serve the poor for free.
He is obliged under Church law to warn his patients of im-
pending death so that they might see to their souls, and
must subordinate his physical therapies to that end. A

---

[31]*Ibid.*, III, 7, 2 (p. 45B in the edition cited). See
also Noonan, "An Almost Absolute Value," p. 26.

physician must be of legitimate birth. He must not boast
about his own achievements or scorn those of his colleagues.
Antoninus ends with a summary list of the sins of doctors
which is similar to those of later post-Tridentine manuals.

In the alphabetical *Summa summarum* of Silvester Mazzolini of Prierio, a kind of composite of previous *summae*
written about 1516, the word "medicus" is included. Here
Silvester speaks of many of the same topics as Antoninus,
whom he cites.[32]

The confessors' manual of Martin of Azpilcueta contains
a special section on physicians which is much briefer than
that of Antoninus. Martin lists neglect of study, injurious
treatment, failure to advise a patient to confess, abortion,
unnecessary dispensation from the fasting laws, overcharging,
and refusal to treat the poor for free as the sins of physicians.[33]

By the time of the Tridentine reform the organizational
rubrics for the systematic investigation of moral theological topics in general and medical-moral topics in particular
had been established. In addition to the commandments, virtues, and sacraments, a special section on physicians had
found its way into the general treatises of practical moral
theology. These treatises were still largely gatherings of

---

[32]Mazzolini, *Summae,* "Medicus" (II, 170-172 in the edition cited). There is also a section on "Hospitale," which
treats the canonical status and regulations of the medieval
ecclesiastical and civic hospice. While this was not a
specifically medical institution, it is interesting to note
that this predecessor of the medical hospital is already
singled out for canonical regulation (I, 383B-387B in the
edition cited).

[33]Azpilcueta, *Enchiridion,* c. 25, nos. 60-64 (pp. 483-
484 in the edition cited). Martin agrees with the opinion
of Antoninus on abortion, that the abortion of a fetus not
animated with a rational soul is licit to preserve the life
of the mother.

cases and canons, and lacked the speculative analysis of
the later manuals. But the rubrics had been set. We will
now turn to a study of the modern period to see how these
rubrics become more and more the selecting and grouping
principles for the topics which will become the content of
medical ethics.

3. The Modern Period (The mid-sixteenth to the mid-
    twentieth centuries)

   — The organizational separation of moral from dogmatic
theology was furthered by the development at the end of the
sixteenth century of the Jesuit *Ratio Studiorum*. This curriculum was drawn up as a response to the plea of the Council of Trent for a consistent and disciplined training of
priests.[34] According to the *Ratio* there was to be, in addition to a professor of scholastic theology whose task was
to teach Thomas' *Summa*, one or more professors of "cases of
conscience" whose responsibility it was "to direct all his
efforts and skill to the training of competent pastors and
administrators of the sacraments."[35] The *Ratio* divided the
study of moral and sacramental-canonical theology into a
two-year curriculum. During the first year the priest-
candidate studied general moral theology, including human
acts, conscience, law, and sin; and the decalogue except for
the seventh commandment. Year two included the seventh commandment (with emphasis on contracts), the sacraments, ecclesiastical censures, and the duties of clerics and of

---

[34]Vereecke, "Moral Theology, History," p. 1121; Häring,
Law of Christ, I, 18; Curran, *Absolutes in Moral Theology?*
p. 13.

[35]Farrell, *The Jesuit Ratio Studiorum of 1599*, p. 37.

certain other states of life.[36]

The *institutiones morales* were the textbooks of moral
theology as taught according to the *Ratio*. The first was
that of Juan Azor, S.J., whose three volume work was published at the beginning of the seventeenth century. It was
the model for several other works which would follow. In
addition to strictly ethical questions, Azor's work includes
long sections on detailed questions of canon law, rubrics,
clerical ranks, and ecclesiastical benefices. Azor includes
the question of abortion in his treatment of the fifth commandment and that of contraception in his chapter on the
sixth commandment.[37]

The *Medulla theologiae moralis* of Hermann Busenbaum,
S.J., was first published in 1648 and had more than 50 printings. After introducing the questions of general moral theology and treating of the theological virtues as "quasi
praeambula Decalogi," Busenbaum organizes his material

---

[36]Vereecke, "Moral Theology, History," p. 1121; Curran,
Absolutes? p. 13. The various versions of the *Ratio* differ
in detail of organization. The 1599 version includes the
study of what we have come to know as "general moral" (human acts, conscience, sin, and law) in the course in scholastic theology as a part of the study of Thomas' *Summa*
(Farrell, *The Jesuit Ratio,* pp. 34-35). The 1586 version
includes general moral in the curriculum of moral theology
(Vereecke; Curran). The 1599 version suggests two separate
two-year curricula for the professor(s) of cases of conscience, one dealing with "the sacraments, the censures, and
the different states of life and their duties . . . [and the
other treating] the ten commandments, including under the
seventh the subject of contracts. . . . He should refrain
entirely from treating of theological questions which have
no essential connection with cases of conscience" (Farrell,
pp. 37-38).

[37]Azor, *Institutionum moralium*, index. Azor includes
as abortive some procedures which would today be considered
contraceptive. Contraception refers to methods and positions of intercourse other than the "missionary" position.

according to the commandments of the decalogue and of the
Church, precepts concerning certain states of life, including that of physician, the sacraments, and ecclesiastical censures.[38]

The first edition of Alphonsus Liguori's *Theologia*
moralis was little more than an edition of Busenbaum's work
and was published in his name.[39] By 1785 the work had grown
to monumental proportions, and was largely the work of
Liguori himself, but Busenbaum's original outline was kept.[40]
It is this outline which, with some variations, has been the
plan followed by most of the moral manuals up to the middle
of our own century. Its central organizational principles
are the commandments, the sacraments, various states of life,
and ecclesiastical censures. There are hundreds of works
organized along these lines, many nearly carbon copies of
their predecessors.[41]

There was no explicit intention in the manuals to write
treatises devoted primarily to medico-moral questions. But
the topics naturally came to be grouped under certain headings, of which four are the most important: first, under the
fifth commandment ("Thou shalt not kill."); second, under
the sixth and ninth commandments ("Thou shalt not commit

---

[38]Busenbaum, *Medulla theologiae moralis* (1652), 1746,
index.

[39]Liguori, *R. P. Hermanni Busembaum . . . theologia*
moralis, 1757. The earliest edition was in 1748.

[40]Liguori, *Theologia moralis,* ed. Gaudé.

[41]Manuals consulted in preparation of this section are
included in the bibliography. Among manuals organized ac-
cording to the commandments are, in addition to Busenbaum
and Liguori: Aertnys-Damen, Ballerini-Palmieri, Davis,
Ferreres, Gabriele da Guarcino, Génicot, Génicot-Salsmans,
Gousset, Gury, Gury-Ballerini, Iorio, Jone, Kenrick, Konings,
La Croix, Marc, Neyraguet, Noldin, Noldin-Schmitt, Sabetti,
Sabetti-Barrett, Scavini, Slater, Zalba.

adultery," and "Thou shalt not covet thy neighbor's wife.");
third, under the sacrament of matrimony; and fourth, under
the duties of various states of life in a special section
concerning the obligations of physicians and other medical
personnel. In addition to these four *loci,* certain other
sections include individual medical ethical issues.

A general survey of the more important of the moral
manuals shows how topics relevant to medicine are in fact
grouped under these headings. We will later demonstrate, in
our description of pastoral medicine and in our lengthy definitional analysis of North American medical ethics, that
these groupings and their organizational headings were of
significance both as grouping and as selecting rubrics for
the topics which were considered part of the material definition of pastoral medicine and medical ethics. For now we
need merely present a brief survey of the four major locations mentioned above and of their contents in the moral
manuals.

Under the fifth commandment come the issues of abortion, euthanasia, suicide, castration, and multilation, especially sterilization. Busenbaum speaks of abortion, mutilation, suicide, and of the means of preserving life.[42]
Liguori adds some clarifications to his opinions.[43] Kenrick
(1860) is similar.[44] Gury-Ballerini (1869) offer basically
a repetition of Liguori.[45] Konings (1880)[46] and Sabetti

---

[42]Busenbaum, *Medulla,* pp. 129-131, 136.

[43]Liguori, *Theologia moralis,* ed. Gaudé, I, 622-629,
644-653.

[44]Kenrick, *Theologia moralis,* I, 66-76. The author was
archbishop of Baltimore.

[45]Gury-Ballerini, *Compendium,* I, 314-318, 326-331.

[46]Konings, *Theologia moralis,* I, 205-206, 209-211.

(1889)[47] do likewise, updating their remarks by including
specific reference to embryotomy and craniotomy. In their
seven volume work, Ballerini-Palmieri (1889-1893) follow
Liguori's outline, adding further detail to his investigation of some of the questions. Several pages are devoted
to the question of possibly injurious asceticism by fasting
and mutilation.[48] The section on abortion is extended.[49]
Sabetti-Barrett (1920) ask about the liceity of ovariotomy
and vasectomy, sterilization of criminals, mandatory sterilization of the innocent, abortion in cases of ectopic pregnancy, Caesarian section, the use of medicine after intercourse to prevent pregnancy, and douching.[50] Ferreres
(1925) includes syphilis under the heading of the fifth commandment.[51] Iorio (1946) includes a section on transplantation, and speaks of hysterectomy during pregnancy, eugenic
sterilization, and euthanasia.[52] Aertnys-Damen (1947) speak
in detail of ordinary and extraordinary means of preserving
life, and add a *scholion* on doing harm to animals, including
the question of animal medical research.[53] Davis (1949)
speaks briefly of medical experimentation, includes extended
sections on sterilization and ectopic pregnancy, and adds an
appendix on "Some Medico-Moral Problems."[54] In this last

---

[47]Sabetti, *Compendium*, pp. 197-198, 203-205.

[48]Ballerini-Palmieri, *Opus*, II, 613-620.

[49]*Ibid.*, II, 647-656.

[50]Sabetti-Barrett, *Compendium*, pp. 270-285.

[51]Ferreres, *Compendium*, I, 360-363. One is obliged
not to do harm to one's neighbor by spreading the disease.

[52]Iorio, *Theologia moralis*, II, 106-107, 112-123.

[53]Aertnys-Damen, *Theologia moralis*, I, 454-455, 473-474.

[54]Davis, *Moral and Pastoral Theology*, II, 155, 156-186,
187-198.

are included various specific problems of pregnancy and
childbirth, euthanasia, embalming, monsters, lobotomy,
transplantation, and shock therapy. Jone (1953) includes a
listing of lawful and unlawful hospital procedures.[55] In
addition to various sterilization and abortion procedures,
Jone lists contraception and artificial insemination.

The fifth commandment section in those manuals which
are organized according to the decalogue becomes, then, an
important *locus* for the grouping of medical ethical topics.
As medical knowledge increases over the years and new procedures are proposed, they are included in this section of
the manuals, and principles previously developed are applied to them.

Under the sixth and ninth commandments is found an entire range of sexual ethical issues which, as we will discover later in our study, are sometimes included among the
topics of pastoral medicine and medical ethics literature.
Busenbaum speaks of extra-marital non-consummated contact,
fornication, rape, adultery, incest, and coitus with a vir-
gin or consecrated celibate; methods and positions of marital intercourse deemed contraceptive (withdrawal, non-vagi-
nal intercourse, and any position other than the approved
position of the husband above the wife); homosexuality and
bestiality; masturbation (including the medically prescribed
expelling of semen deemed poisonous, which is permitted),
and nocturnal emission.[56] Liguori is similar, adding much
detail about the distinction of species of sin and the canonical penalties attached to the various behaviors. He
speaks of intercourse with demons. He insists that any
therapeutic expulsion of poisonous semen be done without

---

[55]Jone, *Moral Theology*, p. 213.

[56]Busenbaum, *Medulla*, pp. 142-151.

touch or other method intended to arouse the passions.[57]
Kenrick,[58] Gury-Ballerini,[59] Konings,[60] and Sabetti[61]
add little to Liguori. Ballerini-Palmieri add some detail.[62] Slater's English manual (1918) is notable only for
the fact that it lapses back into Latin when speaking of sexual matters.[63] Davis (1949) does likewise.[64]

The sacrament of matrimony is a third heading under
which medical ethical issues are discussed. The issues
found here are similar to those treated under the sixth and
ninth commandments, and there is often considerable overlapping, though some distinction is usually attempted.[65]
Busenbaum discusses the moral and canonical implications of
formal betrothal and of marriage itself, the "usus

---

[57]Liguori, *Theologia moralis,* I, 665-707. Liguori's
opinion on therapeutic gathering of semen is important for
later judgements concerning sterility testing ,and artificial insemination.

[58]Kenrick, *Theologia moralis,* I, 81-35.

[59]Gury-Ballerini, *Compendium,* I, 337-358.

[60]Konings, *Theologia moralis,* I, 215-228.

[61]Sabetti, *Compendium,* pp. 208-220.

[62]Ballerini-Palmieri, *Opus,* II, 678-746.

[63]Slater, *Manual,* I, 324-338.

[64]Davis, *Moral and Pastoral Theology,* II, 200-254.

[65]Generally those topics pertaining directly to marriage are included under the sacrament of matrimony. This
is not always true, however, and some issues have been
shifted over the years. For example, it has been noted
above that the earliest manuals spoke of contraceptive methods and positions of intercourse when treating of the sixth
commandment. Later manuals shift this topic to the section
on marriage, and under the sixth and ninth commandments put
far greater stress on "internal" sins against purity than
do the early moralists.

matrimonii," divorce, marriage impediments, and ecclesiastical dispensations.[66] Under the "use of marriage" he
speaks again of positions of intercourse considered contraceptive, and of times for intercourse. Among the impediments to marriage that of impotence is considered, which
will be a common topic for later medical ethics. Liguori
follows Busenbaum, but adds much detail, including, under
the "use of marriage," discussion about intercourse during
pregnancy and menstruation (probably venially sinful) and,
under the impediment of impotence, the question of surgical
procedures for its cure.[67] Gury-Ballerini include an extended discussion on conjugal onanism (withdrawal for contraception).[68] Kenrick,[69] Konings,[70] and Sabetti[71] add little. The entire sixth volume of the Ballerini-Palmieri *Opus*
is devoted to the sacrament of matrimony. The Busenbaum-
Liguori outline is followed. After speaking at length of
the impediment of impotence, the authors add a discussion of
artificial insemination.[72] Sabetti-Barrett ask if double
vasectomy results in canonical impotence, and include a
brief statement of periodic abstinence.[73] Iorio includes a
discussion of various methods of birth control and of neo-
malthusianism in his section on conjugal onanism.[74]

---

[66]Busenbaum, *Medulla*, pp. 471-504.

[67]Liguori, *Theologia moralis*, ed. Gaudé, IV, 3-268.

[68]Gury-Ballerini, *Compendium*, II, 656-661.

[69]Kenrick, *Theologia moralis*, II, 279-342.

[70]Konings, *Theologia moralis*, II, 219-306.

[71]Sabetti, *Compendium*, pp. 642-733.

[72]Ballerini-Palmieri, *Opus*, VI, 658-683, 684-685.

[73]Sabetti-Barrett, *Compendium*, pp. 886, 979.

[74]Iorio, *Theologia moralis*, III, 666-679.

The sixth and ninth commandments and the sacrament of
matrimony thus appear as two important locations for the
grouping of medical ethical topics in the moral manuals.
Together they are the gathering points for the sexual and
marital issues of medical ethics. Many topics which will
be included in works of pastoral medicine and medical ethics are of a sexual nature. Some might seem to have little
direct relevance to medicine as we have come to understand
it today. Their inclusion is at least partially determined
by the fact that the organizational rubrics which are the
sixth and ninth commandments and the sacrament of matrimony
operate as principles of selection.

The fourth principal *locus* of medical moral questions
in the general manuals of moral theology is one specifically devoted to the moral dilemmas of the physician and other
medical personnel. Under the general heading, "Obligations
(or Precepts) of Various States of Life," the manuals consider the duties of specific vocations and occupations.
Much of the discussion concerns clerics and religious, but
most of the manuals contain a short section on the duties of
doctors, nurses, and pharmacists. Without any discussion,
Busenbaum lists the duties of the doctor as acquiring the
knowledge necessary for his profession, following safe medical practice, avoiding harmful or experimental therapies,
refraining from persuading his patients to appeal to super-
stition or to engage in masturbation, and refraining from a
too easy dispensation from the laws of fast and abstinence.
Pharmacists receive like advice. Surgeons are specifically
enjoined not to charge exhorbitant fees for their services
or to drag out the duration of convalescence for their prof-
it.[75] Liguori simply quotes Busenbaum.[76] Kenrick[77] and

---

[75]Busenbaum, *Medulla,* pp. 307-308.

[76]Liguori, *Theologia moralis,* ed. Gaudé, II, 684-685.

[77]Kenrick, *Theologia moralis,* I, 268-269.

Gury-Ballerini[78] add that the physician <u>must not advise an
abortion and insist that he is obliged to inform dying patients so that they might receive the sacraments.</u> Gury-
Ballerini add also that the doctor is obliged to care for
his patients during epidemics. Konings,[79] Sabetti,[80] Ballerini-Palmieri,[81] and Slater[82] have nearly identical sections. Sabetti-Barrett mention medical secrets and sterilization procedures.[83] Ferreres discusses fee-splitting and
rejuvenation operations, and includes in his special section
on doctors reminders about sterilization and mutilation,
abortion, and the use of narcotics.[84] Davis appends a "Hospital Code" to his special section. Included are statements
on birth control, sterility testing, abortion, sterilization,
and preparation for death.[85]

The special section concerning the duties of the medical profession thus provides a final principal *locus* for
the grouping of medical ethical topics in moral manuals

---

[78]Gury-Ballerini, *Compendium*, II, 20-23.

[79]Konings, *Theologia moralis*, I, 420-421.

[80]Sabetti, *Compendium*, p. 373.

[81]Ballerini-Palmieri, *Opus*, IV, 463.

[82]Slater, *Manual*, I, 596-597.

[83]Sabetti-Barrett, *Compendium*, p. 486.

[84]Ferreres, *Compendium*, II, 28-34.

[85]Davis, *Moral and Pastoral Theology*, IV, 400-401.
This addition by Davis demonstrates that by the 1940's it
is no longer merely a question of the individual obligations of doctors, but that ethical issues of the medical
profession as institution have come to be investigated explicitly. By this point in time, of course, we have over-
lapped the period of the emergence of twentieth century
medical ethics as an explicit discipline. A detailed examination must await the next chapter.

organized according to the commandments.   In Roman Catholic
works specifically written as treatises on medical ethics,
the authors borrow heavily from these sections of the manuals.

It has been noted earlier that not all the manuals of
moral theology were organized according to the decalogue.
Some organized their material according to the theological
and cardinal virtues.[86]   Following Thomas Aquinas, they
treated, in addition to the virtues, the obligations of various states of life and the moral and canonical aspects of
the sacraments.   In these manuals the fifth commandment material is discussed under the virtue of justice, and the
sixth commandment issues are found under the virtue of chastity, a sub-heading of the cardinal virtue of temperance.
Thus the same four locations for medical ethical issues are
found in the virtue manuals as in the commandments manuals:
first, under the virtue of justice; second, under the virtue
of chastity; third, under the sacrament of matrimony; and
fourth, under the section on the obligations of medical

---

[86]Among them are Connell, Lehmkuhl, Merkelbach,
Prümmer, Tanquerey, Vermeersch.   Actually the distinction is
not complete, as the commandment manuals include short sections on the virtues, and the virtue manuals often mention
the commandments.
     It should also be noted here that some moralists of
recent decades suggested organizing the issues according to
the virtue of Christian charity (Lottin, *Morale fondamentale,* pp. 16-19).   Gérard Gilleman tried to show how such
an approach might be attempted (Gilleman, *The Primacy of
Charity*).   The best known attempt to write a complete work
on moral theology along these lines is Bernard Häring's *Law
of Christ.*   Today's scholars generally agree that these attempts were transitional, and current work in the field is
interested more in specific methodological (general moral)
and practical (special moral) issues than in an attempt to
produce a supposedly definitive *opus* of solutions to the entire range of moral dilemmas.   Häring's work may well be the
last of the long line of moral manuals begun in the sixteenth
and seventeenth centuries.

personnel.

In both the commandment manuals and the virtue manuals,
individual medical ethical topics may be found outside the
four major groupings. The manuals discuss questions of fetal baptism and anointing of the dying under these respective sacraments. Medical secrets are used as examples of
the professional secret under the eighth commandment ("Thou
shalt not bear false witness against thy neighbor.") or as a
subdivision of the virtue of justice. Under the first commandment ("I am the Lord thy God; thou shalt not have
strange gods before me.") or the virtue of religion are
found discussions of spiritism, magnetism, hypnotism, and
other like methods of healing, which might be considered superstitious or even of diabolical origin. Suicide and mutilation may be treated under the virtue of piety to oneself,
a subdivision of the virtue of religion. Under the precepts of the Church or the virtue of temperance are discussed questions of fast and abstinence pertaining to the
sick. Medical and sexual ethical issues connected with celibacy and consecrated virginity are often treated as part of
the obligations of these states of life.

In addition to the moral manuals, the "Casus Conscientiae" collections contain cases of medical ethical interest.
Most of these works are organized along the same lines as
the manuals. The author is often the author of a moral manual, who follows his own organizational pattern. Thus the
medical ethics cases are grouped under the same headings as
in the author's manual.[87] Similar to these are numerous

---

[87]Examples of these collections of cases are included
in the bibliography. Some are: Bucceroni; Génicot-Salsmans,
Casus conscientiae; Gury, *Casus Conscientiae;* Lehmkuhl,
Casus conscientiae; Palazzini; Slater, *Cases of Conscience;*
Villada. Henri Merkelbach also published a multi-volume
series entitled *Quaestiones pastorales.* Among the volumes,

question-and-answer volumes containing queries about Catholic faith and moral teaching. They often have sections on
morals which include medical ethical topics, sometimes organized according to the commandments.[88]

     Finally, the numerous textbooks of Catholic ethics con-
tain studies of medical ethical issues. These are distinguished from the manuals of moral theology in that they
claim to base their conclusions only on "natural" human reason, excluding any appeal to "supernatural" revelation. In
fact, however, this exclusion is often more nominal than
substantial, and the conclusions reached can hardly be distinguished from those of the manuals of moral theology. The
organization of the ethics texts differs from that of the
manuals, in that the ethics texts cannot use the commandments or sacraments as organizational rubrics. Instead
they treat medical ethical topics under such headings as
life, the body, the family, the virtue of justice, and
others.[89]

---

some speak directly to medical ethical issues (Merkelbach,
*Quaestiones de castitate; Questiones de embryologia et de
ministratione baptismatis; Questiones de embryologia et de
sterilisatione*). Paul Villada's 1885 *Casus conscientiae*
contains a section entitled "Summa notionum de re medica
animarum pastoribus hodiernis praesertim utilis" ("A compilation of medical matters especially useful for contemporary
pastors of souls"). Cases discussed include signs of death
for administering the last sacraments, "embryologia sacra"
(abortion, baptism of fetuses, Caesarian section, Porro section), fasting, Mass attendance for the sick, aphrodisiacs,
hypnotism, informing a patient of coming death, and narcotics (Villada, *Casus conscientiae*, III).

     [88]Examples include Connell, *Father Connell Answers
Moral Questions,* and *More Answers*; Bertrand Conway, *The Question Box;* McCarthy, *Problems in Theology;* Mahoney, *Questions
and Answers;* Rumble, *Radio Replies.*

     [89]Examples included in the bibliography are Fagothey,
Right and Reason; Noonan, *General and Special Ethics;* and

* * *

In our study of the general tradition of moral theology
we have focused our primary attention on the organizational
rubrics for topics of medico-moral discourse. We have discovered that in the pre-scholastic period all ethical teaching, including that of matters relating to medical practice,
was largely topical. The only attempt at organization came
in the *libri penitentiales,* which were little more than
lists of sins and penalties. There was no special recognition of the physician as a select subject for moral investigation. Direct pastoral application was the only organizational principle.

The scholastic period did not reject the principle of
pastoral application, but adopted it, expanded it, organized
it. In the confessors' manuals, as well as in the more
speculative works of the major theologians, headings were
developed according to which the topics of moral discussion

Sullivan, *Special Ethics*. An example of how the exclusion
of "supernatural" revelation is often more nominal than substantive can be found in comparing the various editions of
Fagothey on the birth control issue. Whereas earlier editions condemn all methods of birth control except rhythm on
purely "natural" grounds, the fourth edition, written after
the introduction of controversy by the moral theologians but
before *Humanae Vitae,* suggests that there is some question
here, and that people will no doubt wish to be directed "not
by natural law alone but by natural law as interpreted in
the official pronouncements of the Church to which they have
given their adherence" (p. 299). By this phrasing Fagothey
maintains his nominal exclusion of the revelation-based ecclesial magisterium as source of his argument, but the shift
in his argumentation from earlier editions suggests rather
strongly the influence of moral theology in his thinking.
Generally the ethics texts argue from premises of "natural
theology" or "theodicy" which are scarcely distinguishable
from the tenets of Catholic theology. In later chapters of
our study, works in medical ethics by Catholic moral philosophers will be discussed along with explicitly theological
works. For further discussion of this question, see chapter
three.

were organized. We have found the most important among
them to be the commandments and virtues, the sacraments, and
the obligations of various states of life. In addition we
have seen that during this period special recognition was
given to the medical profession as a select source of moral
dilemmas.

In the modern period we have found an expansion of
these established organizational principles. New topics of
medical-moral discussion were included under the proper rubric. More and more recognition was paid over the centuries
to the specific moral problems of the medical profession,
even in the general treatises of moral theology.

At the risk of some oversimplification, it can be suggested that the basic selecting principle for topics of
medical-moral discourse shifted gradually over the centuries
from what penitents confessed; to what fell under the proper
commandments, virtues, and sacraments; to what the medical
profession was actually doing. Earlier rubrics continued to
serve as selecting principles in later periods, of course.
But the trend is clear. Medical-moral discourse changed its
method of selection. In chapter two we will investigate the
material definition of North American Roman Catholic medical
ethics. There we will study this trend in further detail.

Part Two

Pastoral Medicine

The relationship of medicine and theology has a long
history within the Christian community. The Church has traditionally recognized the importance of healing, both that
of the body and that of the soul, and has long been interested in speaking to the issues arising from the dialogue of
these two arts of healing. Churchmen and women have devoted
their energies over many centuries to medical care. Theolo-

gians and medical scientists have investigated the mutual
influences and interdependences of soul and body. Priests
and religious have practiced medicine; medical doctors have
practiced pastoral ministry; both have investigated the
moral implications of medical practice.

We cannot attempt to investigate, even in a most cursory form, the entire problematic of the interface of medicine
and theology. Rather the purpose of this section is to present a brief overview of the theology-medicine dialogue as
it led to and culminated in the explicitly self-conscious
discipline generally known as pastoral medicine.[90] As we
shall see, pastoral medicine was one of three cognate pre-
disciplines to North American Roman Catholic medical ethics.[91] Together with the general tradition of moral theology, which we investigated in part one of this chapter,
pastoral medicine is the proximate source of twentieth century medical ethics.

Adequate histories of European pastoral medicine are
available in German.[92] While the authors are not in complete

---

[90]In addition, our survey will provide a general picture of the Church's relationship to medicine, which will
lead to a better understanding of the significance of theological principles for theological medical ethics.

[91]The others were medical jurisprudence (or forensic or
legal medicine) and "medical ethics" in the restricted sense
of intra-professional codes of ethics, with emphasis on medical etiquette and professional courtesy.

[92]Pompey, *Die Bedeutung der Medizin;* Niedermeyer,
"Historische Entwicklung der Pastoral-Medizin," in his
Allgemeine Pastoralmedizin, I, 42-82; Karl Franz Hoffmann,
*Christliche Ärzte: Lebensbilder vom 16. bis zum 19. Jahrhun-
dert* (Regensburg: J. Habbel, 1950); Fleckenstein, "Pastoralmedizin." The present overview relies heavily on Pompey and
Niedermeyer. It is not intended here to reproduce their
studies in complete detail. Hence the reader is referred to
them for massively researched and detailed accounts of the
discipline, especially in its early phases. A more general

accord in their judgments of which works have been the most
influential, there is sufficient agreement concerning the
general lines of the discipline's development.

Our study will show that the rubric "Pastoral Medicine"
designates a discipline which, while one of the cognate pre-
disciplines to Roman Catholic North American medical ethics,
is not at all identical to it. We will see that pastoral
medicine developed two rather distinct emphases. As the
discipline investigating the interface of medicine and theology, pastoral medicine took on both a medical and a theological aspect. Included in works of pastoral medicine are
treatises on medicine for the theologian and the pastor, and
treatises from theology for the medical scholar and practitioner. Under the former emphasis (data from medicine for
theology and pastoral care) are found two types of material:
first, medical data presented as a help to the rural pastor
in caring *physically* for people lacking proper medical care
("medicina ruralis"); and second, data from medicine and
psychology which might be of use to the pastor in his *spiritual* task as pastor of souls or to the theologian in his
task of investigating the theological-anthropological or the
moral aspects of the body-soul relationship. Under the latter emphasis (data from theology for medicine) are included
specifically moral treatises from moral theology intended to
inform medical personnel of their ethical responsibilities,
and treatises from various branches of theology intended to
help the physician gain a better knowledge of the spiritual
dimensions of his patient.[93]

---

study of the relationship of medical care to the religious
context of Christianity is found in P. Lain Entralgo, *Doctor
and Patient*, pp. 53-146.

[93]It has been debated whether or not pastoral medicine
is a subdiscipline of pastoral theology. This depends on

The divisions of material within pastoral medicine are
not always clear. Nor is its material definition. The rubric "Pastoral Medicine" has come gradually to be the accepted one for the discipline, and is still used by scholars
today, but many works in the field, especially in its early
phases, do not use it explicitly. Pastoral medicine refers
to one set of contents, then to another, then to a combination of the two. At times it is restricted quite totally to
"medicina ruralis." In other eras it widens its horizons to
emphasize the spiritual dimensions of the pastor's work.
Some authors emphasize questions from metaphysics and speculative theology concerning the relationship of body and
soul. Others investigate the moral issues of medical practice.

Our survey will not find any totally exclusive linear
movement from the one to the other emphasis. We will find
ebbs and flows, as authors are influenced by one and another style of thought. In general we will observe, however,
that the literature of the eighteenth century, written
largely under the influence of the Enlightenment, tends to

---

which emphasis of pastoral medicine is considered as well as
on one's definition of pastoral theology. Certain recent
definitions might exclude pastoral medicine, even in its
more spiritual aspects, and set it rather in the position of
helping discipline, or as a subdiscipline of "pastoral methodology." For a discussion of these somewhat esoteric problems, see Pompey, *Die Bedeutung der Medizin,* pp. 1-5. For a
contemporary opinion on pastoral theology, see Schuster,
"Pastoral Theology," and Brennan, "Pastoral Theology." Much
of the material concerning psychological implications for
pastoral care is part of what we now know as pastoral psychology (see Bier, "Pastoral Psychology"). In its specifically moral aspects, pastoral medicine was and is a subdiscipline of moral theology. The formal and material relationship of moral theology to pastoral theology is itself not
easily determined. Pompey implies (p. 4) that pastoral theology is situated in changing contexts whereas moral theology
can make absolute and lasting judgments. This is surely
problematic, especially in light of the data from sociology
of knowledge.

restrict the newly emerging discipline to the teaching of
rudimentary medicine to rural pastors ("medicina ruralis"),
whereas works written in the nineteenth and early twentieth
centuries insist on broadening the scope of pastoral medicine to include a greater emphasis on spiritual and theological questions. We will also note a tendency in some
writings of the late nineteenth and early twentieth centuries to give greatest emphasis to specifically ethical questions.[94]

The study will be divided into three general sections:
first, the pre-history of the discipline (to the eighteenth
century); second, early works in pastoral medicine (the
eighteenth to the mid-nineteenth centuries); third, later
works in pastoral medicine (from the mid-nineteenth century
to the early part of the twentieth).[95] Through these three
phases the discipline develops in response to the growing
professionalization and secularization of scientific medicine.

1.   Pre-History of Pastoral Medicine (To the eighteenth
         century)

The earliest use of the term "Pastoral Medicine" as a
rubric for an area of study was in the late eighteenth

---

[94]Also to some extent the result of Enlightenment influence. See Pompey, *Die Bedeutung der Medizin*, p. 119. This
late nineteenth and twentieth century process leads to a
growing identification of pastoral medicine with the moral
theology of medical practice. Though never formally a subdiscipline of moral theology, much modern pastoral medicine
in Europe is hardly distinguishable from what we have come
to know as *Medical Ethics*, at least insofar as the latter is
practiced from within a theological methodology.

[95]An adaptation for our purposes of the divisions used
by Niedermeyer (*Allgemeine Pastoralmedizin*, I, 51, 62), and
Pompey (*Die Bedeutung der Medizin*).

century. This newly emerging discipline had, however, a
lengthy pre-history, as the relationship of medicine to religion is as old as either art of healing.

In pre-Christian times the office of healer was most
generally identified with that of priest. In Egypt and
Mesopotamia, in India and in most of the Eastern cultures,
and among the Germans and Celts, the task of physical healing was practiced by holy-men, who used a combination of em-
pirico-rational and magico-supernatural methods.[96]

Among the ancient Greeks, before the time of Hippocrates (460-377), medical methodology was a mixture of "em-
piricism" and magic.[97] By "empirical medicine" is here
meant the mere repetition of successful treatments with no
attempt at defining illnesses or at discovering why certain
remedies are useful. It was Hippocrates who first developed
for Western man a rational approach to medical methodology,
establishing medicine as a "technē," an art or skill based
on the rational investigation of cause and effect, diagnosis and prescription. Thus began the process of distinguishing medical healing from priestly ministry. After the fifth
century in Greece, and later in Rome, there were large numbers of "lay" physicians, doctors who were not official religious leaders.[98]

---

[96]See Pompey, *Die Bedeutung der Medizin,* p. 14; Agnew,
"Medicine, History of," pp. 581-582.

[97]Entralgo, *Doctor and Patient,* p. 15. Also see Agnew,
"Medicine, History of," p. 582; Pompey, *Die Bedeutung der
Medizin,* p. 15.

[98]This development is often called the "secularization"
of medicine. Though Hippocrates did begin a process which
would later lead to such a secularization, recent scholarship suggests that he and his followers remained themselves
quite committed to a religious view of their profession.
The new "art" of medicine was not so much a divorce of medicine from religion--this would not take place till the

As Christianity spread through the Roman Empire, it inherited Roman social and political forms, including the manner of medical practice. Yet, like other Roman institutions,
medicine was transformed by the teachings of the Christian
gospel. The physician understood his profession in a new
way, seeing himself called to the love and service of his
neighbor in imitation of Christ.[99] Asclepius, the Greek god
of medicine, had held the title "sōtēr" (savior), and physicians considered their vocation to be a Christlike service
of salvific healing.[100] To concern for the bodily welfare
of patients was added concern for their spiritual well-being,

---

Enlightenment--as it was an intra-religious reform. Instead
of seeing the immediate workings of an angry god or goddess, the
Hippocratic Asclepiad would see in illness the workings of
"nature." But in his Pythagorean view nature was not at all
a "secular," but rather a "divine" reality (Entralgo, *Doctor
and Patient,* p. 42). The Hippocratic Oath contains elements
both of the older and the newer approaches to nature and religion (*Ibid.,* p. 44). It grew out of a specifically religious Pythagorean cult, and contains within it specifically
cultic elements (Veatch, "Codes of Medical Ethics," p. 143;
see also Edelstein, *The Hippocratic Oath;* Smithies, "On the
Origin and Development of Ethics," p. 583). The new "technical" approach could be characterized as secular in comparison with the older "supernatural" approach, but it would be
better argued that the newer methods represent a theological
as well as a purely medical advance. The gods are no longer
viewed as whimsically responsible for each illness of man.
This would seem to be theologically more accurate than the
older belief. Similar questions are involved in the application of theological principles to medical ethics. A more
detailed analysis must await later chapters. In passing it
might be said that labels like "secularization" are often
used to make facile negative judgments in the theological
or the moral sphere. Such spurious judgments bypass the
real theological or ethical issues, and are neither good
theology nor good ethics.

   [99]Pompey, *Die Bedeutung der Medizin,* p. 17; Entralgo,
Doctor and Patient, pp. 53-57.

   [100]Pompey, p. 17, n. 16.

and in cases of conflict the latter was to take precedence.[101] To *eros* and *philia* as motives for the doctor's
vocation *agapē* was added.[102] Medical treatment was to be
egalitarian, free treatment was owed to the poor, and spiritual healing was to be given along with physical. Thus
physicians were to include spiritual consolation among their
duties, and were to offer aid even to incurable patients.[103]

Until the first half of the seventh century most physicians were laymen. The basic social structure of medical
practice had been inherited from Rome. But as Roman institutions collapsed along with the last vestiges of the Empire, new Christian structures began to take their place.
In the sixth century monasteries began to care for the sick.
Bishops built hospices, where some medical care was given.
During the seventh and following centuries priests and religious took over the medical profession, so that from the
seventh to the twelfth centuries the lay doctor was the

---

[101]Entralgo, p. 54. Entralgo notes that for Christians
physical illness might be seen as a help to spiritual excellence, as in the case of many of the ascetics and mystics.
"Therapeutic and moral value [was] attributed to the endur-
ance of pain. Describing his life in the hospital city of
Caesarea, St. Gregory of Nazianzen said: 'Illness was
patiently borne; misfortune was treated as happiness, and
compassion put to the test by the sufferings of others'" (p.
57). This belief in the spiritual benefits achieved by suffering, when used as a rationale for moral judgments of medical therapy, becomes a theological principle applied in
medical ethics. See below, chapter three.

[102]*Ibid.*, p. 54. This is not to say that medieval doc-
tors always practiced in accord with their theoretical
Christian motivation any more than all Greek physicians
acted according to the highest standards of *philia* or *eros*.
Often greed was the basic motive. Nonetheless the theory of
Christian medicine, followed by the more exemplary of its
adherers, took as its motivating force the imitation of
Christ as healer to all people.

[103]*Ibid.*, pp. 56-57.

exception rather than the rule.[104] This renewed identification of priest and physician was known generally as "medicina clericalis." It was fostered by the theocentrism of
medieval intellectual life and the ecclesiastical nature of
educational institutions, as well as by the missionary activity of monks among the pagan tribes.[105] At first "monks-
medicine" was practiced according to the best science of
Greek medicine, enriched by the knowledge of pagan medicine
brought back by the monks.[106] Gradually, however, this combined learning was rejected, so that medical practice became
a combination of "empirical" therapy, charity, and supersti-
tion.[107] Rather than an art, "technē," medical practice became an office, "officium," where the monk or priest practiced medicine as part of his religious duties. Blood-
letting and baths were combined with prayer and fasting and
the application of relics as medieval medical therapies.[108]

In the twelfth and thirteenth centuries the "medicina
clericalis" of the Early Middle Ages began to disappear, as
laymen (non-clerics) again became dominant in the practice

---

[104]*Ibid.*, pp. 60-62; Pompey, pp. 17-20; p. 19, n. 26.

[105]Pompey, pp. 17-19. The theocentric character of intellectual life of the time distinguished this "medicina
clericalis" from the Enlightenment-influenced "medicina
ruralis" of the eighteenth century. Though priests practiced medicine, they did not intend to become physicians instead of priests. There was thus a personal identification
of priest and doctor, but not a formal theoretical identification of priesthood with medicine. The priest's spiritual
task remained important (*Ibid.*, p. 19). We will discuss
"medicina ruralis" in the next section.

[106]*Ibid.*, p. 18.

[107]Entralgo, p. 70.

[108]*Ibid.*, pp. 65-70; Pompey, p. 19.

of medicine.[109] This transformation during the High Middle
Ages and on into the Renaissance and Baroque periods was not
caused by any radical separation of the natural sciences,
including medicine, from theology. That would not occur until the Enlightenment. The High Middle Ages remained faithful to theocentrism in intellectual life. Nonetheless, various factors emerged which enabled the development of a medical profession no longer bound to the clerical state.

Among these factors were several of a practical nature.
A medical school was established at Salerno which trained
large numbers of secular physicians.[110] Faculties of medicine were included in the new urban universities.[111] A
series of ecclesiastical decrees forbad the practice of medicine by religious.[112]

---

[109]Entralgo, pp. 62, 74.

[110]*Ibid.*

[111]*Ibid.*, p. 62.

[112]The constant repetition of the ban in various forms
indicates the extent to which monks and secular clergy had
engaged in the practice of medicine, and also suggests that
Church officials were not at all convinced of exactly what
to do with the matter. The Council of Clermont (1130) forbad medical practice to monks and regular clerics, but not
to secular priests. The order referred only to those who
intended to earn money at medicine, and the private practice
of medicine within the monasteries was not forbidden (Pompey,
p. 23). Later synods (Montpellier, 1162 and 1195, and Tours,
1163) removed the loophole. The fourth Lateran Council of
1215 extended the ban to all clerics, including the diocesan
clergy, but limited it to surgery, especially by burning and
cutting (*Ibid.*, p. 25). The ordinances were repeated during
the thirteenth century in various forms, sometimes including,
sometimes excluding the seculars. Pope Boniface VIII (1294-
1303) relaxed the ordinance a bit, perhaps, as Pompey suggests, because his personal chaplain was a famous priest-
physician (*Ibid.*, p. 26). Later exceptions were allowed for
missionaries to countries lacking in medical care (Fleckenstein, "Pastoralmedizin," p. 160). The ban is still

Also important in the development of professional and
scientific medicine was the theological integration of Aristotelian philosophy by the scholastic theologians of the
High Middle Ages. This laid the intellectual base for the
reintroduction of medical "technique." Now medical practice
could shift back from an "office" (part of the duties of the
clerical state) to an "art" (a scientific and rational endeavor which develops its own skills). The classical Greek
medical tradition, enriched and transmitted by the best of
Arab doctors, was discovered anew in western Europe.[113] The
scholastic notion of "nature," not unlike that advanced by
Hippocrates,[114] suggested again the possibility of human
intervention for man's betterment. Whereas often in previous centuries there had been a battle between medical practice and religious remedies, and medical techniques had been
opposed as usurpations of God's power,[115] now the scholastic
notions of nature, secondary causality, and "necessitas ex
suppositione" enabled Christians to view such interventions
as part of God's providence for humankind rather than as

---

officially in effect (*Codex juris canonici,* canon 139, 2).
Exemptions are fairly easy to get.
    In any case it is clear that the motivation for the
proscription of medical practice by the clergy was disciplinary more than theological. The "medicina clericalis" of
the Early Middle Ages was ideologically unlike the "medicina
ruralis" of the eighteenth century which, under the influence of the Enlightenment, tended to imply that a cleric,
especially a religious priest, was useless unless he engaged
in some kind of healing which could be rationally and empirically defended. The twelfth century ban was an attempt to
stop priests and religious from earning their living by the
practice of medicine.

[113]Pompey, p. 30; Agnew, "Medicine, History of," p.
583.

[114]See above, pp. 47-48, esp. n. 98.

[115]Entralgo, pp. 78-79.

attacks against it.[116] In this intellectual climate the
physician who was not a cleric could begin to claim his own
vocation and to develop his own skills without separating
himself from the Christian theocentrism of his time. His
call was to use his God-given and God-approved skills, which
he had developed by studying his art, in service of his patients. The lay doctors of the Middle Ages and of the Renaissance and Baroque eras were often very pious men, for
whom the care of the sick was a specifically Christian vocation.[117]

The disappearance of "medicina clericalis" over the
next centuries was a gradual one. Religious continued to

---

[116]*Ibid.*, pp. 83-90. A detailed description of these
processes is beyond our task. The notion of secondary causality admitted the possibility of cause-and-effect in "nature" while retaining God's omnipotence as primary cause.
The concept "necessitas ex suppositione" (conditioned necessity) allowed for the possibility that a reality may be
necessary, or given, only under certain conditions, and that
these conditions may lawfully be altered without interfering
with divine providence. Just as all creation is only conditionally necessary in that God might not have created it, so
some natural realities are seen to be necessary not absolutely, but conditionally. Human "art" can alter them, and this
potential for alteration is a part of God's plan. Paradox-
ically, nominalism also furthered this process, since the
nominalist emphasis on will fostered a growing sense of the
power of human beings over nature (*Ibid.*, pp. 111-112).

[117]Pompey, p. 30; Entralgo, pp. 91-100. Sir Thomas
Browne's *Religio Medici* (1642) is a classic example of how
one Christian physician viewed his vocation in religious
terms (Browne, *Religio Medici*). In this pre-Enlightenment
period both cleric and layman considered the practice of medicine in this manner. For the cleric medicine was, at least
theoretically, subordinate to his primary function as pastor
of souls. For the layman it was his primary task, but it
was seen as an integrally Christian, hence religious, vocation. Again it must be noted that we refer to the best of
the physicians, both lay and clerical. As in any era, many
doctor-priests and doctor-laymen practiced their skills
solely for personal gain.

study and practice medicine through the Middle Ages and into
modern times.[118] Clerics continued to teach medicine in the
universities, using the scholastic method and thus circum-
venting the ban. Rural pastors continued to offer some medical help to their parishioners. But gradually the practice
and study of medicine became more and more a lay profession.

We have already noted that it was during this period
that the confessors' manuals first gave special treatment to
the moral obligations of physicians, thus explicitly recognizing the medical profession as a *locus* of ethical issues.[119]
This recognition of the medical profession in the general
moral tradition coincided with the growing de-clericalization of medical practice.

During the medieval, Renaissance, and Baroque periods,
many works were written at the interface of medicine and religion. In a most general way, these writings prefigure
those of pastoral medicine. Throughout the Middle Ages monks
copied the classical medical treatises and brought back medical knowledge from the pagan tribes.[120] The great theologians not only passed along classical achievements in medical science, but some of them actually carried on experiments.[121] And the theological-philosophical syntheses created by these scholars included, as part of the totality of
human knowledge gathered in them, discussions of theological

---

[118]Pompey, pp. 26-30. The only part of the ban consistently obeyed was that forbidding clerics to practice surgery.
Indeed, few if any educated physicians, lay or religious,
entered surgical practice, where failure was the equivalent
of negligent homicide. Surgery was done by barbers and
stone cutters (*Ibid.*, pp. 27-28).

[119]See above, pp. 24-27.

[120]Pompey, p. 18.

[121]Fleckenstein, "Pastoralmedizin," p. 160. Mentioned
are Albert the Great, Roger Bacon, and Nicholaus of Cusa.

and medical questions concerning human nature and human
health.

Though all of the above types of writings can be said
to prefigure in a general way the works of pastoral medicine, the first work of immediate importance for our purposes is Paulo Zacchia's *Quaestiones medico-legales,* begun
around 1621.[122]   Zacchia has been called the first of the
real forefathers of pastoral medicine, its spiritual father.[123]   He served as personal physician to Pope Innocent X
from 1644 to 1655, and his work earned him in 1644 the title
"General Proto-Physician of the Whole Roman Ecclesiastical
State."[124] His most important contribution to the development of medical ethics was his opinion that the ensoulment
of a fetus takes place at fertilization.[125] The three volume work includes an extensive array of medical-theological,

---

[122]The edition consulted is the Daniel Horst edition
published in Lyons in 1701 (see the bibliography under Zacchia).   Various editions are available, including a reprint
of the Horst edition in Venice in 1789, with different
pagination.   An earlier edition is available in the British
Museum.

[123]Niedermeyer, *Allgemeine Pastoralmedizin,* I, 51-52.
It is interesting to note, however, that K. F. Hoffmann does
not even mention him (see Niedermeyer, I, 61-62), and that
Pompey, whose extensive technical bibliographies list many
works in and around the field, and whose history was written
after that of Niedermeyer, is also apparently unaware of him
(Pompey, esp. pp. 315-316 and 350-352, where Zacchia ought
to appear).

[124]Noonan, "An Almost Absolute Value," p. 35; Niedermeyer, *Allgemeine Pastoralmedizin,* I, 52.

[125]"Foetum humanum nullo unquam tempore alia anima
dotari nisi Rationalis, eamque in ipso primo momento a Deo
creatam & infusam recipere" ("The human fetus is at no time
given any other soul than a rational one, and that one is
received as created and infused by God at the very first
moment." Zacchia, *Quaestiones,* 1701 ed., II, 699 ff.).

medical-canonical, and medical-ethical questions.

In volume one Zacchia begins with a discussion of the
aging process, and then turns to pregnancy and childbirth.
He describes fetal development, pregnancy testing, multiple
births, causes of fetal death, and differences among infants
(a kind of pre-genetics). Next Zacchia turns to mental illness, poisons, and some questions of civil law. He speaks
of sexual impotence and sterility, dissimulation of illness
and epidemics, miracles, virginity, and rape, fasting and
Lent, wounds, mutilation and castration, and ecology.

Volume two considers the physician's liability before
the law for his mistakes, torture and legal penalties for
criminals, and the order of rank between doctors and lawyers.
Zacchia then speaks of monsters, the obligation of hearing
Mass and reciting the Office during illness, the "conjugal
debt" (like the "use of marriage" sections in the manuals,
here limited to asking when the "debt" must be "paid"), and
stigmata. The following section treats of canonical irregu-
larity, medical treatments in general, and monastic cloister.
Then comes the section concerning the ensoulment of fetuses,
Caesarian section and impotence, followed by shorter passages on ecclesiastical benefices, pestilence, tobacco, coffee, liquor, reception of the Eucharist by the sick, annulment and divorce, "female semination," and criteria for determining primogeneity in multiple births.

The third volume is a collection of decisions of the
Roman Rota (the papal marriage tribunal) pertaining to medicine. It is thus a gathering of canonical precedents in the
medical-theological and medical-ethical area.

This summary of the topics investigated by Zacchia
makes it clear that he includes many of the issues of contemporary medical ethics, at least in seminal form. Later
sections of the present work will demonstrate that the
emerging discipline of medical ethics in North America

developed from bases in pastoral medicine, medical jurisprudence, and medical etiquette ("medical ethics" in the
earlier, more restricted sense in which the term was used
within the medical profession). Zacchia touches on all of
these. He introduces to the pastor some basic medical information and speaks to him and to the physician of medical
ethical questions (the two emphases of pastoral medicine);
he discusses the physician's relationship to the law, his
legal liabilities and obligations (medical jurisprudence);
and he includes a short discussion on the social and political honor due the physician ("medical ethics"). Though he
does not himself use any of these terms, Zacchia lays valid
claim to priority in the field.

If Paulo Zacchia can be called the forefather of pastoral medicine, the seventeenth century Belgian moralist Michael Boudewyns deserves the title of forefather of medical
ethics. His 1666 work of some 450 pages, *Ventilabrum medico-*
theologicum, is quite specifically concerned with the moral
questions of medical practice. Whereas Zacchia included
much material intended to inform the theologian and pastor
about the workings of the body (one of the emphases of pastoral medicine), Boudewyns' work is restricted to the presentation of moral theological opinion concerning the practice of
medicine (the second emphasis in pastoral medicine and the
sole area of concern for much of twentieth century theological medical ethics). The title itself sets the tone for the
work. Boudewyns intends to make judgments on "all cases concerning doctors and patients and others," and to do this according to the Church fathers, scholastic principles, and a
safe conscience. He declares that his book is necessary
"for theologians and confessors and especially for doctors."[126]

---

[126]For the complete Latin title, see the bibliography
(Boudewyns, *Ventilabrum*). Neither Niedermeyer nor Pompey
mention Boudewyns, except in their bibliographies.

His emphasis is thus to be on presenting moral theological
data for the use of other theologians in their studies and
teaching, confessors in their sacramental ministry, and
especially physicians in their practice of medicine.

A survey of the topics Boudewyns treats reveals their
remarkable modernity. Though some of them are of antiquari-
an interest only, many are still topical, and others can
easily be transposed with a bit of imagination to today's
medical scene. Boudewyns looks at issues ranging from abortion, contraception, and euthanasia, through issues of sexual-
medical ethics, to questions of medical experimentation, medical secrets, and doctors' fees. A listing of Boudewyns'
topics provides a fascinating look at the medical-moral questions of the seventeenth century, as well as a counter-
balance to the high ethical and religious motivation theoretically subscribed to by the physicians of the time and
doubtless practiced by the best of them.[127]

---

[127]Boudewyns' first part contains fifty questions,
among which are the following. Does a doctor do any good at
all with his art? Is he allowed to hope, or to pray to God,
that many people will get sick? May he use sorcery or super-
stition? Astrology? May he count years, days, hairs, etc.?
May he take away an illness caused by one magic by using
another? May he make use of blood, flesh, fat, human bones,
amulets, pentacles, etc.? Incantations and the like? May
he prescribe love potions? May he use graphology, physiog-
nomy, dreams, etc., to make a diagnosis? May he practice
alchemy? May he prescribe cosmetics? May he order his patient to drink wine and get drunk? May he impede the production of sperm, or destroy the genitals? May he suggest masturbation in order to regain health? May he look at and
touch the shameful parts? May he, for someone's health,
break the hymen? May he advise his patient to marry for
health? May he impede conception? May he castrate a man?
May he order conjugal intercourse? May he procure an abortion? May he undertake the cure of incurable and desperate
patients? May he drag out an illness or use doubtful remedies? May he cure one illness with another? May he omit
necessary remedies because of danger to his reputation? May
he prescribe poisons? May he prescribe medicines to cause

* * *

This survey of the pre-history of pastoral medicine has
discussed in outline form the early stages of the long his-

---

vomiting or defecation? May he mutilate, amputate, make
prostheses? May he accelerate death in order to free a des-
perately ill person from pain? Must he give equal care to
all his patients? May he do an anatomiqal autopsy on the
human body? Must he care for heretics and for those with
contagious diseases? Is he obliged to see to it that the
sick person receive the last sacraments? May a doctor who
is asked about the potency of his drugs cover up or deny?
Is he obliged, when asked, to state that there is danger of
death? Must he reveal secret illnesses? May he relax the
fast or advise something forbidden by the Church? May he
receive a fee for his work? Must he serve the poor for
free? May he bargain with the patient about the price, and
get as much as he can? May he demand more for a remedy he
invented himself, or more from the rich than from the poor?
May one doctor replace another? In consultations is one
doctor allowed, or required, to disagree with the other?
  The second part asks twenty-four questions. May a
prince or a magistrate permit the practice of medicine in
their jurisdiction? Is medicine a licit science for the internal forum? May anyone practice medicine in the internal
forum? Is it the magistrate's task to take care that good
medical care is provided? May he admit Jews to medical practice? What should he do in times of plague? May pharmacists change or omit a doctor's prescription? Must all sick
people avail themselves of medical help? Must the sick obey
their doctor? Must surgeons and other assistants carry out
the doctor's orders quickly and precisely? May the saints
be invoked in times of illness? Is a sick person obliged to
undress and allow the inspection of his obscene parts? May
the impotent marry, and what advice should be given them?
Are any other illnesses impediments to marriage? Are married
people allowed to have intercourse at any time and in any
manner, when health is not at issue? May pregnant women or
nursing women fast, and are they obliged to? Do coffee,
wine, milk, tobacco break the fast? Are Carthusians obliged
by their rule; can they always abstain from meat? Are those
who cannot give birth naturally allowed, or obliged, to submit to a hysterotomy on the living body or to the incision
of the womb, in order to baptize the baby? Must satyrs,
pygmies, hermaphrodites, and similar monsters be baptized?
Is a mother obliged to nurse her child herself? Are the
sick obliged to pay the doctor?

tory of the relationship between religion and medicine. We
have noted a persistent interdependence and overlapping of
the two modes of healing. We have seen the influence which
religious motivation had on medical practice, and the consistent interest shown by theologians in investigating medicine and in applying moral principles to it. We have noted
especially the various shifts during this period in the development of medicine as a special professional sphere.
There was not yet anything approaching a true "secularization" of medicine, but there was in the de-clericalization
process of the twelfth and later centuries a practical separation of physical from spiritual healing. This process of
professional separation coincided with the appearance of the
special section in the moral manuals concerned with the
moral obligations of physicians as a specific class of moral
agent by reason of their special vocation, their state of
life. It was also significant for the development of pastoral medicine as a self-conscious discipline in the eighteenth century, and, as we shall see in the next chapter, for
the definitional emergence of Roman Catholic medical ethics
in North America in the twentieth century.

     The history of pastoral medicine proper begins in the
eighteenth century. Now the theocentric view of the world
which was almost universal in Western civilization during
the Middle Ages will be shattered by the Enlightenment critique. The de-clericalization of professional medicine will
become a true secularization, and the emerging discipline of
pastoral medicine will be affected by this transformation.

2. Early Works in Pastoral Medicine (The eighteenth and

           early nineteenth centuries)

     We noted earlier that pastoral medicine developed two
rather distinct emphases, one medical and the other theological. As the discipline emerged in the eighteenth century

it was the medical aspect which was predominant. The central task of pastoral medicine was to teach the theologian,
and especially the pastoral minister, what he needed to know
from medical science. This emphasis included two dimensions. First, some writings aimed at furnishing the priest,
especially the parish priest in rural areas of Europe, with
a quick course in first aid to enable him to replace the
medical doctor where no physician was available. Second,
some writings aimed at furnishing the parish priest with
data from medicine and psychology which might be of service
to him in his primarily spiritual task as religious leader
and sacramental minister.

The second emphasis of the discipline (theological investigation of the area of medicine, both from the speculative and the moral theological viewpoints) was not entirely
neglected. Nonetheless the central emphasis in pastoral
medicine in the eighteenth and early nineteenth centuries
was by no means on its theological dimensions.[128]

It was in the context of the gradual overshadowing of
theocentric thought systems with anthropocentric ones that
pastoral medicine emerged as a self-conscious discipline.[129]
The movement from theocentrism to anthropocentrism in the
seventeenth and eighteenth centuries led to a formal separation of philosophy and the natural sciences from theology.
Though anthropocentrism and theocentrism can in some sense
be reconciled as complementary within the Christian religion,
the separation of the disciplines which resulted from the
shift from the one to the other often became an alienation
and opposition.[130] The Enlightenment often opposed religion

---

[128]Pompey, *Die Bedeutung der Medizin,* pp. 8-9.

[129]*Ibid.*, pp. 6, 11.

[130]Anthropocentrism itself is not formally identical to

altogether. Recognizing the inadequacy of such a relationship, and drawing on the long history of the theology-
medicine dialogue, eighteenth century scholars produced a
large body of literature which constitutes the early phase
of pastoral medicine.[131]

Many scholars responded to the Enlightenment critique
largely by agreeing with it. Under the influence of the rationalism and materialism which was a part of the Enlightenment movement, much of pastoral medicine restricted itself
to issues of physical healing. These works limited the newly emerging discipline to that of "medicina ruralis," also
called "medicina clerica."[132] They considered the primary

---

a reductionist secularism or materialism, and is, in its
wider dimensions, compatible with Christianity. Indeed,
pastoral medicine is itself an anthropocentric discipline,
as its primary emphasis is on the healing of man (Pompey,
p. 6). In its total scope it is anthropocentric in a non-
materialist way, as its task at the border of medicine and
religion is not limited to the strictly physical process of
healing. In addition, we have already noted that the integration by scholastic theologians of Aristotelian notions of
nature, secondary causality, etc., enabled the science of
medicine, even in its physical, "technical" aspects, to be
seen as part of God's providence for humankind. Medicine,
then, need not be considered "materialistic" or reduction-
istically secular if its task is interpreted as part of God's
plan. In *this* sense anthropocentrism and theocentrism are
complementary rather than antithetic; they offer two alternative approaches to the understanding of human nature and human healing, and neither denies the insights of the other.
Nonetheless the general movement to anthropocentrism included
elements of materialism and reductionist secularism, which
elements also affected pastoral medicine, especially in its
restricted phase of "medicina ruralis."

[131]Fleckenstein, "Pastoralmedizin," p. 160.

[132]Fleckenstein, p. 161; Niedermeyer, *Allgemeine Pastoralmedizin,* I, 15-19, 53-54; Pompey, *Die Bedeutung der Medizin,* pp. 8-12, and generally pp. 33-117, also pp. 295-296.
"Medicina ruralis" and "medicina clerica" are not entirely
synonymous as rubrics for this restricted phase of pastoral

task of pastoral medicine to be the instruction of parish
priests, especially those in rural areas, in practical first
aid so that they might be of use to their parishioners by
offering medical help.

In our study of the pre-history of pastoral medicine,
we noted that in the Early Middle Ages (the seventh to the
twelfth centuries) the practice of medicine was largely in
the hands of clerics, who considered it to be a part of
their duties as consecrated religious ("medicina clericalis"). Now in the eighteenth century, under the influence of
the Enlightenment, clerics were again practicing medicine.
But the context and ideological significance of the newer
"medicina ruralis" differed radically from that of the
"medicina clericalis" of the Early Middle Ages. Whereas in
those earlier centuries the practice of medicine had been
dominated by the clergy, now the practice of medicine was
largely a secular one, dominated by secular physicians in
the cities. Clerics who practiced medicine merely replaced
the lay physician in areas which lacked proper medical care.
In addition, whereas earlier priest-doctors had seen medicine as a largely secondary part of their spiritual vocation, now they were to see it as their primary function,
indeed their only useful task. Materialistic utilitarian
ideology suggested that a priest was quite useless unless
he performed some empirically measurable service to the

---

medicine, but they are similar. "Rural medicine" refers
generally to all treatises on "country medicine" for the
common folk. When pastoral medicine emphasizes this aspect,
it aims most directly at informing pastors, thus "clerical
medicine." "Clerical medicine" is also used simply as a
synonym for "pastoral medicine," including other emphases of
the discipline than merely that of "rural medicine." See
Fleckenstein, p. 161, where "medicina ruralis" and "medicina
clerica" are used synonymously, and Niedermeyer, I, 15,
where a distinction is made.

people.[133]   Accordingly many works in early pastoral medicine were courses in "medicina ruralis."[134]   Unfortunately,
despite the rationalistic and "scientific" bias of these
works, the pastors who practiced "rural medicine" all too
often mixed the newer medical therapies with superstitious
remedies, an influence of the older "medicina clericalis."[135]

Though many works in pastoral medicine of the eighteenth century restricted the discipline to the study of

---

[133]Niedermeyer, I, 15-16. The "ideal pastor" of Josephinism was to be useful in bringing medical care and good hygiene to his people (Fleckenstein, "Pastoralmedizin," p.
161).

[134]Historians of pastoral medicine are not in complete
agreement as to which works should be considered works of
rural medicine. Most of the later nineteenth and twentieth
century pastoral medicine literature contains information
on hygiene and first aid along with more spiritual applications of medical data as well as moral theological material.
Thus the mere inclusion of treatises on first aid for the
pastor is not sufficient to classify a work as a Josephinist
tract in rural medicine. Rather it must be more a question
of emphasis and intent. Generally included as works of
"medicina clerica" or "medicina ruralis" are those of
Leuthner (1781), Lechleitner (1791), Krause (1794), Becker
(1804), Vering (1809), Ritter (1837), Macher (1838), and
Britzger (1848). Also included is the Protestant author J.
Baehrens, whose title, *Beiträge zur Pastoralmedizin*, is the
earliest use of the rubric in a title (1785) that I have
been able to discover (Niedermeyer speaks to this question,
and cites Lechleitner (1791) as using a similar rubric, admitting that the term pastoral medicine was in use previously). The titles of some of these works are indicative of
their scope: "Practical Pastoral-Pharmaceutics for Spiritual
Advisors," "The Medical Rural Pastor: Or Quick Medical Treatment and Healing of Those Sicknesses Which Most Commonly Occur in the Country," "Letter of a Doctor to a Country Pastor," "The Priest as Doctor at the Sickbed," "Introduction
for Country People to Reasonable Health Care . . . A Handbook for Country Ministers . . . Where There Are No Doctors." For a detailed analysis of many of these works, see
Pompey, *Die Bedeutung der Medizin*.

[135]Pompey, pp. 55-73.

practical first aid, some treatises insisted on including
issues of a more directly spiritual nature. These are more
important for our purpose. Among works of a somewhat wider
scope written in the first half of the eighteenth century
were M. A. Alberti's *De convenientia medicinae ad theologiam
practicam* (1732), which has been called "the first general
presentation of the relationship of medicine and theology."[136] the similar treatise *De habitu medicinae ad religio-
nem* by G. M. Matthiae (1734), J. H. Cohausen's *Clericus medicaster* (1748), written in opposition to the practice of
medicine by clerics,[137] and a work devoted to pastoral medical questions of embryology and childbirth, Francesco
Cangiamila's *Embryologia Sacra*. This last work, first published in 1745, had numerous printings[138] and is still of
interest today.[139] The author gives advice to parish
priests on how to help women avoid spontaneous abortion and
other illnesses associated with childbirth. He tells the
pastor how to do a Caesarian section in case of necessity,

---

[136]Niedermeyer, *Allgemeine Pastoralmedizin*, I, 53. "Die
erste zusammenfassende Darstellung der Beziehungen zwischen
Medizin und Theologie stammt . . . von Alberti."

[137]*Clericus medicaster, in quo . . . demonstratur
sacerdotem imprimis curatum praxeos medicae exercitium non
decere*. For a closer analysis of this work, see Pompey, pp.
42-49, and an outline of the book, pp. 315-316.

[138]The work was first published in Palermo, and then
achieved numerous editions throughout Europe. The 1775 Ieper
edition has been used here, and is cited in the bibliography
(Cangiamila, *Sacra embryologia*). For a complete list of
printings see Pompey, p. 155. The numerous editions account
for the different dates assigned to the work by various authors (Fleckenstein says 1751, Niedermeyer 1763). The author was a doctor of theology and a doctor of canon and
civil law (Pompey, p. 155).

[139]Niedermeyer, I, 53. One indication of its importance is its presence in various North American libraries.

and gives instructions for the baptism of fetuses and monsters. The author speaks of the moment of fetal animation,
and cautions the doctor to do everything possible to avoid
the death of the fetus.

The early compendium of pastoral medicine by F. X.
Mezler (1794) broke through the narrow limits of rural medicine, and began a line of such books which continued into
the mid-twentieth century.[140] Mezler's interest was primarily in describing the implications of medical and psychological states on moral behavior and culpability, so as to help
the confessor better understand the behavior of his penitents.[141] He thus moved beyond the physical to the spiritual dimensions of the pastor's ministry, and opened a two-
sided dialogue between theology and medicine.[142] A similar
approach is found in the treatise of F. A. May, which was a
series of sermons on the interrelationship of body and soul,
and on the need for proper diet and proper morals in the
service of physical and spiritual health.[143]

In the third decade of the nineteenth century, the
Protestant physician and quasi-theologian Ernst Joseph de
Valenti wrote a two volume treatise entitled *Medicina cleri-
ca*.[144] Like Mezler, he refused to limit pastoral medicine

---

[140]Niedermeyer, I, 54; Pompey, pp. 134, 164-165. For
an outline of Mezler's work, see Pompey, pp. 326-329.

[141]Niedermeyer accuses Mezler of determinism, in that
he underlines the importance of physical and psychological
determinants of human behavior.

[142]Pompey, p. 167.

[143]*Medizinische Fastenpredigten* (1793). See Niedermeyer, I, 54; Pompey, pp. 140-143, and outline, p. 322.

[144]See Pompey, pp. 186-195, and outline, pp. 338-342.
The subtitle is: *Oder Handbuch der Pastoral-medizin für
Seelsorger, Pädagogen, und Aerzte, nebst einer Diätetik für
Geistliche* ("A Handbook of Pastoral Medicine for Pastors,
Teachers, and Physicians, together with a Diet for Religious").

to "medicina ruralis," and presented it from a wider ethical
and metaphysical standpoint. His work is criticized, however, for excesses in the opposite direction. In the roman-
ticism of his age, he tended to a reductionist supernatural-
ism, and in his reaction against the Enlightenment attempt
to make priests into doctors, he tried to make doctors into
pastors.[145] A similar work is that of the Catholic physician and professor of philosophy Carl Joseph Windischmann,
who spoke in a magical-mystical fashion of illness and its
religious cure.[146]

In most of the works in pastoral medicine of the eighteenth and early nineteenth centuries the medical rather than
the theological emphasis was dominant. Very little emphasis
was given to moral theological investigations of medical
practice. In one work of the early nineteenth century, however, such an investigation is included. This work, *Catechismo*
medico, by the Italian professor of diplomacy and philosophy
Angelo Scotti, was first published in 1821 and translated into German in 1824.[147] It was a transitional work, prefig-
uring later pastoral medicine literature. Scotti divides
his work into three sections. He speaks first of the benefits which medicine has received from religion, second of
the service medicine can offer to religion, and third of the
obligations which religion prescribes for medicine. In this
last section Scotti includes medical ethical issues. He
speaks of the authority of religion to determine the moral
obligations of physicians, the duty of a doctor to be

---

[145]Niedermeyer, I, 55-57. Niedermeyer accuses him of
dualism, and lays the charge to his Lutheran theology of
grace.

[146]Pompey, pp. 181-186, and outline, pp. 335-336.

[147]See Niedermeyer, I, 60-61. The 1836 edition has
been consulted.

properly informed and diligent, and his obligation never to
advise a patient contrary to moral law, such as by advising
drunkenness or illicit sex. Contraception, sterilization,
and abortion are condemned. Questions of truth-telling and
secrets are treated, as are issues of medical experimentation and the obligations of pharmacists and surgeons.
Strictly religious questions connected with medical practice, such as dispensation from the fast laws and the reception of the sacraments in illness are then discussed.
Scotti concludes his work with a treatment of professional
fees and the doctor's responsibility to the poor.

                         * * *

     The early works in pastoral medicine reflect the grow-
ing secularization of medicine under the influence of the
Enlightenment critique. All attempt in some way to re-
establish a relationship between religion and medicine.
Some works, those of rural medicine, make this attempt by
agreeing largely with the materialist emphasis of the age,
reducing pastoral medicine to the study of practical first
aid, and emphasizing the role of religion and religious personnel in specifically physically medical activities. Other
works insist on the importance of spiritual healing, and include material intended to help the pastor in his spiritual
care of souls. Angelo Scotti's work leads us naturally to
the second half of the nineteenth century, when the specifically moral theological concerns of pastoral medicine receive a more important emphasis. Medical treatises continue
to be a part of the literature, but more and more it is the
theological, especially the moral issues, which gain prominence in the discipline. This development is related to the
growing professionalization and secularization of medicine.
More and more the physician is singled out as a subject for
moral guidance in his professional activity.

3. Later Works in Pastoral Medicine (The late nineteenth
       and twentieth centuries)

As the discipline investigating the interface of theology and medicine, pastoral medicine has never limited itself entirely to medical-moral aspects. It is not identical to the moral theology of medicine, to theological medical ethics as that discipline developed in the twentieth
century. Even as pastoral medicine continues today in
Europe, its central task is that of helping the parish
priests and ministers in their pastoral care of souls, which
includes, but is wider than, moral aspects. However,
specifically moral issues come to receive a greater and
greater emphasis within pastoral medicine during the late
nineteenth and early twentieth centuries. Some works in
the field are indeed moral theological writings, limiting
their purview almost exclusively to moral questions. It is
this medical-moral emphasis which most influenced the North
American adaptation of pastoral medicine.

In emphasizing the specifically ethical aspects of the
medicine-theology dialogue, this trend is itself a response
to the Englightenment critique, and reveals a definite Enlightenment influence. By insisting that religion must be
practical in some empirically recognizable form, the Enlightenment accented the ethical importance of religion,
and tended to restrict the validity of religion as such to
its ethical functions. Thus the Enlightenment was at once
influential in restricting early pastoral medicine, as we
have seen, to the "practical" "medicina ruralis" of the
eighteenth century, and in leading later pastoral medicine
to emphasize the equally "practical" ethical questions
posed by medical practice.[148]

---

[148]Pompey, *Die Bedeutung der Medizin,* p. 119. The

A series of manuals of pastoral medicine appeared during the last decades of the nineteenth and the early decades of the twentieth centuries. In many of them, the
growing emphasis on moral matters is evident. The handbook
of August Stöhr (1878) has been called the first modern work
in pastoral medicine.[149] The author includes moral issues,
though this forms a negligible part of his entire treatise.
His emphasis in on correct diet and hygiene. He argues
against materialism and defends priestly celibacy. He insists that the physician be properly trained, and that he
see to it that the dying patient receive the sacraments.
Von Olfers' manual (1881) includes several moral questions,
such as fetal animation, the "usus matrimonii," sins against
the sixth commandment, and abortion. He speaks also of
fetal baptism and advises the pastor on care of the sick.[150]
He specifically excludes courses in first aid from the discipline, reasoning that every popular almanac contains such
an introduction.[151]

The first work in pastoral medicine to appear in English for American readers was the 1878 translation of Carl
Capellmann's *Medicina pastoralis*.[152] Capellmann was influ-

---

author notes the influence of Kant in underlining the ethical value of religion.

[149]Niedermeyer, *Allgemeine Pastoralmedizin,* I, 62. The
German title is *Handbuch der Pastoralmedizin mit besonderer
Berücksichtigung der Hygiene* ("Handbook of Pastoral Medicine
with Special Consideration to Hygiene"). It went through
several editions. See Niedermeyer, I, 62-65.

[150]*Ibid.*, I, 65.

[151]*Ibid.*, I, 19.

[152]The 1882 printing is used here (Capellmann, *Pastoral
Medicine*). The original Latin work went through several
editions and reprints. A comparison of the English translation (1878) with a later Latin edition (1896; see the

ential in furthering the emphasis on moral questions within
European pastoral medicine, and the English translation
fostered the American identification of the field with the
moral theology of medical practice. Because of his importance for the North American discipline, a detailed examination of Capellmann's work is in order.

Capellmann defines pastoral medicine as "the sum of
those explanations anatomical-physiological, as well as
pathological-therapeutical, a knowledge of which is necessary to the priest in the exercise of his pastoral functions."[153] In this definition he reflects the traditional
medical emphasis of the discipline, whereby data from medicine is brought to the pastor. However, Capellmann goes on
to add:

> I prefer to extend the scope of pastoral medicine so
> as to meet likewise the exigencies of physicians.
> Consequently, it will be my aim, in this work, to
> communicate to physicians those dogmatical and moral
> principles, a sufficient knowledge of which is indis-
> pensable to render their professional acts always safe
> and consistent with Christian morals.[154]

Capellmann is thus aware that he is doing something new in
directing his work explicitly and equally to the physician
as to the priest. Surely, as our study has shown, moral
questions are not new to pastoral medicine literature. Nor

---

bibliography. Capellmann, *Medicina pastoralis*) shows some
change in order of treatment, but little in substance.
There is also a later German translation and redaction by W.
Bergmann (1923; see the bibliography, Capellmann and Berg-
mann, *Pastoralmedizin*) and a French translation from the
German by P. F. de Bénéjac (see Payen, *Déontologie*, p. vii).
Niedermeyer discusses the work (*Allgemeine Pastoralmedizin*,
I, 19, 69-70). Capellmann was a German Catholic physician
practicing in Aix-la-Chapelle. The English translator,
William Dassell, was a Pennsylvania parish priest.

[153]Capellmann, *Pastoral Medicine*, p. 1.

[154]*Ibid.*, p. 1. The Latin states simply "tutus atque
honestus" ("safe and proper," *Medicina pastoralis*, p. 1).

is this the first time that the physician has been included
in the intended readership. But most of the literature has
been written primarily for pastors. Capellmann's emphasis
on the physician marks a new departure. Here is a book
specifically entitled *Pastoral Medicine* whose intention is
to serve equally both pastor and physician. Capellmann
cites what he calls the materialism of the age, which
results in a lack of moral theological and ethical training
for physicians. To the priest he will bring data from medicine which will help him in caring for his parishioners,
especially in making moral judgments on medical questions.
To the physician he will bring the principles of moral theology.[155]

Capellmann compares his version of pastoral medicine
to the discipline known as "medical jurisprudence" ("medicina forensis" in the Latin). Just as the medical student
attends lectures and reads books designed to inform him of
what he needs to know of the law, and as law students do
the same in medicine, so "pastoral medicine should, in my
opinion, meet the exigencies of both priest and physician,
the more so as the questions at issue cannot be clearly determined, unless theology and medicine mutually complete
each other."[156]

The "questions at issue" for Capellmann are primarily,
though not exclusively, moral ones. He criticizes previous
works in pastoral medicine:

> The fault of overloading the work with scientific de-
> tail mars nearly all books on pastoral medicine that
> have hitherto appeared. Systematic treatises on anat-
> omy, physiology, dietetics of body and soul, semiotics,
> pathology and therapeutics, even whole sections of
> pastoral theology, were jumbled together. Of these

---

[155]*Ibid.*, pp. 1-2.

[156]*Ibid.*, p. 2.

branches some have no fitting place in pastoral medicine, because physician and priest ought to have a
thorough acquaintance with them. Psychology, for instance. . . . In the same category with psychology
may be placed dietetics of the body and soul. . . .
The same cannot be said of dietary nursing of the sick;
regarding which the information necessary for a priest
must be given, as he may do a great deal of good,
especially in the country, by removing prejudice, re-
forming abuses, or by keeping off noxious agents. For
he generally visits the sick as often as the physician,
sometimes oftener, and may be of service at times, in
controlling somewhat the injudicious nursing of rela-
tives.[157]

He intends, therefore, to eliminate what is extraneous to
the discipline. His emphasis will be explicitly moral.
Yet he will not entirely eliminate questions of first aid,
since such data can be of help to the rural pastor.

The division of material in Capellmann's book follows
his formal intentions. More than two-thirds of the work is
devoted to moral issues. Capellmann explicitly adopts the
commandments and the sacraments as his organizing rubrics.
He divides his material into chapters on the fifth commandment, the sixth commandment, the commandments of the Church,
and the sacraments. His chapter headings thus correspond
closely to the *loci* of medical-moral issues in the general
manuals of moral theology.[158] The last third of the book

---

[157]*Ibid.*, p. 3. In the Latin edition Capellmann adds
a footnote in which he cites Stöhr's work as an example of
an overloaded treatise, and Von Olfers' as one which correctly avoids this defect (*Medicina pastoralis*, p. 3, n. 1).

[158]Under the fifth commandment come questions of abortion, high-risk operations (extraordinary and ordinary
means of preserving health, Caesarian section, the priest's
duty to perform it), narcotic medicines, chloroform in
childbirth (possibly permissible, but not advised; better
to educate the woman to bear the pain, which will increase
her love for the child who caused her to suffer, pp. 39-40),
animal magnetism (forbidden as demonic in origin), vaccina-
tion, wet nurses (usually fallen women who replace lazy

contains data from medicine helpful to the pastor in caring
physically for his parishioners, and in determining the moment of death.

Capellmann's work played an important role in the movement of pastoral medicine in Europe and America toward an
ever-increasing emphasis on moral questions. Other handbooks of pastoral medicine of the period also emphasize
moral aspects, though not all are as clearly defined as Capellmann's, and not all follow the divisional rubrics of the
moral theological tradition.

In 1884 the French physician Ange Ferrand published his
enlarged edition of Pierre Debreyne's *Essai sur la théologie
morale considérée dans ses rapports avec la physiologie et
la médecine.*[159]   In his preface Ferrand describes pastoral
medicine:

Just as there is a *legal medicine,* which studies the

---

mothers wishing to gossip at tea parties, p. 48), drunkenness and its cure (force), hysteria, hypochondria (the "crux
medicorum"), mental diseases, and ecclesiastical burial for
suicides.
The sixth commandment section treats masturbation
("perniciosissimum scelus"), pollution, the "usus matrimonii,"
including onanism, withdrawal, positions and times of intercourse, and immodest looks and touches during medical examination. Many phrases in these sections are not translated
into English. The translator comments in his Preface that
his task is most unwelcome because of the sexual aspects of
the book, and he will maintain a "Latin disguise" when
necessary. In any case, the book is "altogether unfit for
the perusal of the lay or general reader" (p. iv).
The section on the commandments of the Church deals with
the Mass obligation and laws of fast for the sick.
Under the sacraments, the author treats baptism of infants, monsters, abortuses, anointing of the dying, and under
marriage, the question of impotency.
In the later Latin edition the section on the "usus
matrimonii" is transferred from the sixth commandment to the
sacrament of matrimony (*Medicina pastoralis,* pp. 136-169).

[159]Debreyne and Ferrand, *La Théologie morale et les
sciences médicales.*

> relationship of the science and the art [of medicine]
> with the facts of the juridical order, so too there is
> a *clerical medicine* (Capelmann [*sic*]) which has as its
> object the relationship of the science and the art
> [of medicine] with the facts of the religious order.[160]

Ferrand thus sees his work as belonging to the genre of
pastoral medicine. He translates Capellmann's "medicina
pastoralis" into French as "médecine cléricale." As the
title of the work indicates, it is a specifically moral theological book. The first part is an introduction to anatomy,
with an emphasis on brain and nervous system functions, and
human character types. The second part discusses sexual
sins, including masturbation, contraception, and sexual relations with the devil (dismissed as imaginary). Part three
treats of embryology and thanatology, including fetal animation, abortion, Caesarian section, fetal baptism, artificial
insemination, and symptoms of death. Part four discusses
mysticism and science, including questions of hyponotism,
magnetism, revelations and visions, and diabolical possession. The final section concerns the mental status and
culpability of some who commit murder or suicide, the question of miraculous healings, the passions, asceticism, fast
and abstinence, and longevity.

A small book by the French moralist Jean-Étienne-Xavier
Craisson was published in 1875 in Paris and New York.[161] In
this Latin book Craisson presents an examination of sexual
ethical issues, including medical ethical questions of abortion, embryology, and Caesarian section. His purpose is to

---

[160]*Ibid.*, p. iii, translation mine, italics his. "De
même qui'il y a une *médecine légale* qui étudie les rapports
de la science et de l'art avec les faits d'ordre juridique,
de même il y a une *médecine cléricale* (Capelmann) qui a pour
objet les rapports de la science et de l'art avec les faits
d'ordre religieux."

[161]Craisson, *Notiones*.

help confessors decide whether to grant or withhold sacramental absolution.[162]

A more important work in the moral theology of medical
practice was Alphons Eschbach's *Disputationes physiologico-
theologicae*.[163] It first appeared in 1884, and was revised
in 1901 and again in 1915. It was not as such a systematic
treatise in pastoral medicine, but rather a moral ·theologi-
cal examination of several disputed issues. Eschbach states
that he intends to correct the errors which have entered
medical practice as a result of the schism between the natural sciences and revelation, by applying informed moral
principles to newly invented medical techniques.[164] His
first disputation describes human conception and discusses
sterilization, vasectomy, artificial insemination, certain
impediments to marriage, and the times of sexual intercourse.
The second concerns sacramental consummation of marriage and
the impediment of impotency. The third is his "embryologia
sacra," concerning the moment of fetal animation, abortion,
fetal baptism, and Caesarian section. The fourth deals
with therapeutic abortion, embryotomy, and ectopic pregnancy. The fifth discusses clerical celibacy, virginity,
control of carnal concupiscence, masturbation, and contraception by withdrawal. The emphasis in Eschbach's work is
thus on sexual and reproductive dimensions of medical ethics.

The French physician Georges Surbled published a four
volume work on the moral issues of medicine and hygiene in

---

[162]*Ibid.*, p. v.

[163]Eschbach, *Disputationes*. Both the first (1884) and
the third (c. 1915) editions have been consulted. The text
description refers to the third edition, which is slightly
altered from the first. Eschbach was a French moralist,
rector of the French seminary in Rome (Fererres, *Compendium*,
p. xliv).

[164]Eschbach, *Disputationes*, 1915, pp. ix-xi.

the 1890's.[165] It was later translated into German[166] and
one volume of the work appeared in English in 1930.[167] His
purpose is similar to that of Eschbach, in that he intends
to oppose the correct moral teaching of the Catholic Church
to the barbaric materialism of the time.[168] Volumes one
and two concern celibacy, marriage, and sexuality, including abortion, Caesarian section, the use of narcotics in
childbirth, artificial insemination, as well as the whole
range of sexual ethical questions, marital impediments, and
so on. Volume three is on "organic life," and includes
tracts on control of the passions of the heart, fast and
abstinence and other good habits for health, sickness, medical experimentation, miraculous healings, and death and
dying. The fourth volume concerns the moral aspects of psychology, mental health, and psychotherapy.

The German professor of moral and pastoral theology
Ludwig Ruland wrote a handbook of pastoral medicine in 1930,
which was later translated with some changes into English
by an American Augustinian, Tarcisius A. Rattler.[169] Here
moral issues are dispersed among the various sections on
the beginnings of life, the conditions of good health,
drugs, sickness and death, psychology, and sexuality.

---

[165]Surbled, *La Morale dans ses rapports avec la
médecine et l'hygiène.*

[166]By Sleumer; see Niedermeyer, *Allgemeine Pastoralmedizin,* I, 67-68.

[167]Surbled, *Catholic Moral Teaching in Its Relation to
Medicine and Hygiene.* The translation of the entire work
was intended (pp. iv-v). I have been unable to find any
reference to any further volumes in English.

[168]Surbled, *La Morale,* I, xi-xiv.

[169]Ruland and Rattler, *Pastoral Medicine.* A description of the German original is in Niedermeyer, I, 65-66.

Though moral judgments are made, they are often secondary
to the medical advice given the priest for a more healthy
and hygienic environment for himself and his people. In the
section on sexuality, Ruland does emphasize the moral aspects of sexual behavior.

The most important of the manuals of pastoral medicine
of the early twentieth century was Giuseppe Antonelli's
Medicina pastoralis.[170] The work had five editions, the
last of which appeared as a four volume set in 1932. Antonelli, a Roman physician, priest, and professor, covers the
entire range of pastoral medicine issues, both from the
medical and from the theological points of view. The first
volume is a general introduction to anatomy, complete with
colored plates depicting bodily structures, and with an emphasis on reproduction and embryology, including a discussion on the question of fetal animation (judged to be at the
moment of conception). Volumes two and three discuss moral
questions under the headings of the first, fifth, and sixth
commandments, and the sacraments of baptism and matrimony.
The first commandment section contains discussions of spiritism and hypnotism as medical therapies (spiritism is condemned, but Antonelli argues against a diabolical origin
for hypnotism, and allows its use in restricted circumstances). Under the fifth commandment are sections on abortion, sexual organ transplant, alcoholism, morphine, breast
feeding, bodily asceticism (hair shirts, flagellation,
sleepless vigils, fasts), euthanasia, and eugenics. The
sixth commandment section and the section on matrimony include the entire range of sexual ethical questions, those

---

[170]Antonelli, *Medicina pastoralis*, 1920, and 1932.
Both editions are widely available in American seminaries.
Earlier editions appeared in the first two decades of this
century. See Niedermeyer, I, 66-67.

which clearly pertain to medicine, such as contraception
and artificial insemination, as well as those not directly
pertaining to medicine, such as masturbation, nocturnal pollution, times and methods of intercourse, the canonical re-
quirements for marital consummation, and so on.[171] The author adds an appendix on ecclesiastical celibacy. The
fourth volume discusses Church laws of fast and abstinence,
and then goes on to present both a medical and a theological
description of death.[172]

Antonelli's manual thus includes both aspects of pastoral medicine: medical data for priests and theological data
for priests and physicians. It is clear, however, that
Antonelli's primary concern is to deal with the moral issues
of medicine. His principal divisional rubric is that of the
moral manuals (commandments and sacraments), and his section
on anatomy is included as providing the necessary background
information for the rest of the book.[173] Antonelli's work
does not contain any definitions or descriptions of pastoral
medicine. But it is clear from what he does that he sees
the discipline more from the moral theological perspective
than from any other. His influential manual is thus a clear

---

[171]Antonelli has sections on the use of dildoes, sodomy and homosexuality, bestiality, necrophilia, and sex
with statues.

[172]Antonelli is specifically interested in determining
the moment of death for purposes of administering the last
sacraments. His chapter is of wider medical ethical interest, however, in the context of ethical questions surrounding the process of dying, questions which have today found
renewed importance in an age of machines and transplants.
The author also discusses the problem of premature burial,
including a diagram of Louvain Count Karnice-Karnicki's
device for signalling such an occurrence from inside the
coffin (Antonelli, *Medicina pastoralis,* 1932, IV, 132-
133).

[173]Antonelli, *Medicina pastoralis,* 1932, I, v.

example of the change in emphasis within pastoral medicine
of the late nineteenth and early twentieth centuries toward
specifically medico-moral questions.

* * *

These works in pastoral medicine of the late nineteenth
and early twentieth centuries continue the response of theology to the growing professionalization and secularization
of medicine. We have noted that many of the authors explicitly cite the dangers of materialism, which they see as
having led to a divorce of medicine from theology, and thus to
a disregard for the spiritual and moral health of mankind.
The primary emphasis of these later works in pastoral medicine is that of moral theology. Topics included are sometimes grouped according to the organizational rubrics which
we have noted in the general manuals of moral theology (the
commandments and the sacraments) and include many areas
which would not be deemed directly relevant to medical
ethics as that discipline would later develop. The authors
include a whole range of issues which they consider important to the spiritual health of man. In the next chapter
we will see how North American medical ethicists will gradually adopt a more restrictive material definition of the
discipline, emphasizing those topics which are of direct
concern to the professional activity of the physician and
the nurse. In so doing, American moralists continue along
the same direction as the authors we have studied here.
They respond more and more specifically to medicine as a
separate profession, applying to it theological principles
of ethical significance.

By the time of the publication of Antonelli's fifth
edition in 1932, North American Roman Catholic moralists
had already produced a substantial number of works investigating the moral issues of medical practice. From this time

on, the American and European disciplines proceed in a parallel development.[174]

Part Three

"Medical Ethics" and Medical Jurisprudence

Pastoral medicine is by far the most important of the
three cognate pre-disciplines[175] to North American Roman
Catholic medical ethics. The other two, medical jurisprudence and "medical ethics" in the intra-professional sense
in which the term was used until recently, do not require a
detailed examination. A brief description of each will suf-
fice.

1. "Medical Ethics"

In our current usage, the rubric *Medical Ethics* is
generally understood as referring to the study of the moral
(that is, ethical) issues connected with the practice of

---

[174]An investigation of twentieth century European pastoral medicine is beyond the scope of this study. Our purpose has been to overview that discipline inasmuch as it
served as a source for the emerging American literature. A
number of the more important modern European works are included in the bibliography. Among them are Payen, *Déontologie médicale*; Bon, *Précis de médecine Catholique*; Okinczyc,
Humanisme et médecine; Palmieri, *Medicina legale canonistica*;
Ricaud, *La Vie est sacrée*; Tiberghien, *Médecine et morale*;
Pujiula, *De medicina pastorali*; Scremin, *Dizionario de
morale professionale per i medici*; and the voluminous works
of Albert Niedermeyer: *Allgemeine Pastoralmedizin, Handbuch
der speziellen Pastoralmedizin,* and *Compendium of Pastoral
Medicine* and *Compendium of Pastoral Hygiene,* both translated
into English.

[175]The reason for choosing the term "cognate pre-
discipline" will become clearer later in our study. See
especially n. 206.

medicine. In its systematic form it is practiced by moral
philosophers and moral theologians, and by medical personnel
speaking philosophically or theologically or in dialogue
with systematic ethicists. But the term "medical ethics"[176]
can also be used to refer to a field of endeavor which,
while it cannot be separated totally from medical ethics in
the philosophical-theological sense, is in many ways quite
different from it. As we will see in greater detail in the
next chapter, it is only recently that the rubric has been
commonly accepted as applying to the systematic investigation of the moral issues of medicine. In the nineteenth
and early twentieth centuries, the term referred far more
generally to a field of endeavor quite distinct from moral
philosophy or theology. It referred rather to a field of
discussion practiced by physicians among themselves, to an
intra-professional dialogue on issues of etiquette and
"ethics," to the formulation, promulgation, and interpretation of intra-professional codes of "medical ethics." Theological medical moralists often explicitly disassociated
themselves from the rubric.[177] "Medical ethics" was not the

---

[176] In order to avoid some of the confusion which comes
from the double use of the term, I have adopted the device
of putting this word in quotes when referring to intra-professional "medical ethics," the implication being that it
is not really ethics in the philosophical-theological meaning of that term. When not in quotes, the word refers to
the study of the morals or ethics of medicine, our current
usage.

[177] See chapter two, where the investigation of individual Catholic moralists will reveal such disassociation.
Some simply denied that what they were doing was in any way
"medical ethics," and used some other rubric instead. Others used the term, but made it clear that for them medical
ethics meant the ethics or morals of medical practice and
not "medical ethics" in the sense of the word then generally
accepted. One of the clearest examples is found in the work
of the Protestant moralist Joseph Fletcher, whose 1954 work,

systematic study of the moral questions connected with medical care.

On the other hand, inasmuch as "medical ethics" was an
important part of the developing professionalization of modern medicine, it played a significant role in the development of the ethics of medicine. The very notion that there
was a special field of interest called "medical ethics" contributed to the coalescing of our discipline. We have already noted the central importance of the appearance of
special sections in the moral manuals devoted to the obligations of medical personnel, and have seen how this paralleled the growing professionalization and declericalization
of medicine. The specialization known as "medical ethics"
within the medical profession no doubt influenced this
choice of the medical vocation as one worthy of special

Morals and Medicine, is among the earliest important Protestant contributions to the field. Fletcher states: "We are
dealing with the *ethics of medical care.* This means we are
not dealing with medical ethics, a term which is usually
used for rules governing the social conduct and graces of
the medical profession. . . . The extant literature on it
consists for the most part in homilies on the bedside manner
and such calculated questions of propriety and prudence as
shined shoes, pressed trousers, tobacco odors, whether to
drink Madeira, and the avoidance of split infinitives! It
is composed, in a phrase, of manuals or exhortations on com-
petitive success" (p. 5, italics his). Other examples of
disassociation are found in Spalding, *Talks to Nurses,* pp.
14-15; Garesché, *Ethics,* p. 20; Ficarra, *Newer Ethical Problems,* p. xiii; McFadden, *Medical Ethics,* 3rd ed., p. 3 (the
author states that "Medical Ethics" and "Nursing Ethics" are
often not concerned primarily with moral principles; rather
they treat the "etiquette" of the medical profession, including good manners, tact, and personality development);
Kelly, "Medico-Moral Notes," p. 55; Healy, *Medical Ethics,*
p. 13; Hayes, Hayes, and Kelly, *Moral Principles,* p. 4;
Wolkovich, *Norms for Pharmacists,* pp. 17-19; Niedermeyer,
Compendium of Pastoral Medicine, p. 444 ("This latter ["medical ethics"] embraces a series of very heterogeneous norms
which . . . regulate only the external proper conduct of the
doctor within his sphere.").

attention. It contributed to the idea that the physician
was a member of a special profession.

Thus the relationship of the codes and manuals of "medical ethics" to the medical moral discipline known by various rubrics and ultimately simply called *Medical Ethics* is
two-fold. First "medical ethics" is related positively to
the moral investigation of medical practice in that it was
and is a part of the professionalization of medicine. It
clearly contributed to the emerging awareness of the ethical
or moral aspects of the medical profession. The topics it
considered as central to its scope have some definite overlap to the issues which we have seen, and will see again in
more detail in the next chapter, to constitute the topical
array of theological medical ethics. Second, "medical ethics" must be said to have failed to be itself the systematic philosophical and/or moral theological investigation
of medical practice. In this sense, for reasons we will now
proceed to describe, "medical ethics" must be distinguished
from the moral analysis of medical practice.

The criticisms made of "medical ethics" and the reasons
many moralists disassociated themselves from it were basically two, in that "medical ethics" was charged with failing
both materially and formally to be the study of the ethics
of medical care. Materially it was criticized as being pre-
occupied with questions of etiquette to the neglect of more
important moral problems.[178] Formally it was attacked as

---

[178]Examples have been noted in the previous footnote.
Chauncey Leake, in his edition of Percival, states concerning Percival's code and the codes written under his influence: "the chief difficulty . . . is that no clear distinction is drawn between the incidental etiquette of medical
practice, and the fundamental ethical problems of the profession. . . . [There is] considerable emphasis on medical
etiquette. This phase of the matter has since remained in a
position of exaggerated importance" (Leake, *Percival's*

being the discipline engaged in the establishment and en-
forcement of purely intra-professional codes of conduct to
which members of the medical profession were to subscribe.
These codes were criticized as being designed by and for the
members of a particular medical association, and as having
for their primary purpose the enhancement of the profession
and the protection of the association's members.[179]

Medical Ethics, p. 37). Elsewhere the same author charges
that the earliest A.M.A. code was "a set of empirical rules
to assure courteous conduct between physicians and patients;
an early example of Emily Post's style of professional etiquette" (Leake, "Technical Triumphs and Moral Muddles," as
cited in Page, "The Ethics of Heart Transplantations," p.
110). Page, who quotes Leake, does so approvingly. A contemporary critic states: "Two generations ago we knew what
medical ethics was: a genteel code of etiquette among colleagues: do not advertise on billboards, do not air professional disputes in public, do show concern for the welfare
of your patients" (Veatch, "Medical Ethics: Professional or
Universal?" p. 533). See also Romanell, "A Philosophic
Preface," pp. 6-8.

[179]Writing in 1910, an American physician states: "Like
other obsolete codes, it [the A.M.A. code of 1903] contains
many admirable provisions . . . much that is ambiguous and
absurd, and not a few regulations that are palpably selfish,
and in direct opposition to that higher morality which finds
its expression in the Golden Rule" (Barnesby, *Medical Chaos*,
p. 39). In a 1914 article, B. J. Hendrick suggests that the
critics of "medical ethics" of his day believe that "medical
ethics and medical etiquette are really cloaks for a huge conspiracy of silence against the public; when one physician is
attacked, however justly, all the rest run to his support.
'Professional etiquette,' says Mr. [George Bernard] Shaw, 'has
for its object not the health of the patient or of the community, but the protection of the doctor's livelihood and the
concealment of his errors'" (Hendrick, "New Medical Ethics,"
pp. 117-118). Concerning Percival's code, he states: "A
more delectable collection of windy and self-praising plati-
tudes . . . was probably never put together" (*Ibid.*, p. 118).
The 1847 American Medical Association code, according to
Hendrick, sees the doctor as set apart, "like the clergy,
more or less superior to law and conventional morals" (*Ibid.*,
p. 119). A physician writing in the 1930's finds similar
criticism among patients: "To them [our patients], ethics
would seem to mean a fraternal conspiracy to dissemble and

Whether or not the charges were (and are[180]) *entirely*
accurate is problematic. "Medical ethics" has had defend-
ers, both within and without the profession.[181] Surely many

---

cloak our manifold sins and wickedness and to thwart patients in their divine right to hire and fire doctors as
they please. . . . they are mystified by the tender care
with which doctors avoid speaking ill of each other, by our
reluctance or refusal on occasions to accept each other's
patients for treatment, by our aversion to advertising and,
in short, by our ethics" (White, "Doctor's Ethics," p. 498).
A similar critique is contained in a 1945 *Newsweek* article
("What Did the Doctor Say?"). A 1959 book charges that the
codes are basically the work of the elitists among the physicians, who apply them repressively to other doctors
(Beregoff-Gillow, *A Doctor Dares,* pp. 122-128). In the context of the renewal of medical ethics of the past decade,
many have urged a change in the approach to the discipline,
criticizing the earlier "medical ethics." See, among others,
Veatch, "Codes of Medical Ethics," "Generalization of Expertise," and "Medical Ethics: Professional or Universal?";
Ramsey, "The Nature of Medical Ethics,"; Goodfield, "Reflections on the Hippocratic Oaths"; Romanell, "A Philosophic
Preface to Morals in Medicine." A recent editorial in the
Canadian Medical Association Journal states: "So we need not
only an individual ethic, such as the Hippocratic Oath, but
also a social ethic which is much more difficult to frame"
("Finding a Place for Medical Ethics," p. 1159). Scholars
argue for avoiding "erstwhile authoritarian medical dogma"
(Day, *Proceedings: Ethics in Medicine,* p. v), and for a re-
examination of oath-centered and code-centered approaches to
medical ethics (Pellegrino, "Toward an Expanded Medical Ethics," pp. 133-135). For a similar opinion concerning the
ethics of dentistry, see Gurley, *The Evolution of Professional Ethics in Dentistry,* p. vii.

[180]Contemporary criticisms recognize the recent dialogue which has been opened between the medical profession
and moral philosophy. No longer is medical ethics a negative word to the theologian and philosopher. Critics continue to charge the medical associations with serving their
self-interest, however, and in this sense the rejection of
"medical ethics" continues today.

[181]Defenders of the codes argue that they are protective
of the patient and of the general welfare. They consider
"medical ethics" to be indeed a study of the ethics of medical practice. One historian defines it as "that branch of

physicians have been men and women of the highest moral
standards. The medical associations have made important
contributions to advances in medicine and to the welfare of
the people. There have been issues included in the codes
and manuals of "medical ethics" which are "ethical" in the
strictest philosophical-theological meaning of that word.
It is thus inaccurate to imply that intra-professional "medical ethics" can be *entirely* excluded as an ethical discipline as if there were no overlap to moral philosophy or
theology. Nonetheless the history of "medical ethics" as a
field of endeavor--the word "discipline" is here perhaps too
strong--reveals a *general* emphasis on questions of courtesy
and inter-colleague etiquette, as well as a formal perspec-

---

moral philosophy which treats of the duties, responsibilities, and rights of members of the medical profession in relation to the nature of their calling, their relation to
each other and their relation to the whole community" (Davis,
History of Medicine, p. 187). His chapter on the history of
"medical ethics" overviews Hippocrates, Percival, and the
A.M.A. codes, so it is clear that this is what he means by
the "medical ethics" he defines as a branch of moral philosophy. It is precisely this definition which is denied by
the critics of "medical ethics." B. J. Hendrick, already
cited, claims that the reworkings of the A.M.A. code in the
early parts of the century resulted in a new medical ethics
which marked an advance toward real ethics (Hendrick, "New
Medical Ethics," p. 118; and "How Should a Doctor Behave?"
p. 211). Writing in the 1930's, Thomas Verner Moore, a Roman Catholic moralist and physician, refrains from disas-
sociating his work from "medical ethics." He praises the
codes as valuable in enforcing high moral standards for the
profession (Moore, *Principles of Ethics,* pp. 348-350). Willard L. Sperry, writing as dean of the Harvard Divinity
School in 1950, commends the codes and ethical standards of
the medical profession, stating that doctors are, on the
whole, followers of a higher moral standard than ministers
(Sperry, *The Ethical Basis of Medical Practice,* esp. pp. 78-
91). It has been suggested that the self-serving aspects of
the codes are limited to their wording, and that "the
substance of the codes is not seriously wanting" (Garceau,
"Morals of Medicine," p. 64).

tive which is mostly accurately described as self-interest-
ed. For these reasons "medical ethics" can rightly be distinguished from the ethics of medical practice.

Historians of American "medical ethics"[182] generally
trace the discipline from its remote ancestry in the Hippocratic Oath[183] through the code of medical ethics composed
in 1803 by the British physician Thomas Percival,[184] to the
codes of the various American doctors' associations,[185]

---

[182]There is no comprehensive history of "medical ethics." The most detailed history available is a survey by
Donald Konold, who investigates the field in America from
1847 to 1912, spanning the years between the first code of
ethics of the A.M.A. and the 1912 revision. His book ade-
quately describes the state of the discipline as it was at
the time of the earliest American works in Roman Catholic
medical ethics, which is of most importance for this present
study. See Konold, *A History of American Medical Ethics,
1847-1912.* There is a brief overview in Davis, *History of
Medicine,* pp. 187-191, and one in Moore, *Principles of Ethics,* pp. 333-355, who adds a bibliography. Another brief
survey is found in an article by Smithies, "On the Origin
and Development of Ethics in Medicine." Various creeds and
oaths for doctors have been compiled in Etziony, *The Physician's Creed.* There is an historical introduction in
Leake's edition of Percival (Leake, *Percival's Medical Ethics,* pp. 1-57). The history of the ethics of dentistry is
surveyed by Gurley, The *Evolution of Professional Ethics in
Dentistry.* There is a brief survey of "nursing ethics" in
Moore, *Principles of Ethics,* pp. 356-366, with an annotated
bibliography.

[183]For an analysis of the Oath, see especially Edelstein, *The Hippocratic Oath.* Other works are Jones, *'Hippocrates' and the Corpus Hippocratum*; Jones, *Philosophy and
Medicine in Ancient Greece*; Goodfield, "Reflections on the
Hippocratic Oaths"; Entralgo, *Doctor and Patient,* pp. 41-52.

[184]See Percival, *Percival's Medical Ethics,* ed. Chauncey D. Leake. For an argument that Percival's code was of
secondary importance, see Moore, *Principles of Ethics,* pp.
341-348.

[185]Numerous examples of such codes are included in the
bibliography. See American Medical Association, American

especially the American Medical Association, whose code was
first promulgated in 1847.

It is not necessary here to investigate this history
in any detail. We need merely note that the history of
American "medical ethics" provides ample evidence to substantiate the charges of its critics. There was a definite
emphasis on questions of external etiquette.[186] Instead of

Dental Association, American Dental Hygienists' Association,
American Psychiatric Association, American Registry of
Radiologic Technologists, Boston Medical Association, Col-
lege of Physicians and Surgeons of the Province of Quebec,
Graduate Nurses' Association of the State of Pennsylvania,
International Council of Nurses, and National Dental Associ-
ation. Some of the revisions of codes, especially the im-
portant editions of the A.M.A. code, are cited.

[186]The codes themselves often emphasize this aspect.
Attention is paid to methods of advertising and to inter-
colleague politeness. Books and articles in "medical ethics" often show a similar emphasis. In his 1915 manual, Edmund Noyes introduces philosophical ethics (about 130 pages),
but when he shifts to professional ethics for dentists
(about 25 pages), his topics include advertising, fees,
inter-colleague duties, and how to prepare papers for professional association gatherings (Noyes, *Ethics and Jurisprudence for Dentists,* pp. 138 ff.). James Sprague's book
is a series of homilies, poems, codes, and general exhortations about the doctor's nobility. It contains no systematic analysis (Sprague, *Medical Ethics and Cognate Subjects,*
1902). The late nineteenth century work of D. W. Cathell,
generally classified as a work in "medical ethics," includes
the advice that a physician "should, therefore, get a good-
looking horse and a genteel carriage . . . getting it indicates that your practice is growing. . . . If you unfortunately have a bony horse and a seedy-looking, pre-Adamite
. . . buggy, do not let them habitually stand in front of
your office" (Cathell, *Book on the Physician Himself,* p. 27).
The work does contain a section on abortion, but there is no
attempt to analyze the problem. Rather the doctor is cau-
tioned to avoid bringing notoriety on himself (*Ibid.,* pp.
77-79), and to make sure he gets his fee in advance from
"unmarried negresses, ladies of easy virtue, and other low
females" who might try to get off without paying when they
discover he will not abort (*Ibid.,* p. 79). The works of

approaching issues from a universal ethical perspective, the
"medical ethics" codes of the associations often attempted
to enhance the prestige of the association and its membership.[187] The rules of conduct were not based so much on
ethical principles as they were considered to be special
intra-professional codes, whose authority came from the association to which members had pledged loyalty.[188] Much of
"medical ethics" as specified in the early American codes
and commentaries was intended to gain for the association

---

three French-Canadian writers are similar (Desjardins,
Initiations au devoir; Gagnier, *Droits et devoirs;* and
Gauvreau., *Les Médecins au Canada français*). A physician of
the 1920's praises the "medical ethics" taught by the example of senior physicians which results in "quite miraculous" changes in the medical students who enter as "callow
youths, shapeless souls" (Cabot, "Ethics and the Medical
Profession," p. 618). The changes he refers to are mainly
techniques of courtesy and heroic effort. In citing these
often humorous examples, I am not arguing that courtesy is
unwanted in the physician, but merely citing examples sub-
stantiating the thesis that "medical ethics" differs materially from the ethical study of medicine. More recent examples include Gelfand, *Philosophy and Ethics of Medicine;*
and Tenery, "Medical Etiquette."

[187]For a contemporary analysis of universalism vs. pro-
fessionalism in medical ethics, see Veatch, "Medical Ethics:
Professional or Universal?".

[188]Konold traces the codes in America from the middle
of the nineteenth to the beginning of the twentieth century.
He concludes from his study that these codes were basically
as their critics have charged. This is not to say that such
codes did no good. By enhancing the prestige of the medical
profession, they no doubt contributed to the quite valid
advance of medical science for the public welfare. Nonetheless, Konold concludes that "medical ethics" was at heart a
lobbying effort on behalf of the medical association and
professional physicians (Konold, *A History of American Medical Ethics,* p. 75 and elsewhere). A more favorable opinion
is found in Shryock, *Medicine in America,* pp. 13-34. A brief
statement of the issues and arguments is in Titus, *Ethics for
Today,* pp. 293-301.

members a monopoly on medical practice by excluding others
whose methods were not correctly "orthodox" or "scientific."[189] "Medical ethics" discussed the relative strengths
and weaknesses of generalists and specialists, and reflected
the opinions of the dominant body within the medical associations.[190] It guarded the financial interests of the physicians.[191] It often meant opposition to public medical

---

[189]Konold, *A History,* pp. 14-31. Konold shows how this
provision excluded women from membership (p. 23; see also
Shryock, *Medicine in America,* pp. 177-199). He suggests
that, despite the advantages to the public gained from eliminating dangerous forms of quackery, the basic motivation
was not moral but financial. The "regulars" wanted to destroy competition (p. 31). Recent attempts by the A.M.A. to
continue such elimination are noted (p. 72). For examples
of opposition to "irregulars" see especially the various
codes themselves. Also Hooker, *Physician and Patient* (1849),
pp. 1-257; Wilder, "A Conversation" (1901); Pringle,
"Aesculapius in Manhattan" (1927); Roberts, "Medical Ethics"
(1936); Roberts, *Medical Modes and Morals* (1937); and
Smithies, "On the Origin and Development of Ethics in Medicine" (1925), pp. 595-598.

[190]Konold, pp. 32-42. Konold concludes his section on
"The Relation of Research to Medical Ethics" by remarking
that by the turn of the century "physicians had begun to put
aside jealousies which had interfered with their utilization
of scientific resources. *To that extent science had replaced ethics.* Doctors could no longer ignore progress . . .
[they] had to give their patients the best science had to
offer" (p. 42, italics mine). The "medical ethics" of the
time was more interested in establishing domination and defending professional prerogatives than in rendering adequate
medical treatment, so that "ethics" had to be replaced by
"science" in the interests of morality. An example of opposition to codes of ethics is Post, *An Ethical Symposium*
(1883). A discussion is also found in Hamilton, *Conversations* (1884). Thus we find physicians speaking out against
the "medical ethics" of the associations, and doing so on
moral grounds.

[191]Konold, pp. 56-57. The codes insist on the physicians' right to compensation, sometimes suggest minimum fees,
and insist on limits to free service (see especially the
earlier A.M.A. codes) Physicians defend this by stating

insurance,[192] avoidance of public dispute so as to maintain
the prestige and presumed scientific knowledge of the profession,[193] outright concealment of blunders,[194] and cooper-
ative efforts at preventing malpractice suits.[195]

Such was the state of "medical ethics" at the time of
the earliest American writings in the moral theology of medical practice. It is clear why the theologians disassociated themselves from the rubric. On the other hand, many of
the charges brought against the "medical ethics" of the professional associations could also be levied, *mutatis mutandis,*
against the kind of theological methodology in use at the
time. It, too, was often self-serving, ignoring the givens
of the ethical "event" under study in order to remain loyal
to its own professional tradition.[196] All too often the
moral theology of medicine stood as much in the way of the
welfare of the patient as did the "medical ethics" of the

---

that they are not basically out for money (Roberts, "Medical
Ethics," p. 474), or even that they are underpaid and over-
worked (Lindsay, "Ethics of Medical Practice" [1911], p.
513), which was no doubt true for some physicians. It must
also be admitted that pressure has been brought by associations at times to restrict exhorbitant fee-gouging by doctors ("Doctors Who Crack Down on Doctors" [1955]).

[192]A near-constant in "medical ethics." See Konold, pp.
72-73, as well as the codes themselves. Also Lindsay, "Ethics of Medical Practice"; Winslow, "Why Do We Have Medical
Ethics?", who defends the opposition to public medical insurance as protection of the confidential doctor-patient relationship and the free choice of physicians (p. 108).

[193]Konold, pp. 44-48; and the codes. See also an early
critique of the opposition to advertising by his "ethical
colleagues" in Landis, *The Physician and the People* (1924).

[194]Konold, p. 49.

[195]*Ibid.*, pp. 50-51.

[196]These methodological issues will be discussed later.

physicians' associations. Nonetheless, the moralist was at
least formally interested in examining the ethical dilemmas
of medicine from a universal basis. This basis, in its actual formulation, was often inadequate. But it did distinguish the medical moralist from the "medical ethicist," and
it provides an adequate reason for making a distinction between the theological or philosophical study of medical
morality and the intra-professional field of endeavor known
as "medical ethics."[197]

In recent years intra-professional "medical ethics" has
entered into dialogue with more universal approaches to ethics. Today courses in "medical ethics" are apt to be
courses in the ethics of medicine, in medical ethics in the
wider contemporary sense of that term. They may be taught
by a philosopher or a theologian or by a physician knowl-

---

[197] In our discussion we have avoided making the basis
of the distinction reside in the fact that the former proceeds within an explicitly theological methodology and the
latter does not. This would be sufficient to distinguish
"medical ethics" from a Christian moral theology of medical
practice, but insufficient to substantiate the claim that it
has generally failed to be truly an ethical or moral discipline at all. Nor is it so much a question of the lack of a
particular recognizable system of moral philosophy. "Medical ethics" did not fail to be systematically a study of
medical morality because it did not adopt, say, a utilitarian or a natural law point of view, or because it did not
speak with the language of any one theological or philosophical school. It was not the investigation of medical morality because it did not (at least it did not generally)
adopt *any* universal perspective on the problem. In technical terms, "medical ethics" was not the study of the ethics
of medicine because it proceeded unconsciously from an
intra-professional reductionist metaethical relativism.
(For a more detailed analysis, see Veatch, "Medical Ethics:
Professional or Universal?" esp. p. 545. Veatch also makes
the important distinction between metaethical relativism and
ethical situationalism, p. 544. It is not on grounds of a
supposed situationalism that the distinction we are claiming
can be supported.) In addition, it emphasized questions of
etiquette and courtesy to the partial exclusion of more important moral issues.

edgeable in these fields.[198] Moral philosophers and theologians no longer refuse to use the term as rubric for their
field of study. In the next chapter we will note the gradual acceptance of the rubric by American moralists.[199]

---

[198]The debate continues, of course, as it should, concerning the relevance of individual systems of moral philosophy and moral theology for the ethical decisions to be
made. Examples of this debate constantly appear in the literature. See, *e.g.*, Moore, "This Is Medical Ethics?" and
the correspondance referring to that article in *The Hastings
Center Report,* 5 (1975), Nos. 1, 3, 4.

[199]The brief description of "medical ethics" presented
here ought also to include some mention of "nursing ethics."
In a manner not unlike the distinction between "medical ethics" and the ethics of medicine, a distinction can be made
between "nursing ethics" and the ethical study of medical
practice intended for nurses. "Nursing ethics" has consisted largely in the discussion of nursing etiquette. Often known by the rubric "professional adjustments" (see
Price, *Professional Adjustments I,* p. v, where such equiva-
lency is claimed), or, more recently, by the rubric "professional trends," courses in "nursing ethics" deal with the
changes in conduct befitting a nurse as a professional person. As with "medical ethics," it is not possible to separate the field completely from the theological or philosophical study of medical morality, but the general emphasis is
quite distinct.
Manuals of "nursing ethics" and professional adjustments consulted here are cited in the bibliography. See
Aikens, *Studies in Ethics;* Chamberlain, *Orientation;* Dietz,
Professional Adjustments; Fletcher, *Notes for Catholic
Nurses;* Gladwin, *Ethics;* Goodall, *Ethics;* Goodrich, *The Social and Ethical Significance of Nursing;* Kelly, *Dimensions
of Professional Nursing;* Kempf, *The Person as a Nurse;* Lennon, *Professional Adjustments;* Motley, *Ethics;* Murphy, *The
Catholic Nurse;* Parsons, *Nursing Problems;* Pearce, *Nurse and
Patient;* Price, *Professional Adjustments;* Robb, *Nursing Ethics;* Ryan, *Professional Problems;* Sanner, *Trends and Professional Adjustments;* Spalding, *Professional Nursing.*
A good example of "nursing ethics" is Sr. Mary Isidore
Lennon's work, *Professional Adjustments.* The book is not at
all a work in ethics or moral theology, but deals with such
questions as discipline, the religious life of the nurse,
her personal appearance, conversation, conduct in the nurses'
home, classroom, and hospital, her social life, legal

2. Medical Jurisprudence

Medical jurisprudence is the study of the relationship
of medicine and law. Since law can be considered in both
a narrower and a wider sense, medical jurisprudence has been
understood strictly as "the application of the science of
medicine in courts of law,"[200] and more broadly as the study
of a whole range of issues, including "medical ethics" and
questions of medical morality.[201] It is often referred to
as "forensic medicine" or "legal medicine." We have already
noted the French rubric "médecine légale"; in German the
word is "gerichtliche Medizin."

In the strict sense, medical jurisprudence studies the
use of medicine in legal investigations. One of its main
subdivisions is toxicology. The physician or the medical
student is taught how to present legal evidence in criminal

---

responsibilities, budget, job applications, etc. These may
be important issues, but there is a rather clear distinction
between them and the moral questions connected with nursing
practice. For an explicit disassociation of his work from
"nursing ethics," see McFadden, *Medical Ethics for Nurses,*
1946, p. 3.

The same recent criticisms of the lack of universality
that we have noted about "medical ethics" have been made of
"nursing ethics." In this context, for example, the official title of the ethical code of the International Nurses'
Association was changed in 1965 from "Code of Nursing Ethics" to "Code of Ethics as Applied to Nursing." A recent
manual of "nursing ethics" notes: "The concept underlying
the change was that there were no ethical standards *unique*
to nursing, but rather generally accepted ethical standards
that could be *applied* to nursing--or to any other profession,
for that matter" (Kelly, *Dimensions of Professional Nursing,*
2nd ed., p. 22, italics hers).

Some works in nursing ethics written by Roman Catholic
moralists are indeed concerned with the ethics of nursing
practice. They are included for study in later chapters.

[200]Havard, "Medical Jurisprudence," p. 812.

[201]*Ibid.*, pp. 812 ff.; Jones, "Medical Jurisprudence,"
pp. 543-544.

cases, especially in cases of homicide.[202] In Europe a physician must have specialized in medical jurisprudence to be
acceptable as an expert witness in a criminal proceeding.[203]

In a somewhat wider sense, legal medicine includes
questions of the physician's responsibility before the civil
law, therapies which are and are not permitted, the current
status of laws on abortion, euthanasia, medical experimentation, professional licensing, and many other areas.

In its widest usage, medical jurisprudence is the rubric used for the ethical investigation of the medical profession itself, including questions dealing with the codes
of "medical ethics." Medical jurisprudence has been for
some time a recognized rubric for courses in medical schools,
and as such it came to include some discussion of the moral
questions of medical practice. This last area of investigation is today generally referred to as *Medical Ethics* rather
than medical jurisprudence. Until recently, however, as we
have seen, "medical ethics" within the profession was not at
all a systematic study,[204] nor did it include much real ethics. What study there was was therefore often included in
courses of medical jurisprudence.

In the next chapter we will see how medical jurisprudence entered into the emergence of Roman Catholic medical
ethics in North America.[205]

---

[202]Jones, "Medical Jurisprudence," pp. 543-544.

[203]Havard, "Medical Jurisprudence," p. 813.

[204]Writing in 1926, a physician can say that he knows
"no medical school . . . in which professional ethics is now
systematically taught" (Cabot, "Ethics and the Medical Profession," p. 618).

[205]As with "medical ethics," so here, too, we find
works in medical jurisprudence for nurses. Legal problems
of nursing are often included in works of professional adjustments.

* * *

Neither "medical ethics" nor medical jurisprudence can
be identified with the moral or ethical investigation of
medical practice. The former cannot be so identified because, as we have noted, it differs both formally and materially from the discipline now known as *Medical Ethics*. The
latter cannot be so identified because, at least in its
stricter denotations, it is limited in its purview to the
study of the relationship of medicine and civil positive law.

Nonetheless both are important in the emergence of Roman Catholic medical ethics. We will show in the next chapter how each of these disciplines was of direct significance
in the establishment of the name and definition of the discipline. Also of importance, however, was the indirect role
played by them as a result of their importance for the increasing professionalization of medicine. "Medical ethics"
and medical jurisprudence emerged as part of the movement
within medicine toward the establishment of professional associations. These, as we have noted, tended to set the physician apart from others as a member of a special professional group.

This process of professionalization is, as we shall see
in the next chapter, directly related to the fixing of the
discipline's definition. Roman Catholic medical ethics in
North America will become less and less interested in the
whole range of issues treated in the earlier treatises of
pastoral medicine, and more and more restricted to the study
of moral questions met in the daily professional activity of
medical personnel. In this sense intra-professional "medical
ethics" and medical jurisprudence were influential, since
they contributed to the development of the medical profession
as a special sphere of human activity to be studied in and
for itself, and requiring a special discipline which might
apply to it moral theological principles.

Conclusion

Our task in the present chapter has been to locate and
survey the roots of North American Roman Catholic medical
ethics. We have suggested that the discipline arises from
the general tradition of Roman Catholic moral theology. We
have also noted and described three cognate pre-disciplines:[206] pastoral medicine, "medical ethics," and medical
jurisprudence, the most important of which is pastoral medicine.

In the first part of the chapter, we presented an over-

---

[206]This term has been chosen because it is wide enough
to include the diverse relationships which each of the three
had and has to theological medical ethics. Each is in some
way similar to it; each stands in some sort of parallel to
the discipline we are studying; each had an influence, temporary or permanent, of greater or lesser significance, on
it; none is identical to it. The three continue, of course,
in their own development today, and the term "pre-discipline"
is not intended to imply that pastoral medicine, "medical
ethics," or medical jurisprudence have ceased their own separate existence. On the other hand, these three, especially
pastoral medicine and "medical ethics," have been transformed
to a substantial degree in dialogue with theological ethical
emphases. Pastoral medicine, as we have seen, shifted its
emphasis more and more in the direction of ethical questions,
and has become for some authors largely identical to theological medical ethics, though writers in the field still insist
(properly, I think) that the field is formally wider than
medical ethics (see Niedermeyer, *Allgemeine Pastoralmedizin,*
I, 20 ff.; *Compendium of Pastoral Medicine,* pp. 3-16; Fleckenstein, "Pastoralmedizin"). "Medical ethics" continues
within the medical profession, but more and more the physicians are entering into dialogue with moral theologians and
moral philosophers, and thus the earlier emphases on etiquette and professional self-interest are weakening. Medical
jurisprudence continues as a separate discipline in its more
immediately forensic aspects, but it, too, is more and more
in contact with medical ethicists in many of its issue areas.
As we trace the development of North American Roman Catholic
medical ethics in the next chapter, we will see how these
three cognate pre-disciplines influenced its emergence.

view of the general tradition of Catholic moral theology in
its three major traditional phases. There we noted the location of the major groupings of medical ethical topics.
We found a shift in the principles of selection of these issues from purely topical ones (the sins penitents confessed)
to criteria based on the organizational rubrics of the commandments and sacraments (topics grouped under the fifth
commandment, the sixth and ninth commandments, and the sacrament of matrimony), and including a more directly professional criterion according to which topics were chosen as
they related to actual medical practice (the special section
on the obligations of medical personnel). In the next chapter we will see how these principles of selection are significant in the development of the material definition of
medical ethics in North America. We will note an important
shift toward the daily practice of medical personnel as the
primary principle of selection.

In the second part of the chapter, we described the relationship of medicine and theology in Catholic tradition,
especially as that relationship was studied and analyzed in
the discipline generally known as pastoral medicine. We
noted the importance of the de-clericalization and gradual
professionalization of medicine for the development of pastoral medicine. We saw how this discipline included, in its
widest sense, the entire interface of medicine and theology.
In its medical aspect it studied the implications of medicine for pastoral and moral theology. It presented purely
medical data for the rural pastor, so that he might act as
substitute doctor and serve to establish better hygiene
among his parishioners. It taught the pastor and the moral
theologian what they needed to know about human volition,
and gave them the medical data they needed to make moral
judgments. It presented to the speculative theologian data
from medicine and biology which would be of help to him in

formulating theological reasonings about various doctrines.
In its theological aspects it studied the application of
theology to medicine. The doctor was given advice concerning the spiritual dimensions of his patient. Moral theological judgment was applied to medical practice. We have
noted that it was this last emphasis which became predominant in pastoral medicine. In the next chapter we will see
how some of the earliest works in North American medical
ethics are works in pastoral medicine, either in name or in
approach or both, and how gradually both the emphasis and
the rubric shift toward a more restrictively moral theological emphasis. Pastoral medicine as an explicitly self-conscious discipline will largely disappear from the North
American scene, and the practical moral emphasis will dominate in medical ethics.

In the third section, we presented a brief description
of intra-professional "medical ethical" codes and of medical
jurisprudence. In the next chapter, as we trace the development of the name and definition of North American Roman Catholic medical ethics, we will note that both of these cognate
pre-disciplines lend their names to our discipline, one tem-
porarily, the other permanently. We will see how Catholic
medical ethicists distinguish their field both from medical
jurisprudence and from "medical ethics." Nonetheless, these
areas of study were, as we have noted, important to the development of medicine as a specific profession with its own
sense of professional "ethic" and its own need for legal
studies. They advance hand in hand with that very professionalization of medicine which became the basis for the definition of Roman Catholic medical ethics as the moral theological investigation of the ethical issues connected with
the professional activity of medical personnel.

It is in fact this growing sense of professionalization,
common to all three sections of this chapter, which becomes

definitional for Roman Catholic medical ethics in North
America.

CHAPTER TWO

NAME AND DEFINITION OF THE DISCIPLINE

The literature which we will be examining in this and
the following chapters consists of the major works in Roman
Catholic medical ethics written in North America prior to
the Second Vatican Council.[1] This is the period of emergence of the field of study as a self-conscious discipline
with an established name, definition, and methodology. In
the final chapter we will note briefly some developments in
recent scholarship in order to offer a critique of the definition and theological methodology of the discipline in its
pre-Vatican II phase.

Included in the literature to be investigated are works
which are explicitly theological, which claim to be works in
the moral theology of medical practice, as well as some
which define themselves as works in philosophical ethics.
These latter, written by Roman Catholic moralists from within the tradition of Catholic ethics, are distinguishable
from the explicitly theological works only in that they
claim to proceed more from "natural" human reason than from
supernatural revelation. Such a claim is often more nominal
than substantial, however. The authors' conclusions are
identical to those of the moral theologians, and the works
are written from within the perspective of Roman Catholic
moral philosophy-theology. The "ethicists" make use of prin-

_____

[1] A chronological list of these works, together with
their length in pages, is provided at the end of the Introduction.

ciples which are indeed theological.[2]

Works in Roman Catholic nursing ethics are included
where these are indeed studies of the moral questions of
medicine. As such there is no distinction between these
books written for nurses and those written more specifically
for physicians, medical students, and clergy. Indeed, some
of the most important works of the period are written explicitly for nurses and nursing students. This is one of
the professional groups whose practice determines, as we
shall see, the material definition of the discipline. We
will not include, however, works in "nursing ethics" or professional adjustments which, as we have noted in the previous chapter, are not studies of the moral questions of nursing (medical) practice.

In this chapter we will survey the literature to discover the name and definition of the discipline in its emergent (pre-Vatican II) phase. Thus we are interested primarily in what rubrics the authors give to the field, in how
they define it explicitly (formal definition, including
formal statement of purpose), and in what topics they include within it (material definition).[3] We will discuss

---

[2]For a more detailed analysis of this question, see
chapter three.

[3]The formal and material definitions are not, of course,
materially distinct. The formal definition includes formally the field's "comprehension," or the intentionality to include these topics and not those, and thus deals formally
with the principles of selection in accordance with the
formally stated purpose of the discipline. The material
definition is the topical aspect of the formal definition
(as distinguished from the formally stated purpose and, for
our purposes in dividing this from later chapters, as distinguished from the more directly methodological aspect--
the "how" question) viewed materially. It is the definition
of the discipline according to the actual topical array.
Thus the material definition is the material side of one
aspect of the formal definition. The formal definition

in some detail why certain topics are included as relevant
to medical ethics, while others are excluded or deemphasized and how this choice develops over the years. It will
be impossible to eliminate all questions of methodology.
Indeed, questions of name and definition could properly be
called methodological in that they are not substantive. In
addition, in defining the discipline, authors often include
matters which concern their theological methodology. Nonetheless, we will reserve as much as possible for later
chapters questions relating to the application of theological principles. For the moment we are interested in the
more non-methodological aspects of the discipline's definition.

        In the previous chapter we noted the progressive devel-
opment of modern medicine as a secularized profession. We
saw the growing emphasis on distinguishing physical from
spiritual healing, noted that this development paralleled
and was influenced by the shift from theocentric to anthropocentric systems of thought, and briefly mentioned the role
of scholasticism and the recovery of the notion of nature as
influential in this process. In the present chapter we will
discover that it is precisely this developing secularization
and professionalization of modern medicine which comes to
determine the purpose and the topical array of Roman Catholic medical ethics in North America. The moralists who
wrote the texts and manuals which we will investigate came
to be interested primarily in applying moral principles to
the actual daily professional activity of medical person-
nel--of doctors, of general practitioners, surgeons, medical

---

includes as well the purpose of the discipline, the intended readership, and some methodological description. This
last will be reserved as much as possible for chapters three,
four, and five.

specialists, of medical nurses. The topics they came to treat were selected primarily in accordance with this objective. Emphasis was thus given to the physical interventions (operations and drug therapies) which had come to typify modern medicine's approach to physical healing. Formally, of course, the moralists rejected materialistic definitions of health. Their purpose was explicitly to bring moral guidance to these questions, not to help doctors in the purely technical aspects of their work. But from a material perspective (the topics treated in medical ethics, the issues to which moral principles were applied) most North American authors, as we will discover, gave greatest emphasis to physical therapies for physical ailments.

We will discover in our study that some works were exceptions to the prevailing trend. These maintained many of the wider concerns of some of the pastoral medicine literature we have already examined. Treatises on hygiene for clergy as well as detailed examination of moral issues of less than direct importance for the physician, such as the canonical aspects of marriage, questions of individual and marital sexual behavior, moral implications of psychoanalysis for questions of human volition and freedom, etc., were still present in some of the literature. But the largest concentration of this kind of work was, as we will note, in the very earliest years of the discipline's emergence, and constituted an exception to the general trend. Most of the North American authors were interested primarily in the practical application of precise moral principles to the ethical issues arising from professional medical practice. This had become their primary principle of selection.

When topics were included which were of less than direct importance to modern medical practice, often the rationale was introduced that they were necessary as background for more directly "medical" concerns, or that the

physician might encounter them as part of his role as counsellor. Thus questions of sexual ethics, when they were included for discusion, were often introduced with the explanation that the physician might be asked questions by his
patients concerning them. Similarly some questions concerning psychoanalysis were included because a doctor might have
to refer a patient for such treatment. General principles
of sexual ethics were introduced as necessary background for
solving directly medical ethical issues dealing with reproduction, such as artificial insemination, sterilization,
sterility testing, etc.

In our survey of the literature we will note the importance of professional groups such as the Catholic Hospital
Association. We will note the creation of various codes of
ethics for Catholic hospitals and physicians. By emphasizing the practical concerns of physicians and hospitals,
the codes and the groups which promulgated them and wrote
about them contributed to the development of the discipline
and to its primary interest in investigating the procedures
which constituted the professional practice of medical personnel.

With respect to the name given to the discipline, the
general rubric by which it came to be known, we will describe the gradual process by which the term *Medical Ethics*
came to be the generally accepted rubric. We will note that
"pastoral medicine" and "medical jurisprudence," the other
two cognate pre-disciplines whose descriptions we have just
completed, lent their names to the emerging discipline.
But neither of these rubrics suggested the right emphasis
for what medical moralists were doing. "Pastoral medicine"
included aspects of hygienic instruction, speculative theology, psychological theories, etc., which were at most of
secondary importance to the moralist. "Medical jurisprudence" implied an emphasis on civil law which was not the

moralist's central concern. We will note that the term
Medical Ethics was accepted only with reluctance, since
moralists hesitated to identify their discipline with the
"medical ethics" of the medical associations we have described in the previous section. Early authors rejected
the term altogether. Later writers often used the word
only with a definitional disassociation, explaining that
their meaning was different from that of the "medical ethics" codes and manuals. But the term "ethics" had had a
long acceptance within Catholic theology, the alternatives
were inadequate, and the rubric *Medical Ethics* was common
within the medical profession whose structure and procedures were centrally important for the definitional and methodological determination of the discipline. For these
reasons the phrase came to be the generally accepted rubric.

Our description of the emerging discipline will reveal
its relationship to the general tradition of moral theology
and to its three cognate pre-disciplines: pastoral medicine,
medical jurisprudence, and "medical ethics." The central
concern of the field was to apply moral principles to the
daily procedures of professional medical personnel. For
this the special section in the general manuals where the
vocation of the physician was singled out for moral investigation served as harbinger. This became the central principle of selection of topics for inclusion: what the doctor
actually did in his professional calling. The other organizational rubrics of the general manuals, the commandments,
virtues, and sacraments, were of far less significance. We
will discover certain works whose organizational divisions
resembled the manuals to some extent, but the primary criterion for selecting topics for analysis was the practical
medical activity of the doctor and nurse. This central concern also signaled the discipline's emergence from its cognate pre-disciplines. In name, or definition, or both,

Medical Ethics came to distinguish itself from pastoral
medicine, medical jurisprudence, and intra-professional
"medical ethics."

We will divide our study into two major periods, distinguishing the literature written during the papacy of
Pius XII (roughly from 1940 to 1960) from works written
earlier (roughly 1900 to 1940). The reasons for this division will become more apparent later, as they relate specifically to questions of developing theological methodology.
Nonetheless, since this methodological development parallels
and influences the emerging definition of our discipline, a
very brief statement of the most general trends might be
welcome here. Further detail and argumentation is presented
in the next three chapters.

Briefly stated, North American Roman Catholic medical
ethics applied theological principles (principles such as
God's dominion over human life and the redemptive meaning of
suffering in Christ) according to two general approaches or
modalities of application: physicalism and ecclesiastical
positivism. These general modalities became the determining
processes for solving ethical questions of medicine. We
will note a gradual shift in importance from physicalism to
ecclesiastical positivism centered around the time of Pius
XII's accession to the papacy. Hence we divide the study
chronologically into these two periods: the early period,
from 1900 to 1940, in which the physicalist methodology became established; and the later period, from 1940 to 1960,
in which, while physicalism remained important, ecclesiastical positivism took on greater dominance.

For our purposes here it is sufficient to note the harmonious relationship of these two methodological modalities
to the growing professionalization of medicine, and to the
emerging definition of medical ethics as the moral theological investigation of actual medical practice.

The modality of physicalism, as we will describe it
later, operated by arriving at ethical judgments on the
basis of physical criteria, precisely defined physical aspects of the action under consideration (the surgical operation, for example), and thus operated "scientifically,"
enabling the moralist to reach conclusions applicable in
every single instance where the physical action was the
same. In a way similar to the scientific approach used in
modern medicine, this modality enabled correct scientific
answers of a universally applicable nature to be given the
doctor. It was an ideal method for analyzing the kind of
direct bodily interventions (surgery, drug therapy, etc.)
which had become the most widespread therapies of modern
medicine.

The modality of ecclesiastical positivism operated by
arriving at ethical judgments on the basis of the pronouncements of the Roman Catholic magisterium (the teaching authority of the Catholic Church). Though at first sight this
approach would seem to be "unscientific" because "supernatural," we will see in our study that in most cases Catholic
medical moralists claimed *not* to be supernatural moral positivists, but rather proclaimed the authority of the Church
to make universally binding decrees concerning the *"natural"*
law, and applied this law in its physicalist approach to
medical ethical issues. We will have occasion to note the
ambiguities inherent in this argument, but it is clear that
such a claim is generally harmonious with the basic trend
we will discover in the emergence of our discipline's definition as a theologically scientific investigation of medical practice, the kind of scientific investigation which can
bring universally applicable answers to problems. Indeed,
in its emphasis on authority, which authority was defended
"scientifically," Catholic ethics found a harmonious structure with professional medicine, where the medical authori-

ties, speaking with the force of science, were able to find
universally acceptable answers to medical problems. It is
true, as we shall also see, that not each and every medical
question found this kind of solution. But the basic trend
clearly operated in this manner.

In this chapter, therefore, we will describe the emerging discipline of Roman Catholic medical ethics as influenced by and responding to the needs of modern professional
scientific medicine. We will discover how the rubric for
the discipline changes from pastoral medicine to medical
ethics, the name used within the medical profession. We
will see that the discipline becomes formally defined as
the moral theological-philosophical investigation of medical
practice, intended to apply moral principles to the daily
professional activities of medical personnel. And we will
describe in detail how the actual inclusion and exclusion
of topics for discussion (material definition) is influenced by this practical goal.

Part One

Early Works (1897-1940)

1. Charles Coppens: Medical Jurisprudence

The first American work in the morals of medical practice was written in 1897 by the Jesuit classicist and philosopher Charles Coppens.[4] Before the appearance of his

---

[4] Biographical data for the authors studied is gathered
from standard sources, and references will not be given unless the facts are disputed or unusually noteworthy. Among
sources consulted for biographical material are: *The Guide
to Catholic Literature;* Hoehn, ed., *Catholic Authors; The
American Catholic Who's Who; The Catholic Encyclopedia and
Its Makers;* Allaire, *Dictionnaire biographique;* as well as
various biographical articles, obituaries in professional

book, only Carl Capellmann's *Pastoral Medicine,* translated
from the Latin in 1878, had been available in English to
American readers. Capellmann, as we have seen, was influential in furthering the emphasis on specifically moral
questions within European pastoral medicine, and in extend-
ing the scope of pastoral medicine to meet the needs of physicians as well as those of the clergy.[5] The same pragmatic
moral emphasis is central to Coppens' work.

   Unlike Capellmann, however, Coppens does not begin from
within the perspective of pastoral medicine. His book is
entitled *Moral Principles and Medical Practice: The Basis of
Medical Jurisprudence.* As the title indicates, Coppens'

---

journals, etc.
   Book reviews are listed together at the end of the general bibliography, alphabetized according to the author of
the book. In the case of longer critical review-essays,
however, listing is according to the writer of the review,
and the entry is included in the main section of the bibliography. Footnotes will distinguish by noting the latter
under the reviewer's name.
   Charles Coppens was born in Belgium in 1835. After
moving to the United States he entered the Jesuit order in
1853. He was educated in Belgium and in America, and taught
in various Jesuit colleges in the United States in areas of
the classics and philosophy. He authored numerous works in
systematic theology, Catholic apologetics, and spirituality.
He died in 1920.
   His work in medical morals, *Moral Principles and Medical Practice: The Basis of Medical Jurisprudence,* achieved
various editions, with but minor alterations. The second
edition is a reprint of the first, appearing in the same
year, 1897. The fourth edition (1905) is called a "revised
edition" in that it adds a five page appendix of recent decisions of the Holy Office, and, in light of these decisions, makes a slight alteration in the text on page 79. The
1921 edition by Henry Spalding contains major additions, and
will be considered later in this chapter. All references
here are to the fourth edition, but the reader is advised
that, for the most part, the other editions are identical,
even as to pagination.

   [5]Capellmann's work has been described above, pp. 70-74.

perspective is the field of medical jurisprudence. From
1896 to 1905 Coppens was professor of medical jurisprudence
at the John A. Creighton Medical College in Omaha, Nebraska.
His book is the text of the lectures he gave to the Catholic
medical students at Creighton. We have already noted that
systematic courses in "medical ethics" or in the ethics of
medicine were unknown in the medical schools of the time,
whereas the rubric "medical jurisprudence" had long been recognized as an area of formal study.[6] Just as Capellmann
extended the scope of pastoral medicine to meet the needs of
physicians and shifted its emphasis to ethical matters, so
Coppens extended the scope of medical jurisprudence to include moral as well as legal questions.

In his introductory lecture, Coppens describes medical
jurisprudence:

> The science of *jurisprudence* investigates the causes
> or principles of law. It is defined as "the study of
> law in connection with its underlying principles."
> *Medical Jurisprudence,* in its wider sense,[7] comprises
> two departments, namely the study of the laws regard-
> ing medical practice, and, more especially, the study
> of the principles on which those laws are founded, and
> from which they derive their binding power on the hu-
> man conscience.[8]

He goes on to explain that at Creighton the former area is
studied in a course on *medical law,* taught by a lawyer who

---

[6]See above, generally the section on "medical ethics";
also specifically Cabot, "Ethics and the Medical Profession," p. 618; also Callahan, *Recent Activities: 1973,* p. 3:
"in 1969, there were only a handful of people in the whole
country teaching anything that could be remotely called medical ethics"; Gaylin, "Medical Ethics: The Issues," p. 2;
and many others. Also see above, the section on medical
jurisprudence; also specifically Havard, "Medical Jurisprudence," p. 813.

[7]See above, the section on medical jurisprudence.

[8]Coppens, *Moral Principles,* p. 17, italics his.

investigates the state and federal laws germaine to medical
practice, and the problems of a physician who finds himself
in a court of law, either as the accused, or as an expert
witness. The latter area, the study of the underlying principles of law, is the subject matter for a course in *medical
jurisprudence*. Though the lawyer's "field is wide and important . . . the field of *Medical Jurisprudence*, in its
stricter or more specific sense, is wider still and its research much deeper: it considers those principles of reason
that underlie the laws of the land."[9] The teacher of medical jurisprudence "treats of the Ethics or moral principles
of Medical Practice, he deals with what is ever the same for
all men wherever they dwell, it being consequent on the very
nature of man and his essential relations to his Maker and
his fellow-man."[10]

Coppens states that the term "medical jurisprudence"
has fallen into a general misuse, being applied principally
to matters of evidence in law courts and not to matters of
the principles underlying the law. He prefers to use the
term in its genuine meaning. However, "to avoid all danger
of misunderstanding, I will call my subject 'Moral Principles and Medical Practice,' and distinctly style it 'The
Basis of Medical Jurisprudence.'"[11]

The rest of the first lecture is a brief summary of
what we have seen as standard in the "fundamental moral"
sections of the manuals of moral theology:[12] treatises on
human acts, conscience, and law. Coppens underlines again

---

[9]*Ibid.*, pp. 17-18, italics his.

[10]*Ibid.*, pp. 18-19.

[11]*Ibid.*, p. 19, italics mine.

[12]See above, pp. 28-29. This approach of the *Ratio
Studiorum* is in turn based on the *Secunda Pars* of Aquinas'
Summa.

the idea that human laws are dependent on the law of God
for their binding force, and must be judged according to
the norms of the eternal law.

After this brief introduction, Coppens goes on to
treat the following topics: craniotomy, abortion by other
means, including the question of ectopic pregnancy, venereal
excesses, the physician's professional rights and duties,
insanity, and hypnotism and spiritism. Detailed analysis is
limited largely to the abortion issue.

Under venereal excesses Coppens includes the directly
medical ethical issues of contraception and of abortion as
a consequence of unlawful intercourse. In addition, however, he includes a range of sexual ethical issues which
might not seem directly pertinent to medical ethics. Though
he does not use the commandments and sacraments as his explicit organizational rubrics, it is probable that he is influenced to some extent by these principles of selection.[13]
On the other hand, he introduces a more directly practical
reason for treating these questions: the physician is often
called upon to give advice in areas dealing with sexuality.
Thus he includes questions of masturbation and excess of
sexual passion, which the doctor is urged to advise against.
He notes that physicians must not suggest immoral actions.
He condemns extra-marital intercourse and polygamy, and
argues in favor of celibacy, early marriages, and large families.[14]

---

[13]Coppens provides no references. He was clearly familiar with the general moral manuals from his own Jesuit
training, however, and had no doubt read some of the manuals
of pastoral medicine.

[14]Pp. 104-127. Coppens argues that the long lives of
celibates are due to their lack of sexual excitement, but
also urges all others to marry early, as the Irish do, without mentioning the possible deleterious effect this might have

The chapter on the duties and rights of the physician
is divided into three parts: general rights and duties (just
wage, obligations to proper knowledge and diligence, experimentation, secrecy, responsibility to the poor, and respect
for corpses), the duties of Christian and Catholic doctors
(to provide for the sacraments and to refrain from sedation
if the patient is not properly prepared for death), and the
duties of the doctor as a gentleman (to be polite and well-
groomed). The section on insanity includes a chapter advising doctors on how to testify to a person's insanity in
court.

Coppens' approach to his discipline is basically pragmatic, intended to teach the medical professional what he
needs to know in order to practice medicine morally. Though
he includes some material from the forensic aspect of medical jurisprudence (the physician's role in the law court),
and some issues of "medical ethics" (the doctor as a gentleman), his central emphasis is on the moral questions of actual medical practice. He thus continues the trend we have
noticed in our study of pastoral medicine toward more specifically medical ethical issues. He does treat of a range of
sexual issues, but includes as explicit rationale the practical fact that the physician may be called upon to counsel
concerning them. Thus, like Capellmann, he gives greatest
stress to pragmatic ethical questions. Whereas Capellmann
redefined pastoral medicine, Coppens attempts to redefine
medical jurisprudence. Both converge in the same direction:
the ethical investigation of medical practice. In chapter

---

on their life-span. He states that veneral excesses such
as extra-marital intercourse and masturbation cause "a host
of diseases, such as tuberculosis, diabetes, cardial and
nervous affections, epilepsy, hysteria, languor and general
worthlessness, hypochondria, weakness and total loss of reason, and, in married life, impotence and sterility" (*Ibid.*,
p. 105).

four we will show Coppens' use of the physicalist approach
to some of the issues he treats, an approach which is well
adapted to offering practical answers to the questions
posed by daily medical practice.

The rubric used by Coppens for the moral study of medical practice would not be accepted. Later medical moralists
would distinguish their science from that of medical jurisprudence. Contemporary medical ethicists make it clear that
medical ethics is not legal medicine, since the former deals
with ethical issues of right and wrong whereas the latter
treats of the relationship of the physician to civil law.[15]
Though his attempt at including the moral philosophy of
medicine within medical jurisprudence was not lasting, Coppens' work itself achieved a position of eminence. He is
often quoted by other moralists. His book was translated
into French, Spanish, and German,[16] and thus became part of
the development of European pastoral medicine.[17] It was
hailed for its clarity and practicality as giving "the

---

[15]See, among others, Clouser, "Some Things Medical
Ethics Is Not," p. 788.

[16]The French translation was by F. Forbes, with preface
and notes by Georges Surbled, published in Paris by Benziger
in 1901 under the title *Morale et médecine: Conférences de
déontologie médicale*. It is cited by Payen, *Déontologie
médicale*, p. vii. The German translation was by B. Nieder-
berger, with preface and notes by L. Kannamüller, published
by Benziger in 1903 with the title *Ärztliche Moral*. The
Spanish translation appeared in serial form beginning in
1900 under the title *El Criterio Católico en las ciencias
médicas*, in *Revista Mensual de Medicina, Cirugia y Farmacia*,
Barcelona. This data is found in the preface to the fourth
edition, pp. 6-7.

[17]Niedermeyer states that Coppens' work "can lay claim
to a high rating in the literature of pastoral medicine"
(Niedermeyer, *Allgemeine Pastoralmedizin*, I, 65, translation mine). "Das Buch . . . Coppens darf . . . hohen Rang
in der pastoralmedizinischen Literatur beanspruchen."

sound Catholic doctrine,"[18] and was widely used as a text
in medical morals.[19]

2. Alexander Sanford: Pastoral Medicine

Much closer to the earlier medical and hygienic emphasis of European pastoral medicine is the book written by the
Catholic physician Alexander Sanford in 1904, entitled *Pas-*
toral Medicine: A Handbook for the Catholic Clergy.[20] For
Sanford,

> The purpose of Pastoral Medicine is to present to the
> practical theologian facts of physical science, as de-
> veloped by the medical profession, for the purpose of
> applying them in pastoral function and in explanation
> and support of the teachings of faith and morals. Pas-
> toral Medicine has for its object the treatment of some
> branches of the scope of pastoral labors, which, as a
> rule, are but sparingly, if at all, included in the
> clerical student's plan of studies.[21]

Sanford explains that the clergyman must have knowledge of
the body if he is to be a minister to the soul. "He requires this knowledge, furthermore, for the purpose of applying it to the proper care of his own body, and also to
enable him to render judicious advice and practical assistance . . . where, in cases of emergency, a medical man is

---

[18]"Review: Coppens, *Moral Principles*," *America*, 25
(1921), 406.

[19]An obituary notes that Coppens "wrote . . . the first
Catholic text-book on medical jurisprudence . . . still
widely used" (*America*, 24 [1920], 248). We have already
noted the various editions between 1897 and 1905, plus the
edition by Spalding in 1921.

[20]The work first appeared in 1904, and was quickly followed by an enlarged edition in 1905, which included a chapter by Walter Drum, a Jesuit who taught at Georgetown and
Woodstock.

[21]Sanford, *Pastoral Medicine,* p. 5. With the exception
of the appended chapters, both editions are identical.

not immediately at hand."[22]

Sanford compares pastoral medicine to medical jurisprudence:

> The relationship existing between medicine and theology
> also exists between the former and the science of law.
> When applied to jurisprudence, medicine teaches the as-
> pect and influence of medical and physical facts for
> the purpose of the administration of justice. In both
> instances medicine stands in the position of an auxil-
> iary science. Medicine does not undertake to render a
> verdict in judicial matters, and Pastoral Medicine
> does not decide in points of faith and morals. Its
> task is merely to furnish *material* for the formation
> of a correct judgment.[23]

Sanford then gives a brief survey of the historical role of
the clergy in medicine, and refers to the ecclesiastical
prohibition of the practice of medicine by the clergy.[24]
He then concludes his introduction:

> It is not the purpose of Pastoral Medicine to teach or
> to induce the priest to take upon himself the task of
> the practising physician; it merely undertakes to en-
> able him to advise and caution, to protect by hygienic
> and dietetic measures, himself and his flock against
> disease.[25]

Thus for Sanford the purpose of pastoral medicine is
not to aid the priest and the physician in their tasks by
bringing moral principles to bear on medical practice, but
rather to tell the theologian and the pastor what the medical facts are, thus enabling the pastor to better serve the
spiritual and physical needs of his people, and the theologian to judge more accurately concerning doctrinal and
moral issues connected with medicine.

---

[22]*Ibid.*, p. 5.

[23]*Ibid.*, pp. 5-6, italics his.

[24]This has been treated above, pp. 51-52.

[25]*Ibid.*, p. 10.

Sanford's definition of pastoral medicine is reflected
in the topics he treats. The emphasis is clearly not a
moral one. In his first part he discusses hygiene, including the influence on health of natural and artificial
environment, food, and clothing, as well as the symptoms of
death and the correct method of burial.

The second part is entitled "Pastoral Medicine," and
includes two sub-sections. The first, "The Relation of Man
in His Bodily Conditions to Religion and Morality," includes
a brief discussion of abortion, with no systematic investigation of the moral issues. The author then speaks briefly
of the baptism of fetuses, treats of the dangers of consan-
guinous marriages, and speaks in favor of celibacy.[26] The
second sub-section, "Man in Sickness," constitutes the major
portion of part two, and consists of a description of
various physical and mental diseases. Part three of the
book is a brief course in first aid for the injured.

The second edition of the work contains an appendix,
including one chapter entitled "The Fifth Commandment,"
which is explicitly a moral theological investigation of
abortion and related questions. Additional chapters in this
appendix are a chapter by Walter Drum on the moment of death,
intended to inform priests relative to administering the
sacraments, and a chapter on neurasthenia and compulsivity.

With the exception of the appended chapter on abortion
in the second edition, Sanford's work does not emphasize the
moral aspects of medical practice. Unlike Capellmann, and
unlike most of his American colleagues, Sanford's work is in

---

[26]We noted in passing that Coppens shows how priests
and nuns live longer than married persons. Sanford's data
shows that they generally die younger. Whereas Coppens
argues that freedom from sexual excitement results in longer lives, Sanford argues that care for the sick is the
cause of contacting disease among priests and religious.

the tradition of earlier works of European pastoral medicine. Its central emphasis is on providing medical and hygienic advice for the clergy.

3. Andrew Klarmann: Embryonic Man

     It was precisely and explicitly against just this em-
phasis in pastoral medicine that the diocesan priest Andrew
Klarmann wrote his book, *The Crux of Pastoral Medicine: The
Perils of Embryonic Man.*[27] Klarmann intends to limit the
subject matter of pastoral medicine to the question of abortion and fetal care. The clearest description of his intent is found in the preface to the second and third editions. He declares that his approach to pastoral medicine
"set itself at variance with all hitherto acknowledged authors in the same field," and yet was "well received,

---

     [27]Klarmann was born in Bavaria in 1866. He and his
brother sailed to America, and Andrew entered the Abbey of
St. Vincent in Latrobe, Pennsylvania. After a bout with
malaria he left the monastery and was ordained a priest of
the diocese of Brooklyn, New York, in 1892. His writings
include various works of romantic fiction, one of which,
The Princess of Gan-Sar, he wrote as a reaction to the need-
ling of his friends who pointed out the "solid logical content" of his work in pastoral medicine (Hoehn, ed., *Catholic
Authors,* p. 400). In addition to his works, he built a
"large brick church, a school, a convent, and an auditori-
um," and left his parish debt-free. He died in 1931.
     The Crux of Pastoral Medicine was first published in
1905, or late 1904. The standard bibliographical sources do
not list the first edition, but this date can be verified
from lists of "Books Received" in the journals of the time
(the first edition was received by *Catholic World* in July,
1905). The second edition was expanded by some 60 pages,
and appeared in 1905. The identical third edition bears a
1907 date. The fourth edition (1912) adds two chapters.
The fifth edition (1915) is also expanded by one further
chapter. All references here are to this last, fifth edition. The reader is advised that there are some changes in
pagination from earlier editions, but that most of the references are identical.

contrary to expectations and predictions."[28] He decries the
lack of strong stands which theologians might have taken
concerning the central (moral) issues of pastoral medicine.
He suggests that this was due to unnecessary deference on
the part of moralists to physicians, who were presumed to be
in charge of the case from the beginning.[29]

Klarmann continues:

> And thus we find in the various books on this subject
> indications of mutual fear on the part of the authors.
> Few authors, if one, have taken a courageous stand
> against their opponents on the same question. Besides,
> Pastoral Medicine has been held in such scant esteem,
> by the medical profession, at least, that succeeding
> authors contented themselves with copying each other.
> Far from making pretentions to scientific treatment,
> the "crux" of Pastoral Medicine was ever bedded out of
> sight under a heap of hygiene, nursing and sickroom
> regulations, diet and ventilation, signs of death and
> apparent death, lunacy and epilepsy, syphilis, etc.,
> etc. The attempt at sincerity with the dangerous, del-
> icate and troublesome *subject of Pastoral Medicine
> proper, the perils of nascent life*, was only made in a
> half-hearted manner.[30]

Klarmann thus attempts to restrict the subject matter
of pastoral medicine to the one central issue of abortion
and fetal care. In the early editions of the work the entire book is devoted to this question. After an introduction concerning the problems of life and generation (a Tho-
mistic metaphysical analysis of matter and form as related
to cellular life), Klarmann treats in detail of the moral
issues of abortion, including chapters on ectopic gestation,
uterine cancer, clear ova, vomiting, and Caesarian and Porro
section. There is also a chapter on "conjugal onanism,"

---

[28]Klarmann, *The Crux of Pastoral Medicine,* 5th ed., p. 5.

[29]*Ibid.*, pp. vi-vii.

[30]*Ibid.*, pp. vii-viii, italics mine.

which he includes, "not as if it constituted one of the
perils of embryonic man, but rather, because it is so widely
substituted for the remedies of those perils."[31]   An appendix discusses the problem of heredity. A series of Roman
Curial decrees concludes the work.

Later editions of the work do not continue the strict
limitations proposed for the field in the earlier editions.
In the fourth edition (1912) Klarmann extends the topics he
treats without explicitly revising his earlier opinion concerning the "crux" of pastoral medicine. He merely states
in his preface to the fourth edition that he intends to discuss "three questions of vital importance [which] have . . .
forced themselves on the attention of the public,"[32] namely
vasectomy, the moment of death in relation to the sacraments,
and the question of sex education for the young. The fifth
edition (1915) adds a short chapter on psychotherapy. It is
difficult to determine Klarmann's rationale for these later
inclusions within a work which originally was designed to
avoid anything which might overshadow the central importance
of the abortion issue as crux of the discipline. Perhaps
the author simply wished to use the opportunity of reprint-
ing his book for publishing these further essays. To some
extent the material added is of ethical importance to the
medical profession. Vasectomy, of course, is a directly
medical ethical issue. The chapter on sex education might
be helpful to the physician as counsellor, and Klarmann
briefly notes this,[33] but the chief thrust of the essay is
to denounce modern hedonism rather than to aid the physician
specifically. The chapter on psychotherapy is a general

---

[31]*Ibid.*, p. 176.

[32]*Ibid.*, p. iii.

[33]*Ibid.*, p. 210.

description of psychic ills, religion, and the perversity of
the modern age. The additions made in the later editions of
the work thus retreat somewhat from the more strictly practical questions of the earlier editions, where the topic was
one of immediate importance to the physician in his professional practice. Nonetheless these added essays comprise a
relatively small part of the whole work, whose emphasis remains on the ethical medical question of abortion and fetal
care. This question, as we shall see in chapter four, is
resolved largely within a physicalist methodology.

Klarmann's attempt to limit medical ethics to the one
issue of abortion was never accepted. But what was accepted
more and more generally was the growing emphasis on specifically ethical issues as opposed to the other issues included
in earlier works in pastoral medicine. Medical ethics in
North America, though it was not yet known by name, was
gradually emerging as the discipline investigating the actual professional conduct of physician and nurse from a moral
perspective. Less attention was given to teaching the pastor about hygiene. Less discussion was devoted to questions
of dogmatic speculative theology. The "crux" of medical
ethics would not be limited to the question of abortion.
But it would be largely centered on ethical questions of
daily professional interest to medical practitioners.

4.   O'Malley and Walsh: A Compromise

A 1906 work entitled *Essays in Pastoral Medicine* by two
American Catholic physicians, Austin O'Malley and James
Walsh, falls in between the hygienic emphasis of Dr. Sanford
and the restrictively moral emphasis of Fr. Klarmann.[34]

---

[34]James J. Walsh and Austin O'Malley were two of the
more interesting of Catholic laymen of the period. Their

Relative to Sanford and to the earlier European literature,
the book shows a moral emphasis, and is thus part of the
move towards ethical issues in the American discipline.
O'Malley and Walsh do include much medical and hygienic material, however, and a large portion of their discussion is
directed more toward aiding pastors in their work as confessors and spiritual counsellors (the medical emphasis of pastoral medicine) than to specific ethical analysis of medical
procedures (the moral theological emphasis). Direct ethical
analysis is more or less restricted to the question of abortion, and, as we will discuss in some detail in chapter
four, is made within physicalist and ecclesiastical positivist methodologies.

The authors describe pastoral medicine as follows:

---

careers were similar. O'Malley was born in 1858. He was
educated by the Jesuits at Fordham and then at the Gregorian
in Rome. He returned to the United States and entered the
Jesuit order. Deciding he did not have a vocation to the
priesthood, he left the society and studied medicine at
Georgetown and Notre Dame. He was well known as a man of
letters, and wrote both medical and philosophical works. He
died in 1932. An obituary calls him a "versatile genius,"
qualified in "philosophy, theology, asceticism, biology,
medicine, and literature" (*America*, 46 [1932], 453).
    His close friend, James Walsh, was born in 1865. Also
educated at Fordham, he entered the Jesuits, but temporary
poor health caused him to leave the society. He studied
medicine at the University of Pennsylvania, in Paris, and in
Vienna. He taught at Fordham. During his literary career
he published more than fifty books, of which the best known
at the time was *The Thirteenth, the Greatest of Centuries,*
whose central thesis was that man had not progressed since
the time of Thomas Aquinas and Dante (O'Malley, "The Works
of Dr. James J. Walsh," pp. 401-402). He died in 1942 after
a distinguished career in medicine, well known in Catholic
circles for his works in philosophy in defense of the Catholic faith.
    Essays in Pastoral Medicine first appeared in 1906.
There were at least seven reprintings of the work (see
Walsh, "Dr. Austin O'Malley," p. 550).

> The term Pastoral Medicine is somewhat difficult to de-
> fine because it comprises unrelated material ranging
> from disinfection to foeticide.[35] It presents that
> part of medicine which is of import to a pastor in his
> cure, and those divisions of ethics and moral theology
> which concern a physician in his practice. It sets
> forth facts and principles whereby the physician him-
> self or his pastor may direct the operator's conscience
> whenever medicine takes on a moral quality, and it also
> explains to the pastor, who must often minister to a
> mind diseased, certain medical truths which will soften
> harsh judgments, and other facts, which may be indiffer-
> ent morally but which will assist him in the proper con-
> duct of his work, especially as an educator. Pastoral
> medicine is *not* to be confused with the code of rules
> commonly called *medical ethics*.[36]

Clearly included in this definition are both of the emphases

we have noted in pastoral medicine: medical data for the

pastor, and moral theological direction for the physician.

The authors explain that previous works in the field are out-

dated. Those by physicians tend to be "mere popular trea-

tises on hygiene," whereas those written by clergymen "have

some value on the ethical side, but they are incomplete be-

cause the authors had not the necessary medical knowledge."[37]

This has resulted in a general lack of adequate moral guid-

ance for physicians, who therefore follow the medical texts,

> which without exception advise them to take the life of
> a dangerous foetus almost as unconcernedly as they
> might prescribe an active drug, or in any case to put
> utility before justice. There is, therefore, an urgent
> necessity that competent men fix that shifting part of
> ethics and moral theology called pastoral medicine, and
> these essays are presented as a temporary bridge to
> serve in crossing a corner of the bog until better
> engineers lay down a permanent causeway.[38]

---

[35]Precisely the object of Klarmann's complaint.

[36]O'Malley and Walsh, *Essays in Pastoral Medicine*, p.
v, italics mine.

[37]*Ibid.*, p. vi.

[38]*Ibid.*, p. vii.

In addition, pastors are often unnecessarily harsh in their
judgments of moral culpability, and a knowledge of mental
defects will better enable them to carry on their ministry.
It will "widen the bounds of charity and save many that are
more sinned against than sinning from the injury of grievous
misjudgment."[39]

In accordance with their two-fold definition of pastoral medicine, O'Malley and Walsh include both kinds of topics
in their book. There is no logical organization to the order of the topics covered, which include abortion (ectopic
gestation, Caesarian section, craniotomy), pre-natal care,
baptism of monsters, public health, intoxication, heredity,
hypnotism, the moment of death, infectious diseases in
schools, school hygiene, mental diseases, menstrual diseases,
epilepsy, suicide, venereal disease, social diseases, and a
chapter by O'Malley in Latin on the canonical questions of
the impediment of impotence. O'Malley also adds an appendix
on the medical possibility of bloody sweat.[40]

O'Malley and Walsh use the term "pastoral medicine" as
rubric for their discipline. They explicitly disassociate
themselves from the term "medical ethics," which to them
meant merely "the code of rules"[41] we have described earlier.
But the use of "pastoral medicine" as a general rubric was
to fall rather quickly into disuse in Roman Catholic writings in North America. Only the three works which we have
just examined use the term as rubric in their titles.

---

[39]*Ibid.*, p. vii.

[40]A discussion of the possibility and nature of the
phenomenon described in Lk. 22:44. As Jesus prays on the
Mount of Olives awaiting his capture and subsequent passion,
Luke recounts that "his sweat fell to the ground like great
drops of blood" (Jerusalem Bible version).

[41]O'Malley and Walsh, p. v.

Sanford describes the field with an emphasis on medical and
hygienic data for the clergy. Klarmann wishes to restrict it to
its "crux": the question of abortion. O'Malley and Walsh
try to retain both the medical and moral emphases. From
this point on in American writings, authors will search for
a more adequate rubric to describe their field. The term
"medical ethics" is not yet available to them, since it
means something quite different. "Pastoral medicine" means
both too much and too little. It means too much because it
includes questions of hygiene and first aid which the moral
theologians do not consider part of their task. It means
too little, because the hygienic emphasis often results in
the exclusion of systematic moral theological analysis,
which the moral theologians see as the essence of the discipline. Over the next three decades, from 1910 to 1940, authors will use various phrases in their titles. Then, in
the 1940's, *Medical Ethics* will gradually become the accepted
rubric for the discipline.

The various reprints and editions of the works by Coppens, Klarmann, and O'Malley and Walsh appeared during the
second decade of the century. Then in 1919 O'Malley published a book that paralleled that of Klarmann, entitled *The
Ethics of Medical Homicide and Mutilation.*[42] O'Malley had
written most of the ethics chapters in *Essays in Pastoral
Medicine,* and in this book, which Walsh calls "O'Malley's
most important work,"[43] he presents a detailed moral theological study of abortion and sterilization. His purpose is
"to reach all practitioners, to the end that the Natural Law

---

[42]A slightly enlarged version appeared in 1922, called
the "third printing." It included one added chapter on
birth control. References are to this enlarged, 1922 version.

[43]Walsh, "Dr. Austin O'Malley," p. 551.

which binds every man may be observed."[44] He treats in detail of various cases of abortion (ectopic gestation, Caesarian section, cancer, vomiting, syphilis, and other complications of pregnancy), the use of drugs in childbirth,
vasectomy, and birth control.[45] In chapter four we will
discuss O'Malley's methodology.

5. Some Works of the Early 1920's

A work in medical morals and "nursing ethics" intended
for nurses and nursing students was published in 1920 by the
Jesuit professor of ethics Henry Spalding.[46] *Talks to
Nurses: The Ethics of Nursing* is a series of lectures given
by Spalding to student nurses. It includes a few chapters
on central medical moral questions (euthanasia, vasectomy,
abortion, and birth control) as well as chapters directed
more to the personal life of the nurse herself, such as are
found in many texts of "nursing ethics" and professional adjustments.[47] Spalding disassociates himself from "nursing
ethics" in that he charges certain works in that field as
being merely the description of custom and usage, of hints,

---

[44]O'Malley, *The Ethics of Medical Homicide*, Preface.

[45]Reviews of the work call O'Malley "a physician of un-
challenged eminence, a moralist of so high an order that for
years it has been the practice of theologians to ask his advice" (*America,* 21 [1919], 504). Criticism was made, however, of "a somewhat too disdainful attitude towards those
who, on disputable points, disagree with the author" (*Catholic World,* 111 [1920], 690).

[46]Henry Spalding was born in 1865. He entered the Jesuits and was ordained in 1899. He taught at Creighton Medical College (where Coppens was professor of medical jurisprudence), then at Loyola in Chicago, and at the time of his
book was professor of ethics at St. Xavier College in Cincinnati. He died in 1934.

[47]See above, pp. 94-95, n. 199.

suggestions, and advice.[48] Yet a major portion of Spalding's
own lectures are devoted to advising the nurse on habits of
personal etiquette. Nurses are advised to avoid familiarity
with (often dangerous) physicians and interns, to "be sedate,
be prudent, be a lady,"[49] and not to "dissipate your energy
by reading the light literature which you find handy."[50]
Spalding includes in these chapters certain questions of
real medical ethical importance, such as experimentation and
medical secrets, but gives no systematic discussion, and
generally is content with exhortation. The final chapter is
a lecture on the history of Catholic nursing.[51] The book
was praised by reviewers as offering correct moral guidance
to the nurse.[52]

   In 1921 Spalding added three chapters to the original
series of nine lectures which comprised Charles Coppens'
work, *Moral Principles and Medical Practice: The Basis of
Medical Jurisprudence.*[53] The additional lectures, which

---

[48]Spalding, *Talks to Nurses,* pp. 14-15.

[49]*Ibid.*, pp. 93-94.

[50]*Ibid.*, pp. 95.

[51]Pp. 175-189. The author describes how medical care
fell into chaos in Protestant countries while it remained
strong in Catholic lands. He defends Catholic hospitals
against their critics.

[52]One review cites the need that has long existed for
"a thoroughly Catholic book which should set forth in clear
language the right and wrong of the ethical problems with
which the nurse is constantly beset and on which, at the
peril of her soul, she must think aright. It is just such a
book" (*America*, 23 [1920], 332). Another reviewer calls it
"the kind of moral teaching which alone can save this world
of ours from its own folly" (*Catholic World,* 111 [1920],
832).

[53]Listed in the bibliography under joint authorship
(Coppens and Spalding, *Moral Principles,* new ed., 1921).

Spalding delivered to his medical students along with the
original nine, discuss euthanasia and vasectomy, sex education and eugenics, and birth control.

The term *Medical Ethics* is used as a rubric, but without much definitional clarity, in a small pamphlet written
in 1921 by Michael Bourke, entitled *Some Medical Ethical
Problems Solved*.[54] As the title suggests, Bourke does not
include any detailed discussion, but merely gives his answers to certain problems. He divides his pamphlet into
three parts. The first concerns "Questions of Ethics in the
broader, and really inaccurate view of that term,"[55] and includes questions we have seen covered in works of intra-
professional "medical ethics," such as diagnostic incompe-
tency, consultation, recommending physicians, the right to
change doctors, as well as the importance of a doctor's religion to his presence in a Catholic hospital (it is allowed to hire non-Catholics), the presence of a female nurse
at operations on male patients (she should be made to attend
even if prudery causes problems), and the hiring of a known
abortionist (not recommended). The second section treats of
"Questions of Medical Ethics that have to do in the main
with complications in obstetrics and gynecology."[56] Bourke
calls these "the so-called medical ethical problems."[57] He
speaks of abortion (ectopic gestation, and some other cases)
and sterilization. The third section concerns itself with

---

[54]Bourke was superintendent of hospitals for the De-
troit diocese and chaplain at the University of Michigan.
The pamphlet was later included as a chapter in a 1938 an-
thology. See the bibliography (Bourke, *Some Medical Ethical
Problems Solved*). The original pamphlet was 24 pages long.
Page references here are to the reprint in the later anthology.

[55]Bourke, *Some Medical Ethical Problems Solved*, p. 199.

[56]*Ibid.*, p. 199.

[57]*Ibid.*, p. 204.

the sacrament of baptism in medical necessity. Bourke concludes his booklet by urging hospital directors: "And please
see to it that your nurses receive a course of instruction
in medical ethics. This duty some well-informed priest
should be persuaded to undertake."[58] He recommends that the
following topics be covered: the nobility and general duties
of the nursing profession, abortion, baptism, Eucharist in the
sick room, and extreme unction. He suggests that a few topics of nursing jurisprudence might also be added.[59]

Bourke's suggestion that questions of obstetrics and
gynecology constitute "the so-called medical ethical problems" is indicative of the direction we have been describing
in North American medical ethics. We have seen a similar
emphasis in Coppens, and especially in Klarmann. Issues of
this kind grow in importance as modern scientific medicine
develops new physical technologies of intervention. Thus
the definition of medical ethics is influenced by the growing professionalization and specialization of medicine. The
methodology of the discipline is likewise influenced. It is
especially in issues dealing with physical operations such
as abortion and sterilization that the physicalist modality,
which will be described later, is most easily and aptly applied.

We have noted, and will often note again authors who
disassociate their discipline from the term "medical ethics."
Bourke does not. He accepts the rubric as applying to the
ethical investigation of medical practice, especially to
questions of abortion and sterilization. Bourke's usage
demonstrates that in at least some Catholic medical circles,
the term *Medical Ethics* is being used in the way in which it

---

[58]*Ibid.*, p. 219.

[59]*Ibid.*, p. 220.

will come to be generally accepted during the forties and
fifties: as the rubric for the discipline investigating theologically or philosophically the moral issues of medical
practice.

That the rubric "medical jurisprudence" is also in use
during the period is clear from an article written by Bourke
in *Hospital Progress* in 1920. Here Bourke accepts Coppens'
division of medical jurisprudence into a narrower and a
wider aspect. The former "embraces a study of the laws of
the land regulating the practice of medicine." The latter
"includes . . . a review of the principles which lie at the
base of these laws." Thus medical jurisprudence
"scales the heights of theology and philosophy . . . and
falls very properly within the sphere of the priest."[60]
Bourke goes on to treat abortion as one of the topics of
medical jurisprudence proper. He also speaks of sacramental
ministry to the sick, but does not include it within the
proper sphere of medical jurisprudence.[61] Bourke's use of
both *Medical Ethics* and "medical jurisprudence" indicates
that no one term has as yet achieved general acceptance as
rubric for the discipline.

A short work entitled *Acute Cases in Moral Medicine*,
written by Edward F. Burke, appeared in 1922.[62] Burke
treats certain aspects of what he calls the two-fold rights
of man: temporal rights and spiritual rights. Under man's
right to temporal life he includes questions of abortion
(embryotomy, ectopic gestation, and various therapeutic
cases) and certain "special cases," among them euthanasia,

---

[60]Bourke, "Talks to Nurses," p. 47.

[61]*Ibid.*, p. 48.

[62]Burke was professor of moral theology at St. Mary's
Seminary in Cleveland.

twilight sleep (the use of drugs in childbirth), sterilization, "race suicide" (presumably methods of contraception,
which "the doctor and the nurse, far from divulging should
guard as a sacred trust"[63]), and professional consultation.
Under man's right to religion Burke speaks of baptism and
the last sacraments in cases of illness, and of Christian
burial. There is an appendix consisting of decrees of the
Holy Office and some suggestions for the nurse in preparing
for the priest's visit and in providing suitable reading for
the patient. In keeping with his explicit intention,[64]
Burke avoids any real systematic analysis, and contents himself with setting forth a few basic principles and his conclusions. The book is intended for those who care for the
sick, and its purpose is "to mark out a safe line of conduct, brief and readily accessible," in cases of moral medicine.[65] Reviews praised it for achieving this goal.[66] However, Burke's lack of analysis and often of necessary medical and moral distinctions severely limits the value of the
work.

Also in 1922 the Vincentian priest Patrick Finney published his *Moral Problems in Hospital Practice: A Practical*

---

[63]Burke, *Acute Cases*, p. 62.

[64]Burke's preface states that there is to be no "attempt at argumentation; there is, however, ample reference
to authoritative works which discuss at length the conclusions based upon established principles" (*Ibid.*, p. xii).

[65]*Ibid.*, p. xi. A foreword by the bishop of Cleveland
suggests that the work is intended primarily for nurses
(*Ibid.*, p. ix).

[66]The work provided a surprising "thoroughgoing satisfaction." "Nothing better than this, we venture to say, has
ever been done, at least in English" (*Catholic World,* 117
[1923], 140). The work was criticized, however: "At times
. . . the writer seems to slip a point or two in medicine"
(*America,* 28 [1923], 500).

Handbook.[67]   Like Burke, Finney writes to provide quickly
accessible solutions to moral problems. He addresses his
work primarily to nuns in charge of Catholic hospitals, and
secondarily to Catholic physicians, nurses, and seminarians.[68] He explains that the Sister in charge may be unable
to contact the local priest, or that he may be unable to
answer quickly. His handbook is presented so that "a Sister
will have no difficulty in reaching a decision within a few
minutes after a case is presented to her."[69] Accordingly
the work is divided into two parts. The first is a simple
question and answer presentation, in which Finney judges
positively or negatively, with no explanation, concerning
the liceity of certain procedures. Finney explains that the
doctor may wish a justification of the Sister's decision,
and that the second part is written to provide it. Here he
repeats his questions and answers, and adds a brief presentation of the applicable moral principles. He explicitly
avoids any discussion of opposing views, "because it was
judged that such discussions would serve only to create new
doubts, instead of removing those which it was the primary
purpose of the manual to settle."[70]

Almost the entire book is devoted to questions of obstetrics and gynecology. Finney treats of direct and indirect abortion, ectopic gestation, sterilization, and the use
of anesthesia during labor (usually immoral). The only

---

[67]Subsequent editions through the twenties, thirties,
and forties are identical reprints, except for changes in
the introductory material. The 1956 redaction by Patrick
O'Brien is a complete reworking of the original, and will be
treated later. All references here are to the 1922 edition.

[68]Finney, *Moral Problems,* Introduction.

[69]*Ibid.*, Introduction, page two.

[70]*Ibid.*, Introduction, pages three and four.

issue not directly connected to gynecological procedures is
that of baptism, and even here the emphasis is on baptism of
the fetus, and the purpose is that the medical practitioner
might know how to act in case of necessity. Finney thus
continues the trend we have noted in Klarmann and Bourke: in
conjunction with the development of surgical techniques by
scientific medicine, medical ethics, by whatever name it is
to be called, deals with the daily professional activity of
medical personnel, especially as that activity entails actual physical procedure. The physicalist methodology which
will be described later is apt for the analysis and solution
of this type of moral issue.

The book was in considerable demand over subsequent decades.[71] It became known as a rather strict work, especially in the area of ectopic pregnancy.[72] Reviews were mixed,
some hailing it as an invaluable reference tool, others
questioning the ease with which Finney reached his conclusions.[73]

None of these works of the early 1920's were of sufficient detail to constitute important contributions to the
field. Only Finney's work would be remembered in later literature. Not until the later period (1940-1960) would there
be any truly comprehensive manuals of medical ethics, com-

---

[71]See Finney and O'Brien, *Moral Problems*, p. xi.

[72]*Ibid.*, pp. 144-145.

[73]One review criticizes the work at length: "we feel
that he has set himself an impossible task. There is no
royal road to wisdom, and there seems no way of enabling
those who have had no training in moral theology to answer
immediately and categorically some of the most complicated
problems in the field of morals. . . . where the discussion
of any problem has not brought unanimity among Catholic moralists and a doubt still remains, we do not think that
Father Finney is justified in ignoring it" (*Catholic World,*
115 [1922], 831-832).

bining a wide topical array with detailed analysis.

6. Other Works of the 1920's and 1930's

     In 1926 a massive volume appeared, written by an anony-
mous Catholic physician using the pseudonym "Medicus." Entitled *Medical Essays: Compiled from Various Sources, by*
Medicus, the work includes both medical and moral discussion
of various questions connected with sex and reproduction.[74]
In his preface the author states that he "enters an unex-
plored field. He therefore, prefers to remain unknown.
There is nothing in his book for which he hesitates personally to be responsible; but if it fall out that the judgment
of men approve not his work, the lapse into oblivion shall
be easier for an unknown man. . . . As the book is privately
printed and offered to a select public, it demands the privileges of a MEDICAL TREATISE."[75]

     The work is probably best described as one in pastoral
medicine, though even that designation is not entirely apt.
It is limited to the question of reproduction, but it

----

     [74]The first edition was published in 1926. Second and
third editions, each enlarged, appeared in 1928 and 1931.
The first edition has been consulted. The pseudonym "medicus" was a common one at the time (see, for example, the
listing in the *National Union Catalogue: Pre-1956 Imprints*).
No reviews are listed in the standard sources. The book is
not widely cited (I have found no references to it anywhere
in my research) nor is it widely available (I came upon it
in a seminary library). Its three editions suggest that it
achieved some popularity, but the anonymity of its author,
the private nature of its publication, and its general lack of
organization and of specificity of purpose doubtless limited
its impact. The title of the work suggests a compilation of
essays by various authors. In fact each of the chapters appears to be by "medicus," but the text contains long sections in quotes without citation as to author. Presumably
these are the passages "compiled from various sources."

     [75]Medicus, *Medical Essays,* Foreword, capitalization his.

includes both medical and moral aspects. Inasmuch as it
includes much anatomical data and suggests medical treatments of many sexual disorders for the use of physicians,
the work is in part a strictly medical treatise. Yet much
of the work suggests the need for moral guidance, argues
that some disorders of sexual function are due to immoral
practices, and discusses birth control, abortion, sterilization, masturbation, and other behaviors from a moral as well
as a medical perspective. "Medicus" makes no attempt at any
significant organization or systematic ethical methodology.
The work is thus unlike other North American works which are
more specifically interested in limiting their scope to the
development and/or application of moral principles to the
daily professional activity of the doctor and nurse. In
this it is more like the work *Essays in Pastoral Medicine,*
described above, than like most of the other books we have
studied.

A small booklet answering medical ethical questions was
published in 1926 by a French Canadian pastor and hospital
chaplain, Hervé Trudel.[76] In his work, entitled *Éléments de
morale médicale,* Trudel includes a brief summary of general
principles, and then presents a series of answers, with no
detailed ethical analysis, concerning direct and indirect
abortion, ectopic gestation, mutilation and sterilization,
and concerning the administration of the sacraments to the
sick. He ends with a chapter exhorting the physician and
nurse to greater excellence in the virtues of their profes-

---

[76] Trudel was born in the province of Quebec in 1882,
and was ordained in 1907. He served as pastor and as chaplain of St. Joseph's Hospital in Three Rivers. His booklet
first appeared in 1926, and achieved a second edition in
1928, and a third in 1932. A fourth edition, revised and
enlarged by Armand Perrier, appeared in 1940. The second
and fourth editions have been consulted. This last will be
mentioned again in the next section.

sion.

The 1929 book *Ethics and the Art of Conduct for Nurses*
by the Jesuit author Edward Garesché is not a book in the
ethics of medicine, but is rather a combination of a general
introduction to Catholic ethics followed by a manual of
"nursing ethics."[77] Medical ethical questions are treated
briefly in part one in a short chapter on duties to the
bodies and lives of others, and are scattered throughout
other chapters which deal with the whole range of ethical
issues. Part two, "The Art of Conduct," is a "nursing ethics" text, and speaks of the nurse's personality, conversation, dress, and other points of etiquette.[78]

Similar in some ways to Garesché's book, but of greater
importance, is Thomas Verner Moore's *Principles of Ethics,*
first published in 1935.[79] Moore addresses his work to

---

[77]Garesché edited *Hospital Progress* and other journals.
He authored many works in apologetics, spirituality, and
pastoral psychology. He wrote poetry. His book for nurses
saw a second edition, slightly revised, in 1944.

[78]Brief mention ought also to be made of a 1923 work by
the Jesuit Richard Murphy, entitled *The Catholic Nurse: Her
Spirit and Her Duties.* Though the title might suggest it to
be a work in Roman Catholic medical morality, it is in fact
a series of lectures in "nursing ethics."

[79]Thomas Verner Moore was born in 1877. He joined the
Paulists and was ordained in 1901. After earning a Ph.D.
from Catholic University, he taught there, studied medicine
at Georgetown and Munich, and took his M.D. degree at Johns
Hopkins in 1915. He entered the Benedictines in Scotland in
1923 and returned to the United States to found St. Anselm's
Priory in Washington. At the time of his work in ethics he
was professor of psychology at Catholic University. He
wrote numerous works, many concerned with the interface of
religion and mental health. In later life he became a Car-
thusian hermit.
     Principles of Ethics saw four similar editions, in 1935,
1937, 1939, and 1943. Pagination for all is identical, except for the addition in the second edition of a last chapter on teaching medical ethics, and in the fourth of a

nurses, but, like Garesché, he does not limit his topics to
issues of medical or nursing ethics. Moore's work is rather
a general ethics text intended to emphasize the daily ethical issues found problematic in the nurse's own personal as
well as professional life. The book came out of a study of
the personal diaries of ninety-five nurses submitted anony-
mously to one of his students, and then to Dom Moore.[80]
Moore includes these problems as the practical issues discussed in the various chapters. The book includes sections
on general principles, on man's duties to himself, to others,
to the family and state, and to God. Moore concludes with
two brief chapters outlining the history of medical and
nursing ethics, in which he acclaims the codes of ethics as
valuable in enforcing high standards of conduct.[81]

As would be the case in any general text in ethics,
medical ethical topics are scattered throughout the work.
Since the book is intended specifically for nurses, however,
the emphasis on these issues is somewhat greater than would
ordinarily be expected in a general text. In addition there
are two sections where medical issues are specifically gathered: a chapter on the morality of certain operations, limited to the question of abortion,[82] and one on professional
duties, which treats of certain issues of "medical ethics,"

---

concluding chapter on the ethics of war. A so-called fifth
edition appeared in 1959, edited by Gregory Stevens. It is
in fact a new book, and will be noted later. All references
here are to the fourth edition.

[80]Moore, *Principles of Ethics,* 4th ed., p. vii. Also
"Review: Moore, *Principles of Ethics,*" *Catholic World,* 141
(1935), 382.

[81]Moore, 4th ed., pp. 333-366.

[82]*Ibid.,* pp. 159-184.

such as advertising, patents, and medical insurance.[83] Despite this emphasis, however, Moore's work is not as such an
ethical study of the problems of medical practice. Nor is
it sufficiently analytical to serve as more than an introductory text in ethics combined with an abundance of advice
for the student nurse.[84]

In 1938 a book of essays edited by Leo Gregory Fink appeared with the title *Graduate Nurses: Symposium of Ethical
Inspiration*.[85] Essays by various authors discuss contraception, sterilization, euthanasia, and sexual abstinence, and
include a reprint of the article by Michael Bourke already
mentioned. Other essays deal with issues not directly connected to medical morals. The work contains the Surgical
Code for Catholic Hospitals, the Hippocratic Oath, the
Pledge of Florence Nightingale, and the Ten Commandments.
It was acclaimed for its moral exhortation.[86]

7. Two Journals of Medical Morality

In addition to the formal works in the morals of medicine, which we have investigated, the appearance of two Roman Catholic journals devoted to medical matters is of considerable significance. Each was (and still is) published
by an association founded in order to serve as a forum for

---

[83]*Ibid*., pp. 261-272.

[84]One review correctly describes it as "dogmatic" rather than "discursive." "The author, purposely, no doubt,
avoids controversial points" (*Commonweal*, 22 [1935], 222).

[85]Fink was a pastor in the Philadelphia archdiocese.
The copy consulted includes the notation "third edition,"
but this doubtless refers to impression rather than revision.

[86]"In this volume the many errors which are propagated
today . . . are exposed and refuted" (*Sign*, 18 [1939],
251).

discussing and pronouncing on matters relating to medicine
in a Catholic context. The Catholic Hospital Association of
the United States and Canada was founded in 1915, "for the
promotion and realization of progressively higher ideals in
the religious, moral, medical, nursing, educational, social,
and all other phases of hospital and nursing endeavor and
other consistent purposes especially relating to the Catholic hospitals and schools of nursing in the United States
and Canada."[87] The separate Catholic Hospital Association
of Canada began its formal existence in 1954. The Association began publication of its journal, *Hospital Progress,* in
May, 1920. The journal served to inform its readers of medical and of moral matters relating to Catholic hospital and
medical practice. In 1933 the Association was affiliated
with the Catholic hierarchy through the National Catholic
Welfare Conference, and in 1939 the executive board of the
Association joined with a newly formed Conference of Bishops'
Representatives to form the new administrative board of the
Association. Thus the CHA was closely connected to the
formal structure of the North American hierarchy. It continues today in this role.

When the CHA was founded in 1915, there were 541 Catholic hospitals in the United States and 90 in Canada.[88] Since
that time the number has grown (857 and 300 respectively in
1963[89]), and the influence of the CHA in establishing moral
policy within the hospital system has increased. The Association published a brief code of ethics in 1921 which dealt

---

[87]Shanahan, "Catholic Hospital Association," p. 268.
The citation is from the official statement of purpose of
the Association. For the history of the Association see, in
addition to Shanahan, Garesché, "The Catholic Hospital Association."

[88]Flanagan, "Hospitals," p. 167.

[89]*Ibid.*, p. 167.

with operations connected with pregnancy and reproduction.[90]

This surgical code lasted until the appearance of the first set of "Ethical and Religious Directives for Catholic Hospitals" in 1948.[91] The "Surgical Code for Catholic Hospitals" contains two sets of "operations [which] are unethical and may not therefore be performed: One. Operations involving the destruction of foetal life. . . . Two. All operations involving the sterilization or mutilation of men or women, except where such follows as the indirect and undesired result of necessary interference for the removal of diseased structures."[92] Through this and subsequent codes, as well as through its journal, *Hospital Progress,* the CHA was and is largely responsible for setting the actual moral practice in American Catholic hospitals.

The National Federation of Catholic Physicians' Guilds was formed in 1932 "to promote spiritual aims and ideals as they apply to members of the medical profession."[93] Individual guilds had existed for some time on the local level, and guilds were common in England and on the Continent.[94]

---

[90]"Catholic Nurses in Council," p. 296; "Code of Medical Ethics?" p. 492.

[91]These will be discussed in the next section of this chapter.

[92]Catholic Hospital Association, "Surgical Code."

[93]Egan, "National Federation," p. 236. See also McDonald, "Why Catholic Physicians' Guilds?", where the argument is made in favor of the guilds that through them "all Catholics may keep themselves sensitively and fundamentally in touch with sound Catholic principles in questions involving important medico-ethical problems as they arise" (p. 59).

[94]Plater, "Why a Catholic Medical Guild?" p. 311. In England The Guild of St. Luke, St. Cosmas, and St. Damian began publishing *The Catholic Medical Guardian* in 1926 (Plater, p. 314).

In 1932 eleven local guilds joined to form the Federation.
By 1964 there were 104 local guilds with 7,000 members.[95]
The Federation began publication of *The Linacre Quarterly*
in 1932. This journal has consistently emphasized medical
moral issues in its articles. The first International Congress of Catholic Physicians was held in 1935.[96]

These two organizations, the Catholic Hospital Association and the National Federation of Catholic Physicians'
Guilds, are of significant importance in the emergence of
our discipline. We have been noting the growing emphasis in
medical ethics on applying moral principles in order to
solve the ethical questions connected with the actual daily
professional activity of medical personnel. The influence
of these professional groups in this process should not be
underestimated. They are interested in precisely those
questions which affect them as Catholics and as physicians.
They are part of the professionalization of modern medicine.
In the next part of this chapter we will speak again of cod-
ifications of practical rules of moral procedure published
by the CHA. These professional groups are thus influential
in determining the direction taken by medical ethics.

* * *

By the end of the 1930's no term has been generally accepted as rubric for our discipline. The rubric "pastoral
medicine" has been largely unused in American literature
since the very early years of the century, though, as we
have seen in the previous chapter, it continued in general
usage in Europe. Only Sanford, Klarmann, and O'Malley and
Walsh, all writing in the first decade of the new century,

---

[95]Egan, "National Federation," p. 236.

[96]*The Linacre Quarterly*, 3 (1935), 59.

used the term as general rubric in the titles of their
works. We have suggested, in line with what we have seen as
the growing central emphasis in our discipline's definition
on the actual professional activity of modern medical personnel, that the older term "pastoral medicine" fell into
disuse because it meant both too much and too little. It
meant too much because it included questions of hygiene and
first aid intended for the rural pastor as well as some
questions of purely speculative theology which the moral
theologians did not consider to be a direct part of their
task. It meant too little, because this earlier emphasis of
pastoral medicine detracted from the systematic moral theological analysis of directly medical ethical issues.

   We have seen one author, Charles Coppens, who suggested
that the moral investigation of medical practice was a part
of "medical jurisprudence." This term was part of the professional training of physicians, and thus fit in with the
professional emphasis of the discipline. Yet it was too
narrow, in that it was (and is) generally used to refer most
specifically to the interface of medicine and civil law,
especially as doctors are called to testify in courts. This
term thus likewise failed to be accepted as general rubric.

   The rubric *Medical Ethics,* which will become generally
accepted in the 1940's and 1950's, has not yet achieved that
status, since it calls to mind intra-professional codes of
etiquette more than the ethical study of medical practice.
We have seen that the rubric is at times explicitly rejected
(O'Malley and Walsh, Spalding), and that some authors, even
those who no longer subsume their field under the rubric
"pastoral medicine," avoid using any specific rubric to de-
nominate it (Spalding, Burke, Finney). In the second half
of the period we have studied, however, there is evidence
that the term is finding some acceptance. Many titles appear with the word "ethics" in prominence. This term has,

of course, long been used in Catholic literature, and of
itself is of no significance. But its use in specifically
medical moral treatises brings it into contact with the
field, and this is doubtless partly responsible for the
later acceptance of *Medical Ethics* as general rubric. We
have made note of one work where the term *Medical Ethics* is
explicitly used as rubric (Bourke: *Some Medical Ethical
Problems Solved*), and have seen that for him the issues
which are specific to *Medical Ethics* are those concerned
with abortion, sterilization, and similar procedures. The
term also appears, though without any definitional analysis,
in articles written during these years.[97]

In the next part of this chapter we will discover that
later works use the phrase more and more as a general rubric, though often with a definitional disassociation from
the "medical ethics" of the intra-professional codes. Gradually, during the 1940's and 1950's, the term is accepted as
rubric for the discipline investigating the moral problems
connected with medicine.

Definitionally we have seen that our discipline has begun to move toward an emphasis on the actual daily professional activity of medical personnel. To the ethical questions arising from medical procedures moral analysis is applied and correct moral solutions are given. We noted a
similar trend within European pastoral medicine, where the
moral theological emphasis began, in the late nineteenth and
early twentieth centuries, to overshadow rural hygienic and
speculative theological concerns. North American literature
continued this trend, and moved further along the direction
of emphasizing specifically ethical concerns, and of limiting those concerns to practical questions of immediate

---

[97]See "Code of Medical Ethics?"; McDonald, "Why Catholic
Physicians' Guilds?" p. 95.

importance to the professional physician and nurse.[98]   Thus
the earlier organizational rubrics (commandments, sacraments,
etc.) which we noted in our study of the general moral theological tradition, and which we saw to be explicitly operational in some pastoral medicine literature, are of less
direct importance in North American medical ethics.

The newly emerging discipline in North America, in accord with the professionalization of twentieth century medicine, has begun to emphasize the moral aspects of topics related to the newly discovered physical interventions of modern medicine. We have noted the developing secularization
of medicine, the growing split between physical and spiritual healing. The Catholic moralists, of course, as pastors
and theologians, are interested in the spiritual as well as
the material physical health of humankind. Thus they intend
to apply moral guidance to medical practice. But, as the
daily professional practice of doctors and nurses becomes
more concentrated on specifically bodily interventions, the
medical ethicists emphasize more and more topics of this
kind. Thus we have seen during the first four decades of
the century the increased importance given to surgery,
especially to the newly developed procedures in obstetrics
and gynecology, among the topics presented for ethical study.
We have noted authors who limited nearly the entire scope of

---

[98]Despite the general movement within European pastoral
medicine toward this practical moral emphasis, European literature of the twentieth century has continued to discuss
issues not of immediate practical ethical importance for the
physician's practice, and to do so to a somewhat greater extent than North American medical ethics. A survey of European works during this century shows this. See, for example,
Antonelli, *Medicina pastoralis;* Ruland and Rattler, *Pastoral
Medicine;* Payen, *Déontologie médicale;* Bon, *Précis;*
Tiberghien, *Médecine;* Niedermeyer, *Handbuch;* Niedermeyer,
*Compendium of Pastoral Medicine, Compendium of Pastoral
Hygiene.*

their analysis to questions of this kind (Klarmann, Finney),
and others who gave these issues greatest emphasis (Coppens,
Burke), or who saw them as the central questions of medical
ethics (Bourke).

As the notion of healing developed by the medical profession evolved, questions of strictly sexual ethics, that
is, those topics included in many of the works of pastoral
medicine which we saw in the last chapter, but which have
little direct significance for medical professional practice,
such as celibacy, extra-marital sex, homosexuality, masturbation, the canonical regulations concerning the sacrament
of marriage, etc., have come to receive less emphasis in
our discipline. Some of the literature we have examined
does deal with these questions, especially the works which
define themselves generally along the lines of the older
pastoral medicine approach (Sanford, O'Malley and Walsh,
Medicus). But in many of the works we have studied very
little if any discussion is given to those topics (Bourke,
Burke, Finney, Trudel), and some authors who include them
suggest as rationale that the physician must often serve as
counsellor to his patients (Coppens, Klarmann's later editions). In the next part of this chapter we will note the
continued presence of this kind of limitation, and will
again find authors who include sexual material only as it
pertains directly to modern medical practice (in such cases
as artificial insemination, sperm analysis, contraception,
etc.) or inasmuch as the physician might need it as part of
his counselling activity. The place given to topics of
specifically sexual ethics, including topics related to marriage as a sacrament, which we noted in earlier pastoral
medicine literature, is lessened in North American medical
ethics, though these issues are by no means entirely eliminated.

We have seen in this section the role which the profes-

sional associations of Catholic physicians (the National
Federation of Catholic Physicians' Guilds) and of Catholic
clergy and medical personnel (the Catholic Hospital Association) played in the emergence of the discipline. We have
already noted the influence of secular professional organizations when we studied intra-professional "medical ethics."
Special professional groups thus exert a significant influence in determining the direction taken by our discipline.

Later in our study we will discuss at length the theological methodologies used by the medical ethicists of this
period. We have mentioned here the basic methodological approaches of some authors in order to suggest that the discipline's methodology, as well as its definition, is influenced by the growing professionalization and specialization
of medicine. The medical ethicists wanted to present solutions to ethical dilemmas. We have noted in this section
the appearance of a number of works in which all, or most
discursive analysis was explicitly omitted in favor of a
quick and easy set of solutions (Bourke, Burke, Finney).
These works were like ethical cafeterias, where solutions
were served quickly and uniformly to those in a hurry, and
the necessary variety of situational flavor was lost in the
interests of speed and uniformity. In other works of the
early period (Coppens, Klarmann) some analysis is present,
but, as we will see, the analysis is done from within a
methodological approach which itself facilitates clear and
uniform answers to medical ethical dilemmas. In the later
period of the emergence of our discipline (1940-1960) there
will be more and more insistence on detailed analysis, on
the presentation and application of general ethical principles, the establishment of which has begun in the early
period. This analysis will continue to be done from within
a general framework which facilitates arriving at clear and
universally applicable solutions to moral issues. In this

it parallels modern medicine itself, whose scientific approach is aimed at solving in a universally applicable way
man's physical disorders.

The early literature in North American Roman Catholic
medical ethics contains few truly comprehensive works.[99]
Some attempt is made in works we have studied from the first
decade of the century to include a wide topical array as
well as a degree of analysis, but no one book is successful
in both. Most later works of the period are either works in
general ethics with special application to medical personnel
or are too brief to be comprehensive and lack discursive
analysis. This situation changes in the forties and fifties.
In this later period a number of manuals of medical morals
appear, and the emergence of medical ethics as a self-conscious discipline with an accepted rubric, a more or less
consistent self-definition, and an established methodology
is accomplished.

Part Two

Later Works (1940-1960)

1.   Alphonsus Bonnar: An Influential British Work

We began the first section of this chapter by noting an

---

[99]In accordance with the purpose of this chapter, we
have limited our study generally to those works which intend
to examine medical moral issues as a whole, or which at
least investigate a number of them, or which are of importance to the emergence of the name and definition of the
discipline. Mention ought to be made of the fact that a
series of monographs appeared during the period on individual medical moral issues, especially abortion and birth control. The bibliography includes a selection of the more important of these: Bouscaren, *Ethics of Ectopic Operations*
(of considerable methodological significance); Davis, *Birth
Control*; Davis, *Eugenics*; Davis, *State Sterilization*;
DeGuchteneere, *Judgment on Birth Control*; Moore, Edward, *The
Case Against Birth Control*; Sutherland, *Birth Control*.

important European work (Capellmann's *Pastoral Medicine*)
which was influential in the American discipline. Similarly
a British book was of significance in the forties and fifties, and was typical in many ways of the manuals of medical
ethics which appeared in America during this period. *The*
Catholic Doctor, a general text on medical moral problems,
was written by the British Fransiscan priest, Alphonsus Bonnar, and first appeared in 1937.[100] Methodologically it belongs to the later genre of texts rather than to the earlier
period,[101] and its influence extended through the forties
and into the fifties. Hence we include it here rather than
in the preceding section. It was published both in England
and in the United States, and achieved widespread popularity
in both countries.

Bonnar's work is an explicitly moral treatise. "The
book is intended to provide Catholic doctors with a compend-

----

[100]The first edition appeared in 1937, and was re-
printed in 1938 both in England and in the United States.
The 1939 second edition was slightly revised, with changed
pagination, and appeared again in both countries. Reprintings appeared in the following years. A third edition was
published in England in 1944, a fourth in 1948, a fifth in
1951, and a sixth in 1952. These latter editions each contain some revision. The first and second editions were most
influential in North America, no doubt because at that time
there were no contemporary texts of a comprehensive sort
available in English, as we have seen. By the time of the
publication of the later editions, North American manuals
had appeared, and Bonnar's work was of less interest here.
The first and second editions are the most commonly available in American libraries. The first, second, and sixth
editions have been consulted. All references are to the
second (1939) edition, with New York publication. The reader is advised that other editions probably contain identical
material, though perhaps on proximate pages.

[101]The modality of application of theological principles evidenced in the work shows a shift toward accenting
specifically Roman Catholic teaching as authoritative, the
characteristic of works of the later period (see chapter
five).

ious and readable exposition of the teaching of the Church
on medico-moral questions of practical importance."[102]   Bonnar distinguishes two kinds of questions: practical problems
which concern the physician in his daily practice, and issues pertaining more to the philosophical and theological
background needed in order to understand these issues and
make the correct decisions. In addition, the author suggests that there are a few problems which are not yet of
practical importance, but may become so, such as euthanasia
and sterilization.[103]

The work aims at "brevity and completeness." "A rea-
soned exposition of all medico-moral questions would result
in a lengthy and ponderous tome."[104] Yet Bonnar intends to
do more than merely answer the questions raised. He intends
to offer the necessary background as well.

In accord with this purpose, Bonnar begins with a chapter purporting to establish the divinely guaranteed teaching
authority of the Catholic magisterium. Then, in a second
chapter, he defends the possibility and actuality of supernatural miracles. Chapter three offers some background information on general ethics (man's nature, divine law, natural law, and positive law). Chapter four concerns co-opera-
tion in evil, scandal, and double effect. Chapter five is
on the Catholic view of sex and marriage, including divorce,
nullity, and the marriage "debt." These chapters are prefa-
tory to the more "practical" ones which follow: contraception, abortion, other problems of procreation (artificial
insemination, sterility testing by masturbation, ectopic

---

[102]Bonnar, *The Catholic Doctor*, 2nd ed., p. xiii.

[103]*Ibid.*, p. xiii. These issues, clearly, have become
"practical" in the years since 1937.

[104]*Ibid.*, p. xiii.

gestation), baptism, euthanasia and sterilization. Chapter
eleven deals with analytical psychotherapy, and chapter
twelve with Freudian dogma. In these brief sections, Bonnar
points out some of the difficulties he sees in various techniques of therapy. He then goes on to discuss specific
questions of sexuality, especially masturbation and homosexuality, and suggests the need for correct Catholic sex
education. Chapter fourteen treats of scruples. The concluding chapter concerns "the doctor in his practice," and
speaks of the obligation to gain the necessary knowledge, to
serve the poor, to keep professional secrets, and to help in
preparing a patient for death.[105]

The central emphasis of Bonnar's work, as he formally
states it to be, and as evidenced by the topics he discusses,
is to apply moral teaching to issues of practical importance
for the physician. His work also contains discussion of
topics which are of less direct practical import to the physician, however, and in this resembles to a somewhat greater
extent than many North American works the traditional pastoral medicine literature. The best example of this is the
chapter on miracles. Another similar section is that on marriage, where, in addition to material of immediate background
importance for medical personnel, Bonnar discusses Catholic
teaching on nullity and divorce. The rest of the introductory chapters are methodological, and serve to introduce
physicalist and ecclesiastical positivist approaches. We
will discuss this again in chapter five. The short chapter
on Baptism is explicitly included to provide the physician
with sufficient instruction to act correctly in case of

---

[105]The sixth edition (1952) is basically similar. By
this date, however, Bonnar has eliminated his chapter on
Freudian dogma, added one on pain and suffering, and added
two brief sections on tampons and on lobotomy.

necessity during his professional practice.[106] In chapters
eleven through fourteen Bonnar speaks of various topics connected with sexuality and psychotherapy. His treatment of
these issues is not explicitly directed to the daily professional activity of the medical doctor, and thus resembles
the approach of pastoral medicine more than that of North
American medical ethics.

Bonnar's work was widely acclaimed, both in Britain and
in America.[107] By the mid-1940's it was hailed as the "*locus
classicus* for the Catholic doctor."[108] One reviewer called
it "the first book, we believe, in English, which deals pro-
fessedly and minutely with the doctor's duties as a Catholic."[109]

2. La Rochelle and Fink: A Popular Handbook in French and

     English

The first North American work of the period, one which
attempted both comprehensiveness and at least some degree of

---

[106]Bonnar, 2nd ed., pp. 89, 91.

[107]James Walsh, whom we have noted as co-author of *Essays in Pastoral Medicine,* called it "a precious treasure in
a field where there is much need for authoritative treatment.
. . . a definite discussion of all the questions that come
under what is known as pastoral medicine, that is those problems which occur in the borderland between medicine and theology" (Walsh, "Review: Bonnar," p. 506). Of note here is
the use of the term "pastoral medicine," not a current rubric in the late thirties in America. Walsh claims that Bonnar includes all the questions of pastoral medicine, whereas
in fact he does not, even if judged according to the earlier
work which Walsh co-authored, which includes much material
from hygiene and first aid. Bonnar's work is a specifically
moral manual, though he does include some topics at best indirectly related to the ethics of medicine.

[108]*Blackfriars,* 25 (1944), 398.

[109]*Month,* 171, No. 884 (Feb., 1938), 176-177.

analysis, was *Précis de morale médicale pour infirmières, médecins et prêtres*. Written by two Canadian priests, Stanislas La Rochelle and Charles Fink, the original 1940 French book was soon translated into English, and appeared in 1943 under the English title *Handbook of Medical Ethics for Nurses, Physicians, and Priests*.[110] There were numerous reprintings over the next decade, and the book was published both in Canada and in the United States. It was printed in a pocket-sized format of about four by five and a half inches (ten by fourteen centimeters), presumably so that it could be carried easily for quick consultation.[111]

The rubric used in the French title, "morale médicale," is translated into English simply as *Medical Ethics*. It is defined in the context of a professional ethic, for which the common French connotation of *déontologie* is apt.[112]

---

[110]La Rochelle was an Oblate of Mary Immaculate, Fink a Vincentian physician. Eight or more "editions" are listed. The French edition, the second English edition (1943), and the eighth English edition (1948) were consulted. All references are to the eighth English edition, which is substantially identical to the 1943 edition. The reader is advised that references may be found in other editions one or two pages earlier, as at least two minor insertions have been added in the later editions.

[111]A similar manual was the moral theology handbook of Heribert Jone, ubiquitous in seminarians' libraries of many decades. The English edition of this manual was printed in pocket format for easy consultation.

[112]The French usage of *déontologie* differs somewhat from the common English connotation. The emphasis is not on distinguishing a formal, metaphysically based ethic ("deontological ethic") from a more material, teleological ethic ("consequentialist" or "utilitarian ethics") so much as it is on referring to an ethic of professional obligation. As Niedermeyer points out (*Allgemeine Pastoralmedizin*, I, 29, n. 23), in the Romance languages *déontologie* refers in general to professional (medical) ethics with no implications of relativism. In the English version of Niedermeyer's own *Compendium of Pastoral Medicine*, "deontology" is compared to

Deontology is defined as "the science which deals with the
duties of one's state of life."[113] The authors continue:
"If that science be connected with the practice of medicine,
it is called *medical ethics*."[114] The general basis from
which the authors intend to work is that of moral philosophy,
which is correctly taught by the Catholic Church.[115] It is
clear, therefore, that for them the term "*morale médicale*,"
translated as *Medical Ethics*, carries no implications of
intra-professional relativism. In the English version, the
term *Medical Ethics* is thus used simply, and without any
distinction or disassociation as the rubric for the discipline investigating the moral problems of medical practice.
Over the next years this phrase will achieve common acceptance among Catholic authors, though some will continue to
clarify their meaning of the term and to disassociate it
from the "medical ethics" of the medical associations.

The authors state that they had originally intended the
book for registered nurses, but later decided to include
doctors and priests among their readers. Yet their principle readership remains the nurses, who "have as yet no handbook which treats of and sums up the elements of medical
ethics, of their practical application, and of the chief
virtues required in nurses."[116] Physicians and priests, on

"medical ethics" as moral theology is related to philosophical ethics. For Niedermeyer, deontology includes the data
from revelation, whereas "medical ethics" does not (p. 444).
Thus it can be seen that different uses of the word "deontology" and "deontological" are current.

[113]La Rochelle and Fink, *Handbook,* 8th ed., p. 23.

[114]*Ibid.*, p. 23, italics theirs.

[115]*Ibid.*, p. 24.

[116]*Ibid.*, p. 19.

the other hand, have copious volumes and treatises, and for
them the work is intended as a concise survey.[117] It is to
be a "precious vade-mecum."[118]

The topics treated in the handbook reflect the practical intention of the authors. Of particular note is that
the book contains almost nothing which is not of immediate
practical importance in the daily professional activity of
the nurse and physician. The first two chapters are introductory, dealing very briefly with certain principles of
general ethics considered necessary for the solution of medical ethical problems. The approaches used, both physicalist and positivist, will be described in chapter five. The
authors include the moral conscience and the principle of
the indirect voluntary (double effect), the importance of
which in medical ethics will be demonstrated later. The
third chapter discusses various operations and treatments,
including contraception, periodic continence, artificial insemination, abortion including ectopic gestation, sterilization and eugenics, Caesarian section, euthanasia, sedation,
hypnotism, and treatment of psychic disorders. This last
section is considered to be "outside the scope of our present
work. We believe it may be useful to say something here,
however, since doctors and nurses are likely to meet people
suffering from these maladies."[119] Thus again the intention
is a practical one.

The fourth chapter concerns the sacraments. The purpose
of this section is not, however, to give a more or less complete moral and canonical presentation on the sacraments
discussed, as we have seen to be the case with some of the
earlier (especially the European) works. Indeed, the section
does not even speak about matrimony. Rather the authors dis-

---

[117]*Ibid.*, p. 19.

[118]*Ibid.*, p. 21.

[119]*Ibid.*, p. 190.

cuss baptism, confession, the Eucharist, and extreme unction
in the context of illness. Baptism of fetuses and monsters,
of the apparently dead, of unconscious persons of unknown
religion, and of children of non-Catholics are considered.[120]
The nurse is advised on preparing the patient for the sacraments. Questions of receiving Communion, fasting, vomiting,
unconscious patients, and other issues are dealt with. The
fifth chapter concerns "other obligations of justice or of
charity," and discusses cooperation in evil, professional
secrets, professional ability, honesty, medical fees, and
other virtues. There is no discussion of non-medical sexual
ethics, such as masturbation, homosexuality, non-marital intercourse, and the like.

In an appendix the authors add a "Moral Code of Our
Hospitals." We have spoken earlier of the general surgical
code of the Catholic Hospital Association of the United
States and Canada. In addition to that code there existed
various regional codes adopted by individual conferences of
the Association or by individual dioceses.[121] The code included by La Rochelle and Fink is stated to be that of the
Catholic Hospital Association of the United States and Canada, Quebec conference, Montreal section.[122] It bears a 1936

---

[120]The authors suggest that children of non-Catholic
parents be baptized *in extremis*. However, if they survive,
"the Church has the right and is in duty bound to separate
it from its parents, if that be possible, so that it may be
brought up a Catholic" (pp. 235-236). A case of a Jew is
cited. The authors admit, however, that tact often requires
that no mention be made of the baptism.

[121]See Kelly, *Medico-Moral Problems,* Part I, 1949, p. 2.

[122]La Rochelle and Fink, *Handbook,* 8th ed., p. 318. An
almost identical code is cited in McFadden, *Medical Ethics
for Nurses,* 1st ed., pp. 345-346, as "The Moral Code of
Catholic Hospitals," with no further reference. This suggests that the code was in force more generally than only in
Montreal.

approval date. It contains a negative and a positive section. Direct abortions are forbidden, as are male and female sterilization, the giving of information "upon any *contraceptive method* whatsoever," the use of sedatives when
such would make it impossible for the patient to prepare
spiritually or temporally for death, and euthanasia "in all
its forms." The physician must notify his patient of danger
of death, and fetuses must be baptized. The code is in the
form of an oath required for the whole staff of Catholic
hospitals.

The book was generally well received. The large number
of editions attests to its popularity. Reviews were favorable.[123] It was but the first of a number of such works,
many with a greater degree of discursive analysis, which
would bring about the emergence of Roman Catholic medical
ethics in North America.

3. Two Other French Canadian Works

The year 1940 also saw the publication of the revision
by Armand Perrier of Hervé Trudel's *Éléments de morale médicale*.[124] Perrier's definition of medical ethics is much
like that of La Rochelle and Fink, and shows clearly the emphasis on the practical professional activity of medical
personnel. Perrier begins by defining ethics ("la morale")
as "the science which studies human acts to determine whether or not they conform to their final goal which is the

---

[123]"Those to whom the work is addressed will find quickly and easily the key to difficult and complicated problems"
(*Revue de l'Université d'Ottawa,* 11 [1941], 127, translation
mine). "Ceux à qui il s'adresse y trouveront facilement et
promptement la clef des problèmes épineux et compliqués."

[124]Perrier, with doctorates in both theology and philosophy, taught at the University of Montreal.

eternal law of God."[125] Ethics thus defined is distinguished into general and special ethics, the former dealing
with general principles and the latter with specific kinds
of actions. Special ethics in turn can be individual or
social, and this latter can be subdivided into various kinds
of societies, including the family, the nation, the church,
and the profession to which one belongs. "Medical ethics is
thus a division of professional ethics. It has as its subject matter the particular rights and obligations of doctors
and of their assistants in the exercise of their profession."[126] It is clear that Perrier does not intend to imply
by this identification of medical ethics with the professional ethics of physicians the kind of intra-professional
relativism we have seen to characterize much of the "medical
ethics" of the professional codes. Medical ethics is clearly a part of a universalist ethics, and applies the norms of
the eternal law to the specifically professional activity of
medical personnel. Perrier's definition is thus professional and practical, in that he sees medical ethics as the
philosophical/moral theological investigation of the professional activity of physicians and their assistants.

Perrier's topics are basically similar to those of the
earlier Trudel editions which we have already examined.[127]
He adds a chapter on the use of narcotics, speaks of the

---

[125]Trudel and Perrier, *Éléments de morale médicale*, p.
5, trans. mine. "La morale est la science qui étudie les
actes humains (délibérés) pour déterminer quand ils sont ou
ne sont pas conformes à leur fin dernière qui est la loi
éternelle de Dieu."

[126]*Ibid.*, p. 6. "La morale Médicale est donc une
partie de la Morale professionelle. Elle a pour objets les
droits et les devoirs particuliers des Médecins et de leurs
assistants dans l'exercice de leur profession." (Unusual
capitalization his.)

[127]See above, p. 137.

professional secret, and gives the text of some prayers for
use in the spiritual care of the sick.

A similar definition is proposed in a third French-
Canadian work to appear in the early 1940's. In 1943 a Montreal priest, Josaphat-Zéphirin Dufort published a mimeographed text in medical ethics under the title *Éthique professionnelle, morale médicale*. It appeared in book form in
the following year with the title *Application de l'éthique
professionnelle*.[128] Dufort defines "morale médicale" (*Medical Ethics*) as "the science which treats of the obligations
of the nurse."[129] "Professional ethics is therefore the behavior which must be respected--as proclaimed by the natural
law--in relation to one's state of life, in this case: the
professional obligations of the nurse."[130]

Dufort divides his work into four sections. The first
presents general principles, including the human act, conscience, cooperation, and the principle of double effect
(the indirect voluntary). As examples of this last, the author treats briefly of abortions, especially of ectopic
pregnancies, and of the use of anesthetics in childbirth.
He concludes the section with a brief discussion of the role

---

[128]The third edition of the book format has been consulted. Various "editions" and printings carry dates
through the forties and early fifties. The title page of
the 1951 printing notes that 4,000 copies had been printed.
Dufort was born in Montreal in 1877 and ordained in
1901. He served as curate in Montreal parishes and as professor of ethics in hospitals in Lachine and Cartierville.

[129]Dufort, *Application de l'éthique professionnelle*, p.
1, trans. mine. "C'est la science qui traite des devoirs de
la garde-malade."

[130]*Ibid*., pp. 1-2, trans. mine. "L'Éthique professionnelle, c'est donc la conduite à respecter--telle que proc-
lamée par la loi naturelle--en rapport avec ses devoirs
d'état, et en l'occurrence: les obligations professionnelles
de la garde-malade."

of women religious in gynecology and in the care of male
patients. The second section concerns obligations in justice and charity. Under justice are included the obligation
of sufficient knowledge in one's field, as well as the question of anesthesia, euthanasia, informing dying patients,
fees, and the medical secret. Under charity are listed a
number of personal qualities of character needed by the
nurse: devotion, goodness, moral fiber, patience, reserve,
humor, etc. Part three concerns the sacraments. Baptism,
cremation, marriage, the Eucharist, and extreme unction are
treated. Under marriage the author discusses contraception,
sterilization, and artificial insemination. Nurses are instructed in how to baptize, and concerning Church laws regarding Eucharistic fast. The final section concerns again
some general principles which the author suggests as normative for nurses. Included is a section on the need of grace
for salvation.

Dufort's work was less well organized than others of
the time. Though his definition of the field emphasizes the
professional activities of the nurse, he includes discussion
of matters of speculative theology (such as grace and salvation) as well as lists of character qualities which are not
directly germaine to the professional ethics of medicine and
nursing. Topics of more directly medical moral interest are
briefly presented with little analysis, perhaps because Dufort wrote mainly for nurses rather than for physicians.
The book was never translated, and hence its influence was
limited to French Canada.[131]

4. Charles McFadden

The most widely used manual of medical ethics during the

---

[131]Reviews were generally favorable, but little notice
was taken of the work.

forties and fifties was Charles McFadden's *Medical Ethics*.[132]
It surpassed all the others as a textbook for nurses, pre-
medical students, medical students, and seminarians for
nearly twenty years. The first edition appeared with the
title *Medical Ethics for Nurses* in 1946. A significantly
revised and enlarged second edition with the shortened title
Medical Ethics was published in 1949, together with a reference manual for teachers.[133] Subsequent editions appeared
in 1953, 1956, 1961, and 1967, each revised and updated.
McFadden's text became almost synonymous with medical ethics
in the English speaking world. Other authors were of more
significance methodologically. But McFadden's manual was
highly influential in establishing the discipline as a fixed
and recognized field of endeavor.[134]

The first edition of the work was specifically ad-

---

[132]Charles McFadden was born in Philadelphia in 1909.
He was ordained a priest of the order of St. Augustine in
1935. He has been professor of philosophy at Villanova University since the late 1930's and has instructed nurses in
medical ethics at various Catholic colleges. His latest
work appeared recently (1976), entitled *The Dignity of Life*.
    The description presented in these present pages is of
the first three editions (1946, 1949 and 1953). Subsequent
editions will be noted in their proper chronological se-
quence. All editions have been consulted. References will
indicate the proper edition. The reader is advised that editions do differ, but that much of the material is identical,
and may be found on proximate pages in other editions.

[133]The manual contains "answers" to the discussion
cases at the back of each chapter.

[134]The number of editions speaks for itself. Reviews
written both in the United States and in Europe refer to the
widespread use and popularity of the text. I have found the
work to be readily available in just about every Catholic
library. It was well known to seminarians throughout the
period. A 1963 review of the 5th edition states: "It has
been almost universally accepted in the United States as a
text for use in Catholic nursing schools" (*Clergy Review*, 48
[1963], 199).

dressed to nurses. "The primary purpose of a Catholic
Training School is to produce a truly Catholic nurse."[135]
"It is the hope of the author that this work will provide
the basis for the proper moral education of the Catholic
nurse. It is the experience of the author that the matter
is neither too abstract nor too comprehensive for the nurse
to master."[136] In the second edition the subtitle "for
nurses" is dropped because "it is felt that--although the
work is written primarily for the nurse--its content is of
equal value to the medical student and doctor."[137] In the
third edition, "the entire text has been adapted to suit the
needs of pre-medical students, medical students, doctors and
nurses. The earlier editions were directed *solely* to the
nurse, and it was only with some measure of hardship that
the text was used in regular college courses on Medical
Ethics."[138]

McFadden uses the phrase *Medical Ethics* as the rubric
for his area of study. He disassociates himself and his
notion of medical ethics from the courses on medical etiquette commonly taught under that title.

> A cursory glance at many books on "Medical Ethics" or
> "Nursing Ethics" reveals, however, that these works are
> not primarily concerned with moral principles. For the
> most part, they treat of what might be called the "eti-
> quette" of the medical profession. . . . But far more
> necessary and fundamental are proper ethical standards
> for guidance in the very difficult and very real moral
> problems which they [doctors and nurses] constantly
> encounter.[139]

---

[135]McFadden, *Medical Ethics for Nurses,* 1st ed., p. xi
(included in later editions as "Preface to First Edition,"
e.g. see 3rd ed., p. xix).

[136]*Ibid.,* 1st ed., p. xii; 3rd ed., p. xx.

[137]*Ibid.,* 2nd ed., p. xiii.

[138]*Ibid.,* 3rd ed., p. xiii.

[139]*Ibid.,* 3rd ed., p. 3. (In the earlier editions the
reference is limited to nurses and "Nursing Ethics.")

From this point on, the rubric in general use for the
discipline investigating the moral (ethical) issues of medical practice will be *Medical Ethics*. Disassociations such
as McFadden's will continue in the literature throughout the
period, and are still common today. But in general such
disassociations are more distinctions than rejections. Authors may remind their readers that "real" medical ethics is
not the "medical ethics" of the codes of etiquette, but few
now search for a different rubric.[140] Doubtless the success
of the manuals of La Rochelle and Fink and of McFadden, together with the already recognized usage of the term as a
rubric in medical schools and by professional medical associations (though, as we have seen, with a different material
and formal orientation), contributed to the near universal
acceptance of the term.

Like La Rochelle-Fink, McFadden places greatest emphasis
on the practical problems confronting the nurse and the physician in their daily professional activity. In his preface
to the first edition (addressed, as we have seen, to nurses,
but later widened to include physicians and medical students)
McFadden speaks of the need for courses in religion in a
nurse's training. He continues: "But the moral education required by a Catholic nurse is not supplied by ordinary
courses in religion. The first obligation of the Catholic
Nursing School is to train the nurse in the *moral obligations
of her profession*."[141] That is the reason for "a thorough
course in Medical Ethics."[142]

---

[140]An exception is the Protestant ethicist, Joseph
Fletcher, who, in 1954, rejects the rubric completely
(Fletcher, *Morals and Medicine*, p. 5; see above, pp. 82-83,
n. 177.

[141]McFadden, 1st ed., p. xi; 3rd ed., p. xix, italics
mine.

[142]*Ibid.*

McFadden begins with two introductory chapters on general ethical principles, intended as background material.[143]
The first is on the nature of ethics, and distinguishes
philosophical ethics (based on natural reason) from moral
theology (which includes the data of supernatural revelation). The second concerns the foundations of morality, and
speaks of law, conscience, and the principle of double effect. In chapter five we will describe McFadden's methodological approaches, underlying his use both of physicalism
(the principle of double effect) and of ecclesiastical positivism (the use of supernatural authority in defense of natural reason). These methodological approaches, introduced
in these chapters, allow McFadden and other Catholic moralists of the time to arrive at clear solutions to the ethical
questions connected with medical practice.

In chapter three the author treats of Christian marriage. Some of the topics mentioned briefly here do not
pertain directly to the professional needs of physician or
nurse; McFadden speaks of the qualities of marriage, the
ends of marriage, the sacramentality of marriages between
Catholics and non-Catholics, and so on. Yet his rationale
for including them remains a practical one:

> Many of the ethical problems confronting the doctor and
> nurse have a definite relationship to the married
> state. For this reason it is necessary for them to
> have a clear and accurate appreciation of the true na-
> ture of marriage. Such knowledge will furnish them
> with the proper *background* and basis *for the solution
> of* many of their difficult *moral problems.*[144]

He then speaks of artificial insemination, and, in chapters
four and five, contraception and periodic continence.

Chapter six concerns the "Christian philosophy of

---

[143]The second and third editions, both considerably
longer than the first, are described here.

[144]*Ibid.*, 3rd ed., p. 47, italics mine.

suffering," and speaks principally of euthanasia. McFadden
then devotes four complete chapters to the question of abortion.[145] Chapter eleven concerns baptism, emphasizing the
practical questions arising in cases of necessity (baptism
of the unconscious, the dying, fetuses). Chapter twelve
treats of sterilization and mutilation, including plastic
surgery, lobotomy, cornea transplantation, elective appendectomy and tonsillectomy, testicular and ovarian grafts,
and emphasizing eugenic and punitive sterilization. Chapter
thirteen reviews the question of cooperation in immoral operations. McFadden then adds a chapter on property rights,
which seems out of place in a text on medical ethics. Yet
even here his purpose is to deal with an issue of importance
in the daily professional life of nurse and doctor. He
wishes to warn them against stealing hospital property. He
then speaks of truthfulness and professional secrets, and
concludes with a chapter on the last sacraments, intended
principally to inform the nurse and physician of what is
needed to prepare for and assist at the administration of
sacraments in the hospital. The spiritual care of the patient is mainly the responsibility of the priest, however,
and "Ordinarily, medical personnel should not directly inter-
fere in spiritual affairs."[146] In an appendix McFadden adds
a series of documents, including the newly published "Ethical
and Religious Directives for Catholic Hospitals" of the

---

[145]Abortion remains consistently one of the central issues. McFadden divides his treatment into chapters on direct
abortion, therapeutic abortion (direct abortion for medical
reasons), indirect abortion, and ectopic gestation. In chapter five we will show how physicalist principles (double effect) are applied to this question. We can see again here
the importance of surgical techniques, newly developed in
scientific medicine, and solved by physicalist methodology,
in the developing definition of medical ethics.

[146]*Ibid.*, 3rd ed., p. 403.

Catholic Hospital Association,[147] the ten commandments, the
Hippocratic Oath, Florence Nightingale's pledge, "my pledge and
creed," and a rather lengthy section concerning the spiritual care of non-Catholic patients.

McFadden's work thus includes the entire basic range of
issues that constituted the material definition of Roman
Catholic medical ethics of the period. The emphasis is
practical. Most emphasized are questions of direct physical
medical intervention (abortion, mutilation, sterilization,
euthanasia, artificial insemination). Psychological mental
health questions are not included. Questions of marriage
and sexuality are discussed principally as necessary background to directly medical questions such as artificial insemination and contraception. There is no discussion of
such questions as masturbation, homosexuality, etc. McFadden does deal with specifically religious (spiritual) questions which the physician or nurse would be likely to encounter in his or her professional duties. He distinguishes
these "religious" issues from other questions of "natural
ethics," and includes them because a course in medical ethics "must be a preparation for life and it must face reality
by showing the [medical] student how he is to solve the moral problems which he will soon encounter on the level of
both ethics and religion."[148] McFadden's purpose, as seen
both in his formally stated goal and in the matter he treats,
is to analyze and answer the ethical questions connected

---

[147]These will be reviewed in greater detail later.

[148]*Ibid.*, 3rd ed., pp. xiv-xv. This distinction between "ethical" and "religious" issues was furthered by the
"Ethical and Religious Directives" of the CHA which first
appeared in 1949. Both were considered part of the discipline of medical ethics, though the former were more intrinsic to it and the latter included because of the possible
need the physician might have for them.

with the actual professional activity of medical personnel.

The book was well received. Gerald Kelly stated:
"Rating Fr. McFadden's book according to a general impression, the most exacting critic could hardly style it less
than excellent."[149] Criticism to the first editions came
from those who felt it was too deep for the nurse, but other
reviewers defended the layman's ability to grasp the subtleties of ethics.[150]

The 1947 textbook by Joseph McAllister, entitled *Ethics:*
With Special Application to the Nursing Profession,[151] is
not a textbook in medical ethics, but rather is similar to
the book by Thomas Verner Moore which we have already noted.
It is an introductory work in general Roman Catholic ethics
addressed to nurses. McAllister does emphasize the problems

---

[149]Kelly, "Review: McFadden," p. 616. Kelly points out
the need for a manual, which McFadden added with the second
edition. Other reviews call it the most extensive and
scientific thus far (*Homiletic and Pastoral Review*, 46 [1946],
719); "a splendid contribution" (*American Ecclesiastical Review*, 115 [1946], 155).

[150]An Irish review states: "The author's sweep is deep
as well as wide. Too wide, much too deep, perchance, for
most of the readers to whom the book is primarily addressed"
(*Irish Ecclesiastical Record*, 69 [1947], 171). An American
reviewer argues: "As a teacher, Fr. McFadden is an optimist.
He does not subscribe to that defeatist theory that Catholic
laymen are incapable of grasping sharp theological distinctions" (*Sign*, 25 [May, 1946], 56).

[151]McAllister, a diocesan priest of the archdiocese of
Baltimore, taught philosophy at Catholic University for many
years. He was for a time associated with the Sulpicians.
The work was received as a general ethics text, and was far
less well known than McFadden's work. It was less widely
reviewed, and is less generally available in library collections. One review speaks of it as a general ethics text,
and adds: "The illustrations are drawn from situations, attitudes, and ideals familiar to the nursing profession.
However, this feature in no way makes the book less valuable for the general reader" (*Sign*, 27, No. 1 [Aug., 1947],
55).

of nurses, and his practical cases are taken from their
daily personal and professional lives. He begins with a
lengthy section on general ethics (human act, law, conscience, double effect, and the virtues). His special ethics section is divided into four parts: ethics regarding
self, other persons, God, and the family and state. Included in these chapters are, among other issues, medical
ethical ones. They are given greater prominence than would
be the case in a general ethics text not designed specifically for nurses. Under obligations to self are included the
questions of preserving life and health. Abortion, euthanasia, and sterilization are treated under the rights of others. Here McAllister also deals with various contractual
issues of professional interest to the nurse. He includes
the problems of spiritual and sacramental care of patients.
The section on the family (marriage) includes questions of
contraception and artificial insemination.

A second, revised edition of the manual appeared in
1955 with a revised subtitle: *With Special Application to
the Medical and Nursing Professions.* Various medical ethical issues were updated, but the basic format of the work
remained unchanged. McAllister's work is of insufficient
depth to qualify as an important contribution to the field.
He often misses important distinctions, fails to give any
real analysis of difficult issues, and contents himself with
presenting his own opinion on questions which were in dispute even among his contemporary Catholic moralists.[152]

Three brief pamphlets on medical ethics were published

---

[152]This is perhaps understandable for a work in introductory general ethics. Examples include the brief treatment of euthanasia (2nd ed., pp. 218-220), his opinion on
the spiritual care of the non-Catholic (1st ed., p. 319, revised without any discussion in the 2nd ed., pp. 285-286),
his brief treatment of ectopic gestation (2nd ed., pp. 228-
229), etc.

in the late 1940's, one by an American priest, Timothy O'Connell, entitled *Morality in Medicine*,[153] and two by an Australian apologist, Leslie Rumble, entitled *Quizzes on Hospital Ethics for Nurses, Doctors, Priests, and Sisters*, and
Ethical Guide for Nurses.[154] The pamphlets briefly answer
questions concerning medical ethics. There is little or no
analysis. There are, as would be expected, instances of
disputable questions answered with no mention of the fact of
dispute.[155]

5. Gerald Kelly and the "Ethical and Religious Directives"

The most influential of American Catholic medical ethicists of the 1950's was the Jesuit moralist Gerald Kelly.[156]

---

[153]O'Connell was (and still is) a priest of the diocese
of Worcester, Massachusetts. I wish to acknowledge here his
bibliographical help in the preparation of this present work.
His pamphlet first appeared in 1949. There was a second edition in 1953, and a revised, third edition in 1959.

[154]Rumble was a well known Australian convert who wrote
many works in Catholic apologetics and was in charge of the
Australian Radio Apostolate to non-Catholics in Sidney. His
Radio Replies in defense of Catholic doctrine achieved popularity in America. *Quizzes* appeared in 1946, and *Ethical
Guide for Nurses* in 1947. The former was "recommended for
wide distribution" (*American Ecclesiastical Review*, 118
[1948], 399).

[155]One example among many is O'Connell's treatment of
the release of amniotic fluid in cases of hydramnion. O'Connell calls it direct abortion, whereas the issue had been,
and would continue to be, controverted.

[156]Kelly was born in Denver, Colorado, in 1902 and ent-
ered the Society of Jesus in 1920. Ordained in 1933, he
earned an S.T.D. degree from the Gregorian University in
Rome in 1937. He taught for 26 years at St. Mary's College,
St. Mary's, Kansas, and gave summer courses at St. Louis,
Creighton, Marquette, and other colleges. With John C. Ford
he authored *Moral Theology under Pius XII* and the two volume
Contemporary Moral Theology (1958 and 1963), an influential

Beginning around the time of the promulgation of the new
"Ethical and Religious Directives for Catholic Hospitals" by
the Catholic Hospital Association of the United States and
Canada in 1949, Kelly contributed a regular series of articles to *Hospital Progress* and other journals which were later gathered in a set of five booklets entitled *Medico-Moral
Problems*. They appeared over a span of years from 1949
through 1954. Then, in 1958, many of the original articles
were combined with some new ones and published again as *Medico-Moral Problems,* this time as one volume with continuous
pagination.[157] Though other works in medical ethics were
also being published during the years 1949 through 1958, we
will consider Kelly's work as a whole first, and then return
to the works of other authors written during these years.

---

transitional work for the years just prior to the Second Vatican Council. From 1947 to 1953 he wrote the "Notes on Moral
Theology" for *Theological Studies,* which has consistently
been one of the best sources for gaining a critical understanding of contemporary moral thinking. Kelly was generally
considered the foremost medical moralist of his time, at
least among American Catholics. His articles were constantly
cited as sources for opinions presented by Catholic authorities and by other authors. His style was lucid, and his
analysis critical. He died in Kansas in 1964. For further
details on his life, see McAuliffe, "Kelly, Gerald Andrew."

[157]The publishers fail to make the necessary distinctions between editions. Some of the articles appear in the
booklets in slightly revised form from their original journal
appearance. The booklets themselves were changed from earlier to later printings. The changes are described, but there
is no simple bibliographical way to identify the edition used
(no use of "second edition," for example). The earlier set
of booklets and the later one-volume edition are identically
titled with no notation of edition. The booklets were bound
in sets of four, and published as a unit, then bound later as
a set of five, all with the same title, some with revisions.
Libraries did their own binding. The reader is advised of
these complications. References here will specify the earlier set of booklets by stating the date and the part number
of the booklet cited, and by specifying "1958" when referring
to the later volume.

We have already noted the importance of the Catholic
Hospital Association, and described the "Surgical Code for
Catholic Hospitals."[158] In the late 1940's it became apparent that this code was inadequate as a guideline for Catholic hospital practice. Accordingly, a committee was appoint-
ed by the CHA, with Kelly as its chairman,[159] to formulate a
revised set of directives. Kelly himself suggests the reasons for such a code. Catholic doctors have need of and the
right to proper moral guidance as taught by the Church.
"Many of them have never had a course in medical ethics; for
these a statement of correct moral principles and sound applications is certainly necessary. And the need is not confined to this group; even those who have studied medical ethics are prone to get 'rusty' and to be at a loss without some
handy summary to which they can refer."[160] Kelly considers
the "Surgical Code" inadequate in that it was limited to surgery. He notes that various dioceses had formulated their
own codes, an indication of a need for revision.[161] Finally,
he suggests that such codes cannot be static, even though the
principles themselves do not change, because of the progress
of medical science.[162]

The Catholic Hospital Association's "Ethical and Reli-

---

[158]See above, pp. 141-142.

[159]McAuliffe, "Kelly, Gerald Andrew," p. 146.

[160]Kelly, *Medico-Moral Problems,* Part I, 1949, p. 1.

[161]We have already described the code adopted by the
Quebec Conference of the CHA in 1936, which became the official code for the dioceses of the Province of Quebec (see
above, pp. 157-158). A slightly altered version of that same
code appears in McFadden's 1946 edition entitled "The Moral
Code of Catholic Hospitals" (McFadden, *Medical Ethics for
Nurses,* pp. 345-346), indicating a wider usage of the code.

[162]Kelly, *Medico-Moral Problems,* Part I, 1949, p. 2.

gious Directives for Catholic Hospitals" were first formulated in 1949, revised in 1955, and again revised in 1971.[163]
They were not intended to be binding on individual dioceses
unless the ordinary so directed, but were rather to serve as
guidelines for dioceses which did not have their own
codes.[164] They quickly became the accepted code for Catholic hospitals in Canada and the United States.

After a brief introduction, the "Directives" are divided
into two general sections: a longer first section on ethical
directives, and a shorter second section on religious directives. The former directives "concern all patients regardless of religion, and they must be observed by all physicians, nurses, and others who work in the hospital."[165] The
latter concern the spiritual care of Catholic patients.

The ethical directives are divided into general and
specific directives. The general directives require that
the patient give his consent to therapeutic procedures, that

---

[163]The "Directives" appeared by themselves as a small
pamphlet published by the CHA in 1949, and in the March, 1949,
issue of *Hospital Progress*. They also were printed in the
July-October issue of *Linacre Quarterly* for the year 1948.
The date here is confusing, since this July-October, 1948,
edition includes an exact reference to an article dated Feb-
ruary, 1949 (see p. 9, note 17 of the *Linacre Quarterly* edition), and must therefore have been printed after the latter.
The Directives can be found in McFadden's 2nd, 3rd, and 4th
eds., in Kenny's 1st ed., and in McAllister's 2nd ed. Reference here is to the printing in *Linacre Quarterly*.
The 1955 "Directives" were issued as a pamphlet by the
CHA. They can also be found in McFadden's 5th and 6th eds.,
in Kenny's 2nd ed., in O'Donnell's 2nd ed., and in Healy.
Since this version is numbered sequentially by paragraph,
reference will be to paragraph number.
The 1971 version is available from the United States
Catholic Conference, and is listed in the bibliography under
the U.S.C.C.

[164]Catholic Hospital Association, "Ethical and Religious Directives," *Linacre Quarterly*, p. 1.

[165]*Ibid.*, p. 3.

the physician inform a dying patient, that there be adequate
consultation, that the doctor inform the hospital administration of the precise nature of any intended treatment,
and that all organs removed be sent to the pathologist.[166]

The specific ethical directives forbid direct abortion
while permitting indirect abortion, forbid euthanasia "in
all its forms" while allowing the use of sedatives once a
patient is properly prepared for death, forbid artificial
insemination with a donor's sperm and by masturbation or unnatural intercourse, forbid contraception by sterilization
or by any other means save continence while allowing sterilization for other purposes (indirect sterilization), forbid
masturbation and unnatural (condomistic) intercourse for
sterility testing, allow skin grafts and blood transfusion
and admit that the question of organ transplantation is still
debated, allow incidental appendectomy, lobotomy as a last
resort, narcotherapy with proper safeguards, and operations
to correct uterine malposition.

The religious directives concern only the Catholic patient, and no mention is made of the spiritual care of non-
Catholics. Baptism is to be given in cases of emergency,
and the chaplain must be called if possible. The other sacraments are to be available frequently, but without coer-
cion. Amputated members are to be buried if possible, otherwise burned. Fetuses should be buried unless a serious sani-
tary reason demands cremation.

Throughout the directives notation is made to various
articles by Kelly which had appeared in *Hospital Progress*
during 1948 and early 1949.

The "Ethical and Religious Directives" were influential
in the development of the material definition of medical
ethics. We have seen in many of the works studied that

---

[166]*Ibid.*, p. 3.

chapters on the specifically religious care of patients are
included along with chapters on more strictly ethical issues. The directives make a clear distinction between what
is "ethical" and what is "religious." "Religious" issues
continue to be a part of the Catholic medical ethical discussion, but they are distinguished from other "ethical" issues, and their inclusion is clearly based on the practical
need of medical personnel working in Catholic hospitals.
The directives give greatest emphasis to surgical questions,
especially to those pertaining to obstetrics, gynecology,
and reproduction.

The 1955 version is, for the most part, identical.
Under general ethical directives a statement is added concerning professional secrets (No. 11). The paragraph on
artificial insemination is altered to clarify that the use
of a cervical spoon as an aid to fertilization after normal
marital intercourse is permitted (No. 39). Directives are
added on human experimentation (consent is required), ghost
surgery (forbidden), psychoanalysis (allowed with restrictions on sexual activities and on asking patients to reveal
what they cannot), shock therapy (allowed), and unnecessary
operations (forbidden).[167]

The religious directives contain a provision for the
care of non-Catholic patients which was of significance when
it appeared.[168] It specifically permits calling a non-

---

[167]Nos. 42, 43, 46, 47, and 48.

[168]There had been some confusion on whether it was allowed for a Catholic to call a non-Catholic minister, as it
was held that this would be participation in heretical worship. For some further discussion, see Kelly, *Medico-Moral
Problems,* 1958, pp. 320-324. McFadden added a paragraph in
his second edition which allows the practice (McFadden, *Medical Ethics,* 2nd ed., pp. 407-408). However, his first edition specifically forbids a Catholic nurse to "summon the
official of any other religion for the express purpose of

Catholic minister and suggests "avoiding odious prosely-
tism" (No. 58).

Some mention should be made here of other codes based
on the "Ethical and Religious Directives." The "Moral Code"
of the Catholic Hospital Association of Canada was approved
by the Canadian hierarchy in 1954. The Canadian code was
based on the 1949 directives, but contains some of the
changes of the 1955 revision.[169] There was also in circula-
tion a brief version of the "Ethical and Religious Directives" called the "Code of Medical Ethics for Catholic Hospitals." It was available in pamphlet form and as a chart
for framing and posting. It, too, was written in 1954, and
became the official code for many American dioceses.[170]

Kelly's articles concern the directives and the ethical
(and religious) issues considered by them. Taken as a whole,
the five booklets or the later one volume edition constitute
a comprehensive treatise on medical ethics. In the five
booklets, Kelly does not follow any logical order. In part
one he speaks first about the code itself, its authority and

---

having him minister to members of his Church. To do so would
be a direct encouragement and aid to another in the practice
of a religion which she believes to be false" (McFadden, *Medical Ethics for Nurses*, p. 333). There is little doubt but
that the new approach brought relief to the many doctors and
nurses and chaplains who found it intolerable to refuse this
service. Of course, the Catholic could always request that
a non-Catholic family member make the call, and no doubt the
spiritual care of non-Catholics by their own clergy was seldom if ever actually hindered in Catholic hospitals. But
the attitude was odious, and its passing welcome.

[169]See Catholic Hospital Association of Canada, *Moral
Code*.

[170]This code is described in Lynch, "Medico-Moral
Notes," p. 24, n. 1. See also Kelly, *Medico-Moral Problems*,
1958, pp. vii-viii. For a brief description and comparison
of the 1949 and 1955 directives and the 1954 codes, see
Kelly, "Review of Existing Codes."

its applicability to non-Catholics. He then treats of ectopic gestation, sterilization to arrest cancer, problems of
uterine bleeding, incidental appendectomy, lobotomy, narcotherapy, baptism, and disposal of amputated members. Part
two begins with further introductory words about the code,
and then deals with truth-telling, the use of ergot for
hemorrhage during pregnancy (a question of possible abortion), sterility testing and artificial insemination (no
masturbation allowed), female castration for breast cancer
(permitted as an indirect sterilization), rhythm, Caesarian
hysterectomy (not permitted routinely as a sterilization
after multiple Caesarian births, but permitted if otherwise
necessary), vasectomy with prostatectomy, and a second chapter on lobotomy. Part three considers euthanasia, therapeutic abortion, delivery of hydrocephalic infants, organ
transplantation (debated and not settled), lobotomy for pain
relief (allowable only as a last resort), cooperation in illicit operations, and adult baptism. Part four treats of
the code, patient consent, consultation, the relation of the
doctor to his supervisor (the supervisor should see to it
that the doctors do not perform illicit surgery), the obligation of sending removed organs to the pathologist, cleido-
tomy (an operation which breaks a baby's clavicle to permit
birth--permitted if for the child's benefit), the use of
demerol in a threatened abortion, aspiration in hydrocepha-
lus, induction of early labor, rhythm, some further cases of
hysterectomy, unnecessary surgery, and the Eucharistic fast.
The final part considers the ordinary and extraordinary
means of preserving life, abortion and rubella, abdominal
(ectopic) pregnancy, contraception and sterilization, rhythm
again, presacral neurectomy, psychosurgery and Pius XII,
shock therapy, experimentation, fertility testing, and,
again, the Eucharistic fast.

In the 1958 version, the same basic topics are treated,

with some combinations and omissions. Additions include
ghost surgery, hypnoanalysis, hypnosis as anesthesia, and
the question of calling a non-Catholic minister. Kelly also
adds an appendix of statements by the Holy See on medical
issues.

We have listed the topics Kelly treats in detail because
the work is helpful for a description of the definition of
Catholic medical ethics of the period. The discipline is
here defined in a pragmatic way. The older organizational
rubrics (the commandments and sacraments) do not play any
recognizable role. Kelly, and the "Directives" he wrote,
are interested primarily in the ethical (and "religious")
issues besetting the physician and the nurse in their daily
professional activity. By far the largest emphasis is on
questions of surgery connected with reproduction: abortion
and sterilization. Other surgical techniques are stressed:
transplants, appendectomy, ghost surgery. Even in his discussion of mental disorders, Kelly gives greatest stress to
those procedures which are most directly surgical or which
involve related kinds of techniques: lobotomy, narcotherapy,
hypnotherapy, shock therapy. He is most interested in what
medical practitioners actually do. Gone is any consideration of the personal morality (as distinguished from professional conduct) of the nurse or doctor. Gone are treatises
on hygiene or first aid intended for the pastor. Gone is
any lengthy treatment of the canonical questions pertaining
to the sacrament of marriage. Gone is speculative theological analysis on the doctrinal issues pertaining to body and
soul.

Gone, too, is most discussion of purely sexual ethics.
The exclusion of these topics is not complete, however, since
some discussion is needed in the context of directly physical
medical procedures, such as artificial insemination, fertility testing, sterilization, and artificial contraception.

But Kelly avoids any lengthy treatment of extra-marital sex, homosexuality, masturbation (except in the context of sterility testing and artificial insemination), and other similar questions. One topic which could possibly be seen as an exception to this is that of non-"artificial" contraception, birth control by periodic continence, which Kelly, like many other moralists, includes among his topics. Here there is no question of a direct medical intervention. Yet this procedure is closely linked with other directly medical interventions as constitutive of the contraception question, and is thus included in the discussion. An additional important reason for its inclusion is the role that the medical doctor often plays in explaining the rhythm method to his patients. Kelly states: "These topics are closely connected with the question of what the physician may do as regards giving information, advice, and help to couples who wish to avoid or space children."[171] Again an explicitly practical motivation is apparent.

Like other moralists, and in keeping with the "Ethical and Religious Directives," Kelly includes some questions of a religious nature, such as baptism of fetuses, of the dying, Eucharistic fast in cases of illness, burial of amputated limbs, etc. They are included because they concern the hospital practitioner in his profession. And they are distinguished from the "ethical" questions which constitute the core of medical ethics.

Kelly's work was hailed by critics for its depth and its breadth.[172] Doubtless this was partly due to his role

---

[171]Kelly, *Medico-Moral Problems,* 1958, p. 176.

[172]An Irish review of parts one, two, and three states that Kelly is "one of the foremost moral theologians in the United States. He is a writer of outstanding merit and clarity. His frequent articles and notes . . . are consist-

in writing the directives, which originally carried references to his articles. But Kelly also had an ability to
speak precisely and without mystifying jargon. He said what
he thought was right, and also admitted it when he did not
know the answer to a case. This is not to say, however,
that he was ever able to transcend the rigid physicalist and
ecclesiastical positivist aspects of the methodology of his
time. Indeed, as we will see in chapter five, he was one of
the strongest proponents of these methodological modalities,
and responsible (with others) for their widespread dissemi-
nation and acceptance. Kelly's influence was of central importance in the emergence of Roman Catholic medical ethics
in North America. When he died in 1964 the pill controversy
was just beginning. Kelly did not live to see the radical
transformation which occurred after Vatican II.

---

ently amongst the best. . . . All his writings bear the
stamp of mature and painstaking scholarship. . . . On the
few points on which there is some room for disagreement of
opinion Father Kelly . . . makes handsome concessions to
the views and arguments of others" (*Irish Ecclesiastical
Record,* 77 [1952], 289-290). Another reviewer says: "No
medical man will set these articles down without the feeling
that the subject has been handled honestly and fairly. No-
where does Kelly assume a dogmatic role, imposing morality
upon medicine" (*Theological Studies,* 13 [1952], 287). In
his index to medical moral problems, John Lynch gives references to Kelly's articles first. "Several reasons urged
this 'primacy of honor,' among them the hope that no Catholic physician would be without these priceless works"
(Lynch, "A Topical Index," p. 87). "We have here the professional theologian at work," states yet another, "not the
mere redactor of a handbook for doctors and nurses. . . .
First, it is characterized by judicious interpretation of
the directives of the Holy See, especially the prolific pronouncements of Pius XII. . . . Second, it is distinguished
by broad knowledge of matters medical . . . Lastly, it is
noteworthy for a wisdom and prudent judgment born of long
years" (*Theological Studies,* 20 [1959], 146).

6.   Some Manuals of the Early 1950's

The decade following the appearance of the "Ethical and Religious Directives for Catholic Hospitals" saw the publication of numerous manuals of medical ethics by American and Canadian Catholics. The influence of Pius XII, who issued a large number of statements on medico-moral questions, was of significance for the emphasis given to the area by Catholic moralists.[173] In most of the manuals of the period the same pragmatic approach to defining the discipline is found as is apparent in Kelly and McFadden, though in some authors topics are included whose practical importance for the daily activity of medical personnel is less immediately apparent.

Of less significance and popularity than the works of La Rochelle and Fink, McFadden, and Kelly were two books written in 1951 by Catholic physicians. In comparison with the major works of North American medical ethics of the period, one of these books shows some resemblance to the pastoral medicine literature we described earlier, and the other includes topics we have seen to be typical of works in intra-professional "medical ethics."

Marriage, Morals and Medical Ethics was written by two Catholic physicians, Frederick Good and Otis Kelly, the latter being also a priest.[174] Many of the issues included in the work are of little or no practical importance for the physician. Medical advice is mixed with moral dicta. In

---

[173]A more detailed study of this aspect of the discipline will follow in later chapters.

[174]Frederick Good was surgeon-in-chief at Boston City Hospital and consultant to the marriage tribunal of the archdiocese of Boston. He had previously taught at Harvard and Tufts. Otis Kelly, a priest of the Boston archdiocese, as well as a physician and psychiatrist, was also consultant to the Boston tribunal. He taught psychology at Regis College in Weston, and was at the same time pastor of a local parish.

this the book has some resemblance to earlier works in pastoral medicine. But the book is not at all well defined.
There is a lack of consistency regarding the readership to
which it is presumably addressed. Some topics are included
which have little relevancy to the authors' supposed subject
(medical-ethical problems of matrimony), while other issues
of more direct relevancy are neglected.

The authors describe their own work as "a discussion of
medico-moral problems in matrimony confronting priests, physicians, nurses, social workers, hospital administrators,
and all those who need responsible information."[175] The
first chapter is an introduction to Christian marriage, and
includes questions of contract, sacramentality, ends of marriage, premarital instruction, canonical impediments (not
limited to "medical" ones, such as impotence, but including
questions of ecclesiastical form, consent, annulment procedures, etc.), and canonical procedures for marital validation
and legitimization of children. All these questions are
handled in a cursory fashion, with little critical discussion. The second chapter introduces the principle of double
effect, questions of cooperation and scandal, and conscience.
Chapter three is a basic introduction to the structure and
function of the sex organs, and speaks of masturbation and
sex education for adolescents, and the climacteric. The next
chapter is a description of conception, pregnancy, and labor.
The authors then describe various complications of pregnancy,
and suggest therapies. There is little moral discussion of
abortion here. The seventh chapter speaks of birth control,
arguing for rhythm and against other means, but with little
real analysis. Artificial insemination is mentioned. Chapter eight is entitled "About Psychiatry," and speaks briefly

---

[175]Good and Kelly, *Marriage, Morals and Medical Ethics*,
p. xi.

of a whole range of issues pertaining to mental illness.
The authors then speak of how to give medical testimony before an ecclesiastical court, and, finally, on administering
the sacraments to the sick.

Some parts of the book are entirely too superficial for
professionals. Other sections are of use only to a spefific
class of professional (to physicians and clergy called to
give tribunal testimony, for example). There is no material
integrity. The authors fail to include any real treatment
of many medico-moral issues pertaining to marriage and pregnancy, but do include much that has little or no direct connection to their topic, such as psychiatry and the sacraments
for the sick. The work is more medical and canonical than
moral, and ethical analysis is almost entirely lacking. Reviews ranged from highly positive to completely negative, a
phenomenon not often encountered among Catholic reviews of
medical ethical books of the period.[176]

---

[176]An English reviewer asks: "How do Americans manage to
do things so well? . . . This is a straightforward account
. . . written in simple convincing language, which can be recommended to all who have to apply Catholic principles to
marital problems" (*Tablet,* 200 [1952], 272). A physician attacks the book for its numerous technical errors and adds:
"In conclusion this critic must conclude that the book is
valueless for those who have no previous medical training because they would not recognize its numerous technical errors
and of little value to those who are medically trained because it does not contain an adequate discussion of moral
principles and their application. It could be dangerous if
taken literally because of the numerous unsupported statements which have no scientific basis" (*American Ecclesiastical Review,* 128 [1953], 76). Theologians question some of
the conclusions and lack of analysis (*Theological Studies,* 13
[1952], 286-287; *Furrow,* 4 [1953], 357-358), and criticize
the disjointedness of the work: "One would like to have a
general textbook of medical ethics from such competent authors. Alternatively one might wish that, having set their
limits, the authors had more closely observed them. . . .
There is a haphazard note discernible in the order of the
work" (*Irish Ecclesiastical Record,* 79 [1953], 78-79).

The year 1951 also saw the publication of a medical
ethical work by the Catholic physician Bernard Ficarra entitled *Newer Ethical Problems in Medicine and Surgery.*[177]
The book covers most of the issues common to general texts
in the field, but gives somewhat more detailed treatment to
those the author considers especially pertinent to his time
(contraception, euthanasia, and artificial insemination),
and includes many issues more generally found in the intra-
professional manuals and codes of "medical ethics." Ficarra
explains:

> In the majority of discourses and texts on pastoral
> medicine, stress has been placed on abortion, ectopic
> pregnancy and mutilation. At the present time there is
> no great moral problem associated with these subjects
> because the wisdom of years has confirmed the Catholic
> concepts on these moral transgressions. The present
> day concern centers about newer ethical problems which
> have found advocates among the laity and the medical
> profession. Such topics as contraception, euthanasia
> and artificial fecundation are the topics of major im-
> portance. . . . For this reason, the former group (abor-
> tion, etc.) will be discussed briefly and are included
> in this treatise for the sake of completeness and to
> reaffirm our belief in the accepted dogma. A more ex-
> tensive study and discussion, therefore, will be given
> to the more recent group of medico-moral problems.[178]

Ficarra includes brief statements on direct and indirect abortion and ectopic gestation, on mutilation, sterili-

---

[177]Bernard Joseph Ficarra was born in Brooklyn in 1914.
He earned his M.D. at Georgetown in 1939, and served as
surgeon and chief of staff in various hospitals. He taught
experimental physiology at St. John's University.

[178]Ficarra, *Newer Ethical Problems,* p. xix. Ficarra's
opinion on the relative importance of these issues is open
to question. The problem of ectopic gestation was generally
less disputed and less urgent now than formerly, but other
issues of abortion, and the problem of sterilization and
mutilation were still of concern. It is interesting to note
the use of the rubric "pastoral medicine" in Ficarra's introduction. As we have seen, no recent American works have
used it. Yet it has not completely disappeared.

zation, and the improper use of drugs. His chapters on contraception, euthanasia, and artificial insemination are
longer, but even these contain no real philosophical or theological ethical analysis. Ficarra does present some detail
about the legal aspects of these practices. His sources
generally are more from the legal and medical disciplines
than from moral theology. The last three chapters deal with
issues of professional ethics. Chapter ten argues against
any sort of socialized medicine in America, defending the
American medical miracle, and supporting the program of the
American Medical Association. Chapter eleven concerns autopsies and the legal and moral consent needed for them.
The next chapter considers the "Moral Aspect of Professional
Conduct," including questions of advertising, patents, legal
restrictions, secrecy, and other issues. The final chapter
is on compensation medicine (the medical treatment of those
covered by workmen's compensation laws), and discusses choice
of physicians, fees, insurance, and other questions.

Ficarra's work is not as such a work in the moral theology of medical practice. Written from a physician's perspective, it discusses various legal and ethical aspects of
medicine in support of conclusions reached by Catholic moral
theology and by professional "medical ethics." There is
little analysis of the ethical principles used.[179]

A 1952 work by the Dominican moralist John Kenny is
specifically intended to be a one semester textbook in medi-
ical ethics. It is entitled *Principles of Medical Ethics*.[180]

---

[179]The work was seen to be valuable in that it was addressed to the medical profession in general, and did not
overly stress specifically Catholic arguments, while maintaining adherence to Catholic teaching (*Clergy Review*, 38
[1953], 126).

[180]Kenny was born in Providence, Rhode Island in 1909,
entered the Dominicans in 1930, and was ordained a priest in

Kenny states:

> The need for moral guidance in the medical and nursing
> professions was the inspiration for writing this book.
> Since the problems encountered by the practicing physi-
> cian and nurse are not treated in religion and general
> ethics courses, medical and nursing students need to be
> well instructed in the principles of medical ethics.
> Their curriculum should include a course which will not
> only give the answers to medico-moral problems, but which
> will also explain the reasons why certain operations
> and procedures are lawful and others are unlawful.
> This book was written with this twofold objective in
> view.[181]

Kenny's double objective is thus essentially practical:
to provide solutions to the medical ethical problems of medical practitioners and to explain these solutions by describing general principles of morality from which they are derived. In general, Kenny gives greatest emphasis to those
topics which pertain to the professional activity of nurses
and physicians. He does include some discussion of issues
which recall the codes and literature of "medical ethics" and
"nursing ethics," however, such as topics of intra-professional etiquette and personal morality.

Kenny's first chapter concerns general principles of
morality, and is introductory and quite brief. His purpose
is to present them as background necessary for their later
application to practical problems: "The application of these
principles to the many and varied problems of medical practice constitutes the subject matter of medical ethics."[182]
He names four postulates of ethics (epistemological possibil-

---

1938. He taught at Dayton, Notre Dame of Maryland in Baltimore, and at Providence College. A second edition of his
book was published in 1962. Descriptions of both editions
are given in the text. References distinguish the editions.

[181]Kenny, *Principles of Medical Ethics,* 1st ed., pp.
vii-viii; 2nd ed., pp. ix-x.

[182]*Ibid.,* 1st ed., p. 1; 2nd ed., p. 1).

ity of certain knowledge, the existence of God, free will,
and immortality of the soul), speaks of human acts, the principle of double effect, law, and conscience. In chapter five
we will discuss Kenny's use of physicalist and ecclesiastical
positivist methodologies. It is within these frameworks that
Kenny applies theological principles to medical ethical questions. They enable him to arrive at clear universal solutions to ethical dilemmas.

Chapter two deals with certain questions of justice and
charity pertaining to medical practice, such as lying, secrecy, cooperation in evil, and restitution. The third chapter
treats of certain professional duties and rights of medical
personnel, and is an attempt to apply general ethical principles to some of the "medical ethics" norms of the professional associations. The physician must be properly trained. He
has a right to a just fee, but must not overcharge. He has
an obligation to uphold the honor of the medical profession,
which means he must follow the American Medical Association's
code respecting advertising and patents. Kenny simply as-
sumes this is ethically correct. Both doctor and nurse must
live a personally virtuous life. The nurse, especially, must
avoid impure thoughts and language, be honest, and maintain
loyalty to her superiors, to physicians, and to her nursing
school. She is to carry out the doctor's orders ("He gives
the orders and it is the duty of the nurse to fulfill
them."[183]). She should never criticize the physician.

Chapter four is entitled "Morals and Marriage." Here
are found topics of medical-sexual ethics. It is not Kenny's
purpose, however, to deal with all the issues of sexual morality or to treat of canonical issues of marriage as such,
as was often the case with the manuals of pastoral medicine.
Kenny states regarding the chapter:

---

[183]*Ibid.*, 1st ed., p. 55; 2nd ed., p. 63.

>It is not proposed as an exhaustive study of the con-
jugal society, for its purpose is to furnish those
interested in the medical profession with a knowledge
both of the fundamental concepts of Christian marriage
and the morality of certain situations which arise in
wedlock. Needless to say, the material of this chapter
is of importance for those in the medical profession
since they may be called upon to explain the morality
of these various procedures to their patients.[184]

Kenny's purpose is thus primarily practical: to discuss marriage and sexual morality in order to furnish the physician
and nurse with necessary background material for their own
practice, and in order to help them in counselling others.
He deals with the nature of marriage, the nature of sex and
love, the purpose of intercourse, the marriage debt, impotency, sterility, sterility testing, artificial insemination,
contraception, douching, and periodic abstinence.

Chapter five is on "Questions Arising from Man's Right
to Life." He treats of suicide, homicide, mutilation, blood
transfusion and skin grafts, amputation and burial of amputated members, autopsies, organ transplantation, lobotomy,
sterilization, euthanasia, drugs, and hypnotism. The sixth
chapter concerns specific questions of childbirth, including
abortion, Caesarian section, ectopic gestation, and painless
childbirth. The final chapter is on the administration of
baptism in the hospital. An appendix includes the "Ethical
and Religious Directives."

The book was revised and a second edition published in
1962. It follows the same basic format as the first, except
that the section on the right to life is extended and a separate chapter added on various questions of mutilation. The
question of means of preserving life is discussed, as are issues of psychotherapy. Organ transplantation is more thoroughly discussed, since kidney transplants were now possible.

---

[184]*Ibid.*, 1st ed., p. 57; 2nd ed., p. 67.

The appendix includes several additional codes of ethics.

Kenny thus includes topics from the whole range of medical ethics. In accordance with his formally stated purpose,
the needs arising from the daily professional practice of
medical personnel constitute his primary criterion of selection. General principles serve as background necessary for
solving these problems. Sexual ethical discussion is presented as background for more directly medical interventions
or for the physician's role as counsellor. In comparison
with most of the other medical moralists of the period, however, Kenny includes more discussion of professional etiquette and personal morality. Also of particular note is
his uncritical acceptance of some of the norms of the professional codes of "medical ethics" and "nursing ethics."
Reviewers praised his emphasis on principles, but were generally critical of the brevity of the work.[185]

Direct influence of European medical ethical literature
during this period was somewhat limited. The American authors were conversant with some of the European works, some
had studied in Europe, and as moral theologians they were
familiar with the general manuals of moral theology published
on the continent.[186] Nonetheless, the primary circle of

---

[185]"The emphasis is on principles . . . and that emphasis is good and timely" (*Thomist,* 17 [1954], 101). Another
reviewer offers "a qualified welcome" to the work. "Father
Kenny's work belongs to the first ranks of the possible textbooks from which the teacher of medical ethics has to select
his choice." But qualifications include a criticism of the
work's brevity and its neglect of some problems (*Homiletic
and Pastoral Review,* 53 [1953], 853-854). Other reviews are
similar (see the review section of the general bibliography).

[186]References in the American texts are almost totally
limited to other American works, though some of the authors
make occasional reference to the general European manuals
(See O'Donnell, *Morals in Medicine,* for examples of such citation; McFadden, Kenny, and Kelly give almost exclusive

dialogue was largely limited to North American authors, with
the occasional inclusion of an English language work from
Britain. An exception to this isolation was the appearance
in English of a series of volumes consisting of articles
translated from the French *Cahiers Laënnec* and edited by the
English Benedictine physician Peter Flood. The series consisted of four volumes entitled *New Problems in Medical Ethics,* which were published over the years from 1953 to 1960.[187]

The volumes might have had more impact on American medical ethics had they been more unified within themselves or
had they been limited more to topics of current interest in
the North American discipline. As it was, the volumes included some topics of current practical interest to American
medical moralists, but also dealt in considerable depth with
issues of no immediate importance for medical ethics as that
discipline had come to define itself in North America.

The first volume, or first series, includes four "studies": the sexual problems of the adolescent (masturbation),
intersexuality (homosexuality), abortion, and the miraculous
cures at Lourdes. Volume two discusses artificial insemina-

---

attention to other American works in their references). An
exception is the French Canadian work by Jules Paquin, to be
studied later in this present section.

[187]Flood was a physician, civil lawyer, and Benedictine
monk. He was educated in Paris and Rome. He wrote a number
of works in moral and pastoral theology.
        Cahiers Laënnec was begun in 1934 in Paris to serve as
a forum for discussion of problems of medical ethics (*déontologie médicale*--see above, pp. 154-155). The journal approached each problem from different disciplinary perspectives: medical, legal and moral.
        New Problems in Medical Ethics consists primarily of
four volumes, or "series," published respectively in 1953,
1954, 1956, and 1960. The reader is advised, however, that
the same title was used for a subsequent series of smaller
works, published in the early 1960's, and consisting of the
same articles in different order.

tion, narcoanalysis, medical responsibility (three articles
on the legal responsibilities of physicians under French
law), the medical secret, and preparation for death. The
third series treats of castration, ecclesiastical marriage
annulments, psychoanalysis, psychasthenia (a continental
term for a neurosis often called the disease of ecclesias-
tics, consisting of a general malaise and indecisiveness--a
lack of psychic energy[188]), pain, and euthanasia. Volume
four discusses the psychopathology of birth control, the
treatment of alcoholism, and various metapsychic (parapsy-
chological) phenomena and their connection to Christian miracles.

It is clear from this general listing that the topics
include many which were of direct interest to pastoral medicine but not of practical importance to medical ethics. Data
from medicine for speculative theology was part of pastoral
medicine, for example, and thus questions of miraculous cures
were included in its definition. But this issue was never an
essential topic for North American medical ethics. Critics
of the series praised its depth and its openness to newer
psychoanalytic data, but pointed out the irrelevance of some
topics to medical ethics, the lack of unity of purpose within
each volume, and the lack of applicability of French law and
terminology to the American situation.[189] Despite these

---

[188]See Flood, ed., *New Problems,* III, 149 ff.

[189]The method followed, says one reviewer, "is to have
the various subjects dealt with by experts from the different
relevant aspects--usually the legal, medical and theological
aspects. This indeed, is a comprehensive way of treating a
particular problem . . . But inasmuch as it is the legal
practice in France that is mainly envisaged the legal dimensions mean comparatively little elsewhere" (*Irish Ecclesiastical Record,* 83 [1955], 73). Another states that "there is
no real unity of point of view. . . . [the volume treats of]
such various matters as masturbation and the discernment of

limitations, however, the works were widely disseminated in
North America, and are easily found in Catholic and secular
libraries both in the United States and Canada.

In addition to the four volumes we have described,
Flood edited two smaller individual volumes, each also con-
sisting of a series of articles translated from *Cahiers
Laënnec*. Both appeared in 1955. One volume is entitled
Medical Experimentation on Man, and the other *The Ethics of
Brain Surgery*.

Two books appeared in 1954 consisting of proceedings of
professional gatherings. In the Spring of that year the
Western Conference of the Catholic Hospital Association of
Canada held an Institute on Medico-Moral Problems in Regina.
The Association published the proceedings in a volume entitled *A Workshop on Medico-Moral Problems*.[190] There are five
themes treated in the book. The first deals with general
principles and their application to medical ethics. The second is on abortion and related procedures. The third considers mutilation, including sterilization. The fourth considers mental illness and the fifth treats of the religious care
of patients (various sacraments and questions of burial).

In the summer of the same year an international gathering of Catholic physicians was held in Dublin. Its published
proceedings were entitled *Transactions of Congress: Sixth
International Congress of Catholic Doctors, Dublin, June*

---

the miraculous, all under the common heading of 'Medical Ethics'" (*American Ecclesiastical Review,* 131 [1954], 430). A
British reviewer praises the French for avoiding the polemics
common in England where Catholicism is a minority religion.
In France "they are concerned less with the establishment of
Catholic principles, which are taken for granted, than with
their application in practice" (*Tablet,* 202 [1953], 38).

[190]Listed in the bibliography under Catholic Hospital
Association of Canada.

30th to July 4th, 1954, and were edited by John Fleetwood.[191]
The theme of the Congress was demography. Topics considered
include abortion and birth control, geriatric issues (euthanasia, telling the dying patient, and sedation are briefly
mentioned) psychological problems in demography (birth control and psychosurgery), and social and nutritional problems
connected with population trends.

7.   Jules Paquin: An Exception

An exception to the general trend in North American literature is the extensive volume published in 1955 by the
French Canadian Jesuit, Jules Paquin, entitled *Morale et
médecine.*[192]   Here the influence of European works in pastoral medicine is directly evident.[193]   Though the author organizes his material in a more practical fashion than many
of the European works, and in that sense participates in the
American pragmatic approach, there is much in his work which
is generally not included in North American manuals of medical ethics.

In a two-part article appearing in *Hospital Progress* in
1954, while he was writing his book, Paquin proposes a description of what a course in medical ethics should be. He
first enumerates three conditions which must be fulfilled

---

[191]Listed in the bibliography under Fleetwood.

[192]Paquin was professor of moral theology at the Jesuit
Scolasticat de l'Immaculée Conception in Montreal and taught
medical ethics in the Faculty of Medicine at the University
of Montreal.   There was a second edition in 1957 and a third
in 1960, both slightly revised.   The book was translated into
Italian in 1958 by A. M. Di Marina, S.J., under the title
Morale e medicina.   References here are to the 1955 French
edition.

[193]His bibliography contains a wider sampling of French
works than is common to English speaking North American authors (Paquin, *Morale et médecine,* pp. 468-471).

for an effective course: first, the student must be convinced of the importance of the subject; second, there must
be a profound background knowledge of religion and dogma;
third, the student must have a developed personal spiritual
life.[194] He then goes on to insist that a course in professional ethics must recognize

> two complementary aspects: the theoretical aspect and
> the practical aspect. Since it is a true *science,* eth-
> ics cannot be conceived in isolation from its funda-
> mental principles; and the course in ethics will be
> primarily an exposé of these principles. But as a *prac-*
> *tical* science, ethics is oriented towards action, and
> the course in ethics, without slipping into hair-split-
> ting casuistry, should anticipate certain typical cases
> to exemplify a judicious application of principles.[195]

An emphasis on principles is necessary in order to avoid
utilitarianism and the "new morality." Paquin admits that
nurses often have trouble understanding principles, but insists on their importance for an effective course in medical
ethics. Without this explanation of the "why" of moral judgments, ethics becomes mere casuistry.[196] On the other hand,
Paquin recognizes the importance of including "typical cases"
in his course, in order that the student may learn to apply
principles correctly.[197]

In the second part of the article, Paquin offers some
suggestions for a course outline. These are, of course,
basically similar to the division of his manual. He begins

---

[194]Paquin, "A Course in Medical Ethics: Three Conditions," pp. 68-69.

[195]*Ibid.,* p. 69, italics his.

[196]In our study thus far, we have noted a number of the
less important American works which are indeed merely casuistic catechisms, where the ethical explanation is minimal
or entirely lacking.

[197]Paquin, "A Course in Medical Ethics: Three Conditions," pp. 70-71.

with an "introduction on the nature of natural and theological ethics and the general relations that should exist between ethics and medicine."[198]   The rest of the course he
describes as follows:

> To summarize--the division I use for the course in pro-
> fessional ethics distributes the whole subject in seven
> parts: 1) fundamental principles; 2) general profes-
> sional duties; 3) respect of the supernatural rights of
> the patient: the sacraments; 4) respect of his internal
> rights: life, integrity of the body and its functions,
> the genital powers, health, mental health; 5) respect
> of the mixed rights: right to the truth and secrecy;
> 6) respect of material property; and 7) a few comple-
> mentary questions.[199]

In keeping with his intention to emphasize principles,
Paquin's first part, concerning fundamental principles, is
more extensive than that of most North American works.   He
includes three sections: the rules of morality (man's end,
law and "the different elements that give our concrete actions their morality; the action considered in itself, the
circumstances, the effects of our actions [double effect],
the satisfaction that accompanies them, and the intentions
of the one that performs the action,"[200] as well as conscience, the subjective rule of morality), moral responsibility (modifiers of the voluntary in the light of the discov-
eries of depth psychology[201]), and the question of supernatural merit, not generally included in medical ethical works.
     Part two treats of general professional duties.   Paquin
here speaks of the greatness of the medical profession, the
qualities of virtue needed by its practitioners, the virtues
of justice and charity, cooperation in evil, obligations to

---

[198]Paquin, "A Course in Medical Ethics: Practical Suggestions," p. 85.

[199]*Ibid.*, p. 87.

[200]*Ibid.*, p. 85.

[201]*Ibid.*, p. 85.

the poor, and the question of patient consent to treatment.

The next four parts concern "the major particular professional duties of the nurse [and physician]."[202] Part
three addresses those duties which respect the patient's
supernatural rights, that is, the question of sacramental
care of Catholics (baptism, confirmation, extreme unction,
penance, and the Eucharist), and the spiritual care of non-
Catholics.[203] Part four is the longest section, and treats
of the "internal rights" of the patient. In the manual it
includes parts four and five.

> In *the fourth section* many problems are treated. Con-
> cerning life: euthanasia, embryotomy or any form of
> foetus killing, curettage, inducement of labor, ce-
> sarean section. Concerning the integrity and function-
> ing of the body: mutilation and in particular, sterili-
> zation. Concerning actuation of the genital powers:
> artificial insemination, contraceptive [*sic*], the safe
> period method, incomplete coitus, venereal diseases and
> sexual relations, spermaculture [sterility testing],
> treatments with sexual reactions [treatments which may
> cause arousal], sexual literature and purity in general.
> Concerning health: choice of drugs, narcotics, seda-
> tives, anesthetics, and human experimentation in medi-
> cine. Concerning mental health: hypnotism, narco analy-
> sis, psychoanalysis, shock treatment, psycho-surgery.
> Concerning positive care of life and health: the obliga-
> tion to seek treatment and care.[204]

Parts five and six (combined in the manual to form part
six) concern the "mixed rights" and material rights of the

---

[202]*Ibid.*, p. 86. In his article, Paquin envisages the
nurse as student for his course. The manual itself addresses
both nurse and physician.

[203]Paquin's approach to this last issue is very cautious.
If a Catholic nurse is asked to call a non-Catholic clergyman,
she may do so only if no-one else is available, and using a
formula which Paquin suggests to avoid any chance of cooperation in false worship (Paquin, *Morale et médecine,* pp. 186-
188).

[204]Paquin, "A Course in Medical Ethics: Practical Suggestions," p. 86.

patient. Here the author treats the patient's rights to
truth, the professional secret, and questions of payment.
Part seven, to which Paquin gives "the rather vague title of
'complementary questions,'"[205] would include certain of the
Church's positive laws, such as burial, and the obligation
of Mass attendance, fast, and abstinence for the sick. In
the manual these are not gathered in one place, but are
treated in other sections.[206] Paquin suggests a chapter on
the states of life, including marriage and celibacy, which
are briefly treated in part four of the manual.[207] The manual concludes with brief chapters on the professional oath
and codes of medical ethics. Paquin notes that the professional codes often include directives which are not part of
morals in the strict sense, and adds: "It is regretable
that matters of such diverse value are included under the title *Medical Ethics.*"[208]

Though Paquin's longest sections concern the physical
medical procedures which we have seen to constitute the
greatest emphasis in North American medical ethics, he includes more detailed consideration of certain other questions
than is commonly found in the medical ethics manuals we have
studied. His section on fundamental principles emphasizes

---

[205]*Ibid.*, p. 87.

[206]Paquin, *Morale et médecine*, pp. 350-352, 392-397.

[207]*Ibid.*, pp. 267-283. His treatment of celibacy is
very brief, limited to noting its objective superiority to
the married state. The manual does not consider questions
of "medical contra-indications to priesthood and religious
life" as suggested in the article outline ("A Course in Medical Ethics: Practical Suggestions," p. 87).

[208]Paquin, *Morale et médecine,* p. 462, n. 2, translation mine, italics his. "Il est regrettable que l'on englobe
sous le titre d'*Éthique médicale* des choses de valeur aussi
diverse."

the psychological determinants of freedom. This often appears very briefly in the manuals as part of the section intended to introduce the principles which will later be applied to more practical questions. But Paquin's emphasis
and relatively lengthy discussion recalls the earlier, medical aspect of pastoral medicine, where data from medicine
(here from the allied field of psychiatry) were brought to
the pastor for use in his work as confessor and spiritual
director. Paquin includes a section on supernatural merit,
not generally treated in the North American manuals.

His treatment of the sacraments is longer than in most
other works. Though much of his discussion pertains to the
practical questions of administering the sacraments to the
sick, he also includes some discussion of the significance
of medical data for sacramental theology, an aspect of pastoral medicine not usually included in North American medical
ethics texts.[209]

Included in the section on questions connected with reproduction are issues not of a directly medical nature, such
as impurity in looks, touch, thought, desire, reading, etc.
His section on the sacrament of marriage gives greater detail
concerning sacramental and canonical questions than is common
in the manuals. Whereas other North American authors may include a brief description of marriage and sexual morality, it
is usually in the context of providing necessary background
information to the physician as surgeon or as counsellor.
Paquin treats these issues in detail as pertaining intrinsically to his discipline. It is probable that he is influ-

---

[209]One reviewer states that "the author examines with
special attention the contributions of medicine to the doctrine of the sacraments, so much so that one could consider
this part as a complete *medicina pastoralis*" (*Jurist,* 19
[1959], 272). The reviewer misunderstands the scope of pastoral medicine as we have discovered it to be, but he correctly senses the pastoral medicine aspects in Paquin's work.

enced here by the European literature of pastoral medicine, where the commandments and sacraments serve more directly as organizational rubrics and principles of selection than they do in the North American manuals. In these latter, as we have consistently noted, it is the daily professional activity of medical personnel which serves as primary, often as sole criterion of selection. This activity, in turn, is influenced by the growth of professional secular medicine, where physical healing, as contrasted with spiritual healing, is most emphasized. By way of contrast, Paquin includes greater discussion of sexual issues and of other questions (the psychological determinants of freedom, for example) which pertain more to human spiritual-moral-mental health than directly and exclusively to one's bodily welfare. In this, Paquin resembles pastoral medicine scholars, whose discipline was never restricted to the degree found in North American medical ethics to questions of practical importance for the modern medical practitioner.

Reaction to the book was quite favorable. Reviewers praised it for its depth and its emphasis on principles, as well as its use of Freudian psychology.[210] It was never translated into English, however, and thus its direct influence in North America was limited largely to French Canada. In chapter five we will speak of Paquin's theological methodology, of his application of general principles to medical ethical questions.

---

[210]"It is gratifying to see the stress which P. has put on principles. . . . This approach, while perhaps less popular in appeal, has a much more permanent value. . . . [It is] the most thorough treatment of medical ethics which has appeared in French or English since Payen's *Déontologie médicale*" (*Theological Studies,* 17 [1956], 121-122). Similar notices are found in other reviews.

8.   Five Works in 1956

The year 1956 saw the appearance of three new manuals
of medical ethics, as well as new editions of two others.
The new manuals were by two Jesuit moralists, Edwin Healy
and Thomas O'Donnell, and by a trio of writers of the archdiocese of Newark, Edward J. Hayes, Paul J. Hayes, and
Dorothy Ellen Kelly. The revisions were the fourth edition
of McFadden's *Medical Ethics* and the redaction by Patrick
O'Brien of Patrick Finney's 1922 work.

Healy's manual, entitled simply *Medical Ethics,* is a major treatise.[211] It was written "primarily as a textbook
for use in Catholic medical schools and as a reference book
for use in Catholic hospitals," but also addresses non-Catholic physicians with Catholic patients.[212] Healy accepts
the term *Medical Ethics* as rubric, but distinguishes ethics
in the strict sense ("the science of moral duty") from ethics in the broader sense such as it is understood in the
codes of professional associations. The practices prescribed
in the codes "may set an ideal which is in every way to be
commended; but if they do not involve a strictly moral issue,
they do not fall within the scope of the present work."[213]

Healy's first chapter is on fundamental principles, and
sets out three postulates as a necessary basis for ethics:

---

[211]Edwin Healy was born in Detroit in 1897. He entered
the Society of Jesus in 1919 and was ordained in 1931. He
studied at Weston, Massachusetts, and at the Gregorian University in Rome. He taught at Loyola University in Chicago,
and then for many years at West Baden College in Indiana. He
also taught moral theology in Rome and served as theological
consultant to the Vatican tribunal. He produced three textbooks in ethics and moral theology: *Moral Guidance* (1942),
Marriage Guidance (1948), and *Christian Guidance* (1949), in
addition to his *Medical Ethics*. He died in 1957.

[212]Healy, *Medical Ethics,* p. ix.

[213]*Ibid.,* p. 13.

that there is an infinitely wise and good Creator; that He
rewards and punishes men for their acts; that man's soul is
immortal and his will free. He then speaks of the natural
law, and presents some fundamental principles of medical ethics. The first chapter is very brief, and contains no analysis.

Chapter two concerns the general obligations of the physician. Here Healy treats some of the more directly moral
issues often found in professional works of "medical ethics."
Included are professional competence, the use of drugs, ghost
surgery, fees, fee splitting, truthfulness, secrets, and unnecessary surgery.

Chapter three returns to the question of general principles, but includes specific medical ethical applications and
cases. Here Healy discusses the problem of ordinary and extraordinary means to preserve life, self-defense (not a valid
principle in cases of abortion, but applicable to attacks by
the mentally ill), the double effect principle, cooperation,
and the avoidance of scandal. In chapter five we will discuss Healy's methodology, showing how he applies general
principles to practical dilemmas.

Chapters four through eight concern specific medical
ethical problems. Healy first treats certain issues connected with surgery, including non-sterilizing mutilations,
preventive surgery (incidental appendectomy, etc.), cosmetic
surgery, transplantation of organs (Healy hesitates to offer
an answer concerning living donor transplants), autopsies,
and animal experimentation (licit). He then discusses some
problems of married people, such as sterility testing, artificial insemination, and birth control. Chapter six concerns abortion and sterilization.[214] The seventh chapter is

---

[214]Sterilization is commonly included as a mutilation.
Healy puts it in the context of reproductive questions.

on delivery problems: drugged childbirth, Caesarian section,
and other issues. The eighth chapter includes a number of
"unclassified problems," including hypnotism, euthanasia, *in
vitro* fertilization, douching after rape, and menstrual hygiene.

The ninth chapter concerns mental disease and psychiatric treatment, and speaks of diabolical possession, homosexuality, and sterilization of the unfit. In chapter ten,
Healy speaks to the physician as counsellor, and includes
discussion of sexual ethical issues. Pre-marital counselling, marriage instruction, the sex education of children,
and masturbation are discussed, along with problems of adop-
tion and of care of the aged. Chapter eleven concerns the
spiritual care of patients by administration of the sacraments, and discusses the laws of fast, abstinence, Mass attendance, and recitation of the official prayer of the Hours,
all in the context of cases of medical illness. An appendix
includes several codes of ethics.

Healy's primary principle of selection, in keeping
with his stated purpose, is the practical one we have seen
develop in the North American discipline. In the interest
of quick solution, he includes in his text 171 numbered
cases, to which he gives a solution and a brief explanation
of the principle applied. By far the greatest number of
these concern physical operations and other direct bodily
interventions, many related to reproduction.

When Healy does speak of other kinds of issues, such
as psychiatric treatment in chapter nine and some sexual
ethical questions in chapter ten, he does so for explicitly
practical reasons. He makes it quite clear that psychiatric
issues as such are of secondary importance, not related intrinsically to medical ethics as he defines it, but of some
use to the medical doctor who may need to refer patients for
therapy. And he includes sexual ethical issues as part of

the discipline for a similarly practical reason: the physician may be called upon, as part of his professional activity, to counsel concerning sexual matters.

Thus Healy introduces his ninth chapter on mental disease:

> It is not our intention to go deeply into the subject of psychiatry. The science is advancing with amazing rapidity and new procedures and therapies are constantly being developed. A separate treatise would be required for a complete discussion of all the moral problems connected with psychiatric counseling and treatment. Our purpose is not to present such a discussion, but rather to treat briefly those things that the general practitioner should know and keep in mind before he refers a patient to a psychiatrist and when he chooses the psychiatrist to whom he will refer his patient.[215]

Healy gives a brief discussion of Freudian psychotherapy, adds two paragraphs on diabolical possession, and speaks of homosexuality as a psychiatric disorder. The rest of the chapter treats of more directly physical kinds of interventions, such as psychosurgery, shock therapy, narcotherapy,

---

[215]Healy, *Medical Ethics*, p. 280. Healy suggests one such treatise in a footnote (a work entitled *Psychiatry and Catholicism*). Other similar works were available, for example Moore, *The Nature and Treatment of Mental Disorders;* Moore, *Personal Mental Hygiene;* Moore, *Heroic Sanctity and Insanity;* Hagmaier and Gleason, *Counselling the Catholic.* This last work, written in 1959, emphasizes precisely those issues which we have seen to constitute an intrinsic part of pastoral medicine (and to be emphasized in such works as Paquin and Good and Kelly, which resemble pastoral medicine), but which have been deemphasized in medical ethics texts. North American medical ethics has defined itself in such a way that these issues are the proper concern of pastoral theology, pastoral counselling, and specific works on religion and psychiatry, for example, as well as works in specifically sexual ethics. Hagmaier and Gleason speak at length about the psychiatric modifiers of human freedom, and discuss explicitly masturbation, homosexuality, alcoholism, scrupulosity, mental illness, and their moral implications. The discipline to which their work belongs is explicitly that of pastoral counselling (p. xii), not medical ethics.

and sterilization of the unfit.

In a similar way Healy introduces some sexual ethical issues in chapter ten, which he entitles "The Physician as Counselor." He notes that the medical doctor is called upon more and more frequently "to counsel individuals and groups of individuals on problems pertaining to marriage, the care of children, and the correction of undesirable sex habits in children."[216] He sees this as an important responsibility for the physician. "The purpose of this chapter is not, of course, to supply him with any of the medical knowledge he needs, but solely to discuss certain matters in which moral issues are involved."[217] The purpose of the chapter is thus once again to apply moral principles to the questions arising from the daily professional activity of the medical doctor.

Reviews were generally favorable.[218] Critics appreciated the clarity and depth of the manual. Healy's work was one of many similar manuals now on the market, however, and this fact reduced its importance and its influence.

A second new manual to appear in 1956 was *Morals in Medicine* by Thomas O'Donnell.[219] The author proposes to include

---

[216]*Ibid.*, p. 310.

[217]*Ibid.*

[218]"This book could well become a standard manual . . . It succeeds unexpectedly in covering the whole of the ground without any of that abridgement of reasoning or paucity of detail which one normally accepts as the inevitable price of comprehensiveness" (*Clergy Review*, 42 [1957], 114). Other reviews are listed in the bibliography. One outstanding characteristic, noted by reviewers, was the book's physical appearance. It was printed cleanly on high-gloss paper, which resulted in a compact size for this work of some 440 pages.

[219]O'Donnell was born in Baltimore in 1918. He entered the Society of Jesus in 1938 and was ordained in 1950. He studied at Georgetown and Woodstock, and taught at Georgetown University School of Medicine. *Morals in Medicine* was

data from three disciplines in his work: ethics ("an investigation into the goodness or evil of human actions in the light of natural reason"), moral theology (which "investigates the morality of human actions against the background of man's supernatural life and destiny, and with the added assistance of divine revelation"), and canon law ("an investigation into the meaning and interpretation of the positive ecclesiastical law which governs the external conduct of the baptized as members of the Church"). He continues:

> Each of these disciplines . . . is concerned primarily with human conduct. The purpose of this book is to select some of the salient features of these three disciplines as they apply specifically to the conduct of the medical profession. The moral aspects of medicine are, briefly, a study of right order in the professional conduct of the doctor, as learned from human reason and divine revelation, in his relationships to his God and to his fellow men.[220]

O'Donnell does not use the term *Medical Ethics* as a rubric, nor does he disassociate himself from it.

O'Donnell's approach is consistent with that of the majority of American manuals. He begins with a chapter on fundamental truths, in which he speaks of God and the soul. In keeping with his explicitly theological intentions, he adds a section on revelation, and a brief defense of the authority of the Roman Catholic Church and of papal infallibility. The second chapter speaks of basic principles, including law, conscience, the human act, double effect, and cooperation. We will return to these questions in chapter five. There we will discuss at some length O'Donnell's use

---

enlarged in a second edition which appeared in 1959. References here will distinguish editions. A third edition, entitled *Medicine and Christian Morality,* appeared in 1976. This revision, which is largely a restatement of earlier positions, is outside the scope of our present study.

[220]O'Donnell, *Morals in Medicine,* 1st ed., p. xv; 2nd ed., p. xix.

of ecclesiastical positivism, and will show how this approach, together with a physicalist methodology, enables him
to solve the moral issues he raises.

Chapter three discusses the obligation to preserve life
(ordinary and extraordinary means). Chapter four concerns
mutilation, including sterilization, transfusion, incidental
appendectomy, psychosurgery, hypnotism, and human experimentation. Ghost surgery is also treated here. He then speaks
of abortion including ectopic pregnancy. He presents the
canonical aspects of ecclesiastical excommunication for cooperation in abortion.

Chapter six is entitled "Medico-Canonical and Medico-
Moral Aspects of Marriage." Here O'Donnell includes material
which is not of immediate importance to the practicing physician. His reason for doing so, however, is that it might
serve as necessary background for the physician in his surgical and counselling practice.[221] O'Donnell speaks at some
length of the canonical concept of impotence, and of the definition of "true seed" needed for valid marriage. He mentions as well the other canonical impediments to marriage
which would have little or no direct interest for the physician. These are rarely found in North American medical ethics texts. He treats briefly of marriage guidance and pre-
marital instruction, and, in the second edition, adds brief
sections on masturbation (included for the physician's benefit in his role as counsellor[222]) and menstrual hygiene (not
to discuss the hygienic aspects, but to ask if the use of
tampons is allowed despite possible erotic stimulation--yes,
provided the woman does not desire the stimulation). More
directly medical ethical issues included are contraception,

---

[221]*Ibid.*, 1st ed., pp. 177, 201, 203, 211, 213; 2nd ed.,
pp. 237, 269, 271, 285, 287.

[222]*Ibid.*, 2nd ed., p. 314.

sterility testing, and, in the second edition, artificial
insemination.

Chapter seven concerns professional secrecy. Chapter
eight discusses terminal illness. Here O'Donnell discusses
the administration of the sacraments to the dying, and the
doctor's obligation to inform a patient of his condition.

A second edition was published in 1959. It follows the
same basic format, but some sections are substantially expanded. The chapter on mutilation includes sections on cosmetic surgery, surgery by residents, shock therapy, animal
vivisection, and organ transplants (not yet clear, but probably licit). The chapter on marriage adds sections on artificial insemination, breast feeding, masturbation, and tampons. An appendix contains the 1955 version of the "Ethical
and Religious Directives."

In keeping with his formal goal, "a study of right order in the professional conduct of the doctor,"[223] O'Donnell
emphasizes those topics which pertain to the professional
practice of the medical doctor. Surgical procedures and
other direct physical interventions, especially those pertaining to reproduction, receive the most analysis. O'Donnell does not speak of mental illness or psychological theory in any detail, limiting his discussion to brief statements on such more or less direct interventions as psychosurgery, narcoanalysis, shock therapy, and hypnotism. He
does include, as we have noticed, some canonical aspects of
marriage and some sexual ethical issues which are of little
direct interest to the practicing physician, but even here
he suggests the rationale that these are necessary as background for the physician's role as counsellor. His discussion of baptism and extreme unction (the "religious" issues)
are in the context of providing these sacraments to the

---

[223]*Ibid.*, 1st ed., p. xv; 2nd ed., p. xix.

dying, where the doctor might be required to help in preparation or in emergency administration. O'Donnell's emphasis
is thus on those topics of importance to the physician's
practice.

Reviews of this further addition to the now sizable number of contemporary manuals were quite favorable. Some critics asked for more detail on certain problems.[224]

The third new work which appeared in the same year,
1956, was the brief *Moral Handbook of Nursing* by two priests
of the Newark archdiocese, Edward J. and Paul J. Hayes, and
a nurse, Dorothy Ellen Kelly. The authors describe the book
as "complete enough to form the basis of a good course, yet
brief enough to be used for ready reference. . . . medically
up to date, inexpensive, well indexed, and of convenient
handbook size."[225] The work is divided into two sections:
the moral and ethical principles of nursing, and the nurse's
spiritual life. The first section, of about 100 pages, is a
brief overview of Catholic medical ethics of the period.
The authors treat the general principles of ethics, including
the nature and sources of ethics, the natural law, conscience,
and double effect. In this context medical ethics is defined
as "the particular aspect of the science of ethics which
guides our judgment concerning the goodness or badness of
human acts in the medical profession."[226] The authors dis-

-----

[224]One reviewer suggested more treatment of fee-split—
ting, homosexuality, and the moral responsibility of neurot-
ics and psychotics. He praised the work as clear, objective,
and authoritative (*Homiletic and Pastoral Review*, 57 [1957],
958-959). Another states: "Although *Morals in Medicine* is
limited by the practical purpose it is meant to serve, the
author has given evidence throughout of a capacity for producing a much more thorough treatise on the subject" (*Priest*,
13 [1957], 222). The second edition doubtless answered somewhat these aspirations.

[225]Hayes, Hayes, and Kelly, *Moral Handbook*, p. ix.

[226]*Ibid.*, p. 5.

tinguish this from medical etiquette.[227] Particular topics
of later chapters include issues concerning the origin of
life (contraception, artificial insemination, and sterility
testing), problems relating to the destruction of life
(abortion and euthanasia), and problems connected with some
operations (cooperation in evil operations; discussion of
mutilation, sterilization, and organ transplantation is too
brief to be of much help). The section concludes with a
chapter on the nurse's responsibilities to her patient,
including secrecy and the spiritual and sacramental care of
patients, both Catholic and non-Catholic. The second part
of the book includes a spiritual exhortation on the meaning
of suffering and a series of prayers for the nurse.

The same authors also published a revised edition in
1964, under a new title, *Moral Principles of Nursing*. All
of the ethical discussion is expanded, especially the section on general principles, which constitutes part one of
the work. The chapter on operations is enlarged. A glos-
sary of medical and theological terms is appended.

Patrick Finney's *Moral Problems in Hospital Practice:
A Practical Handbook* originally appeared in 1922. In 1956
it was revised and enlarged by Patrick O'Brien and published
under both names with the original title.[228] O'Brien

---

[227]"Often there is confusion on this point because
medical ethics is sometimes considered as dealing primarily
with medical etiquette. Medical ethics correctly understood deals with *moral conduct*" (*Ibid.*, p. 4, italics
theirs).

[228]O'Brien, like Finney, was a Vincentian priest. He
earned his S.T.D. at Catholic University and taught at St.
John's Seminary in San Antonio, Texas. He also wrote *A
Handbook for Catholic Chaplains,* a manual on hospital chap-
laincy and ministry to the sick. For a description of
Finney's work, see above, pp. 133-135.

describes the purpose of the work:

> What Father Finney had in mind we have undertaken to
> continue: the presentation in simple and direct fashion
> of the moral solutions to medical problems that occur
> in hospital practice. Both the example of Father
> Finney and mature contemporary advice have served to
> restrain us from the citing of divergent opinions and
> to strengthen our resolve to provide a useful solution
> to problems for those who are not specially trained to
> make their own or for those who want an immediate solu-
> tion to a pressing problem.[229]

Finney's first section (his list of question-and-answer
solutions) is eliminated. O'Brien adds a chapter on general
principles (morality, human acts, double effect, conscience,
law, cooperation in evil) which includes a section on professional secrets. The order of the rest of the book is
generally that of Finney, whose text O'Brien partially repeats, with his own substantial additions. Thus he speaks
of abortion in four chapters (including direct and indirect
abortion and a lengthy section on the question of ectopic
gestation), mutilation and sterilization, and certain other
issues. O'Brien adds a chapter on administrative problems
of the hospital. Here he includes questions of burial, experimentation, obligation to preserve life, sterility tests,
contraception, and preparation for death.

O'Brien spends much of his work defending Finney's
strict opinion concerning operations in cases of ectopic
pregnancy against the more general opinion of his contemporaries.[230] Reviews were generally favorable. Critics noted
the confusion resulting from O'Brien's defense of Finney,
but praised the work for its brevity and clarity.[231] The

---

[229]Finney and O'Brien, *Moral Problems,* p. xi.

[230]*Ibid.*, pp. 160-190.

[231]"We welcome the return to the market of this very
popular and standard work . . . One is struck by the clarity,

book was never as influential as its more popular competi-
tors. Its analysis is uneven, with much discussion given to
some issues, little to others. Finney's original work was
not designed to be a textbook, but rather a "handbook" for
quick consultation. O'Brien's revision adds some textbook
characteristics (the chapter on fundamental principles, the
detailed treatment of ectopic gestation), and the result is
a work which was not truly adequate either as textbook or as
reference manual. We will return to O'Brien's use of theological principles in chapter five. There we will note his
strict application of physicalist criteria, enabling him to
arrive at clear and universal scientific solutions to the
issues (mostly surgical) which he analyzes.

One final work to appear in 1956 was the fourth edition
of McFadden's *Medical Ethics*. The author changes the order
of his chapters and adds a new chapter concerning man's duty
to preserve his life. Here McFadden discusses ordinary and
extraordinary means of preserving life, human experimentation, and non-sterilizing mutilations (formerly treated in
the chapter on sterilization). The chapter on euthanasia,
formerly titled "The Christian Philosophy of Suffering," is
retitled "Man's Life--The Inviolable Creation of God," but
is substantially identical to that of earlier editions. The
references at the end of each chapter were dropped, a fact
regretted by reviewers.[232]

---

the concise presentation and the attractive format of the
book. . . . On the matter of detail there are many points on
which we should beg to differ" (*Homiletic and Pastoral Review*,
57 [1957], 955-956). The review goes on to criticize
O'Brien's treatment of ectopic gestation: "The ghost of the
original author hovers over the answers too persistently and
to little advantage" (*Ibid.*, p. 956).

[232]*Irish Ecclesiastical Record*, 88 (1957), 140.

9. Other Works of the Late 1950's and Early 1960's

We have already noted the appearance in 1954 of the
"Moral Code" officially approved by the Canadian Catholic
bishops for application in Canadian hospitals. It was based
essentially on the "Ethical and Religious Directives for
Catholic Hospitals" of the Catholic Hospital Association.[233]
In 1957 two Canadian priests, Edgar Godin and John O'Hanley,
published a commentary on this code entitled *Hospital Ethics:
A Commentary on the Moral Code of Catholic Hospitals*.[234]
The authors explain that "it has been written primarily as a
textbook of medico-moral for the student nurse, but intended,
too, as a vade-mecum of medical ethics for the medical doctor, and even the inexperienced hospital chaplain."[235] The
authors explicitly avoid any analysis or "expositions of
medical and moral theories, and other material that belongs
more to the realm of speculation than to that of practice."[236] The book follows the code article by article,
citing also the relevant paragraphs of the "Ethical and Religious Directives."[237] Brief explanations are given of
each of the prescriptions in the code.

In 1959 the Benedictine priest Gregory Stevens wrote a
textbook in general ethics published as the fifth edition of
Thomas Verner Moore's *Principles of Ethics*.[238] Since the

---

[233]See above, p. 176.

[234]The work also appeared in French, under the title
Commentaire du code de morale pour les hôpitaux (Montreal:
Wilson and Lafleur, 1957).

[235]Godin and O'Hanley, *Hospital Ethics,* p. vii.

[236]*Ibid.*, p. vii.

[237]For a description of the "Directives" see above, pp.
173-176.

[238]Like his predecessor, Stevens taught at Catholic

work is substantially a new one, it is difficult to understand why Stevens kept Moore's name and title. In any case
the work is not a text in medical ethics, though it does,
like Moore's earlier editions, address itself specifically
to nurses, and thus emphasizes medical ethical issues more
than would a text with a less specialized readership. The
chapters on the right to life, on truthfulness and secrecy,
and on civil law and the nurse are focused especially on medical ethics and "nursing ethics."

A brief manual in ethics for pharmacists was written in
1962 by William Wolkovich, a Boston priest, entitled *Norms of
Conduct for Pharmacists*.[239] Wolkovich notes the existence of
several codes of ethics of pharmaceutical associations, and
makes the distinction we have become familiar with between
ethics in this sense and ethics in the stricter philosophical
sense of the normative science of human conduct.[240] In order
to avoid confusion, he explicitly rejects the use of the term
"ethics" in his work.[241] In his first section he outlines
briefly some general principles. The second section applies
them to pharmaceutical practice. Among issues included are
birth control, abortion, and various kinds of drugs, as well

University and at St. Anselm's Priory. For a description of
Moore's original editions, see above, pp. 138-140. The bibliographical listing here is found under Moore and Stevens.

[239]Wolkovich wrote his book while working as assistant
pastor in the Archdiocese of Boston. His interest in phar-
macy ethics was an avocation.

[240]Wolkovich, *Norms of Conduct,* pp. 17-18. "Ethics"
can be used in the "strict sense" to mean "the practical
normative science of the rightness and wrongness of human
conduct as known by natural reason" (quoted from Fagothey,
Right and Reason), or in a "broader scope" to mean "the etiquette, rules or standards of ideal personal or professional
conduct" (p. 18, italics deleted).

[241]*Ibid.*, p. 19.

as a number of topics relating to the professional ethics of
the pharmacist (advertising, relations to physicians, secrecy, etc.). He appends two papal addresses to pharmacists,
a statement of the hierarchy on birth control, and some ex-
cerpts from United States civil law.

Brief mention should be made of the appearance in the
early 1960's of several British and European works available
to North American readers. In 1960, the British physician
John Marshall wrote a brief summary of medical ethics entitled *Medicine and Morals*.[242] For him, "Medical ethics are
not a series of commands and prohibitions, they are a plan
for the positive health for the Mystical Body of Christ and
for each of its members."[243] He includes general principles
(the nature of man, law, and the doctor's role in the Mystical Body), and applies them to specific issues. Included
are discussions of the genesis of life (contraception), in-
fertility, sterilization, abortion, the preservation of life,
the end of life (pain, leucotomy, euthanasia, and preparation for death), and psychiatry. Discussion is brief and
analysis scant.

The British Catholic lawyer Norman St. John-Stevas
wrote *Life, Death and the Law* in 1961.[244] His work is an
attempt to describe and comment on the legal aspects of some
medical ethical issues. Its approach is closer to that of
works written during and after the Second Vatican Council,

---

[242] It was published as volume 129 of the *Twentieth Century Encyclopedia of Catholicism*. Marshall taught at the
University of London and wrote several books on marriage
counselling and family planning.

[243] Marshall, *Medicine and Morals,* p. 26.

[244] The author earned doctorates in both law and philosophy. He has been active in English politics. The book
appeared with different subtitles in its British and American publications.

and it belongs more to that period than to the period of our
present study. His book *Law and Morals* (1964) examines legal
questions relating to various ethical issues, most of them
connected with the practice of medicine.

We have already had occasion to cite the works of Albert
Niedermeyer in our study of European pastoral medicine. Two
of his volumes were translated into English in the early
1960's. They are *Compendium of Pastoral Medicine* and *Compendium of Pastoral Hygiene*. The former is a compact summary
of Niedermeyer's basic German work, the two volume *Allgemeine
Pastoralmedizin* and *Handbuch der speziellen Pastoralmedizin*.[245] The latter concerns questions of hygiene.[246] American and British reaction was mixed. Though they praised the
work for its vast scope, reviewers found much of it to be of
little practical importance to their needs and interests.
They criticized the technical language and the presence of
cautious Latin phrases. European pastoral medicine did not
meet North American (or British) expectations in medical ethics.[247] Rather it included detailed discussions of non-

---

[245]All the works mentioned here are listed in the bibliography.

[246]We have already noted how pastoral medicine included
in its scope questions of practical hygiene for the priest.
Niedermeyer suggested a distinction between pastoral medicine
(dealing with medicine--the curing of the sick) and pastoral
hygiene (dealing with hygiene--keeping the healthy healthy).
He states: "In older works of pastoral medicine such a distinction was not common . . . Whether this was good or
whether the present trend of complete separation is better
must be judged by the results" (*Compendium of Pastoral Hygiene*, p. iii).

[247]Referring to the *Compendium of Pastoral Medicine*,
one reviewer stated that it was an excellent and vast work,
but that it was too wide, and lacked adequate explanations
for the non-expert (*Irish Ecclesiastical Record*, 97 [1962],
128). See also *Clergy Review*, 48 (1963), 200-201. Another
critic states: "The result is a bewildering assemblage of

medical ethical questions, such as sexual biology, evolu-
tionary theory, the theory of various schools of psychology,
supernatural phenomena and mysticism, miracles, as well as
the whole area of personal hygiene in the life of the priest.
It was clear that North American medical ethics had, in its
emerging phase, limited its scope to more immediately practical problems in the professional activity of medical personnel.

The two final editions of McFadden's *Medical Ethics*
will bring our survey to a close. More than any other single work, McFadden's manual spanned the entire period of the
papacy of Pius XII, the definitive period in the emergence
of Catholic medical ethics in North America. In the preface
to his fifth edition (1961), McFadden notes "the almost universal acceptance of this text in our schools."[248] By the
time of the publication of the sixth edition (1967), much
had changed in Roman Catholic medical ethics, and McFadden's
text was largely dated. Nonetheless the author can still
refer to "the widespread acceptance of this text in medical
and nursing schools, not only in the United States, but also
in Canada, England, Australia, New Zealand, and Spain (in
its Spanish translation)."[249]

---

highly technical matters far beyond the capacity of the ordinary priest" (*Downside Review*, 80 [1962], 191).
    Reviews of the *Compendium of Pastoral Hygiene* were even
more critical. Reviewers considered Niedermeyer's long sections on the hygienic characteristics of church buildings to
be generally irrelevant, and his "discussion of the relative
hygienic merits of the Roman vs. the Gothic chasuble to be
almost ludicrous. . . . Doctor Niedermeyer is very definite
on some points . . . he advises us sternly not to drink coffee after 4 p.m. We are allowed more latitude when it comes
to tea. Its deadline is 5 p.m. What American priest can
read such advice and keep a straight face?" (*Priest*, 20
[1964], 619-620).

    [248]McFadden, *Medical Ethics*, 5th ed., p. xiii.

    [249]*Ibid.*, 6th ed., p. xi.

In the last two editions, McFadden follows his basic
outline. The fifth edition contains an additional chapter
on the rights of the patient in the spiritual order. Here
the author focuses on patient consent to treatment, on information owed to a dying patient, on the spiritual care of
non-Catholics, and on the problem of hypnosis. The chapters
on contraception and direct abortion are rewritten. Various
topics are added to the text, including the question of oral
contraceptive pills (a grave offense against moral law if
used to prevent conception[250]), and kidney transplants
(allowed hesitatingly, despite McFadden's opposition to corneal transplants from living donors[251]). The chapter on
ectopic gestation is eliminated, and the arguments summarized in the section on abortion. Reviews begin to note
that some of McFadden's opinions are no longer acceptable
without nuance.[252]

The sixth edition brings us beyond the emerging period
of our discipline. The chapter on contraception is again
rewritten, this time in light of magisterial hesitation with
respect to oral contraception. McFadden retreats from his
earlier negative position, and offers only a hesitant condemnation of the pill.[253] The chapter on man's duty to

---

[250]*Ibid.*, 5th ed., p. 81.

[251]*Ibid.*, pp. 266-268.

[252]One reviewer asks for more consideration of oral contraception (*Blackfriars,* 43 [1962], 442). Marshall calls it
"reprehensible" that McFadden includes "traditional statements which should long ago have disappeared from responsible
books. . . . Even worse is the statement that contraception
'has frequently resulted in nervous disorders, sterility,
chronic invalidism, and even death.' There is not a shred of
evidence to support this melodramatic statement" (Marshall,
"Review: McFadden," p. 315). O'Donnell reacts to being
called a proponent of abortion (O'Donnell, "Review: McFadden," p. 159).

[253]McFadden, *Medical Ethics,* 6th ed., p. xii; pp. 86-88.

preserve life is divided into two chapters, the additional
one entitled "Man's Body--Respect for Its Integrity." Surgical sex alteration, the use of the body for research, and
cremation are topics added in this doubled chapter.

Before turning to a concluding summary of the present
chapter, mention should be made of two other sources of medical ethical material available to American scholars. The
first consists of the various collections of papal pronouncements on medical ethical issues. Some of the works we have
examined include references to many such speeches and writings of popes, especially of Pius XII. We will have reason
to return to this in the following chapters. In addition to
these, and to the standard translations in periodical form
of papal speeches and writings, books were written which
collected papal teachings on medical issues. Among them
were the two collections gathered by the monks of Solesmes
and published in English under the titles _Papal Teachings:_
The Human Body, and _Papal Teachings: Matrimony._[254]

The second source consists of the "Notes on Moral Theology" which appeared annually or semi-annually in _Theologi-_
cal Studies from the first issue in 1940 and continuously
since then. Most of these articles include medical ethical
issues, and some emphasize the field. This is hardly surprising, since the Jesuit authors of the series over the
years included several who wrote much in the field, among
them Gerald Kelly.[255]

Later printings of the sixth edition include reference to
"Humanae Vitae," Paul VI's encyclical condemning oral contraception, and urge that the conclusions be accepted (_Ibid._,
some printings, "Addendum" on p. xvii).

[254]Listed in the bibliography under _Papal Teachings._
They appeared in English in 1960 and 1963.

[255]A complete listing of these articles, consulted in
connection with this study, is in the bibliography. See

Pius XII died on October 9, 1958. With the preparation for and the opening of the Second Vatican Council (1962-1965) under his successor, John XXIII, the period of emergence of Roman Catholic medical ethics ended. A time of critique began which would radically alter the discipline.

Conclusion

It has been the purpose of this chapter to trace the emergence of Roman Catholic medical ethics in North America with respect to its name and definition. We have surveyed the literature of the field[256] during its period of emergence into a self-conscious discipline with a generally established rubric, self-comprehension, and extension. In the course of this survey we have also discovered the nominal and definitional relationship of the discipline to its three

---

Ford, Kelly, Connery, Farraher, Lynch, McCormick, and Springer for their respective surveys. No detailed analysis of these articles is given here, as the topics included in them are generally identical to those in the works we have surveyed, and since there is never any attempt to present an inclusive study of the field.

[256]We have not directly studied works concerned only with an individual issue. As we have listed above some of the more important of these written during the early period (p. 149, n. 99), so we refer the reader now to some books of this type written during the later period: Biltz, *The Obligation to Preserve Life*; Cunningham, *The Morality of Organic Transplantation*; Glover, *Artificial Insemination*; Hughes, *A Moral Judgment Concerning the Transplantation of Organs*; Lohkamp, *The Morality of Hysterectomy Operations*; Shinners, *The Morality of Medical Experimentation*; Sullivan, *The Morality of Mercy Killing*. Many of these are dissertations. All are included in the bibliography. Some will be included in the discussion in chapter five. The many works in sexual and marriage ethics include discussion of contraception and some other medical ethical issues. No attempt has been made to include these works specifically in our study. They are in any case largely identical to the works we have examined.

cognate pre-disciplines:[257] pastoral medicine, intra-professional "medical ethics," and medical jurisprudence.

We have described the process by which the term *Medical
Ethics* came to be the generally accepted rubric. We noted
that the earliest literature of the late nineteenth and early
twentieth centuries used the rubrics "medical jurisprudence"
(Coppens) and "pastoral medicine" (Sanford, Klarmann, and
O'Malley and Walsh). These terms were never totally accepted
as general rubrics for the discipline.[258] They meant something different from what medical moralists were doing.
"Medical jurisprudence" implied an emphasis on civil law
which was not the central concern of the moralists. "Pastoral medicine" included aspects such as the teaching of hygiene, various speculative theological issues, psychological
theories, etc., which were at most of secondary interest
to medical practitioners and, hence, to the moralists who
wrote primarily for them.[259]

We have discovered why the term *Medical Ethics* was not
accepted without hesitation. In the early literature some
authors rejected the rubric altogether (O'Malley and Walsh,
Spalding), since for them it indicated the professionally
relativistic codes of etiquette of medical associations.
During the twenties and thirties no rubric was in general
use. Often titles did not include one (Spalding, Burke,
Finney). The word "ethics" by itself often appeared, however, and one work used the rubric *Medical Ethics* (Bourke).
In the later period, 1940-1960, the majority of scholars

---

[257]For the meaning of the term "cognate pre-discipline,"
see above, p. 98, n. 206.

[258]Though some authors still used the term "pastoral
medicine" here and there in their writings (Ficarra; Walsh,
"Review: Bonnar," p. 506, etc.).

[259]See above, pp. 143-144.

came to accept the term as general rubric. Some disassociated themselves from the "medical ethics" of the professional codes, but now the disassociation was usually one of distinction rather than rejection (McFadden; Kelly, "Medico-
Moral Notes," p. 55; Healy; Hayes, Hayes, and Kelly). *Medical Ethics,* or its closest French translation "Morale Médicale," was used as rubric in the titles of many books (La
Rochelle and Fink, Trudel and Perrier, Dufort, McFadden,
Good and Kelly, Kenny, Flood, Healy). Other authors, whose
titles did not include it, used it in their texts as name
for the discipline (Kelly, Paquin, Ficarra). Its acceptance
was due to the inadequacy of the alternative terms "medical
jurisprudence" and "pastoral medicine," to the traditional
acceptability of the term "ethics" within Catholic moral
philosophy and theology, and to the widespread popularity of
the term "medical ethics" both in intra-professional and in
general usage.

In our survey of the literature we have discovered that
North American Catholic medical ethicists came to define
their discipline as the moral theological-philosophical investigation of medical practice. Their purpose was to apply
moral principles to the daily professional activity of medical personnel, in order that they, as well as the clergy and
laity who might be concerned as moral guide, chaplain, or
patient, would know and carry out correct moral procedure.
We have seen this definition formally stated by many authors
(Coppens, Burke, Finney, La Rochelle and Fink, Trudel and
Perrier, Dufort, McFadden, Kenny, Paquin, Healy, O'Donnell,
Finney and O'Brien, Hayes, Hayes, and Kelly, and Wolkovich).

The inclusion and exclusion of topics for the discipline
(material definition) depended to a large extent on its purpose. The primary principle of selection for North American
Roman Catholic medical ethics came to be the actual daily
professional activity of medical personnel.

When we examined the general moral theological tradition as a source of medical ethical topics, we discovered a
gradual shift in principles of selection from the sins penitents confessed to the organizational rubrics of the commandments and sacraments, including a section concerned with the
actual daily professional problems of medical personnel (the
section concerned with states of life, in which the vocation
of physician was included). In the general manuals, of
course, this last never became the central principle of selection, since their scope was never limited to medical ethical issues. But the inclusion of a special section concerned with the physician, which accompanied the development of
professionalized and secularized medicine, is significant
for the definitional development of medical ethics. This
latter discipline came to emphasize precisely this concern:
the daily professional activity of medical personnel. The
purpose of the discipline was to offer moral guidance to the
physician and the nurse in their professional conduct. In
this singling out of the medical profession for special concentration, medical ethics could point to the special section
of the moral manuals as an already well established example.

When we studied the development of European pastoral
medicine, we noted a similar process. The field came to emphasize more and more the practical moral aspects of the interface of theology and medicine. Pastoral medicine itself
was never limited to these aspects, since its definition included other areas of interest. Yet the shift in emphasis
was apparent. As medical ethics in North America emerged
from its pre-disciplines, the non-moral emphases of pastoral
medicine were all but eliminated. Treatises in hygiene and
first aid for the priest were relegated to secular works in
popular medicine. Data from medicine intended to help the
pastor in his spiritual care of souls were relegated generally to works in pastoral theology and pastoral psychology.

Medical material applied to questions of speculative theology was relegated to the various areas of that discipline. These three aspects of the medical emphasis, of pastoral medicine appeared as central concerns only in the relatively small number of North American works which approached the field more from the wider pastoral medicine perspective than from the more common and more restricted perspective adopted by most North American authors. These works, as we have seen, were exceptions to the general definitional determination of medical ethics as it emerged in North America.

We have discovered, then, that North American medical ethics emerged as the discipline investigating the moral rightness and wrongness of the daily professional activity of medical personnel. It was interested primarily in what the medical doctor and nurse did in their professional conduct. Thus, in conjunction with the development of modern medical technique and specialization, medical ethics came to give greatest emphasis to those direct physical and surgical interventions which typified modern medicine. We have noted in numerous authors that much, sometimes virtually all, of the discussion centered around surgical procedures, especially those connected with reproduction, obstetrics, gynecology. This emphasis was nearly universal in North American authors (Coppens, Klarmann, Bourke, Burke, Finney, La Rochelle and Fink, Trudel and Perrier, McFadden, Kelly, Kenny, Paquin, Healy, O'Donnell, and Finney and O'Brien). The "Ethical and Religious Directives" also gave primary place to this kind of issue.

In arriving at this emphasis, North American moralists accepted materially if not formally the modern medical notion of health, where the accent for medicine was placed on physical interventions and physical cures of bodily disorders. The moralists were not, of course, formally content with materialistic definitions of health. Their purpose was

explicitly to bring moral spiritual guidance to these questions. But from a material perspective (the topics treated,
the issues to which moral guidance was brought) most North
American authors gave greatest emphasis to specifically physical procedures. These procedures constituted the core of
the professional activity of the nurse and physician, which
activity served as the primary criterion of selection of
topics for discussion.

     In keeping with this emphasis, questions of psychiatry
and mental illness occupied a generally secondary place,
since they were seen as extrinsic to the professional activity of the medical doctor, the surgeon, the general practitioner, the medical nurse. The application of moral principles to specifically psychotherapeutic issues was thus relegated on the whole to other than general medical ethical literature, to works in pastoral counselling, pastoral psychology, or to specific treatises devoted to the relationship of
morality, religion, and various psychotherapeutic techniques.
In the medical ethics texts and manuals these questions were
not considered intrinsic to the discipline, since they were
not a direct part of the professional activity of the medical
practitioner to whom the works were addressed.

     Some questions of mental health are discussed in certain
of the books we have studied. We have noted, however, that
in those works which form part of the emerging discipline of
medical ethics in North America (as distinguished from the
relatively few works which continue to resemble European
pastoral medicine, such as the very early books of Sanford,
O'Malley and Walsh, and Medicus, or the later works by Paquin
and Good and Kelly) the topics receiving most emphasis are
those involving strictly physical interventions, such as
psychosurgery, narcotherapy, and shock therapy, in which the
medical doctor would be likely to participate, and the similar, if less direct procedure of hypnotherapy (McFadden: no

mention of psychiatric issues at all except for lobotomy and,
in the fifth, 1961 edition, hypnosis; Kelly; Kenny: lobotomy
and hypnosis only in the 1st, 1952 edition, and a few paragraphs on other less physical treatments in the 1962 edition;
Healy; O'Donnell). We have also seen instances in which authors have considered their discussion of mental health questions to be explicitly extrinsic to their work (Healy: the
doctor might have to refer a patient to a psychiatrist; La
Rochelle and Fink: this is outside our scope, but the doctor
might meet a mentally ill patient). Thus these issues, even
when they are included briefly in the discussion, are clearly
of secondary importance.

In a somewhat similar manner, and also in keeping with
the emphasis on topics of interest to the professional medical practitioner, questions of strictly sexual ethics, that
is, those topics included in many pastoral medicine works as
an intrinsic and central part of that discipline, but which
have little direct significance for medical practice, such
as the canonical regulations of marriage (especially the non-
medical ones), extra-marital sex, homosexuality, masturbation, sexual thoughts, etc., came to occupy a generally secondary place in North American medical ethics. We have noted
some works in which these issues continued to receive considerable discussion: the works written in North America
which resemble European pastoral medicine to a greater extent
than do the majority of North American texts (in the early
years Sanford, O'Malley and Walsh, and Medicus; in the latter
period Paquin and Good and Kelly). But by far the greater
number of authors restrict topics of this kind to a secondary place or eliminate them altogether (Klarmann's first
edition, Bourke, Burke, Finney, Trudel, La Rochelle and Fink,
McFadden, Kelly, Kenny, Healy, and Finney and O'Brien).

This is not to say, however, that all discussion of sex-
ually connected topics could be avoided. Some presentation
of sexual ethical norms was required in the texts since

often these were the norms which were applied to medical procedures concerning reproduction, such as artificial insemination, sterility testing, contraception, and sterilization.
Thus sexual ethics in general was often discussed as part of
the background needed for understanding the moral solutions
given for more directly medical ethical dilemmas. We have
seen authors who explicitly give this rationale for including
a discussion of sexual ethics (McFadden, Kenny, and
O'Donnell).

A second reason often suggested for the inclusion of
topics connected with sexuality is that the physician might
need a knowledge of sexual ethics in order to correctly counsel his patients. As the one to whom people turn for bodily
health, the physician is often questioned about sexual behavior, and, since this involves questions of morality, his
counselling cannot be limited to merely medical data. In
this context questions of strictly sexual ethics, such as
homosexuality, pre-marital sex, masturbation apart from the
context of sterility testing, and some of the canonical and
sacramental aspects of marriage are sometimes discussed because they pertain to the physician's professional activity
as a counsellor. We have noted authors who give this explicitly as a reason for treating topics of this kind (Coppens, Klarmann, Kelly, Kenny, Healy, and O'Donnell).

The practical needs of medical personnel also influenced
the inclusion of the more strictly "religious" issues in the
literature. Since there were ethical questions traditionally
connected with sacramental administration, and with the spiritual care of Catholics and non-Catholics, and since nurses,
doctors, and hospital chaplains would often encounter such
situations, these "religious" problems were treated. They
were often formally distinguished from the more strictly
"ethical" issues, however. We have noted here the influence
of the "Ethical and Religious Directives for Catholic

Hospitals."

The question is probably unanswerable as to exactly how much the older organizational rubrics of the general moral manuals and the manuals of pastoral medicine influenced later works in medical ethics. We have seen that one of those rubrics, the special section concerned with the vocation of the physician, served to single out the medical practitioner as a subject for special moral analysis. In so doing it was of clear significance in the emergence of medical ethics as a separate discipline. And the topics discussed by medical ethicists reflected precisely this criterion of selection: the professional activity of medical personnel. With respect to the other rubrics of the general moral manuals, the answer is less clear. North American authors naturally tended to group similar topics together. Thus issues pertaining to life might be gathered in one section, as might issues pertaining to reproduction, "religious" or sacramental issues, or issues not fitting into any of these categories but still of importance to professional medical practice, such as professional secrets, fees, ghost surgery, etc. These groupings recall to some extent the earlier organizational rubrics of the manuals, where the fifth commandment (life questions), the sixth and ninth commandments (sex questions), the sacraments (marriage questions and other sacramental issues), and the special section on the obligations of physicians were the ordering principles. It is also true that these later writers were conversant with the moral manuals and had studied according to their rubrics. Some influence must be assumed. But the formal definitions of purpose as well as the formats used in the later texts of medical ethics suggest a far greater influence of the pragmatic professional activity of medical personnel as the primary principle of selection. The one older rubric from the manuals which clearly exerted influence was the special section devoted to the

physician. What the doctor did had become the primary principle of selection. As we have seen in our survey, there
was no one standard method of grouping topics. Some authors
followed the life history from birth to death. Others
grouped according to various rights or goods. Many grouped
minor topics together, and treated major issues separately.
Some followed no logical order. Though the authors may have
read the moral manuals, they worked with physicians and
taught in hospitals and medical and nursing schools. By the
end of the period of emergence, the definition of medical
ethics was basically pragmatic. *Medical Ethics* was the moral theological investigation of the ethical issues connected
with the professional practice of medical personnel.

We have now completed our study of what is meant by the
ethical issues of medical practice. For an analysis of what
is meant by moral theological in this context, we turn to
the next three chapters. There we will discuss at length
the development and application of two generally pervasive
methodological modalities, namely physicalism and ecclesiastical positivism, both of which proved to be apt vehicles
for arriving at universal "scientific" solutions to medical
ethical questions. These approaches were especially adapted
for analyzing just those questions which we have seen to be
the core topics in the material definition of the discipline:
the physical surgical interventions which formed such a large
part of the physician's professional practice. They also
enabled the medical ethicist to develop and defend a scientific, universally applicable methodology which paralleled
the scientific method used by the modern medical profession.
Thus the definition of the discipline, which has been the
subject of this chapter, and its theological methodology,
which is the subject of the next, are both best understood
in the context of the growth of modern professional medicine.

CHAPTER THREE
INTRODUCTION TO THE THEOLOGICAL
METHODOLOGY OF THE DISCIPLINE

The issues we investigated in the previous chapter, the
name and definition of the discipline, were methodological
ones to the extent that they concerned structure and process
rather than data and conclusions. As we have seen, the authors used some sort of method in adopting names and formal
definitions for the field, and in choosing certain topics
and rejecting others. To this extent, the previous chapter
dealt with "methodological" questions. In the present section of our study (the next three chapters), we will be
speaking of questions of theological methodology in a
stricter sense of the term. We are interested in how theological principles, norms, and statements were applied to
medical ethical issues. Were any theological principles of
primary importance in medical ethics? *How* were principles
derived from theological tradition applied to the ethical
problems which constituted the topical array of medical ethics? Were there any general trends which might be said to
have constituted the *modality* or *modalities* according to
which such application was generally made? Like the last
chapter, these next three will examine the literature of the
period from 1900 to 1960, the period which saw the emergence
of Roman Catholic medical ethics as an established discipline in North America. This present chapter will introduce
the basic issues. Chapter four will study the methodology
of the discipline from 1900 to 1940, and chapter five will
continue from 1940 to 1960.

1. Two Dominant Modalities: Physicalism and Ecclesiastical
        Positivism

It is the thesis of this section that the application
of theological principles to medical ethical issues was determined largely by the operative influences of two pervasive and dominant theological ethical approaches. These approaches were physicalism and ecclesiastical positivism.
They served as determining modalities of application for
theological arguments. Other theological principles were
not applied directly to the issues, as themselves determinative of the rightness or wrongness of the medical procedures
in question, but were rather used as *supportive* of conclusions reached according to these two modalities of application.

As we survey the literature of the emergent (pre-Vatican II) period, we will note the presence of both of these
modalities. The history of Roman Catholic medical ethics in
North America discloses a gradual shift of emphasis from
physicalism to ecclesiastical positivism during the papacy
of Pius XII (from about 1940 to 1960). The Second Vatican
Council marks the beginning of a far more radical shift away
from both these modalities to a more personalistic application of theological traditions to the question of the meaning of human life. Chapters three, four, and five will discuss the modalities of the emergent period (1900-1960).
Chapter six will include a brief critique of these modalities based on the personalist approach of medical ethics of
the last ten to fifteen years.

While a detailed discussion of the two methodological
modalities (physicalism and ecclesiastical positivism) may
await the study of the period in which each achieves paramount place, it is necessary here to present a brief definition of each. This will be helpful to the reader in following the sometimes complex argument of our subsequent

analysis. In addition, since the modalities are not at all
totally exclusive of one another, and since the development
of the discipline is not such that any one modality arises
anew at a particular point in time, such definition is
needed before proceeding further. Our present introduction
will be brief, however, since more detailed discussions will
be presented later.

By physicalism is meant that modality of application of
theological principles whereby the emphasis is placed on the
physical *finis operis, objectum,* or actual physical proper-
ties, motions, and goals of the action under consideration.
Within a static natural law understanding of human nature,
the ethical judgments arrived at are considered to be universally applicable to all situations involving the same
physical act. Physicalist criteria are used to determine
the *finis operis* (the "end" of the "act-in-itself") or the
objectum, and the resulting judgment is programmed into the
double effect principle which serves as a framework for
making moral judgments.[1]

By ecclesiastical positivism is meant a specific kind
of theological voluntarism or metaethical supernatural absolutism. It is that modality of application of theological
principles whereby the emphasis is placed on God's will
(theological voluntarism in its ethical ramifications) as
that divine will is seen to be expressed in a specific
source of revelation, the authoritative pronouncements and
interpretations of the Roman Catholic magisterium. An action is right or wrong according to its acceptability to
this authority. We will discover that ecclesiastical positivism was seldom adopted as a *theoretical* modality of application, but that it served in fact as the often primary

---

[1]A more detailed analysis is presented in part one of
chapter four.

practical methodological modality in the discipline.[2]

The approaches to theological methodology which we have
chosen to call modalities of application of theological
principles could be called, and have been called, themselves
theological principles. We would not disagree with this
judgment. The principle of double effect, which, as we will
see, serves as a framework for the application of physicalist criteria, has traditionally been known as a principle of
moral theology. Theological voluntarism, of which practical
ecclesiastical positivism is a species, is certainly a theological principle, and carries with it ancillary principles
and arguments from apologetics and ecclesiology, and from
the fundamental theology of faith and revelation.

Nonetheless, for our purposes in describing the theological methodology of our discipline, we have decided to view
these approaches as modalities of application within which
other theological principles are applied and *to which these
latter are subordinated*. A theologically critical analysis
of the methodological modalities of medical ethics reveals
that these theological modalities are in fact super-princi-
ples, or guiding frameworks within which other theological
norms and statements are applied.

2. Sovereignty and Suffering: Two Subordinate Principles

What, then, are these "other theological principles"?
No complete listing would be possible. Nor would such an
attempt be helpful. Various authors have tried to produce
lists of principles, and we will have occasion to mention
some of them. The lists are generally arbitrary, and the
individual items might have been reduced to one another, or
further subdivided and distinguished. Though a number of
principles or theological statements might thus be distin-

---

[2]A more detailed analysis is given in part one of chapter five.

guished as relevant to medical ethics, two such principles
or sets of principles are central. The first set of principles concerns God's dominion over human life, and purports
to judge concerning the obligation of men and women, faced
with various ethical dilemmas, to respect God's sovereignty.
The second principle or set of principles concerns the redemptive meaning of suffering, and purports to judge concerning one's obligation to join one's own suffering love
to the redemptive sacrificial love of Jesus.

Though these theological principles may be formally
distinguished for purposes of discussion and analysis, they
are not in fact separate, but rather two aspects of one central theological axis: what is one's relationship to the
creator? To what extent is one a creature; to what extent
a co-creator, or at least a co-agent with God? The two
principles we have defined as central to medical ethics both
can be placed in the context of this axis. Is it God's will
that we try to "create a better world," that we join with
our creator as co-sovereigns over life, that we eliminate
suffering (and even death) to the extent that we can? Or is
it rather God's will that we respect the sovereignty of God
alone, that we accept our position in resignation to God's
will, realizing that our suffering love is redemptive if ac-
tively joined to the redemptive suffering of Jesus? What
are the relative weights of one's co-creativity and creatureliness in ethical application? When does an emphasis on
co-active powers lead to blasphemy; when does an emphasis on
creatureliness lead to fatalism and despair?

From the point of view of speculative or mystical theology, the very formulations we have used for presenting
this central axis and these theological principles imply an
either-or dichotomy which does not consider sufficiently the
dimension of paradox, mystery, and myth inherent in these
central truths. Clearly one is both creature and co-agent
with God. Suffering is an essentially mysterious reality in

human life, and no one-dimensional answer to the question of
the presence of evil in God's creation has ever been satisfactory. An attempt to probe the theological meaning of
these issues in and for themselves would, however, be far
beyond the scope of our study. We must be content here to
describe these theological principles, not in their mystical,
spiritual, ascetical, and mysterious dimensions, but merely
in their medical ethical applications during the period of
emergence of our discipline, for such is our task.

In the emerging (pre-Vatican II) phase of Roman Catholic medical ethics in North America, the two "theological
principles" we have mentioned, namely the principle of God's
sovereignty over life and the principle of the redemptive
value of suffering, find ethical application to the rightness and wrongness of medical procedures *not* (at least not
generally) in their dimension of mystery, but rather as motivating principles or ancillary arguments used to support
ethical conclusions reached in accordance with the dominant
methodological modality (physicalism and/or ecclesiastical
positivism). As we will discover, therefore, the application of these theological principles is most often not an
independent or direct one, but rather depends on prior[3] ethical decisions made according to the framework modalities we
have mentioned. In chapters four and five we will demonstrate and describe this process.

In the final chapter we will note that with the emergence of Christian personalism[4] in medical ethics after

---

[3]The priority here is one of logical primacy and not
necessarily of temporal priority.

[4]By personalism is meant an approach whereby the emphasis is placed on the entire personal complexus of the act in
its human dimensions and circumstances. In contradistinc-
tion to the modalities which preceded it (physicalism and
ecclesiastical positivism), personalism does not limit its

Vatican II, a more direct application of the principles of
sovereignty, co-agency, and suffering becomes possible. In
contemporary Catholic medical ethics these principles are
more often used to suggest answers to the "bio-significance"
question: what is the meaning of human life? In this context, the dimensions of mystery we have mentioned play a
more significant and direct role.

3. The Use of Scripture

In the course of our methodological survey of the literature we will have occasion to note the use of Scripture
in the process of ethical argumentation. It is difficult to
situate precisely the exact significance of the Scriptures
in this process. Generally the Scriptures are used in various ways as ancillary proofs of the decisions reached according to the dominant modality framework. For example,
Scriptural texts may be used to support one or another of
the theological principles we have mentioned, to demonstrate
God's dominion over life or the redemptive value of suffering. In this context the Bible becomes a source for the
theological principles which are themselves subordinate, in
actual medical ethical application, to the dominant ethical
approaches of physicalism and ecclesiastical positivism. Or
Scripture may be used to prove the divine authority of the
Roman Catholic magisterium, and thus to serve as a theological defense of ecclesiastical positivism. Finally, in some

---

scope to the physical or biological qualities of the action,
but rather extends its purview to psychological, social, and
spiritual dimensions. It does not emphasize one or several
specifically defineable sources of revelation, but rather insists on a wider (theoretically on the "total") spectrum of
human experience, which includes, but is not limited to and
often does not emphasize, either Scriptural or magisterial
ethical judgments. A more detailed analysis will be given
in the final chapter as part of our critique of the methodology of Catholic medical ethics in its emergent phase.

cases Scriptural quotations are used in direct application
to immediate medical ethical issues. Even here, however,
the use of Scriptural arguments is generally of secondary
importance.

4. Theology and Natural Ethics

We have stated that the purpose of these chapters is to
describe the practical operative significance of "theological" principles. Yet our methodology does not permit us to
give any *a priori* answer to the highly problematic question
as to the exact formal and material definition of "theology"
itself. Such a discussion is beyond our task. It must be
left to speculative fundamental theology. For our purposes
we must be content to recognize that Roman Catholic medical
ethicists wrote from within the complex tradition of Catholic moral theology-philosophy, and to describe and analyze
the primary methodological modalities which they in fact
utilized. Any attempt to posit a clear line of division
within areas of or approaches to medical ethics, defining
some as "theological" and others as "philosophical" requires
a definition of theology which would be problematic at best,
and which would not in any case be justified by the factual
development of the discipline. A brief discussion of some
of the issues involved will clarify this point.

Within Roman Catholic moral thought the problem of distinguishing moral theology from philosophical ethics was
traditionally "solved" by defining "ethics" or moral philosophy as the natural science of human conduct based on natural human reason without the use of supernatural revelation
or of the doctrinal teachings of the Church.[5] It included,

---

[5]This distinction is found in many works. See, for an
example, the work in general "natural" ethics by Austin
Fagothey, *Right and Reason*, 2nd ed., p. 23; 4th ed., p. 4.

however, data from "natural" theology (theodicy) such as
data concerning one's natural relationship to God as
creator and final end. Moral theology added direct data
from the Christian Scriptures and from the doctrinal tradition of the Church. It dealt not only with one's "natural"
end but with one's supernaturally revealed end: salvation in
and through Christ. This distinction was, however, more
nominal than substantial. The conclusions reached in "natural" theology were consistent with, and had emerged from, a
specifically Christian and Catholic thought universe. The
conclusions arrived at as to the ethical rightness and wrongness of human actions were almost always the same as those
arrived at by scholars who explicitly claimed to be moral
theologians. And the methods of argumentation were generally quite similar. Manuals of moral theology and texts in
ethics both argued from the same rational bases.[6] And both
in fact used the decisions of the magisterium as authoritative guarantees of conclusions thus arrived at, though the
texts in natural ethics did so with less emphasis and often
with more subtlety.[7]

Within Roman Catholic medical ethical literature in
North America during the period of our study, we have noted
and will note again works which make the traditional dis-

For a brief statement of the traditional distinction, without any acknowledgment of the difficulties involved, see
Ramirez, "Moral Theology," pp. 1115-1116.

[6]The principle of double effect, for example, whose
great importance we will demonstrate in the next chapter,
served to provide the same answers for the "ethicists" as
for the moral theologians.

[7]We have already noted such a use in Fagothey concerning birth control, where the author changed his opinion on
the issue in accord with the pronouncements of the magisterium (see above, pp. 40-41, n. 89).

tinction between moral theology and natural ethics.[8] Some
of these works imply that their process of argumentation is
to be primarily "ethical" or "natural." They insist that
the conclusions reached are binding on all according to
natural law, and are not based on religious doctrines peculiar to Catholics or even to Christians. Yet unlike some of
the texts in general ethics, none of the major works in
Catholic medical ethics which we are studying claim to be
strictly "natural," to avoid completely all appeal to specifically Christian teaching and all mention of specifically
religious issues.[9] Some works, of course, claim explicitly
to be works in moral theology.[10] In these, much appeal is
made to natural, rational processes of argumentation, along
with specific appeal to Christian teaching and to Church
pronouncements.

     With respect to the methodological modalities and the-
ological principles themselves, we have made note of two
specific principles of theology which would be accepted as
"theological" without much dispute: the principle concerning
God's dominion over life and the principle of redemptive
suffering. We have also mentioned the use of Scripture in
medical ethics. These three issues concern one's relationship with God rather directly, and their theological relevance is apparent. Of the two modalities of application of
theological principles dominant during the period of our
study, that of ecclesiastical positivism would probably be

---

     [8]For example, see McFadden, *Medical Ethics*, any edition,
p. 2.

     [9]See McFadden, *Medical Ethics*, 2nd ed., p. 6; 5th ed.,
pp. 5-6.

     [10]For example, see O'Donnell, *Morals in Medicine*, 1st.
ed., p. xv; 2nd ed., p. xix; Paquin, *Morale et médecine,*
p. 11.

accepted as a "theological" principle.[11] It might be disputed as to whether or not the approach is correct theology,
or "good" theology, or faithful to the message of Christ,
but it would generally be considered to belong within the
realm of theological debate. The other modality is more
problematic. What is "theological" about the principle of
double effect or about the physicalist modality of application? Is not this rather a principle of "natural" or philosophical ethics?

It is impossible to give a totally satisfactory answer
to this question. From an *a priori* perspective, one might
argue for a strict definition of theology, and relegate
physicalism, the double effect principle, and, indeed, many
other processes of ethical argumentation found in the manuals and textbooks of moral theology to the area of non-theological discourse. Or one might more accurately argue that

---

[11]Though it is, as we have noted, also operative even
in the general ethics texts which claim to proceed solely
from natural reason. The argument that in these works the
authoritative guarantee of the magisterium is merely a natural one, guaranteeing what everyone knows anyway (or ought
to know) from natural reason, fails to satisfy. When the
more subtle points of the natural law require authoritative
pronouncements of a Church body in order to be known, and
when ethicists switch arguments, not according to their own
reasoning process, but in accord with such pronouncements,
it is hard to accept the notion that ecclesiastical positivism in such cases can be purely "natural." It is clear
that directly theological issues are involved, such as the
theological question of infallibility, Christ's intentions
concerning his Church, the action of the Spirit, etc. It is
quite possible, of course, that the same conclusion "ought"
to be reached by all philosophers. But when the direct
authority of the Church is brought to bear, and when the
conclusion reached is in fact arrived at and formulated in
accord with this authority and primarily on account of this
authority, it is no longer possible to claim that merely
"natural" reasoning processes are operative. For a discussion, see St. John-Stevas, *Life, Death and the Law*, pp. 29-
30; Curran, "Natural Law and the Teaching Authority of the
Church," p. 82.

human reason and emotion and experience are indeed theologically relevant when presented within the context of an ethic
open to issues of human relationship to God. All theology
must of necessity rely on "human" or "natural" factors. Indeed, the attempt at such a dichotomy in the first place is
highly problematic. In any case, our present methodology
does not permit any such *a priori* answers. Our task is to
describe what were indeed the modalities of argumentation of
medical ethics used by Roman Catholic moralists. We shall
discover the pervasive importance of physicalism as a modality of application of theological principles. In the final
chapter we will have occasion to argue that both the modality of physicalism and the modality of ecclesiastical positivism hindered the theologically correct application of the
theological principles of God's dominion and of redemptive
suffering. We shall argue that whereas these principles
ought to have been applied in their dimension of theological
mystery, the influence of the two modalities of application
to which they were generally subordinated made such a theologically correct application impossible. But this is not
the same as arguing that such modalities, or the use of human reason in general, are non-theological.

The relationship between natural ethics and supernatural moral theology is thus problematic. The problem is part
of the wider issue, surely never solved, of the relationship
between philosophy and theology, reason and revelation, nature and grace. A study of this relationship cannot be our
task here. Our purpose is rather to investigate the methodology of Roman Catholic medical ethics, a methodology which,
as we have already seen, emerged from a theological thought
system and from sources in moral theology and pastoral medicine. Despite the nominal distinctions often made between
ethics and moral theology, the fact is that Roman Catholic
moral thought in general, and medical ethics in particular,

emerged from a philosophical-theological complexus where any
satisfactory substantive dichotomies are impossible. It is
this complexus which has historically constituted the discipline known as "moral theology," and it is in this sense
that we refer to "theological" methodology in medical ethics.

* * *

It is not necessary, or even desirable, to survey again
in these chapters the entire body of literature which the
previous chapter has investigated. Here we are interested
in locating the central methodological modalities and in
showing how theological principles are applied within these
frameworks. Thus our selection of works to be studied will
be according to a different criterion than that used for
chapter two. Here we are interested in investigating those
works which were of importance either in developing one or
another modality or in establishing that modality in general
acceptance. Hence we will examine only those authors whose
methodological analysis was creative as well as those whose
influence was such that through them a methodological approach became widely known and generally accepted. Accordingly only the most influential of the manualists will be
reviewed, along with a few authors whose works in specific
problems of medical ethics were methodologically significant.[12]

Nor will we attempt to show how theological principles
were applied to each and every question in medical ethics.
Our purpose is to demonstrate the general patterns of operation of theological principles. Hence it will be our task
to select the more important paradigmatic examples from the
literature to show how theological principles were applied.

---

[12]A chronological list of these works is provided at
the end of the Introduction.

Our study of the theological methodology of the discipline will be divided chronologically into two chapters. Chapter four will study the earlier works, those written from approximately 1900 to 1940. In chapter five, we will study the works written during and immediately after the papacy of Pius XII, who was elected pope on March 2, 1939, and died on October 9, 1958. We will show that the earlier works in medical ethics in North America disclose an emphasis on as well as a development of the physicalist modality of application of theological principles, whereas the later works demonstrate a clear and significant increase in emphasis on the role of the Church's magisterium in legislating answers to medical ethical dilemmas (the modality of ecclesiastical positivism). There is no chronological dichotomy between these two methodological modalities. The role of the magisterium is apparent and significant in the earlier period (and had been in previous centuries, as we have seen in our study of the general moral theological tradition and of pastoral medicine), and does not appear for the first time in the 1940's. Nor does the central significance of the physicalist modality cease in the later period. Rather there is, as we shall see, a gradual shift in the relative importance of these two approaches, so that ecclesiastical positivism takes on a more and more explicit and direct significance in the medical ethics of the 1940's and 1950's. As a result, the critical analysis and development of physicalism is set more and more within the positivist framework, and it is the latter which achieves dominant place.

Each of the two chapters will begin with a somewhat detailed systematic description of the methodological modality which typifies that period. Thus we turn now to a description of physicalism, and will begin chapter five with an analysis of ecclesiastical positivism. Following these systematic descriptions, each chapter will then demonstrate, by

an analysis of the literature of its respective period, the
presence and significance of the approaches as modalities of
application of theological principles to medical ethical
issues.

CHAPTER FOUR

EARLY WORKS (1897-1940): THE DEVELOPMENT OF PHYSICALISM

The purpose of this chapter is to investigate the theological methodology of Roman Catholic medical ethics in
North America from its beginnings around the turn of the
century up through the 1930's, the period during which physicalism was the dominant methodological approach. We will
begin with a lengthy and detailed systematic analysis of
physicalism and then turn to the literature to describe how
this modality developed and operated in the medical ethics
of the period.

Part One

Physicalism in the Double Effect Framework

The "physicalism" of which we speak as a modality of
application of theological principles to medical ethical issues refers to an emphasis on the specifically physical and
biological aspects of actions and their consequences. This
emphasis is dominant to the neglect of other aspects present
in human actions, such as the social, spiritual, relational,
and psychological components of human behavior.

"Physicalism" defies precise definition. Contemporary
moral theologians suggest various strands of influence which
led to it, as well as various nuances which compose it.[1]
Physicalism is based partly on a static and essentialist definition of human nature. Human nature for the scholastics

---

[1]See especially two important analytical articles by
Charles Curran: "Absolute Norms and Medical Ethics," and
"Natural Law and Contemporary Moral Theology."

was essentially changeless, and change was accidental to the
underlying substantial form. In this classic world view
historical processes and influences were of secondary importance, both epistemologically and psychologically.[2] In addition, scholastic rational psychology saw man in terms of
distinct faculties, each created by God with a particular
goal or purpose, defined in terms of the physical structure
of the faculty. Often the purpose of a faculty or of a
human behavior was identified with the physical purpose of
the similar faculty or behavior as found in sub-human
animals.[3] Within this static natural law[4] understanding
of human nature, ethical judgments were arrived at according
to physicalist criteria and were considered universally
applicable to all cases involving the same physical action.

---

[2] See Curran, "Natural Law," esp. pp. 116-120, 130-136.

[3] The result of the influence of Ulpian on Thomas and on
later scholastics and manualists. See Curran, "Absolute
Norms and Medical Ethics," pp. 115-120; "Natural Law and Contemporary Moral Theology," pp. 105-110; *Medicine and Morals,*
pp. 8-13.

[4] Natural law theory need not be static. In its widest
and most acceptable sense, the natural law refers to that
law "written in men's hearts" (Rom. 2:15), to the moral
sense inherent in created man. It need not assume a static
or essentialist picture of human nature. It need not ignore
cultural and social variations, nor assume the total and exact repeatability of human situations according to physical
criteria. It need not assume that what is "natural" for man
is that which is common to him and sub-human nature (Ulpian-
ism). Nonetheless, there is no doubt that natural law theory in the general Roman Catholic tradition has been, until
recently, based on a "nature" which was static, in that "nature" was seen to transcend any specific incarnation in the
stages of salvation history, to be independent of any historical situatedness. Knowledge of the "natural law" in this
sense presupposed an extra-temporal standpoint from which to
acquire truth concerning historical man and to evaluate ethical behavior. In his excellent and important work on the
natural law, Josef Fuchs puts it this way: "In Catholic theology the natural law concept referring to nature in general
or nature taken absolutely as an ultimate foundation, posses-
ses qualities that have always been attributed to natural
law. It is valid for every salvation situation and always

For our purposes in demonstrating the significance of
physicalism as a modality of application for theological
principles in medical ethics, a description of the actual
operation of physicalism will be sufficient. We will attempt no detailed history of the various threads which led
to and constituted this multifaceted phenomenon. In the
context of this chapter, the best way to demonstrate the
operational significance of physicalism as well as to present a description of it in its ethical implications is to
describe it as it actually functioned within its ethical
framework: the principle of double effect. It was the double effect framework which served as the organizing structure for the application of physicalist criteria to medical
ethical topics. Double effect made it possible to make
clear linear distinctions between right and wrong actions
using physicalist criteria. It was precisely the use of a
physicalistically restricted application of double effect

---

has an actual validity and a possibility of being applied.
It has these attributes because it is related to these absolute elements and is not conditioned by the particular situation" (Fuchs, *Natural Law,* p. 51). It is a moot point
whether or not the concept "natural law" is so thoroughly
tied to an extra-temporal standpoint of this type that it
becomes simply misleading to use it in an historically
grounded theological ethic. Personally, I would argue for
its usefulness as emphasizing a metaethically empirical ethic rather than one metaethically rationalist, intuitionist,
or supernaturalist. In theological ethics the notion "natural law" can, if delivered from its abstract staticism, imply a creatively balanced, if tension-filled, position between a reductionist secular humanism with no room for
transcendence or for the sovereignty of God and a radically
supernaturalist ethic with no room for human reason, where
supernatural revelation in Scripture is seen as the sole
source of ethical knowledge (see Curran, "Natural Law and
Contemporary Moral Theology," pp. 98-102, 138-139; Curran,
"Natural Law and Moral Theology," pp. 171 ff.; Fuchs, *Natural Law,* pp. 42-52). For the classic criticism of extra-
temporal standpoints, see Karl Mannheim's work in the sociology of knowledge, especially Mannheim, "The Problem of a
Sociology of Knowledge," pp. 78-103.

in medical ethical areas (and in areas of sexual ethics)
which distinguished these areas methodologically from Catholic social ethics. The clear distinctions made possible by
the use of this modality were not present in social ethical
areas. Hence Catholic medical (and sexual) ethics was able
to achieve a casuistic precision never found in other areas
of Catholic moral theology.

In the pages which follow, we will first present the
principle of double effect and describe and analyze its four
conditions, showing their relationship to physicalism. We
will then argue that double effect is better seen as a general framework than as one principle among others. We will
conclude with a brief series of examples of how double effect physicalism was applied to medical ethical topics.

1. The Double Effect Principle and Physicalism

The principle of double effect,[5] often called the principle of the indirect voluntary or the *voluntarium in causa*,[6]

---

[5]For further analysis and description of the double effect principle and of the history of its development, see
Kramer, *The Indirect Voluntary*; Mangan, "An Historical Analysis of the Principle of Double Effect"; Michel, "Volontaire";
Ghoos, "L'Acte à double effet"; Knauer, "The Hermeneutic
Function of the Principle of Double Effect"; Connell, "Double Effect"; Janssens, "Ontic Evil"; Curran, "The Principle
of Double Effect."

[6]The various wordings denote no substantive differences.
Since one of the effects of the act with double effects (the
evil effect or effects) must be willed only indirectly, or
willed "negatively," or willed inasmuch as it is necessarily
caused by the act in question, the principle can be referred
to in any of these ways. Practically, the various formulations are identical (Michel, "Volontaire," col. 3306). For
an analysis of the causal process involved, see Kramer, *The
Indirect Voluntary,* esp. pp. 53-63. The identical meaning of
the various formulations seems not to have been present in
Thomas, but this is a problem beyond our own task. (For a
critique of Kramer on this point, see Ghoos, "L'Acte à double
effet," p. 31.)

can be applied to any morally problematic act (or any act
at all, for that matter[7]) which results in both good and bad
effects. "Good" and "bad" here refer to pre-moral, non-moral, physical, or "ontic" evil, not to moral evil.[8] The

---

[7]All acts of human beings, since they are by definition
temporally and spacially limited and limiting, must of necessity cause some "bad" effects in the ontic sense. The bril-
liant analysis of the relationship between moral and ontic
evil by Louis Janssens demonstrates this conclusively. Janssens refers (and consistently did so in his classes at
Louvain, which I was fortunate to attend) to the simple case
of man who goes for a walk. He may intend recreation, exercise, even an act of charity, but he must of necessity wear
out the soles of his shoes (Janssens, "Ontic Evil," p. 136).
Clearly there are more important evils in life than wearing
out shoe soles, and this is hardly a morally problematic
case. But moral dilemmas are in fact moral dilemmas because
human acts often cause harm as well as benefit. If one were
obliged to avoid any and all activity which would bring
about some deleterious effects to others, however remote,
human action would be impossible. In this sense the double
effect principle is for Janssens the basic paradigm for all
moral judgment.

[8]Janssens uses "ontic evil" to distinguish the concept
both from moral evil (an evil which one has a moral obligation to avoid) and from physical evil (a harm which affects
the physical health of society or individual). "Ontic evil"
includes psychological and spiritual harms as well as physical damage (Janssens, "Ontic Evil," p. 133). Richard
McCormick prefers the term "nonmoral" (McCormick, "Notes,"
1976, pp. 76-78; also "Notes," 1975, p. 90). In some cases
of application of double effect, such as in questions of
material versus formal scandal, and in questions of cooperation in evil actions, the evil effect might be called morally evil, but only in the sense that another agent might be
led to perform an immoral action or helped in its perform-
ance. The evil effect remains an "ontic" or pre-moral evil
with respect to the act which is itself analyzed by the double effect. That is, if the conditions of double effect apply, the human act under analysis does not bring about moral
evil in the sense that this evil must be avoided by the
agent, who would otherwise act immorally. The "ontic evil"
caused by the action may nonetheless be or bring about moral
evil on the part of another agent within the context of
another human act. Thus, for example, a nurse may cooperate

moral question is whether or not one may licitly (morally)
perform an action from which two effects or sets of effects
flow, some of them "ontically" good, others "ontically" evil.

In itself the double effect principle is not limited to
the modality of physicalism. Today's moralists maintain it.
Some argue that it is the central principle of all morality.[9]
In its original form in Thomas Aquinas, it is not physicalistically restricted.[10] Nonetheless, as developed by the
moralists after Thomas, the double effect principle served
as framework for the application of physicalism.[11]

The principle, as formulated by the moral manuals[12] and

"indirectly" in an immoral operation provided that the four
conditions of double effect are met, even though another
agent (the physician who is the principle agent) is presumably committing an immoral act. (See McFadden, *Medical Ethics*, 2nd ed., pp. 307-308.) This will all become clearer in
the course of the present section.

[9]For example, Knauer, "The Hermeneutic Function of the
Principle of Double Effect," p. 132.

[10]As proved by Janssens, "Ontic Evil." See also McCormick, "Notes," 1975, pp. 89-92; Curran, "The Principle of
Double Effect," pp. 174-182.

[11]Our point in this present chapter is that the double
effect principle was applied in a limited fashion. As we
shall see, physicalist criteria were of paramount importance,
and the double effect principle, in its four-condition formulation, provided the framework for the application of those
criteria. Nonetheless, there is a genius in the principle
of double effect, once it is released from this physicalist
restriction. Inasmuch as it contains within it both a deontological and a consequentialist ethic, it has a high potential as a framework for doing effective ethics.

[12]The controversy surrounding the history of the double
effect framework is of great significance in moral theology.
As we will note in the final chapter, contemporary scholars
reject the way in which the manualists developed the principle. The four-condition principle of double effect is a
product of 16th and 17th century development, and was finally formulated in its modern version by Jean Pierre Gury in

as found in our medical ethics texts, contains four conditions which must be met if an action which results in both
good and bad effects is to be morally lawful. Though different wordings are used by different authors, and though the
conditions are often found in a different order, the wording
used by Gerald Kelly is typical, and his order is the one
which will best permit analysis.[13] Kelly describes the

---

the mid-19th century (Connell, "Double Effect," p. 1021;
Mangan, "An Intellectual Analysis," pp. 58-61). The premises of the double effect principle can be found in Thomas
Aquinas, in his discussion of self-defense against unjust
aggression (*Summa theologica,* IIa IIae, q. 64, a. 7). Thomas
states: "It must be said that nothing prohibits one act from
having two effects, of which only one is intended, while the
other is apart from the intention. But moral acts obtain
their [moral] species according to that which is intended,
and not according to that which is apart from the intention,
since it is accidental" (*Ibid., in corp.,* trans. mine.
"Dicendum quod nihil prohibet unius actus esse duos effectus,
quorum alter solum sit in intentione, alius vero praeter
intentionem. Morales autem actus recipiunt speciem secundum
id quod intenditur, non autem ab eo quod est praeter intentionem, cum sit per accidens."). For Thomas, the good effect is preservation of life, which is proper according to
the natural law. The evil effect is the death of the assailant, which is apart from the agent's intention. It is not
part of the end of the human act. The act is morally lawful as long as the evil effect does not become an intended
end itself and as long as there is a due proportion between
the act and the intended end (the good effect). For a bril-
liant analysis of double effect in Thomas, including a critique of later physicalist distortions of Thomas' original
insights into human acts, see Janssens, "Ontic Evil." From
this beginning in Thomas, various further applications and
nuances were added. Historians cite Azpilcueta (Navarre),
Cajetan, Medina, Vasquez, Lessius, Sanchez, the Salmanti-
censes, and John of St. Thomas as the 16th and 17th century
scholars who contributed to the development of the principle
(Mangan, "An Historical Analysis," pp. 52-59; Ghoos, "L'Acte
à double effet," pp. 33-51).

[13]The order we choose is that used by many, though not
all moralists. Kelly, McFadden, Kenny, and Hayes, Hayes,
and Kelly, among others, use this order. Another common ar-
rangement (Burke; Finney and O'Brien; Shinners, *The Morality*

principle of double effect as follows:

> The principle of the double effect, as the name itself
> implies, supposes that an action produces two effects.
> One of these effects is something good which may be
> legitimately intended; the other is an evil that may
> not be intended. . . . Granted the presupposition of
> good and evil effects, an action is permitted, accord-
> ing to the principle, if these conditions are ful-
> filled:
> 1) The action, considered by itself and independ-
> ently of its effects, must not be morally evil. . . .
> 2) The evil effect must not be the means of pro-
> ducing the good effect. . . .
> 3) The evil effect is sincerely not intended, but
> merely tolerated. . . .
> 4) There must be a proportionate reason for per-
> forming the action, in spite of its evil consequences.[14]

The first condition requires that the act-in-itself not
be morally evil. Many authors express this positively by
insisting that the act-in-itself be morally good or at least
morally indifferent.[15] If the act considered in itself is
morally evil, then no good effect can make it lawful, since
the end cannot justify the means. Thus, for example, since
masturbation is seen to be morally evil in itself, it can
never be used as a means to obtain semen for sterility test-

---

of Medical Experimentation; Connell, "Double Effect"; and
others) is to reverse the second and third conditions. Some
authors combine the four into three, and O'Donnell adds a
fifth (that there be no alternative way of achieving the
good effect), which most would presume as included in the
original four. Kelly's order, which we will use consistently here, is best for analysis, because, as we shall see, the
first two conditions present the context for application of
physicalist criteria, whereas the two latter conditions are
not physicalistically limited, and are, in fact, maintained
by post-Vatican II moralists.

[14]Kelly, *Medico-Moral Problems,* 1958 ed., pp. 12-14.

[15]Among others, Burke, *Acute Problems*, p. 16; Michel,
"Volontaire," col. 3307; Healy, *Medical Ethics,* p. 98;
Shinners, *The Morality of Medical Experimentation*, p. 59;
O'Donnell, *Morals in Medicine,* 2nd ed., p. 44; Connell,
"Double Effect," p. 1020.

ing, despite the good effect of the test.

The second condition is similar to the first, and often reducible to it. It requires that the causal chain from action to effects not include a causal link whereby the bad effect is cause of the good effect. The good effect must proceed with at least as much immediacy from the causing act-in-itself as the evil effect. Some authors use wording which might imply that this is a question of temporal priority.[16] But the condition is best understood as requiring that there be no causal relationship from bad effect to good effect.[17] The reason for this second condition is identical to that suggested for the first: the end cannot justify the means.

The second condition is merely another way of stating the first condition. The choice of which condition to apply to a given case depends on an often arbitrary decision as to how to specify what precisely is the "act-in-itself." What *physical* structure is to be identified with the act? Though authors reach a general consensus concerning this specification in most traditional cases, no totally sufficient reason is given which might provide an *a priori* logical explanation of why an act-in-itself should be specified in this rather than in that precise physical way. The act-in-itself is specified in various ways for various purposes and in various circumstances. We have noted, for example, that in the context of sperm acquisition for sterility testing the act-in-itself is specified as one of masturbation, which

---

[16]McFadden's second condition, for example, is worded this way: "The good effect of the action must precede the evil effect or at least be simultaneous with it" (*Medical Ethics,* 2nd, 3rd, 4th eds., p. 33).

[17]See, e.g., Shinners, *The Morality of Medical Experimentation,* p. 59. Also McFadden's own explanation, *Medical Ethics,* 2nd, 3rd, 4th eds., p. 34.

is itself considered evil. Hence the first condition is
violated when masturbation is used for acquiring sperm testing, since "the action, considered in itself . . . must not
be morally evil." But if the act-in-itself had been specified as one of simple touching of the genitals, then the
pleasurable emission of sperm would follow as first effect,
from which would come in turn the availability of the sperm
for testing. In this case the second condition would be the
one violated, since the good effect (availability of sperm
for testing) would be caused by the bad effect (pleasurable
emission of seed outside of the marriage act).[18] The first
two conditions are thus only two ways of stating the same
principle: the end cannot justify the (*physically specified*)
means.[19]

---

[18] Such a definition of the act-in-itself is not as unlikely as it seems. A parallel case, common in traditional
moral theology, concerns the possibility of orgasms resulting
from touches while bathing. The touches are justified according to the double effect framework. In this case the
act-in-itself is specified precisely as simple touching,
from which come, with equal causal immediacy, both cleanliness and orgasm. Since the cleanliness does not result from
the orgasm, the second condition is met. But if the cleanliness had indeed been the effect of the orgasm (as the availability of sperm for testing is the result of orgasm), then
the good effect would have been caused by the bad effect, and
the second condition violated.

[19] The problem involved in the process of specifying the
act-in-itself is highly complex, and cannot be dealt with
fully here. To some extent, the intention of the agent plays
a role in the specification. This would not be a problem in
itself, since for Thomas and for today's moralists the *finis
operis* (the end of the act-in-itself) can never be specified
apart from the *finis operantis* (the intention of the agent,
or the end of the total human act) (see Janssens, "Ontic
Evil," pp. 116-133). The problem arises when the act-in-
itself, thus specified, is considered *apart* from the end of
the agent. Moralists often confused the two terms, failing
to clarify what it was that they were in fact doing with the
act-in-itself.

Some examples from non-medical ethical areas will be
helpful in clarifying this question. We have already had
occasion to note that the premises for the double effect
principle can be found in Thomas' analysis of killing in
self-defense (see above, pp. 249-250, n. 12). Ironically,
however, once the first two (physicalist) conditions were
added to the double effect principle, it became impossible,
without some incredible verbal quibbling, to apply double
effect to killing in self-defense. What would be the act-in-
itself? It could not be the killing of the assailant, since
then the killing would not be indirect, but direct, and,
presuming direct killing to be evil, killing in self defense
would not be justified. Thus the act-in-itself had to be defined in greater physical specificity as a "thrust" or a
"wound"or as the pulling of a trigger, from which there resulted two equally immediate effects: the death of the assailant (the bad effect) and the stopping of the assailant
(the good effect). Authors insisted that the stopping hap-
pened before the death, that the stopping did not result
from the death, but that the same causal immediacy occurred
in each case. Thus the double effect conditions were met,
and the indirect killing could be justified. Thus, to cite
one author who applies double effect in this case, Michael
Cronin states: "The order of aims in such a case is the following: to strike or wound the aggressor [act-in-itself] in
order to stop his charge, and to save one's own life [good
effect]. If as a result of the blow or wound delivered, the
death of the aggressor [bad effect] should follow as well as
paralysis of movement [good effect], the former consequence
is quite beside the intention of the agent; it in no wise
enters into his aims either as means [by this, Cronin means
to imply the first two conditions of the double effect] or
as end [the third condition]; it is caused by the agent indirectly only" (Cronin, *The Science of Ethics*, II, 100).
Cronin tends to confuse the various conditions here, but he
is at least clear in recognizing that the four-condition
double effect principle requires such specification in order
to be applicable in this case. It should be noted that most
authors, who applied four condition double effect in medical
and sexual ethics, refused to apply it here, insisting that
the killing was direct, and that it could be justified by a
collision of rights. (See Fagothey, *Right and Reason*, 2nd
ed., p. 291; Lohkamp, "Self Defense," p. 61.) One medical
ethicist who explicitly applies double effect to this case
is John Kenny (*Medical Ethics*, 1st ed., p. 103). Kenny, as
we will see, is consistent in using the four-condition double
effect principle for medical ethical application.
A classic case of double effect often given as an example is that of two shipwrecked sailors hanging onto a plank
which can support only one of them. Though no one has the
right to take his own life directly (God alone is sovereign

The third condition simply requires that the agent not intend the bad effect, but merely tolerate it. That is, he must not wish, desire, rejoice in, or aim at the bad effect. Properly understood, this condition is maintained in contemporary versions of the double effect framework. No agent may morally seek even ontic evil, in the sense that it forms part of his purpose or desired intention. If an alternative way of achieving the good effect were available to him, which would eliminate the evil effect, then he would be obliged to use it. If "sincerely intend" is understood in this non-physicalist way, then the third condition of the double effect framework is not intrinsically linked to physicalism, and it has in this connotation been maintained by today's personalist moralists. Theoretically, even for the physicalist medical ethicists, this third condition was independent of the first two. In practice, however, there was constant confusion as to the exact meaning of the "intention" of the agent. Intention was often confused with the physical effect of the act.[20]

---

over life), the sailor may let go the plank as long as he does not intend his own death thereby but merely permits it. The death must not be the cause of the saving of the other sailor's life. Thus the act-in-itself is the letting-go-of-the-plank. To kill himself by other means (a gun, for example) would be a direct act, and the first (or second) condition of double effect would be violated. Similar definitions of acts-in-themselves would be jumping-out-a-window which results in escaping a fire and hitting the ground, setting-an-ammunition-dump-ablaze which results in destroying the arms and in one's own death (but one would never be allowed to take a suicide pill before setting the fire), cutting-out-a-fallopian-tube-with-a-fetus-inside (but never removing the fetus "directly" from the tube), etc. (For other examples and some further discussion, see Van der Poel, "The Principle of Double Effect," pp. 194-195.)

[20]We noted in the last footnote that this notion of intention of the agent is often confused with that of the immediate physical goal of the act, so that the end of the

The fourth condition of the double effect principle is
the most flexible and the least susceptible to physicalist
limitation. It is included both in the traditional four-
condition formulation of double effect and in today's

---

agent is reduced to the "direct" physical result of the act-
in-itself. For this reason, it is often impossible to determine which notion of "intention" a moralist means when he
uses such phrases as "the agent must not directly intend,"
or "the bad effect cannot be the direct object of the intention." Though theoretically the four conditions were to be
understood as independent of one another, often the notion
of intention was reduced to that of physical *finis operis*.
(See, for example, the section cited from Cronin on self-defense, *The Science of Ethics,* pp. 97-103.) Van der Poel
makes this precise point in his critique of physicalist double effect: "Of course, the morality of an act is directly
connected with the human will [third condition], but the human will is so inseparably connected with the individual
(material) result [second condition] that in practical application the material result became the final determinant of
what the agent intended by his action. Therefore in fact
(though not in theory), the physical aspect became the ultimate determinant of the morality of the action" ("The Principle of Double Effect,"   p. 188, italics his).   Janssens has
demonstrated that such a confusion was not present in Thomas,
at least in his general moral section on the human act ("Ontic Evil," pp. 116-133).   The question cannot be solved simply by insisting that the agent's intention includes both
the end and the means. It must still be determined what precisely is the means. If the means is specified in its physical structure alone, then the agent's intention, as it is
directed to the means, is still identified with the physical
structure and goal of the act-in-itself, an identification
not found in Thomas' analysis of human acts. It should also
be noted that a reverse confusion can result in the reduction
of the physical cause and effect chain to a supposed interior
intention of the agent. In this case, effects which would be
seen as "direct" according to the first two conditions might
be changed to "indirect" status if the agent did not "intend"
them. This kind of reduction is unacceptable according to
the physicalist criteria of four-condition double effect,
since the first two conditions are supposed to stand by themselves, and a change in the agent's "intention" does not
alter the physical facts. It does seem to be closer, however, to what Thomas had in mind when he first applied the
notion of "two effects" to self defense (see above, pp. 249-
250, n. 12; pp. 253-254, n. 19).

moral methodologies. The fourth condition requires that
there be a sufficient reason for permitting the evil effect.
The goodness of the good effect must be at least equivalent
to the goodness lost by permitting the bad effect. Today's
personalist moralists state this by speaking of "due proportion,"[21] "commensurate reason,"[22] "the principle of proportionality,"[23] etc.

It is the first two conditions of the double effect
principle which serve as framework for the emphasis given to
physical structures and aspects as a modality of moral
methodology in medical ethics. It is, as we have noted,
these two conditions which require some sort of physical
specification of the act-in-itself. This specification is
often problematic. The first two conditions theoretically
demand a specification of the act-in-itself which must be
made independently of other factors, such as the effects of
the act and the intention of the agent. In some cases this
kind of specification seems to be realized. In others, the
act-in-itself is specified in such a way as to include *certain* aspects of effects, intentions, and circumstances, and
to exclude others. We have already cited examples of this,
and will give further cases in the following pages. The

---

[21]Janssens, "Ontic Evil," p. 144 and generally. Janssens also words it this way: "[The act] must be found without an intrinsic contradiction between the *means* (exterior
act as material element) and the morally good *end* of the in-
ner act of the will (formal element)" (p. 142). That is,
there must be a due proportion between the act, which of
necessity causes some ontic evil, and the morally good end
or effect intended. This is a more intrinsic way of stating
that there must be a due proportion between good and bad
effects.

[22]Knauer, "The Hermeneutic Function," pp. 133, 137, and
generally.

[23]Maguire, *Death by Choice,* pp. 115, 126-129.

exact specification of the act-in-itself, thus highly problematic, becomes crucial for the ultimate moral judgment
made, since the violation of the first two conditions is in
itself sufficient to vitiate the entire act.

In addition to emphasizing the physicalist specification of the act-in-itself, the first two conditions constitute the framework for an emphasis on the physical end or
purpose of each human "faculty" or biological function, considered in itself. This emphasis, as we shall see, finds
its full force only in the reproductive faculty. The primary end of marriage is the physical procreation of children
and each genital act must include a direct and immediate
openness to this purpose. Whereas all other human faculties
may be "directly" thwarted (we will demonstrate this in a
few pages when we speak of mutilation), the reproductive
faculty must always be allowed to attain its primary physical
or biological end. This insistence on the strictly physical
purpose of the reproductive faculty is a result of the influence on Catholic moral theology of the identification of
natural law with the natural functions common to humans and
sub-human animals, an identification made by Ulpian and accepted by Thomas Aquinas.[24]

Both of these aspects of the physicalist modality (the
emphasis on the act-in-itself as physically specified and
the restrictive emphasis on the biological end of the human
reproductive faculty) find their application to medical ethical issues within the double effect principle, especially
in the application of its first and second conditions.

---

[24]Ulpian was a third century Roman lawyer (170?-228)
who distinguished the *jus gentium* (the law proper to men)
from the *jus naturale* (the law common to all animals).
Thomas accepted Ulpian's definition (Curran, "Absolute Norms
and Medical Ethics," p. 116), though he also accepted other
definitions which differed (Curran, "Absolute Norms in Moral
Theology," pp. 76-79).

2. Double Effect as General Framework

We have now completed our description of the traditional double effect principle. We have described and analyzed
its conditions, and have shown how physicalist criteria are
central to their application. We must now approach the question as to whether the double effect principle itself is one
principle among many, applicable in certain cases and irrelevant in others, or whether it is rather better understood
as a framework which was applied to most, if not to all,
medical ethical issues by Catholic moralists. This question
must be asked of the four-condition double effect as we have
described it in traditional Catholic medical ethics. Today's
moralists have reformulated the double effect framework so
that it forms a basic hermeneutic device for "doing ethics."[25]
But can the same general applicability be attributed to the
double effect principle in its traditional four-condition
formulation? In medical ethics it seems that it can be.
The double effect principle was indeed a general framework
applied to most problems of medical ethics.

The choice of whether or not to consider double effect
a framework applicable to most problems in medical ethics
rather than one principle among many, applicable to some few
cases but irrelevant in others, depends on two rather subtle
points. First, is double effect to be said to apply only
when its four conditions are met, or also when one or more
of them are violated? Second, how is the act-in-itself to
be specified?

---

[25]The best example is Knauer, "The Hermeneutic Function
of the Double Effect Principle." Also Janssens, "Ontic
Evil." Other modern moralists propose principles which
could be accepted within a non-physicalist formulation of
double effect (for example, McCormick, "Notes on Moral Theology," 1975, pp. 85-92; Maguire, *Death by Choice,* pp. 77-
129, etc.).

With respect to the first point, many authors insist
that the double effect principle is applicable only in a minority of cases. By this they mean that one of the four
conditions is *not* met in most instances. Hence the double
effect principle cannot be applied, in the sense that the
procedure at issue cannot be justified by the principle.
Here the double effect principle is viewed only in its
strictest sense, as a principle which justifies certain procedures, rather than in its slightly wider sense, as a principle which can be applied both to permit and to proscribe
an action. This narrower view is the more prevalent formal
or technical response to our first question. Substantively,
however, it would seem that a moral principle can rightly be
said to apply to a case both in the positive and in the negative sense. If a procedure is examined in light of the double effect principle, and found wanting because one of its
conditions is violated, it seems that the principle can
rightly be seen as operative in the moral analysis, even
though not applicable in the strictest sense, due to the
failure of the procedure to meet one or more of its conditions.

For example, the removal of a cancerous uterus is traditionally justified by the principle of double effect. The
principle of double effect is said to "apply" to the case,
since the act-in-itself (removal of the uterus) causes with
equal immediacy the good effect (removal of the cancer and
the woman's health) and the bad effect (loss of reproductive
function). Thus the first two conditions are met. Presuming
the woman does not delight in her loss of fertility (third
condition), and accepting the due proportionality of effects
(fourth condition), the procedure is justified and double effect "applies." On the other hand, if a woman discovers that
future childbirth will threaten her life, she is not allowed
to have the procedure performed, and the principle of double

effect is said *not* to apply. In this latter case the act-in-
itself is the same (unless differently specified here so as
to include the sterilization aspect in the act-in-itself--we
have seen a parallel case earlier), but this time the good
effect (the woman's health) is caused by means of the bad effect (loss of reproductive function). The double effect
principle is said *not* to apply, since the second condition
is violated. Substantively, however, the double effect
principle has served as a framework in both analyses. For
our purposes in analyzing the operational significance of
physicalism as a modality of application of theological principles to medical ethics, the double effect can best be seen
as a framework for the operation of physicalist criteria,
both in permitting and in proscribing a procedure.

With respect to the second point, we have already had
occasion to mention the highly problematic nature of specifying the act-in-itself. If the act-in-itself is specified
in a larger fashion, then double effect may be omitted from
the direct analysis of a procedure to which it would be directly applied if the act-in-itself had been specified in a
more restricted sense. Again the example of mutilation, this
time of non-sterilizing mutilation, may be cited. Those authors who attempt to decide the question of mutilation (removal of a leg or arm, lobotomy, etc.) according to the
principle of double effect, directly applied, consider the
act-in-itself in such a way that the mutilation or loss of
function is seen as indirect, a result of the act-in-itself,
which is defined as one of simple cutting or removal.[26]

---

[26]This is an exact parallel to the case of killing in
self-defense which we detailed earlier. (See above, pp. 253-
255, n. 19.) Authors who apply double effect directly to
non-sterilizing mutilations include O'Malley, *The Ethics of
Medical Homicide and Mutilation,* pp. 26-27, and Finney,
Moral Problems, pp. 146-148.

Most authors, however, specify the act-in-itself to be a
direct mutilation, and justify it according to the principle
of totality.[27] The double effect principle does not apply
since the act has been specified in such a way as to include
the mutilating aspect in the act-in-itself. Nonetheless,
double effect applies to similar cases with slightly different act-specifications, and in this sense is still influential in the analysis of the procedure at issue. In addition,
it should be noted that even though the double effect principle is not directly applied by most authors to the case of
non-sterilizing mutilations, the principle which is directly
applied, the principle of totality, does not itself escape
from the physicalist modality. With one highly significant
exception,[28] the principle of totality is applied in a
strictly physicalist manner. Hence, even though the traditional double effect framework is to some extent eliminated,
the modality of physicalism is still operative in this question area.

Our study of the double effect principle as framework
for the application of physicalist criteria suggests four
degrees of operational presence of the principle, ranging
from direct and explicit applicability of double effect phys-

---

[27]A part of the physical body may be mutilated if necessary for the physical health of the whole organism. We will
describe this principle in greater detail later.

[28]The exception was Bert Cunningham's non-physicalist
interpretation of the totality principle as applied to organ
transplantation. His 1944 thesis was the first breakthrough
in this area. Cunningham insisted on allowing organ transplants according to a spiritual interpretation of totality.
We will return to Cunningham's thesis in the next chapter.
It should be noted here that Cunningham never allowed transplantation which would cause a sterilization in the donor.
We will show that this resulted from his willingness to
subordinate his own (non-physicalist) principle to papal
pronouncements, which were explicit as to sterilization.

icalism through to complete rejection of this methodological
modality.

First, in its strictest sense double effect physicalism
is operative when the (physicalist) four-condition principle
is said to permit an action since its conditions are met.
Thus, for example, a cancerous womb may be removed. The
sterilization is indirect, and the double effect principle
applies explicitly.

Second, in a slightly wider sense, double effect physicalism is still substantively operative when a procedure is
rejected precisely because one of the physicalist conditions
of double effect (generally one of the first two) is said to
be violated. Thus, for example, a non-cancerous womb of a
woman whose heart condition makes future pregnancies dangerous may not be removed, precisely because the second condition of the double effect principle is violated. The bad effect causes the good effect.

Third, physicalism is still operative, even though the
four-condition double effect principle is not specifically
involved, when a procedure is analyzed according to another
principle, which latter principle is still physicalistically
limited. Thus, for example, the amputation of a leg is allowed according to the physicalist principle of totality. As
we have noted, however, the double effect principle is still
influential here, in that it is directly applied to other
similar cases which adopt a slightly different act-specifica-
tion.

Fourth, physicalism is no longer operative when an action is analyzed either in accord with a non-physicalist
formulation of double effect,[29] or according to

---

[29]We will return to these contemporary personalist formulations in the final chapter. Generally, as we have noted,
the first two conditions are eliminated, and the last two
kept.

"another"[30] principle, such as the principle of totality,
interpreted without physicalist restrictions. Thus, for example, "direct" or positive euthanasia is said to be permitted if and when there is a proportionate reason.[31] Or, as
another example, the mutilation of an eye for purposes of
transplant is permitted, since the principle of totality is
said to include inter-personal love and is thus not restricted to the one physical body.[32]

3. Examples of Double Effect Physicalism in Medical Ethics

We have now completed our analysis of the double effect
principle as framework for the operation of physicalist criteria in medical ethics. As we have done so, we have included many clarifying examples. In concluding this section,
before turning to the literature itself, a more inclusive
and systematic listing of medical ethical issues to which the

---

[30] I have put "another" in quotes here, since the non-
physicalist formulation of the principle of totality is merely another way of stating the double effect principle in its
non-physicalist, modern formulation. The action can be
posited if there is a commensurate reason for so doing.
Knauer states this explicitly and correctly: "In my opinion
the principle of totality is in reality not distinguishable
from the principle of double effect. The latter bears not
merely on the passive permission of an evil [traditional
four-condition formulation] but relates to the most active
kind of permission; concretely the act itself may cause or
effect the evil; the evil is not direct unless it is willed
without commensurate reason" ("The Hermeneutic Function," p.
150).

[31] Maguire, *Death by Choice*. Maguire's argument is a complex one, but he eliminates any restriction to physicalism,
and argues basically that the central issue is that of proportionate reason (generally, pp. 55-129).

[32] Cunningham, "The Morality of Organic Transplantation."
My purpose in citing this and other examples is not to imply
my personal judgment of approval in each instance, but merely to give examples of non-physicalism in medical ethics.

physicalist modality was applied is in order. We will make
no attempt here to describe the various stages of argumentation among moralists which preceded the final consensus as
to the application of physicalist criteria with the resulting
moral judgment. These stages will be noted when we examine
the literature itself. Not each and every issue considered
by the Roman Catholic medical ethicists we are studying was
explicitly decided by double effect physicalism. But many
of the most important issues were approached from within this
framework.

    The most obvious example, and one of the most consist-
ently important issues in medical ethics, is that of abortion.
Gradually Roman Catholic medical ethicists arrived at a consensus as to the exact application of double effect physicalist criteria, which enabled them to make clear and precise
judgments in each kind of abortion situation. "Direct" abortions were those in which the act-in-itself was the removal
of the fetus "directly" from the body of the woman, or the
"direct" killing of the fetus by any other means while still
within the mother's body. These acts were never permitted,
and were considered gravely immoral, identical to murder.
"Indirect" abortions were, however, permitted according to
the principle of double effect. Here the act-in-itself was
specified as an operation or other procedure whose directly
intended effect was the preservation or restoration of the
mother's health. The foreseen but unintended death of the
fetus was "indirect." The two classic cases were the removal of a pregnant cancerous uterus and the removal of a
fallopian tube in the case of ectopic gestation. Other
cases were the use of certain medications or operations
where there was some danger that the fetus might die as a
result, but where the procedure was directed at some other
effect. Thus, for example, an appendectomy might be performed on a pregnant woman, even though some (perhaps even

great) danger existed of a consequent abortion (miscarriage).
It was clear, however, that the fetus itself could never be
"directly" attacked. Thus, though the cancerous uterus might
be removed with the fetus inside, the fetus could never be
removed from the womb if its presence was itself the cause of
a woman's dangerous ailment (severe vomiting, eclampsia,
hemorrhage, etc.) The pathological fallopian tube might be
removed with the fetus inside, but the fetus could never itself be removed from the tube, even if (a practical impossibility) the tube might be saved as a result. This latter
act-in-itself would violate the first two conditions of double effect.

     Likewise, "direct" euthanasia was forbidden. That is,
any act which of itself brought about or hastened the death
of a dying person was forbidden. On the other hand, drugs
could be given which would lessen pain, as long as these
drugs would not "directly" hasten death. Likewise "negative"
euthanasia was permitted. That is, extraordinary means were
not required to preserve or prolong life, and such means,
once begun, might be stopped. In this latter case, the distinction between ordinary and extraordinary means was not at
all physicalistically restricted, and provided a very flexible principle in the care of the dying. It could be applied,
however, only within the double effect framework. That is,
any "direct" killing or hastening of death was to be avoided.
Similarly "direct" suicide was forbidden, whereas "indirect"
suicide was permitted.[33]

---

     [33]We have already given examples of this distinction.
A person might escape a fire by jumping into the lake, even
though he knew he could not swim and would drown. He was
not allowed to shoot himself in a similar situation. His
escape from the flames thus depended morally upon the presence of a nearby lake into which (or at least a window from
which) he might "jump."

The case of mutilation presents an extremely complex
set of issues. Distinctions were made between non-sterilizing mutilations (amputations of limbs, lobotomies, appen-
dectomies, etc.) and sterilizing mutilations (hysterectomies,
vasectomies, etc.) Further complications arose when the purpose of the mutilation was for organ transplantation to
another person or for medical experimentation.

Non-sterilizing mutilations were sometimes judged explicitly according to the principle of double effect. The
act-in-itself had to be specified in such a way as to exclude
the mutilating aspect from the cause, and relegate it to the
(indirect) effect. Moralists who did so thus specified the
act in a way similar to the specification we have noted in
the case of self-defense.[34] The act-in-itself was a cutting,
or some similar procedure which resulted both in a mutilation and in the health of the patient. Thus the first two
conditions of double effect were seen to be met. There was
generally confusion here, however, and often the notion of
"intention" of the agent was confused with the "object," or
direct act-in-itself.[35] Seldom if ever was there any complete explanation of how an operation to remove a limb, for
example, was only "indirectly" a physical (first two conditions) mutilation.

Most authors ultimately accepted the fact that all mutilations were "direct" in the physical sense. They were justified according to the principle of totality, which holds
that a part of a physical body may be mutilated if it is
necessary for the physical health of the whole individual

---

[34]See above, pp. 253-255, n. 19.

[35]See, for example, O'Malley, *The Ethics of Medical
Homicide,* pp. 26-27; Finney, *Moral Problems,* pp. 146-148.

physical organism.[36] This principle was physicalistically
restricted, but the limitations were of no consequence in
simple non-transplant, non-sterilizing mutilations.

Sterilizing mutilations were lawful only if "indirect."
Here the act-in-itself had to be specified in such a way
that, although the "mutilating" aspect could be a part of
the act-in-itself, and the "mutilation" direct, the "sterilizing" aspect had to be excluded from the act-in-itself and
the "sterilization" indirect. Thus a direct mutilation for
removal of the uterus would only be an "indirect" sterilization, providing that the good effect was not the result of
the sterilization but only of the mutilation. A woman was
thus permitted to have her uterus removed if it was cancerous or otherwise diseased. The removal (a direct mutilation)
caused with equal immediacy the good effect (restoration of
health) and the bad effect (sterility). On the other hand,
a woman with a series of Caesarean sections whose womb was
dangerously weak was (generally) not permitted a hysterectomy, since in this case only future pregnancy would bring
about any difficulty, and the good effect (the preservation
of health or the avoidance of danger) was caused by means of
the bad effect (sterility), and thus the second condition of
the double effect principle was violated.[37] Similarly, a

---

[36]The principle of totality can be found in Thomas
Aquinas, *Summa theologiae*, IIa IIae, q. 65, a. 1.

[37]This opinion was not universal. Some authors argued
that the pathological condition of the uterus was a present
one, thus justifying the operation as indirect. The argument
of those who opposed the operation as a direct sterilization
was more consistent with the second condition than that of
their more liberal colleagues, who tended to argue more from
external factors (some moralists allow it and there has not
been an explicit Church decree on it, hence it is a probable
opinion which may be followed) than on internal reasons concerning the procedure itself. For a list of moralists on
both sides of the issue, see Kelly, *Medico-Moral Problems*,

woman with a heart condition was refused hysterectomy or
other sterilizing operation, since the good effect (avoidance of heart strain) was caused by the bad effect (sterility). Her health was preserved by keeping her from being
pregnant, which made the procedure a direct sterilization.
A man could be castrated if his testicles were diseased (indirect castration), but castration for his spiritual good,
to remove the danger of sexual sin, was forbidden, since the
sterilization would be the cause of the decrease in tempta-
tion, and would thus in itself be direct.

It is clear that sterilization was seen to constitute a
special case of mutilation, to which the normal rules would
not apply. Moralists here insisted that the direct and primary end, the *finis operis*, of the sex act, and of marriage
itself, was the biological procreation of children. No individual sex act could be posited which would directly thwart
that end. Nor could any operation be performed which would
directly thwart that particular faculty of a man or a woman.
The generative faculty was thus given a special set of controls which were not applied to man's other faculties.[38]
Often moralists explained that the reproductive faculty was
"social," for the good of the whole race, and not just individual. Nonetheless, moralists were consistent in rejecting
any "social" arguments for sterilization or other forms of
birth control, such as eugenic or demographic arguments. Regardless of the social effects, the generative faculty could

---

1958 edition, pp. 215-217.

[38]For example, transplants of healthy organs were permitted except for those which would sterilize the donor
(Cunningham, *The Morality of Organic Transplantation,* pp.
101-106). Similarly, capital punishment and punitive non-
sterilizing mutilations were permitted, but punitive sterilization, such as castration, was forbidden (La Rochelle and
Fink, *Handbook,* 8th ed., pp. 153-156).

not be directly thwarted. The various (non-sterilizing)
methods of contraception were included in this context.
With the exception of total or periodic abstinence (rhythm),
all methods of contraception were "direct" attacks upon the
operation of the generative faculty. Though oral contraceptives might be used when their contraceptive or sterilizing effects were indirect, they could never be used for
the purpose of avoiding children.[39] This was a direct
sterilization.

Organ transplants added yet a further complication. At
first all organ transplants were forbidden, since they were
direct mutilations of one person's body for the sake of
another person's body, which was not allowed by the physicalistically limited principle of totality. In 1944, as we
shall see later, Bert Cunningham proposed that the principle
of totality *not* be restricted to one physical body, but that
it be extended to apply to all men in the Mystical Body of
Christ. This thesis marked the first time in which physicalism was explicitly rejected by a Catholic medical ethicist. Yet Cunningham himself continued to insist that sterilizing transplants would always be wrong, since "direct"
sterilization was always forbidden. Thus Cunningham allowed
the donor to accept total blindness in giving his eyes to
another, but forbad the donor to sterilize himself to give

---

[39]Oral contraceptives were unknown until very late in
the period we are studying. It was the "birth control controversy" which provided the locus for the ultimate attack
on traditional modalities of medical ethics (both physicalism and ecclesiastical positivism). Traditional moralists
refused to allow the use of the pill as a "direct" sterilization. The exception was in the case of the use of the
pill for the regulation of a woman's cycle, in order to restore her fertility, or for some other organic reason. In
these cases the sterilization was only the indirect result
of a medication taken for other, non-sterilizing reasons,
and thus the pill might morally be used.

another fertility.[40]

We have noted the use of the double effect framework
in questions of sterility testing. If masturbation was
used to attain sperm for the testing, since masturbation
was a directly immoral act-in-itself, the procedure was forbidden. The intrinsic immorality of masturbation was in
turn supported by arguing that this was a direct misuse of
the generative faculty. Sperm for sterility testing could
be acquired only by removing some semen from the wife's vagina some time after conjugal intercourse. The use of a
perforated condom was also allowed by some, with much dispute as to the number and size of the holes required so
that the sex act be not directly thwarted in its biological
end.

Artificial insemination was forbidden for similar reasons. If a donor other than the husband was used, the procedure was considered adulterous in addition to the other
difficulties. Masturbation could not be used to gather the
husband's sperm. Thus only the use of a cervical spoon to
inject the semen more deeply into the wife's reproductive
tract was permitted. All other methods were seen as direct
misuses of the generative faculty.

All of the cases we have cited thus far involve some
kind of surgery or at least medicinal therapeutic intervention. The other issues of medical ethics generally were

---

[40]Cunningham, *The Morality of Organic Transplantation,*
pp. 101-106. We shall note later, when we return to
Cunningham, the importance of papal pronouncements in
Cunningham's thesis. He merely accepts the physicalist
criteria of direct and indirect in the case of sterilization because papal documents have decreed that direct
sterilization is immoral. Since no similar decrees were
available concerning non-sterilizing mutilations, the rest
of Cunningham's thesis, though hotly contested, was accepted as a "probable" opinion, that is, as one which
might be held and taught by Roman Catholics.

not solved by the use of the physicalist modality. Thus,
for example, there was no application of physicalism to the
problem of an ignorant or greedy physician, or to the question of the medical secret. One exception was the case of
truth-telling. Here the Catholic moralists had a traditional principle drawn from the double effect framework which
could be directly applied: the principle of mental reservation. Though all "direct" lies were forbidden, it was allowed to posit an act-in-itself consisting of the physical
utterance of a series of words which might be misunderstood
by the hearer but which in themselves were not directly untruthful. Thus a nurse could say to a patient, "The doctor
is not in," even though the doctor was in the office, since
the physical words might (by an astute listener) be correctly understood as meaning "The doctor is not in *for you*."
Similar evasion techniques could be applied to questions
which a physician might not wish to answer. Thus a doctor
might say, "I don't know," even though he did know, since
the words could mean "I don't know *anything I can tell you
about*." The speaker would mentally withhold or reserve the
explanatory clause, and the listener would presumably mis-
understand. Moralists insisted that the speaker drop enough
of a hint as to what he was reserving so that there was at
least a decent chance for the listener to understand "correctly," that is, to grasp the factual truth.[41]

---

[41]An excellent example of this kind of approach to
truth-telling is in Kenny, *Principles of Medical Ethics*,
either edition, pp. 19-21. Janssens correctly points out
the absurdity of this kind of quibbling. He analyzes human
speech in its wider, social dimensions, and shows how the
notion of mental reservation was more of a game to be played
by the verbally sophisticated than a valid moral respect for
real human truth ("Ontic Evil," pp. 146-148). An additional
criticism would be that the third condition of the double
effect principle would seem to be violated by all "mental
reservations," since the agent clearly intends, wants, the

One final application of the double effect framework was in the case of cooperation in an evil procedure. For example, what part could a nurse take in the care of a patient who was to undergo or had undergone an abortion or other immoral operation? To what degree could she be a part of the procedure itself? Moralists distinguished between direct and indirect cooperation. Immediate or direct participation in the immoral act was forbidden. The nurse was allowed, however, to perform duties that were not in themselves evil, provided there was a sufficient reason for so doing. Often the same principle was applied to cooperation in (evil) non-Catholic worship. Some moralists, as we have already noted, forbade the calling of a non-Catholic minister by a Catholic nurse. Later most writers accepted this as indirect cooperation at worst.

* * *

We have now concluded our necessarily lengthy description of physicalism as a modality of application of theological principles to medical ethical issues. We have described what we mean by physicalism as it was actually used within its framework of application: the double effect principle. We have analyzed the traditional four-condition double effect, and shown that physicalist criteria are applied according to its first two conditions. We have demonstrated that this principle is more aptly viewed as a framework of medical ethical methodology than merely as one principle among many. We have enumerated and described the most important of the medical ethical issues to which double effect physicalism was applied. In the next section we will trace the process by which, in the literature of the earlier

---

physically untruthful interpretation to be accepted by the listener.

period of North American Roman Catholic medical ethics,
physicalism came to be the established theological modality.

Part Two

The Literature of the Early Period

Our purpose in this section is to describe and demonstrate the operation of theological principles in the medical ethical literature of the early period of our discipline
(1897-1940). As we have already proposed it, our thesis is
that the application of theological principles to medical
ethical issues was determined largely by the influence of
two pervasive and dominant theological ethical approaches:
physicalism and ecclesiastical positivism. Other theological principles and arguments, such as the principle of God's
dominion over life and the principle of redemptive suffering,
were of secondary importance because they were consistently
subordinated in their application in medical ethics to these
two methodological modalities.

The modality of physicalism operated by arriving at
ethical judgments on the basis of physicalist criteria within the double effect framework. We have just finished a detailed description of this process. Ecclesiastical positivism operated by arriving at ethical judgments on the basis
of pronouncements of the Roman Catholic magisterium (the
teaching authority of the Catholic Church), generally those
of the pope or of his administrative body, the Vatican curial agencies. Ecclesiastical positivism is, at least in its
immediate medical ethical ramifications if not in its speculative theological aspects, far less complex than physicalism. Though we will give a more detailed description of it
as introduction to the period when it achieved its greatest
importance in medical ethics (1940-1960), the definition we
have already given is sufficient to enable us to discover

its presence as we survey the literature of the early period. We will note how medical moralists often cite papal documents as answers to medical ethical questions, and even as determinative of the ethical principle which must be applied to the case.

The theological principles of God's sovereignty over life and of the redemptive importance of suffering in Christ are, as we shall note in this and the following sections, used primarily as ancillary ethical and motivational principles within the modalities of physicalism and ecclesiastical positivism. The ethical judgment is first arrived at by the use of physicalist and/or positivist criteria, and the theological principles, if they are used at all, are then added as supportive ethical arguments or as motivations for doing what has been judged as the good. For example, the principle of God's dominion over human life is consistently used as the reason why one may not take one's own life or that of another. But this theological principle does not enter directly into the ethical process whereby a judgment is made as to the rightness or wrongness of a specific abortion or euthanasia procedure. The latter is determined by the decision as to whether or not the act is a direct or an indirect killing. God's sovereignty over life is said to be violated by direct killings, but not by indirect ones. The ethical distinction is made by physicalist criteria, and the theological principle of God's dominion is quite secondary to the actual ethical method. Similarly, when a magisterial decree is the central criterion used in solving an ethical dilemma, the theological principle of God's dominion over life is often cited by the medical ethicist. But here, too, the actual distinction between right and wrong procedures is not made on the basis of God's dominion, but on the basis of the authority of the magisterial pronouncement. A procedure which is forbidden by authority is said to violate God's

dominion, but the same is not true of one which the magisterium permits. The theological principle of God's dominion
is thus applied differently according to prior ethical pre-
cisions arrived at by the use of the positivist approach.

In general the principle of redemptive suffering finds
similar application. We have already noted that the two
theological principles of God's dominion over life and of
redemptive suffering are, in their medical ethical applications, but two aspects of one theological axis: the axis
which attempts to define one's relationship as creature and
co-creator with God. Thus when a procedure is judged to be
immoral, it is one's obligation to recognize God's sovereignty and to accept whatever suffering may result from
avoiding the immoral act. On the other hand, as God's co-
agent, acting in imitation of Christ the physician, one is
obliged to eliminate needless suffering by moral means.
Thus the rightness or wrongness of the procedure, as determined by other criteria, in turn determines how the theological principles are to be applied. If the procedure is
judged licit, then one is seen to be God's co-agent in eliminating suffering. If the procedure is illicit, then the
suffering which results must be accepted as redemptive.
Thus the theological principles are subordinated to the basic physicalist and positivist modalities of ethical argumentation. This subordination, though not operative in each
and every medical ethical issue, constitutes the general
pattern of theological methodology for the discipline.[42]

---

[42]There are exceptions. One of the most common is the
complex case of the spiritual care of the dying patient,
where both "ethical" and "religious" aspects are directly
pertinent. In this case, theological principles, including
that of redemptive suffering, were applied by some moralists
as themselves determinative of the rightness or wrongness of
a medical procedure. The question was whether or not pain-
killing drugs might be given to a dying patient. Of course,

By choosing one or the other pole of the creature co-
creator axis as supportive of an ethical judgment already
reached by other criteria, the intriniscally mysterious and
paradoxical nature of the theological principles of dominion
and suffering is ignored. Thus the axis is exploited by
being shorn of mystery when it is applied as supposedly supportive of the sharp ethical distinctions made between right
and wrong procedures on the basis of physicalist or positivist criteria.[43]

---

all direct euthanasia was forbidden, but here the central
question was the patient's consciousness, so that he might
prepare spiritually for his day of judgment. It was sometimes urged that the patient be allowed to suffer more before death so that he might suffer less in Purgatory after
death. In addition, principles from Catholic sacramental
theology were directly applied to determine whether or not a
pain-killing drug which would cause unconsciousness could
ethically be given. Though such drugs were considered in
themselves licit (according to the double effect principle),
if a Catholic patient had not gone to confession, they were
not to be given, since the patient must remain conscious for
possible conversion. The case of non-Catholic patients was
somewhat more difficult, since there was less direct evidence as to the state of his soul. This ethical issue is
thus an exceptional case, where explicitly theological
principles, such as redemptive suffering, the spiritual
state of the patient's soul, his religious affiliation, the
presence of a priest, etc., were directly determinative of
the rightness or wrongness of the use of pain relieving
drugs. The patient's own choice in the matter, which would
be generally used as determinative today, was secondary to
the supposedly objective religious criteria of the reception
of the last sacraments.

[43] It is not yet the proper place to attempt explicitly
an evaluative criticism of the methodology of pre-Vatican II
medical ethics. It is in order here, however, to make one
precision to avoid misunderstanding. I am not arguing that
the theological principles of God's dominion over life and
of redemptive suffering *ought* to be applied immediately to
medical ethical dilemmas, if by immediate application is
meant the use of these principles by themselves to make precise distinctions between right and wrong medical procedures.
Such an application is simply not valid. These theological

As we survey the literature of Roman Catholic medical
ethics in this and the following chapters, we will discover
a shift in the relative importance of the two modalities we
have defined. The early period of the discipline, which is
our present subject, emphasizes and develops the modality of
physicalism, whereas the later period places greater emphasis than the earlier period on ecclesiastical positivism.
We have already noted that this shift was by no means dichot-
omous. Both modalities are of significant operational importance in both periods.

We will discover that during the early period of the
discipline the physicalist approach is gradually developed
and refined. Certain points of contention among authors

---

principles are mystery-laden theological statements, and as
such they would be misused if given the burden of making
precise ethical procedural distinctions. As we will see in
the final chapter, the inadequacy of traditional medical
ethical methodology lay not in the failure of these authors
to apply these principles more "immediately" (in the sense
defined here), but rather in their use of the principles,
shorn of mystery, to support ethical procedural distinctions
made as a result of other criteria which were themselves inadequate. My criticism of the subordination of these theological principles to the modalities of physicalism and
positivism is thus *not* that they are not applied "immediately" to procedural distinctions--they can never be used validly in this way--but that they are subordinated to and
mediated by inadequate methodological modalities in such a
way that they are applied to the ethical dilemmas in an im-
poverished fashion. We will note in the final chapter that
today's Catholic medical moralists are more apt to use a
less restrictive personalist modality which provides a context for the use of theological principles in a more authentic fashion. The principles are applied directly to the
bio-significance question. Thus theological principles are
used to approach theological questions: the questions of
Christian anthropology. They are not mediated by distorting
modalities, and are in this sense more immediate. On the
other hand, they are less immediate in that their direct
context is, as it should be, not the precise distinctions
between medical procedures, but the wider context of the
meaning of human life.

writing at the turn of the century are solved, so that by
1940 the physicalist modality and its application is established in most of the important medical ethical topics.

1.   Coppens and Klarmann: Developing Physicalist Categories

Charles Coppens' 1897 work, the first Roman Catholic
medical ethics text written in North America, shows the importance of the physicalist approach to medical ethical
analysis. It also demonstrates, however, that some of the
more exact distinctions which will be made by later moralists are not available to Coppens, so that double effect
physicalism is not applied as precisely as it will be by
later moralists, nor to as many different medical ethical
topics.

The only issue to which Coppens devotes any real analytic detail is that of abortion. In this issue the importance of the physicalist modality is clear. He outlines the
double effect principle with its four conditions, and then
applies it to various cases. Coppens insists that all direct abortions are forbidden because God alone has dominion
over human life.[44] This theological principle is supported
at some length with passages from Scripture, and is applied
also to questions of suicide and euthanasia, neither of
which are treated with any precision.[45] Indirect abortions
or miscarriages are justified explicitly by the physicalist
criteria of the double effect principle. Coppens' first example is that of a woman who needs to be given some medication for an illness, which medication might cause an abortion:

I answer with this important distinction: you can give

---

[44]Coppens, *Moral Principles*, pp. 38-48.

[45]*Ibid.*, pp. 38-39, 45-48.

such medicine as will act on her system, her organs, in
a manner to save her life, and you may permit the sad
effects which will indirectly affect the child; but you
cannot injure the child directly as a means to benefit
her indirectly; that would be using a bad means to
obtain a good end.[46]

Coppens then goes on to show that an abortion used to save
the life of a woman suffering from severe vomiting is forbidden, since it would be a direct abortion.

Abortion is then the means used to stop the vomiting.
Are you justified in using that means? Abortion is the
dislodging of the child from the only place where it
can live and where nature has placed it for that purpose. Therefore abortion directly kills the child, as
truly as plunging a man under water kills the man. Can
you thus kill the child to save the mother? You *cannot*.
Neither in this case nor in any other case can you do
evil that good may come of it.[47]

Finally Coppens applies the physicalist modality to the
question of ectopic pregnancy, one of the paradigmatic cases
for the application of double effect physicalism. At the
time there was still some controversy over the issue, controversy which will later be largely, though not completely,
settled. We have already noted the final consensus of most
traditional moralists when we included the case in the list
of medical ethical topics to which physicalism was applied.
That consensus would be that it is allowed to remove the tube
with the fetus inside, but not to remove the fetus from the
tube. This distinction depends on a precise specification
of the act-in-itself. Though the elements for such a specification are present in Coppens, he introduces other factors
which lead to some confusion.

The first of these is his distinction between cases in
which there is a doubt as to whether or not the "interior
growth" is a tumor or an ectopic fetus, and cases in which

---

[46]*Ibid.*, p. 69.

[47]*Ibid.*, pp. 69-70, italics his.

it certain that the "growth" is, or contains--this last distinction is important, and is not always precise in Cop-
pens--a fetus. For later moralists, this question as to
doubt will be of less importance, since it will be the precise nature of the act-in-itself (cutting out the tube with
the fetus inside as opposed to cutting the fetus out of the
tube) which will bear the central weight of the moral distinction. Coppens also insists on the physical nature of
the act-in-itself, but does not develop this specification
to the same degree of precision as will later Catholic moralists.

If there is doubt as to the nature of the growth, the
double effect principle applies directly and explicitly.[48]
The doctor must wait until there is an immediate crisis.[49]
But if fatal consequences are imminent, and there is still
doubt as to the nature of the growth, the operation may be
performed. Coppens insists, however, even in this case,
that the act-in-itself be such that the abortion, if such it
is (since it may not be a fetus at all), be indirect. He
states: "The evil is not [to be] made the means to obtain
the good effect. . . . This last condition would not be
verified if it were proposed, not to cut out the cyst, but
to destroy its contents by an electric current. Then, it
would seem, the foetus itself, if there be one, would be

---

[48]*Ibid.*, pp. 78-79.

[49]This insistence on waiting will persist until the
1930's, when the thesis of T. Lincoln Bouscaren will demonstrate the pathological condition of the tube from the beginning of the ectopic gestation. It is Bouscaren who fixes
the precise specifications and distinctions needed for
solving the case of ectopic pregnancy. Even then, some controversy will continue over the need to wait until a crisis
is immediate, that is, until the tube has burst, or is about
to burst, and the hemorrhage has begun or is imminent.

directly attacked."[50]

In cases where no doubt exists as to the nature of the
growth, Coppens refrains from giving any clear answer. He
merely cites the opinions of other Catholic moralists, and
concludes: "Gentlemen, when such authorities disagree, I
would not presume to attempt a theoretic decision."[51] Later
moralists will answer this question by insisting more than
Coppens does on the specification of the act-in-itself.
Thus, even though it is certain that the growth is an ectopic gestation, it may be removed "indirectly," that is, along
with the removal of the tube itself.[52]

Coppens' use of the modality of ecclesiastical positivism can also be demonstrated in his treatment of ectopic
gestation. He puts it this way:

> In Jurisprudence, reason must be our guide when it af-
> fords us evidence of the truth. But when our reason
> offers arguments on both sides of the question, so that
> we can arrive at no certain conclusion, then we act
> prudently by invoking the authority of wiser minds who
> make moral questions a specialty, and we are perfectly
> safe if we follow the best authority available. A
> Catholic physician has here a special advantage; for he
> has in cases of great difficulty the decisions of Roman
> tribunals . . . Non-Catholics are, of course, not
> obliged to obey such pronouncements; yet even for them,
> it cannot be injurious, but rather very useful, to know
> the views of so competent a court on matters of the
> most vital interest in their learned profession.[53]

---

[50]*Ibid.*, p. 78.

[51]*Ibid.*, 1st ed., p. 79.

[52]Actually, Coppens himself proposes this precise argument, but only in the appendix of the later editions, and only
as citing, with approval, the opinion of an unnamed surgeon.
He does not introduce this precision into the body of his
text, and all editions of the work refuse to make any definitive answer. (See his fourth edition, pp. 226-227.)

[53]*Ibid.*, any edition, p. 80.

For Coppens the modality of ecclesiastical positivism
is not dominant. His basic arguments are from the natural
law,[54] and he uses magisterial pronouncements only secondarily. Unlike some later moralists, who will devote much detail to a defense of the teaching authority of the Roman
Catholic Church, Coppens avoids any primary appeal to this
source.[55] Ecclesiastical positivism is operative in Coppens,
however, as can best be seen by comparing the early editions
with the last two. In the preface to the fourth edition,
Coppens states: "In this fourth edition, owing to a late decision of the Roman Congregation of the Holy Office, one
passage, p. 79, has been rewritten, not to change the former doctrine, but to emphasize it more by reference to that

---

[54]*Ibid.*, pp. 29-32.

[55]It must be noted here, in order to avoid confusion
later, that our conclusion is not based on the fact that
Coppens *states* that the decrees of the magisterium are of
secondary importance, and are to be used only when reason is
inadequate. Later moralists for whom ecclesiastical positivism is a primary modality often make the same claim.
Coppens does in fact appeal to ecclesiastical authority only
occasionally, and does not give it any totally definitive
significance in arriving at his judgments.
    The question concerning the authority of magisterial
decrees for non-Catholics must be seen in a similar fashion.
For Coppens, these decrees are not obligatory for non-Catholics, either in theory, as the passage we have cited shows,
or in practice, since his use of the decrees is in fact secondary to his physicalist natural law arguments. But for
some later moralists whom we will study, it is precisely
the decrees of the magisterium which are the primary source
for determining the rightness or wrongness of procedures.
These judgments, in turn, are said to bind everyone, including non-Catholics, since they are derived from the "natural" law. We will return to this *practical* ecclesiastical
positivism later. For the moment we might mention simply
that if the "natural" law is in fact discovered only by
reading and accepting the decrees of the magisterium, then
in practice these decrees are binding on all people, even
though in theory it is the "natural" law which is said to
be binding.

authoritative pronouncement."[56]   The exact passage changed
is not at all central.   Coppens merely states that Catholic
moralists no longer allow the use of the unjust aggressor
argument in the case of ectopic gestation, as a result of
the Roman decree.   Nonetheless, the fact that this is the
one change made in the later editions shows the definite,
if not dominant, influence of ecclesiastical positivism.[57]

The theological principle of God's dominion over life
is thus used by Coppens within the physicalist double effect
framework.   Because God alone has such dominion, direct
killings such as suicide, euthanasia, and abortion, are forbidden.   In certain situations, however, indirect killing is
permitted, according to the principle of double effect.   The
theological principle is thus significant, but the actual
ethical distinctions are made according to physicalist criteria.

In a similar manner, Coppens applies the theological
principle concerning the meaning of suffering.   The clearest
example is in the context of contraception, which the author
rejects as contrary to the legitimate purpose of the marriage act, the procreation of children.[58]   Having thus concluded to contraception as immoral, Coppens brings up the

---

[56]*Ibid.*, 4th ed., p. 7.

[57]The fourth edition also adds an appendix which contains the substance of the new decrees of 1898 and 1902
(pp. 223-227).

[58]Either edition, p. 116 and elsewhere.   Coppens cites
the divine condemnation of Onan in Genesis 38 as a Scriptural proof of the immorality of contraception.   He also adds
a lengthy series of debilitating consequences which flow
from sexual immorality, such as a host of physical and mental diseases.   It would seem, however, that these are offered as supportive arguments, since even if it could be
shown that contraception might prove physically healthful in
a given case, it would still be forbidden.

case of a wife whose first childbirth was so difficult that
the doctor suggests a second might be fatal. Coppens be-
rates the physician for making the prognosis, since he might
thus be the cause of immoral practices. In addition, had he
not done so, the woman might have born a healthy and numerous family. He continues:

> For we must trust in Divine Providence. If a husband
> and wife do their conscientious duty, there is a God
> that provides for them and their family more liberally
> than for the birds of the air and the lilies of the
> field. And if He should so dispose that the worst be-
> fall, well, such temporal dangers and sufferings as at-
> tend child-bearing are the lot of womankind, just as
> the dangers and hardships of the battlefield, the mine,
> the factory, the forest, and the prairie are the lot of
> the men. The man who shirks his duty to family or
> country is a coward; women, as a rule, are brave enough
> in their own line of duty, and patiently submit to
> God's sentence pronounced in Paradise, "I will multiply
> thy sorrows and thy conceptions . . ."[59]

Thus the theological principle concerning the meaning of
suffering is used as a motivation for avoiding the commission of an act judged immoral according to other, largely
physicalist, criteria.[60]

The physicalist modality of application of theological
principles is thus clearly present in Coppens' book. Though
all the precise specifications are not yet present which
will later enable the application of physicalist criteria
more clearly and to a wider scope of medical ethical issues,
the basic elements are operative. Ecclesiastical positivism

---

[59]*Ibid.*, pp. 123-124.

[60]There is one example of the direct application of the
theological principle of redemptive suffering. We noted it
above. It is the case of suffering in preparation for death
and judgment. The patient should not be rendered unconscious until the priest arrives, since to do so "would be
not kindness but cruelty. A little suffering more in this
life may save much suffering in the next" (*Ibid.*, p.
145).

is of less significance. The theological principles of
God's sovereignty and of redemptive suffering are important,
but are subordinated in the actual decision-making process
to physicalist criteria.

In Andrew Klarmann's ethical analysis of abortion as
"*The Crux of Pastoral Medicine*," the physicalist modality is
clearly dominant. Like Coppens, Klarmann does not yet apply
the precise distinctions of later moralists to all cases,
and remains somewhat confused on the question of ectopic
pregnancy.

Klarmann begins by insisting on the principle that God
is the author of life. He applies this immediately to direct acts of abortion.

> Whatever may endanger the life she consents to bear in
> her womb, is an offense against her state of life, an
> act of immorality, if the cause of that danger is di-
> rect, and under her control. With that life she holds
> a pledge from God, which He alone can redeem, the Au-
> thor of life.[61]

He cites the fifth commandment and the curse of Cain, the
sensus communis, and the teaching of the Catholic Church as
sources for arguments against abortion.[62] He then goes on
to treat cases of spontaneous abortions or miscarriages, insisting that most of these are immoral, in that the cause
could have been avoided by more diligence on the part of the
woman.[63] Klarmann also rejects the use of medicine during
pregnancy which would cause abortion. In doing so he seems
to reverse Coppens' central example of an indirect, and thus
permissible, abortion. Klarmann's reasoning, however, is
that it is never medically necessary to use doses of any
medicine which would bring about an abortion, and that for

---

[61]Klarmann, *The Crux of Pastoral Medicine*, 5th ed., p. 32.

[62]*Ibid.*, p. 36.

[63]*Ibid.*, pp. 37-38, 58-63.

this reason such medications are immoral.[64]

The clearest application of double effect physicalism
in Klarmann is in his analysis of the removal of a cancerous
uterus from a pregnant woman. The author states that "the
solution of this case must proceed from the answer to this
question: 'Is the death of the child in this case the *direct*
consequence of the excision or not?'"[65] Klarmann does not
state the four-condition double effect principle explicitly,
but its criteria are clearly the decisive ones. "Abortion,"
he says, "may be called direct in two ways: 1) when it is
procured as the immediate *object* of both the operator [this
would be a violation of the third condition] and the operation [a violation of the first condition]; 2) when it is
procured as the *means* of achieving the object of the operation [here the second condition would be the one violated]."[66]
He continues by arguing that "in the excision of the pregnant womb, the operation tends toward the killing of the
fetus neither of its nature, nor of its object. . . . Now
the excision of the womb does not aim *directly* at the death
of the fetus; therefore the death of the fetus is not the
direct effect of the operation."[67]

Klarmann goes on to contrast the case of "locked uterus"
(retroflexed uterus) during pregnancy. The question is
whether or not the amniotic sac may be perforated in order
to release the womb by emptying its contents. Klarmann, in
opposition to Capellmann, argues that such an operation would
be direct.[68] He puts it this way:

---

[64]*Ibid.*, pp. 70-71.

[65]*Ibid.*, p. 115, italics his.

[66]*Ibid.*, p. 115, italics his.

[67]*Ibid.*, pp. 116-117, italics his.

[68]*Ibid.*, pp. 73-89, 118-128.

Now, the direct effect of an operation is not that
which may be first in the mind of the operator (except
as to its morality), but that which is the first and
immediate effect of the operation, considered as a
means to procure the object intended by the operator.
. . . In the "classic" process of the perforation of
the fetal membranes, no matter for what purpose or with
what intention or fiction, the first and immediate effect is this: to withdraw from the fetus the vital element, the amniotic fluid . . . Therefore, the direct
effect of the perforation of the fetal membranes is the
killing of the fetus.[69]

The distinction between the morally permissible hysterectomy and the forbidden perforation of the amniotic sac is
clearly based on the physical structure of the act-in-itself,
on the physical chain of cause and effect.   Klarmann argues
that God's dominion over life is violated in the latter case,
but not in the former.   Indirect abortions "do not clash
with the prohibition of God: 'Thou shalt not kill!'"[70]   Direct abortions, on the other hand, like all direct killings,
are in violation of the principle that "*human life is sacred*,
that is, that it has a value set upon it by God, who created
it for a supernatural purpose.   He has so often signified
that He would never surrender His dominion over human life,
except for the good of the race, in particular cases."[71]

The clarity of the physicalist criteria which Klarmann
applies to the cases of a cancerous uterus and a retroflexed
uterus is not found in his analysis of ectopic pregnancies.
He quotes Coppens at length, including his confusing distinction as to whether or not there is a doubt concerning the
nature of the growth.   In cases of doubt, Klarmann seems to
accept Coppens' conclusion that the operation is indirect.
Where there is no doubt, however, Klarmann indicates that

---

[69]*Ibid.*, pp. 121-122.

[70]*Ibid.*, p. 126.

[71]*Ibid.*, pp. 126-127.

the operation would be a direct abortion. He does not give
the distinctions available as to act-in-itself specification
which would make it possible to allow the removal of the
tube with the fetus inside (in like manner as the removal of
the cancerous womb was allowed) and to forbid the removal of
the fetus from the womb (similar to the case of emptying the
retroflexed uterus). In this context, he suggests the redemptive value of suffering:

> In a truly *desperate* case, where no help can be expect-
> ed at the hands of man, it should not be so difficult
> to implore help from God; and if He, too, declines to
> interfere, a Christian mother must rise to the solemn-
> ity of the occasion, and make herself a willing martyr
> to her conjugal vows. Martyrs are made not only by
> dying for the Faith, but also by dying for duty and
> virtue.[72]

The authority of the Roman Catholic magisterium is also
operative in Klarmann, though it is not as important as
physicalist criteria. One of the sources for arguments
against abortion is "the ruling and teaching of the Church,
commissioned by God to be the teacher of mankind in His
stead."[73] Klarmann often cites decrees of the Holy Office,
and includes the complete Latin texts of five of them in his
appendix.[74] He agrees with Coppens that Catholics may not
use the unjust aggressor argument, because of Roman pronouncements.[75] He explicitly gives weight to the decrees of
the Church in arguing against operations for definite ectopic pregnancies.

> But the positive ruling of the Holy Office concerning
> the removal of the *ectopic conceptions, dummodo et
> foetus et matris vitae, quantum fieri potest, serio et*

---

[72]*Ibid.*, p. 101.

[73]*Ibid.*, p. 36.

[74]*Ibid.*, pp. 290-298.

[75]*Ibid.*, pp. 87-89.

> *opportune provideatur*," given as late as 1898,
> precludes the possibility of an operation by which the
> fetus must die, although it be only in consequence of
> its inviability.[76]

And again, he states: "The ectopic fetus enjoys the same

protection of its right to life, as the normal conception,

as the best authorities agree, and the Holy Office has de-

cided."[77]

Both modalities are thus operative in Klarmann's analy-

sis. The more important of the two is physicalism, to an

explanation of which he devotes much of his effort. This

relative emphasis in the actual operation of the two modal-

ities corresponds with Klarmann's theoretical presentation

of his intentions in the book. In the preface, he states:

> It occurred to us, then, that the writing of a new book
> in English required more than a mere compiling of cases,
> decisions and quotations. We thought it feasible and
> necessary, to put Pastoral Medicine on its own feet,
> lending a pedestal from Christian biology and from the
> philosophy and ethics of the greatest philosopher, St.
> Thomas; and then chisel away "for dear life" at the
> new goddess, until she should take form and feature,
> spurring our efforts with the principles of these
> sciences, and guiding them with authoritative decisions,
> as far as they are on hand.[78]

The decisions of the magisterium are thus of definite signi-

ficance, but the greatest emphasis is on physicalism. The

theological principles of God's dominion over life and of

redemptive suffering are used as ancillary principles and as

-----

[76]*Ibid.*, p. 96. The Latin reads "as long as serious
and opportune provision is made, as much as can be done, for
the life both of the fetus and the mother."

[77]*Ibid.*, p. 108. The importance of Church decisions
can also be seen in one of the reviews written of Klarmann's
book. The reviewer states: "Many of the problems are still
under discussion among theologians, some of them have been
definitely settled by Church decision" (*Catholic World*, 95
[1912], 258).

[78]*Ibid.*, pp. viii-ix.

motives for following the judgments thus arrived at.

2. Austin O'Malley: Physicalism and Ecclesiastical
Positivism

Both modalities of ethical analysis are present in the
writings of Austin O'Malley. This Catholic physician is
often confused as to the exact applications and specifications of physicalist distinctions, but gives them great
weight. In addition, he attaches significant importance to
the decrees of the magisterium when they are available.

The case of hysterectomy as surgery for cancer of the
womb during pregnancy testifies to the importance of double
effect physicalism. O'Malley distinguishes this permissible
indirect abortion from craniotomy, a direct abortion.[79]
O'Malley's analysis also demonstrates the importance for him
of the decisions of the Vatican.

> Such cases [hysterectomy for cancer] differ from crani-
> otomy, or the *direct* killing of a foetus (which were
> formally forbidden by the Holy Office on May 28, 1884,
> and August 19, 1888, and always forbidden by the natu-
> ral law) in several factors: first, in craniotomy the
> child is *directly* killed, although it is not an aggres-
> sor, in the hysterectomy it is permitted to die, it is
> *indirectly* killed; secondly, in craniotomy there is a
> viable child, in the hysterectomy, an unviable child;
> thirdly, in craniotomy there is a killing that is a
> means toward the end of saving the mother's life, in the
> hysterectomy there is a permitted hastening of the foe-
> tus's death, and this is only a circumstance inseparably
> joined to the act; fourthly, in craniotomy the killing
> is utterly uncalled for, because the caesarean section
> . . . will do instead, in the hysterectomy, because the
> child is not viable, there is no alternative way out of
> the difficulty; fifthly, formal judgment has been pro-
> nounced by the Holy Office in craniotomy, no formal

---

[79]Craniotomy and other forms of embryotomy were used before the relative perfection of Caesarian section to reduce
the size of the infant when labor could not be completed.

judgment has been made as regards this hysterectomy.[80]
The operation of both physicalist and positivist criteria is
clear in this analysis. The hysterectomy is allowed and the
craniotomy forbidden because the former is indirect and the
latter direct. O'Malley's first and third reasons are merely restatements of the first two conditions of the double
effect principle. His fifth reason is an explicit example
of the significance of ecclesiastical positivism. His
fourth reason merely points to the fact that now there is an
alternative to craniotomy. In the absence of such an alternative, the operation would still be immoral, however, and
thus the conclusion does not depend on this fourth reason.
The second reason is really irrelevant to O'Malley's analysis, since for him life begins at the moment of conception,
and it is quite as immoral to directly kill an unviable as a
viable fetus.[81]

O'Malley uses similar arguments to forbid other cases
of direct abortion. Direct abortion is forbidden in cases
of severe vomiting, even if the mother and child must both
die as a result.[82] A similar proscription applies in cases
of eclampsia.[83] The fetus may not be directly attacked even
in order to save the mother's life.

In these cases O'Malley's application of physicalist
criteria is clear. While direct abortions are forbidden,
the removal of a cancerous uterus is permitted, since the

---

[80]O'Malley and Walsh, *Essays in Pastoral Medicine*, pp.
42-43, italics his. O'Malley wrote all of the chapters
which we will cite in this section. Each chapter of the
book is signed by its respective author.

[81]O'Malley, *The Ethics of Medical Homicide,* pp. 33-82,
esp. pp. 39, 62, 76.

[82]*Ibid.,* p. 181.

[83]*Ibid.,* pp. 162-169.

killing of the fetus is merely an indirect consequence of
the removal of the womb. The same clarity is not present,
however, in O'Malley's analysis of ectopic pregnancies. As
we have seen in Coppens and in Klarmann, the precise physicalist specifications distinguishing the act-in-itself of
removing the tube directly with the fetus removed indirectly, from the act-in-itself of removing the fetus directly
from the tube have not yet been totally clarified. Lacking
this precise distinction, O'Malley, like Coppens and Klarmann, is unsure as to the exact morality of medical procedures in cases of ectopic gestation. For O'Malley the question is solved by the authoritative decrees of the magisterium.

In his earlier work, the 1905 *Essays in Pastoral Medicine*, O'Malley presents two different cases. One is the
case of a ruptured fallopian tube, the other of a tube which
has not yet ruptured. O'Malley first examines the decrees
of the Holy Office, and concludes that they can admit of
various interpretations: "Since the decree concerning lapar-
otomy in extrauterine pregnancy is by no means clear, we may
discuss the question until the law has been fully promulgated, ready to conform to the real meaning of the decree
whenever it is explained."[84]

O'Malley explicitly applies the principle of double effect to the case of a ruptured tube. The act-in-itself is
the clamping off of the blood supply to the hemorrhaging
tube, which results in two effects: the saving of the mother's life and the hastening of the fetus's death. It is
therefore permissible.[85]

O'Malley's analysis of the second case, where an ectop-

---

[84]O'Malley and Walsh, *Essays in Pastoral Medicine,* p. 22.

[85]*Ibid.*, pp. 20-28.

ic pregnancy is discovered before the tube has ruptured, is
totally confused. He argues that the operation is allowed
because the fetus is an unjust aggressor, and thus the mother may act in self defense. Nonetheless the action to be
taken must still be an indirect killing. Thus O'Malley concludes his section: "The practical rule, then, is that the
ectopic foetus will die anyhow, and operation [*sic*] only
indirectly (mark the word) accelerates the inevitable death
of a materially unjust aggressor, while it gives the mother
the best chance for her life, which is in very grave
peril."[86]

By 1912, the year of publication of his second book,
The Ethics of Medical Homicide, O'Malley has changed his
mind about the second case. He no longer considers it moral
to remove an ectopic fetus before hemorrhage has occurred.
The reason for this change he explicitly states to be a
clarifying decision of the Holy Office.[87] In 1902 the Holy
Office declared that it was not allowed to remove an unviable
ectopic fetus from the mother's body. In accord with this

---

[86]*Ibid.*, pp. 34-35, italics his. O'Malley's reason for
introducing the unjust aggressor theory is hard to determine.
He is confused as to whether or not a "direct" means may
ever be taken to hasten the fetus's death. In one place he
says it may be taken, in another he denies this. Thus, approving the theory that the ectopic fetus is a materially
unjust aggressor, he states that therefore "the direct hastening would be licit according to Cardinal de Lugo" (*Essays*,
p. 26--the problem here is that de Lugo approved only indirect means even in cases of self-defense against formally
unjust aggressors, and defined the act-in-itself in terms of
"blows" and "striking" [see Fagothey, *Right and Reason*, p.
290], so that O'Malley misrepresents de Lugo and confuses
the meaning of direct and indirect). On the other hand, in
the passage we have cited in the text, he specifically insists that the means be only indirect. This contradiction
is due in turn to a confusion of the intention of the agent
with the physical direct effect of the act-in-itself.

[87]O'Malley, *Ethics*, pp. 129-130.

decision, O'Malley rejects his previous appeal to the unjust
aggressor theory.[88] He contrasts the removal of the fetus
as direct killing to the removal of a cancerous uterus as
indirect killing.[89] He concludes that once rupture has occurred the blood supply may be cut off, indirectly
killing the fetus. But until rupture has occurred, any removal of the ectopic fetus constitutes a direct attack on
the fetus, forbidden by the decree of the Holy Office.

Another example of the importance of physicalist criteria for O'Malley is in his analysis of mutilations.[90] Yet
here, too, O'Malley's confusion as to the exact meaning of
his terms is apparent. He distinguishes direct and indirect
mutilations, and allows the latter according to the four-
condition double effect principle, which he here states explicitly.[91] What he does not explain, however, is how a
mutilation can ever be indirect in physical terms. He then
goes on to permit direct mutilation in accordance with the
physicalistically limited principle of totality. Thus a direct mutilation may be permitted when it is for the physical
good of the patient's own body, but not for any other reason.
"Therefore," he says, "direct mutilation is not permissible

---

[88]*Ibid.*, pp. 130-131.

[89]*Ibid.*, p. 130. Throughout his entire analysis in both
volumes, O'Malley confuses the intention of the agent and the
direct physical effect of the act. This confusion, coupled
with those we have already mentioned, makes it nearly impossible to arrive at any satisfactory understanding of O'Malley's analysis. Thus he states: "As great an authority as
de Lugo holds that in such defense, whether the aggressor is
formally or only materially such, the victim may *directly*
kill, but direct killing is never necessary, *as it is all a
matter of intention*" (*Ibid.*, p. 131, italics mine).

[90]*Ethics*, pp. 23-32.

[91]*Ibid.*, pp. 26-27.

to effect immediately a spiritual good, or the good of the
soul. We may not castrate a man, or do vasectomy on him, to
preserve his continence, because there is no immediate subordination and connection between the members of the body and
the salvation of the soul."[92] It would seem, then, that
O'Malley allows "direct" mutilations: "The good of the body
is the sole cause that renders direct mutilation licit."[93]
Yet, in confusing the intention of the agent and the direct
physical effect of the act, he contradicts himself when he
says that "it is permissible to mutilate directly to save the
whole body. Direct mutilation, however, is never unavoidable
because *the agent* can always correctly order his *intention*
before the operation."[94] This constant confusion concerning
terms makes O'Malley's analysis nearly impenetrable. Nonetheless, the author insists that these distinctions between
direct and indirect are important.

> This is not hairsplitting in the opprobrious sense of
> that term. The bases of all sins are absolutely ab-
> stract principles, and because abstract principles can-
> not be pinched or weighed, they have often little mean-
> ing for the opposition in an argument. There is only
> the width of a hair between Heaven and Hell at many
> places along the frontier, and there is only the differ-
> ences between a direct or an indirect volition sepa-
> rating murder and a good deed.[95]

Physicalist criteria, however confused they may be in
O'Malley's analysis, are of clear operational significance.
The authority of magisterial decisions is also of great importance. We have noted that O'Malley changes his mind in
the case of a non-ruptured ectopic pregnancy explicitly

---

[92]*Ibid.*, pp. 27-28. For more detail on vasectomy, see
pp. 260-263.

[93]*Ibid.*, p. 27.

[94]*Ibid.*, p. 27, italics mine.

[95]*Essays,* p. 25.

because of a new Roman pronouncement. In this case, ecclesiastical positivism is the dominant modality. O'Malley explicitly states his reason for citing magisterial decrees:
"Decrees of the Catholic Church are cited in these pages, not
because morality is an asset of the Catholic Church alone,
but because it alone pronounces officially on these medical
subjects after careful consideration by competent specialists."[96] It is clear that O'Malley gives total adherence to
these decrees whenever they are available. However, as he
goes on to state, "The Church has made decisions in comparatively few medico-moral cases, and the questions still undecided authoritatively are very numerous."[97] For this reason,
most of O'Malley's analysis is done within the physicalist
rather than the positivist framework. In later years, magisterial pronouncements concerning medical ethical questions
will multiply, and the positivist modality will achieve
greater importance.

The theological principle of God's dominion over life is
used by O'Malley in much the same way as in Coppens and Klarmann. The direct killing of an (innocent) man is forbidden
because "he belongs to no one except to God, who made him."[98]
O'Malley goes on in the same section to explain, however,
that a man may be killed indirectly. Similarly he argues
that only God can order a man to take his own life directly,
since only God has "supreme dominion over human life . . .
God, however, does not by the natural law confer on man the
right thus to kill."[99] That is, God can, by a directly supernatural revelation, order an individual to take his own

---

[96]*Ethics,* Preface [p. 2].

[97]*Ibid.,* Preface [p. 2].

[98]*Essays,* pp. 17-18.

[99]*Ethics,* p. 9.

life. But apart from such a case, man is not allowed to
kill himself directly, since God alone has dominion. He may,
however, take his life indirectly.[100] Similarly, direct
abortion is "an enormous subversion of the order of the natural law, as it is a usurpation of the dominion over life
possessed by God alone."[101] An indirect abortion, as in the
case of hysterectomy of a cancerous uterus, is permitted,
however. Thus the actual distinction between right and
wrong medical procedures is made according to physicalist
(and positivist) criteria. O'Malley does not give any significant role in his ethical analysis to the redemptive value
of suffering.

Other examples could be given of the importance of physicalist and positivist criteria in O'Malley's medical ethical
methodology, but these constitute the most important. We
have seen that O'Malley is often confused in his definitions
and specifications of physicalist terms and distinctions.
Later moralists will draw out the implications of these criteria more clearly and consistently. We have noted that
O'Malley gives primary place to the decrees of the magisterium when they are available, but that in his day relatively
few are specifically applicable to individual medical ethical
issues. Later moralists will give great importance to the
numerous decrees pronounced specifically on medical moral
topics. Finally, we have seen that O'Malley uses the theological principle of God's dominion over life as a general
principle, but that in its specific application to medical
procedures, it is of ancillary importance to physicalist and
positivist criteria.

---

[100]*Ibid.*, pp. 9-10.

[101]*Ibid.*, pp. 111-112.

3. Burke and Finney: Strict Physicalism

Edward Burke's brief 1922 work contains little detailed
analysis, but it offers an example of simple application of
physicalist criteria. Burke's use of magisterial decrees is
confined to an appendix listing.

Burke distinguishes direct and indirect killing. He rejects any argument for abortion based on a conflict of
rights.[102] Direct abortion is always immoral, regardless of
the circumstances. Thus abortions in cases of pernicious
vomiting, eclampsia, or any other medical circumstance, are
forbidden.[103] An indirect abortion is permitted if the four
conditions of the double effect principle are met.[104] Thus
medicines may be given for other illnesses, even if there is
some danger of an abortion being caused.[105] Likewise operations for appendicitis or other ailments are permitted.[106]
The direct emptying of the womb in cases of placenta previa
or hydramnios is forbidden.[107] Burke allows hysterectomy in
cancer cases as indirect, quoting the argument of O'Malley.[108]
The case of ectopic pregnancy is still not solved in the way
in which later moralists will be able to do so, distinguishing simply between direct removal of the fetus from the tube
(immoral) and the removal of the (pathological) tube with the
fetus inside (moral). Like O'Malley, Burke insists that a

---

[102] Burke, *Acute Cases in Moral Medicine,* p. 10.

[103] *Ibid.,* pp. 25-28.

[104] *Ibid.,* pp. 28-32.

[105] *Ibid.,* pp. 33-34.

[106] *Ibid.,* pp. 35-36.

[107] *Ibid.,* pp. 36-42.

[108] *Ibid.,* pp. 44-48.

ruptured tube may be treated by stopping the blood supply,
but that nothing can be done until the rupture occurs.[109]

Burke's use of the positivist modality is secondary to
the physicalist modality. He does list some of the Vatican
decrees in an appendix, but explains that they are not definitive.

> The Holy Office is the Roman Congregation which deals
> with faith and morals. It consists of a college of
> Cardinals under the presidency of the Pope. They are
> assisted by numerous consultors of different nationali-
> ties. They are not endowed with the prerogative of in-
> fallibility, hence their decrees are provisional and
> not definitive. Needless to say these decrees do not
> formulate a new morality; they simply apply the eternal
> principles of morals to specific cases.[110]

This restriction in the importance of the Vatican decrees is
remarkable. Not until the 1960's will moralists again make
explicit restricting arguments of this kind. It is impossible to tell, of course, whether Burke in fact grants a
greater importance to these pronouncements than he gives
them in theory. All of his actual conclusions are in accord
with the decisions of his day. Nonetheless his ethical
analysis is a physicalist one, and no direct importance of
the operational significance of ecclesiastical positivism
can be ascertained in his method.

Patrick Finney's 1922 manual is similar to that of
Burke, in that he gives greatest emphasis to the application
of physicalist criteria in his ethical analysis. He begins
by defining direct abortion as "that which is procured as an
end, or as a means to an end. . . . First, abortion is direct, when it is procured as the immediate end or object of
both the operator [this would seem to refer to the third condition of the double effect principle] and the operation

---

[109]*Ibid.*, pp. 48-54.

[110]*Ibid.*, p. 111.

[the first condition]. Secondly, abortion is direct, when
it is procured as a means for the attainment of some end
[the second condition would then be violated]."[111] Finney
goes on to state that the "moral principles which determine
the morality of direct abortion may be reduced to two: First,
'Thou shalt not kill.' Second, 'Evil must not be done that
good may come of it'; or, in other words, 'A good end does
not justify an evil means.'"[112] This second principle is
merely the second condition of the double effect principle.
The first Finney shows to be not merely a divine precept but
also a mandate of the natural law. He goes on in this context to appeal to the principle of God's dominion over life:
"God alone has dominion over the life of the human fetus,
and He has made its right to life sacred and inviolable, both
by the natural law and by divine precept."[113] Thus the theological principle of God's sovereignty is used as a reason
for forbidding direct abortion, but the actual ethical distinction between those procedures deemed direct and those
deemed indirect is made according to physicalist criteria.

Finney goes on to reject other arguments which might be
applied to the abortion issue so as to permit, in some cases,
direct abortions. He thus rejects the unjust aggressor theory, the argument that the mother has a prior right to life
(there can never be such thing as priority in rights to
life), the norm that one must choose the lesser evil (physical direct abortion is a moral evil, and can never be done
regardless of the physical [ontic] evil thus avoided), and
the argument that necessity knows no law.[114] Finney then

---

[111]Finney, *Moral Problems,* p. 28.

[112]*Ibid.,* p. 30.

[113]*Ibid.,* p. 30.

[114]*Ibid.,* pp. 35-47.

forbids a series of medical procedures because they are direct attacks on the fetus. The fetus may never be killed in
cases of retroflexed uterus, pernicious vomiting, eclampsia,
hydramnios, or placenta previa.[115] Embryotomy and craniotomy
are forbidden, as are all other procedures whose direct effect is the destruction of the fetus, such as abortion by
electric shock or x-rays.[116]

Indirect abortions are permitted, however, according to
the principle of double effect, whose four conditions Finney
lists.[117] The author defines an indirect abortion as one
"that results from the employment of means that are used for
some other end than the expulsion of the fetus, although it
is foreseen that they may unintentionally cause the expulsion
of the fetus. . . . Abortion, therefore, is indirect, when it
is not made the end either of the operator [third condition]
or of the operation [first condition], or when it is not made
a means of achieving even the ultimate end of the operator or
of the operation [second condition]."[118]

According to the double effect principle, operations
such as appendectomy or other surgery during pregnancy are
allowed as is the judicious use of medication.[119] It is not
permitted to give unnecessarily large doses of medicines,
however, or to perform unnecessary treatments. Similarly,
hysterectomy of the cancerous womb is permitted, provided it
is necessary for the mother's life.[120]

---

[115]*Ibid.*, pp. 56-78.

[116]*Ibid.*, pp. 79-95.

[117]*Ibid.*, pp. 97-98. Finney seems to reduce the intention of the agent to the physical direct effect of the act
(pp. 98, 104).

[118]*Ibid.*, pp. 96-97.

[119]*Ibid.*, pp. 105-116.

[120]*Ibid.*, pp. 117-124.

Finney's analysis of ectopic gestation contains all of
the elements needed for precise physicalist distinctions of
the various situations. Like the authors we have already
studied, Finney allows an operation once tubal rupture has
occurred. In this case the operation is aimed at stopping
the hemorrhage, and the death of the fetus is indirect.[121]
Likewise, an enlarged tube may be removed when there is doubt
as to the nature of the growth.[122] When there is no doubt,
however, nothing can be done which would directly attack the
ectopic fetus. Here, however, Finney distinguishes two different kinds of surgical procedures. He first asks, "is it
lawful to remove an inviable ectopic fetus? *Answer:* No, it
is not lawful."[123] Then he asks, "is it lawful, before the
term of viability, to remove the unruptured tube with the
living fetus . . .? *Answer:* No, it is not lawful. Such a
removal is a direct killing of the fetus, and is therefore
forbidden."[124] This distinction is the very one which later
moralists will use to justify the removal of tube-with-fetus
even before rupture has occurred. Thus Finney's analysis
contains the elements necessary for that later judgment.
Finney himself, however, does not come to the same conclusion.
Nor does he further explain *why* he considers the second operation to be a direct abortion. Perhaps it is because of the
decree of the Holy Office of 1902, which he cites.[125] Yet
later moralists will be able to interpret this decree as not
applying to the "indirect" abortion which results from the

---

[121]*Ibid.*, pp. 138-140.

[122]*Ibid.*, pp. 137-138.

[123]*Ibid.*, p. 135, italics his.

[124]*Ibid.*, p. 135, italics his.

[125]*Ibid.*, p. 134.

removal of the enlarged tube. Perhaps it is because Finney
feels it necessary to wait until the danger to the mother
is present, that is, until it is caused by the actually
bleeding tube, and not by the mere presence of the fetus.
Arguments around this precise point will continue in the literature for many years. In any case, though Finney does not
allow the more liberal conclusion of most later moralists
(permitting the removal of the unruptured tube with the fetus inside as an indirect abortion), his analysis contains
all of the precise specifications and distinctions needed for
the traditional solution of the case.

In the issue of mutilation, Finney quotes O'Malley, and
thus continues in the same confusion concerning direct and
indirect mutilations as his predecessor. Indirect mutilations are allowed by the double effect principle.[126] How a
mutilation can ever be indirect is not explained. Direct
mutilations are permitted if they are for the physical good
of the whole body, according to the principle of totality.[127]
Direct sterilizations are never permitted, since the good effect (the prevention of a future danger from pregnancy) is
the result of the bad effect (the sterilization), and thus
the good end justifies the evil means, which violates the
second condition of double effect.[128] Sterilizing operations
may be done, however, if they are indirect, that is, if the
organ is diseased, and its removal necessary for health. In
this case the good effect does not result from the loss of
fertility.[129]

Physicalist criteria are thus central in Finney's analy-

---

[126]*Ibid.*, pp. 146-147.

[127]*Ibid.*, p. 148.

[128]*Ibid.*, pp. 149-155.

[129]*Ibid.*, pp. 155-166.

sis. With the exception of one brief mention of a magisterial decree, there is no appeal to Church authority. The theological principle of God's dominion is applied generally to
the question of killing, but there is little insistence on
it. There is no mention of redemptive suffering.

4. T. Lincoln Bouscaren: An Important Physicalist

Specification

It was T. Lincoln Bouscaren who "solved" the problem of
ectopic pregnancies in a thesis he wrote in 1933.[130] Working
from the various physicalist criteria we have described, he
concludes that an operation to remove a non-ruptured pregnant
fallopian tube is an indirect abortion, and hence permissible
according to the double effect principle. His precise thesis
is this:

> The removal of a pregnant fallopian tube containing a
> non-viable living fetus, even before the external rup-
> ture of the tube, *can be done in such a way that the*
> *consequent death of the fetus will be produced only in-*
> *directly.* Such an operation may be licitly performed
> if all the circumstances are such that the necessity
> for the operation is, in moral estimation, proportionate
> to the evil effect permitted. But in all such opera-
> tions, if the fetus be probably alive, care must be
> taken to baptize the fetus immediately, at least condi-
> tionally.[131]

---

[130]Bouscaren was born in Cincinnati in 1884. He studied
law and served in Oklahoma as an assistant District Attorney
from 1911 to 1913. He entered the Jesuits in 1916 and was
ordained in 1925. He received his doctorate in theology from
the Gregorian in Rome, and taught Canon Law there and in the
Chicago seminary. He was co-author of a text on Canon Law
which served for many years as *the* seminary manual in Canon
Law for American students. His book was his thesis at the
Gregorian, re-edited and published in English in 1933, with a
second revised edition in 1943. The major changes in the
1943 edition consist of an updating of medical procedures.
The moral conclusions do not differ.

[131]Bouscaren, *Ethics of Ectopic Operations,* 1st ed.,

The core of Bouscaren's argument is based on the physicalist
specification of the act-in-itself, defined as the direct
removal of the tube including indirectly the removal and
death of the fetus. He insists that the fallopian tube is
pathological from the beginning of an ectopic pregnancy, and
that its removal may thus be allowed in order to save the
mother's life.

Bouscaren begins by tracing briefly the history of the
abortion controversy. He notes that recent decrees of the
Holy Office have ruled out any appeal to various arguments
that might be used to support direct abortions, such as the
unjust aggressor theory.[132] He then presents some of the
arguments used for and against the removal of an unruptured
fallopian tube, and concludes that "several great moral theologians have failed to provide an adequate and satisfactory
solution. The primary reason seems to have been a certain
vagueness of concept or at least of expression, in regard to
the physical nature of the operation."[133] It is this very
vagueness which we have seen reflected in the North American
moralists we have studied thus far. Bouscaren then proceeds
to analyze the double effect principle, and concludes:

> Accordingly, if an objection to our solution of the
> problems of ectopic pregnancy be based fundamentally
> on a failure to understand or a refusal to accept the
> principle itself of double effect, then we say simply
> that that objection is in conflict with the whole trend
> of Catholic moral teaching for more than six hundred
> years. It is practically impossible to call that prin-
> ciple into question.[134]

This is clear testimony to the central importance of double

---

p. 2; 2nd ed., pp. 1-2, italics mine.

[132]*Ibid.*, 1st ed., pp. 5-22; 2nd ed., pp. 4-16.

[133]*Ibid.*, 1st ed., p. 28; 2nd ed., p. 20.

[134]*Ibid.*, 1st ed., pp. 51-52; 2nd ed., p. 37.

effect, with its physicalist criteria, to Roman Catholic
medical ethical methodology.

The author goes on to mention various arguments which
might be used as reasons for permitting direct abortions.
He rejects these, and includes among his reasons the theological principle that "God alone has direct and complete
dominion over every individual human life,"[135] as well as
the decisions of the magisterium.[136] Bouscaren is clear in
accepting the binding authority of the decrees: "We admit in
general the binding character of these decisions. As far as
their subject matter is concerned, it is evident that they
present Catholic doctrine on morals, and they are therefore
within the general competency of the Holy Office."[137] But
he insists that these decrees are meant to apply only to
cases of direct abortion, and do not forbid procedures which
cause abortion indirectly.[138]

Bouscaren then goes on to distinguish two possible operational procedures in treating unruptured tubal pregnancies.
The first, and most common medically, is to remove the swol-
len tube with the fetus inside. The second, which Bouscaren
claims to be medically obsolete, is to kill the fetus first
by removing the amniotic fluid or by drugs or electric shock,
or to slit open the tube and remove the fetus, and then remove the tube itself. These procedures he considers to be
certainly direct abortions. "It is one thing to remove the
tube containing the fetus; it is another thing to remove the
fetus directly."[139] The former is allowed according to the

---

[135]*Ibid.*, 1st ed., p. 71; 2nd ed., p. 52.

[136]*Ibid.*, 1st ed., p. 71, pp. 80-85; 2nd ed., p. 52,
pp. 58-62.

[137]*Ibid.*, 1st ed., p. 81; 2nd ed., p. 59.

[138]*Ibid.*, 1st ed., pp. 82-85; 2nd ed., pp. 60-62.

[139]*Ibid.*, 1st ed., p. 140; 2nd ed., p. 102.

double effect principle, the latter is forbidden.

There remains one objection to Bouscaren's thesis, which he ascribes to Finney. Finney, as we have seen, insisted that the removal of the unruptured tube was a direct abortion, and that the physician was obliged to wait until tubal rupture, at which time an operation to stop the bleeding would be an indirect abortion. In a 1928 article Finney gives as reason for this conclusion that in the case of an unruptured tubal pregnancy "it is the pregnancy, and not some pathological condition of the tube apart from the pregnancy that threatens the mother's life."[140] Bouscaren answers the objection by specifying the physical causal chain obtaining both in the disease and in the operation. The pregnancy is the cause of the pathological condition of the tube, but the object of the operation is not the pregnancy, but the tube, which is already pathological due to the presence of the ectopic fetus. Since the direct physical effect of the operation is to remove the diseased tube and not to kill the fetus, the operation is allowed. The fact that the cause of the tubal pathology is the pregnancy is irrelevant to the solution of the case.[141] As long as there is due proportion for the operation (the mother's life is threatened), the removal of the tube with the fetus inside is permitted, since the killing of the fetus is only indirect.

With Bouscaren's thesis the precise physicalist distinctions and specifications needed for medical ethical application are fixed. Though some controversy continues concerning ectopic operations, the argument always proceeds from within the physicalist framework.

---

[140]Finney, as cited in Bouscaren, 1st ed., p. 160; 2nd ed., p. 154.

[141]Bouscaren, 1st ed., pp. 160-162; 2nd ed., pp. 154-155.

The modality of ecclesiastical positivism is also significant in Bouscaren's analysis, though not as central as
the physicalist modality. We have noted that he cites magisterial decrees and accepts their binding authority. In
aruging for his own interpretation of these decrees, he
states: "We admit that this interpretation can be made absolutely certain only by a further authentic declaration of
the Sacred Congregation itself."[142] It is significant for
the thesis of our next chapter to note the changes Bouscaren
made in his second edition, published in 1943. He adds this
sentence to his foreword: "From the doctrinal standpoint it
is scarcely necessary to add that the author wholeheartedly
submits in advance to any decision which might at any time
in the future be issued by authority of the infallible
Church upon any moral doctrine or conclusion contained in
this book."[143] This kind of explicit declaration is typical
of the medical ethics literature of the 1940's and 1950's,
when the modality of ecclesiastical positivism becomes more
and more dominant.

* * *

We have now traced the literature of the earlier period
in the emergence of Roman Catholic North American medical
ethics. Our purpose has been to describe the operation of
theological methodology in its actual application to medical
ethical questions. We have seen the dominant importance of
physicalist criteria within the double effect framework. We
have noted the process by which these criteria were developed
more and more exactly and applied with greater and greater

---

[142]*Ibid.*, 1st ed., p. 83; 2nd ed., p. 61.

[143]*Ibid.*, 2nd ed. only, p. viii.

precision to the central questions of medical ethics of the
period. The exact physical structure of the specified act-
in-itself, the precise causal chain by which good and bad effects result from the causing procedure, and the physical or
biological goal or purpose of human faculties have been seen
as playing dominant roles in the theological method. We have
also noted the importance of the decrees of the Roman Catholic hierarchy, and the various degrees of submission given
to them by Catholic moralists. Within these two modalities
we have seen the operational significance of the theological
principle of God's dominion over human life and, to a lesser
extent, of the principle of redemptive suffering. These
principles are applied within the modalities of physicalism
and ecclesiastical positivism.

By 1940 the physicalist modality is largely fixed in application to medical ethical issues. It continues to be of
great operational significance in the second period of our
discipline. Now, however, the explicit use of authoritative
decrees of the Catholic Church takes on a greater and greater
importance. It is to this second period that we now turn.

CHAPTER FIVE

LATER WORKS (1940-1960):

THE SHIFT TOWARDS ECCLESIASTICAL POSITIVISM

With the general acceptance by the 1930's of physicalism in double effect theory, the basic traditional methodology of medical ethics was fixed. It would continue in force until the time of the second Vatican Council. With few exceptions, conclusions as to the rightness and wrongness of specific medical practices would remain as they had been decided according to double effect.

The later period of the emergence of Roman Catholic medical ethics in North America gives evidence of a sometimes subtle but nonetheless clear and significant increase in emphasis on the role the visible Church structures play and ought to play in deciding issues. Working from within the physicalist modality, the moral theologians of the forties and fifties begin to emphasize the active role of the magisterium in making definitive ethical decisions. The medical ethics manuals rely more and more heavily on Church decisions, and this reliance often overshadows other forms of argumentation. It is this shift in methodological modality which will be the focus of this chapter. As in the last chapter, we will begin with a systematic analysis of the modality itself and then turn to the literature of the period to describe how it developed and operated in medical ethics.

Part One

Ecclesiastical Positivism

Ecclesiastical positivism in medical ethics (or in moral

theology in general) is not a new creation of the 1940's and
1950's. In the previous chapter we have seen instances of
scholars who emphasized the decisive role of the Catholic
magisterium in determining moral judgments. With the accession of Pius XII to the papacy, however, a period begins
which gives evidence of a greater degree of emphasis on this
approach than is present in previous decades. There is no
clear dividing point between the time of the development of
physicalism in medical ethics and the time of its defense by
appeal to ecclesiastical authority. Just as in the earlier
period appeal was made to Church authority, so in the 1940's
and 1950's the physicalist interpretation of the double effect principle continues as the key operative principle in
Catholic medical ethics. The study of the literature of the
later period does demonstrate, however, a growing emphasis on
explicit appeal to magisterial decisions. Whereas in the
earlier period the emphasis was on working out the fundamental principles for universal application, on bringing added
precision to the definitions and specifications needed for
application to difficult cases, now there will be a shift
toward a defense of the principles and specifications thus
developed. Whereas earlier literature is directed generally
to Roman Catholic audiences, and presumes the agreement of
its readers, the medical ethical literature of the later period is more consciously aware of the diversity of its audience. Both Catholics and non-Catholics may need convincing.
Catholics are urged to show their allegiance to the inerrant
authority of the Church, which is emphasized as a primary
guarantee of the conclusions presented, conclusions often
disputed in the general medical profession whose opinions
Catholics confront daily. Non-Catholics, too, are urged to
respect magisterial decisions. Though not expected to accept theoretically the authority of the Church, they are
told that only Catholic authority can correctly interpret

the natural law. This law binds all people, regardless of
religious affiliation, since it does not depend intrinsically on supernatural revelation. But since it can be understood completely only by divinely guaranteed Church authority, non-Catholics are in practice urged to accept the ethical authority of the Catholic Church.[1]

One of the causes for this shift in emphasis was the
increasing integration of Catholics into the mainstream of
American life. In 1900 there were an estimated 12 million
Catholics in the United States.[2] By 1940 the number had
probably risen to 30 million, though the official *Catholic
Directory* figure for the year was 23 million.[3] 1921 marked
the first of a number of restrictive immigration laws, which
led to a relative stabilization of the American Catholic population.[4] John Tracy Ellis notes that "if the first generation of these ethnic groups clung to their respective ghet-
tos, their children were much less content to do so, and
their grandchildren broke entirely with the Old World framework and sought--with striking success--to enter the mainstream of American life."[5] The Catholic Hospital system grew
to be an important part of American medical care, and took on

---

[1]We will have occasion to note examples of this as we
survey the literature of the period. An excellent statement
of this position is that by Gerald Kelly, whose opinion certainly represents that held by the mainstream of Catholic
moral thinkers of the time, though other moralists were often
not as forthright in expressing it. See Kelly, *Medico-Moral
Problems,* 1958 ed., pp. 2, 26-35; and *Medico-Moral Problems,*
Part I, 1949, pp. 5-9. Some subtle changes over the years
between these two articles are of interest. We will speak of
Kelly later.

[2]Ellis, *American Catholicism,* pp. 124-125.

[3]*Ibid.*

[4]*Ibid.,* p. 129.

[5]*Ibid.,* pp. 167-168.

an ever increasing role in offering medical services to non-
Catholics, who began to participate more and more officially
in it. The Second World War brought about increased cooperation across denominational lines in medical matters. American Catholic scholars were just beginning to join the intellectual dialogues of wider circles. Thus what had been
previously presumed as needing little defense in a literature directed largely to strictly Catholic readers now came
to require a more explicit apologetic.

The great interest shown by Pope Pius XII (pope from
1939 to 1958) in medical ethical issues also contributed to
the accent on ecclesiastical positivism. Whereas in previous decades there had been relatively few direct magisterial
pronouncements in the area,[6] now the new pope and his curial
agencies will issue large numbers of statements of various
kinds, including encyclicals and addresses to various groups,
on medical ethical topics. Writing in 1955, Gerald Kelly
estimated that there were to that moment about sixty different statements on medical ethics by Pius XII.[7] The importance given by Catholics to these statements can be demonstrated by the large number of lists of such statements added
to texts in medical ethics, as well as a number of antholo-
gies devoted primarily or exclusively to the pope's addresses
on medical ethics.[8] We will note the use of these papal

---

[6]We have already noted how one early (1919) moralist
noted the paucity of authoritative decisions and the large
number of still undecided questions (O'Malley, *The Ethics of
Medical Homicide,* Preface [p. 2]; see above, p. 297).

[7]Kelly, "Medico-Moral Notes," 1955, p. 57.

[8]For example: "Pope Pius XII and Medicine: List of Discourses on Medical Topics"; Werth and Mihanovich, *Papal Pronouncements on Marriage and the Family;* De Letter, "The Pope
on Medical Questions"; Kothen, *Directives récentes de
l'Église concernant l'exercice de la médecine; Papal Teachings: The Human Body; Papal Teachings: Matrimony;* and Pius
XII, *Discorsi ai medici.* These last three contain the texts

statements by many medical moralists.

Our introductory description of physicalism as applied
to medical ethical issues in the double effect principle was
of necessity lengthy. The various subtle specifications
used in conjunction with the principle were seen to be of
immediate practical importance in distinguishing right from
wrong procedures. Since our task has been to demonstrate the
operative importance of theological principles, we were able
to pass over the theoretical questions of the natural law and
of Christian anthropology, and to concentrate on the way in
which double effect physicalism was in fact used to judge
medical procedures.

The same approach will be used here. Ecclesiastical
positivism, however, unlike double effect physicalism, is
far easier to understand in its practical aspects. The theoretical questions connected with it are vast and complex,
but from the point of view of its actual ethical applications it is rather easy to describe. Practical ecclesiastical positivism is a practical species of theological voluntarism (theonomous moral positivism) or of metaethical supernatural absolutism,[9] according to which an action is to be

---

of most of the important documents.

[9]This latter term is commonly used by moral philosophers. It refers to the theory according to which a given
act, together with its attendant motives, situations, and
circumstances, can be judged as right or wrong. The judgment
can, at least in theory, be universally verified. (This distinguishes all metaethical absolutist theories from relativ-
ist and non-cognitive metaethical theories.) Its verification is possible by discovering that God has in fact willed
it to be right or wrong. This latter aspect distinguishes
supernatural metaethical absolutism from metaethical abso-
lutisms of the rational, intuitionist, or empirical type.
The traditional Catholic natural law approach would be closest to the empirical type of metaethical absolutism, since,
at least in theory, ethical judgments are made by right reason examining the action in itself and in its circumstances

considered right or wrong as it is or is not acceptable to
the teaching authority of the Church. It will be the purpose of the second part of this chapter to demonstrate the
operative importance of this approach in the medical ethics
of the period. First, however, a brief discussion of some of
of the theoretical questions of ecclesiastical positivism is
in order.

It must be noted that Catholic moralists consistently
claimed *not* to be ecclesiastical positivists. In the *theoretical* definition of moral positivism in the strict sense
this was indeed the case.

The first distinction that must be made here is between
moral positivism and legal positivism. Legal positivism refers simply to the right of a society to pass positive laws
for its members. There is no implication that the positive
laws thus passed are morally required in themselves. A society may decide that driving is to be on the right side of
the road with no insistence that this is a moral law in itself. Of course the citizens may now be morally obliged to
follow the law, but their moral obligation comes from the
moral good to be sought by not harming their fellow drivers.
There is nothing intrinsically immoral about left-side
driving. Driving on the right might just as well have been

---

and motives in relationship to human nature as God created
it to be. Empirical metaethical absolutism need not be non-
theistic. It need only be not a theological voluntarism,
not a theonomous moral positivism. For a typology and description of metaethical theories, the one which we have
used here, see Veatch, "Does Ethics Have an Empirical Basis?"
pp. 52-58. Veatch does not discuss the process by which men
might discover God's will, however. Presumably the supernatural authority of a Church would be one such way. Veatch
does not explicitly exclude an examination of human nature
as another way, but this latter would presumably be closer
to what he means by empirical metaethical absolutism. The
exact lines of demarcation between the various metaethical
approaches are not clear, and thus some confusion must inevitably result.

forbidden. The Catholic Church has traditionally insisted
on its own right, as a society, to make such laws. Laws of
fast and abstinence, Sunday Mass laws, and some of the canonical marriage laws are examples. Though Catholics may be
said to be obliged in conscience to follow them, they are
merely human positive laws, in the sense that the Church may
change them. Often the word "disciplinary" has been used to
refer to laws of this type. Moral positivism, on the other
hand, refers to the theory that moral right and wrong is established, created, by the positive willing of some law
giver.[10] Actions are right or wrong, not according to some
intrinsic quality which renders them such (deontological
ethics), nor according to their consequences (consequential
ethics), which quality and consequences are somehow discovered in the ethical entity, but according to the positing of
the law giver. The law giver can be God, in which case we
speak of theonomous moral positivism or theological voluntarism, or men, in which case we have autonomous moral positivism.[11] The characteristic common to both is that an action
is right because commanded or wrong because forbidden rather
than commanded because right or forbidden because wrong.

Catholic moralists seldom adhered *theoretically* to a
strict theonomous moral positivism. There have been adher-
ents of the theory among nominalists,[12] of course. But the
general moral tradition of Catholic thought has been opposed
to theoretical nominalism and voluntarism, and has emphasized
a natural law theory. Within the medical ethical literature
we are studying we have seen this clearly, and will continue

---

[10] See González, "Positivism, Moral."

[11] *Ibid.*, p. 1257.

[12] The history of nominalism and voluntarism is beyond
the scope of this chapter. Clearly nominalist influence is
operative in the theory of theonomous moral positivism.

to do so in the literature of the later period. Actions are
held to be right or wrong according to their own intrinsic
nature and the nature of man, which nature can be determined
by the analysis of right reason. Moral law is not created
by the arbitrary whim of God, but rather is imbedded by the
creator in human nature as he created it to be.[13]

Nonetheless, in a less strict sense a *de-facto* or *practical* moral positivism operated extensively as a modality of
application of theological principles in medical ethics.
Though theoretically acts were right or wrong according to
the natural law, which law every man ought to know by his
right reason, in practice it was often considered necessary
for the Church to teach God's will in disputed matters.
Only the Church was given such authority by Christ. Thus in
practice it was often the pronouncements of the magisterium
which determined the conclusions reached by Catholic moralists.[14]

Thus we have a generally consistent denial of the theory
of strict theonomous or ecclesiastical positivism, together
with a concomitant affirmation of the right of the Church to
interpret natural law. The problem as to how a moral law
could be a natural law and still require the direct intervention of a supernatural body for its explanation was never
sufficiently explained. At times emphasis was placed on the
scientific ethical expertise of Catholic moralists,[15] but

---

[13]Again see Kelly, *Medico-Moral Problems,* 1958 ed., pp.
28-30; *Medico-Moral Problems,* Part I, 1949, pp. 6-7.

[14]We have already spoken of the distinction made between
moral theology and "natural" philosophical ethics. We noted
that even in works explicitly claiming to be based solely on
natural reason, theological and ecclesiastical authorities
were in fact utilized (see above, pp. 236-241).

[15]See Kelly, *Medico-Moral Problems,* 1958 ed., pp. 33-35;
Medico-Moral Problems, Part I, 1949, pp. 7-8.

this failed to explain why these moralists changed their
opinions in accord with and explicitly on account of authoritative pronouncements. Thus there was a tension, not always acknowledged, between the theoretical rejection of
strict moral positivism and the theoretical and practical
affirmation of ecclesiastical positivism in another sense,
in the insistence on the right of the Church to be the sole
authoritative interpreter of the natural law. Often the destructive influence of sin on man's capacity to understand
the natural law was cited. But this explanation, while perhaps correct in itself (sin does indeed hinder one's intel-
lect), did not alter the fact that a supernatural body was
required to judge concerning God's law, which could hardly
now be called a purely "natural" law, since the natural law
was supposed to be a law written in creation and in fact
discoverable by man's reason without any direct supernatural
revelation. Yet only the teaching Church, with its divine
mandate, was said to be the authoritative interpreter of
natural law. It was often pronouncements of the magisterium
which determined the conclusions reached by Catholic moralists. Thus, though the theory of theological voluntarism or
theonomous or ecclesiastical moral positivism in the strict
sense is rejected, in a less exact sense it is affirmed, and
in practice it operates as a dominant approach in medical
ethics of the period.[16]

---

[16]As will be shown in the next section. For a clear
statement of some of the difficulties we have noted concerning the traditional answer given to charges of positivism,
see St. John-Stevas, *Life, Death and the Law*, pp. 29-31. He
writes: "Such an answer, while consonant in theory, certainly carries little conviction in practice. . . . Catholics
would be acting more reasonably if . . . they treated the
morality of birth control [his topic, but the same applies
to other ethical issues under dispute] as within the sphere
of moral theology, a science based on revelation and the
teaching authority of the Church, rather than on natural

Other theoretical issues connected with ecclesiastical
positivism are of obvious importance. The entire problematic of the divine institution of the Church and of its teaching authority, ordinary and extraordinary magisterium, infallibility of the Church and of the pope, the work of the
Spirit in ecclesial inerrancy, the extent to which sin hind-
ers knowledge of the natural law, and the difference between
dogmatic and moral matters in authoritative (or infallible)
pronouncements is of great theoretical interest as well as
of practical importance for Catholic moral thought. The
literature on these issues in recent years is extensive.[17]
Our own task lies rather in describing the actual operative
influence of this and of other theological principles in
medical ethics.

---

ethics" (p. 30). The problem is that even the explicit moral theologians claim, as we have seen, to argue primarily
from a natural law position and to reject moral positivism;
they claim that their conclusions apply to everyone, not
only to Catholics. Thus the problem which St. John-Stevas
correctly points out applies to moral theologians of the
period as well as to Catholic moral philosophers. In any
case, we have already pointed out that the nominal distinction made between "ethics" and moral theology, a distinction
which St. John-Stevas uses in his analysis, fails to lead to
any real substantive difference in the two disciplines, and
that in medical ethics such a distinction is of no practical
importance either as to method used or conclusions reached
(see above, pp. 236-241). For another statement of the ambiguities we are describing, see Baum, "The Right to Dissent," pp. 72-73. We will discuss this further in chapter
six, part two.

[17]Among more specifically moral works, see Curran, *A
New Look*, pp. 89-106, 125-143; *Catholic Moral Theology in
Dialogue*, pp. 150-183; "Natural Law and the Teaching Author-
ity of the Church"; *Ongoing Revision*, pp. 37-65; Maguire,
"Moral Absolutes and the Magisterium."

Part Two

The Literature of the Later Period

1. Alphonsus Bonnar: The Importance of Church Authority

The emphasis on ecclesiastical positivism as a modality of application of theological principles is clear in the work *The Catholic Doctor* by the British scholar Alphonsus Bonnar, which, as we have seen, achieved widespread popularity in America. Bonnar intends his work to be an "exposition of the teaching of the Church on medico-moral questions."[18] Decrying the current pagan atmosphere as more dangerous than the Protestant ethos of which Newman complained in 1842, Bonnar states, "The Catholic alone stands secure, the only complete rationalist, firm upon the rock which Christ gave him."[19] Bonnar's insistence on the importance of ecclesiastical authority is most clearly demonstrated by the fact that he devotes his entire first chapter to a defense of the authority of the Catholic Church. He considers this to be "part of [the] necessary intellectual background" needed for understanding medical ethics.[20] Thus an acceptance of Catholic authority is explicitly proposed as central to a correct understanding of medical morality. The author presents in this chapter a brief defense of the Catholic teaching authority based on divine guarantee as found in the New Testament teaching of Christ. He distinguishes infallible from non-infallible pronouncements, but insists on both internal and external assent to the latter as well as the former in almost all cases, except where an

---

[18]Bonnar, *The Catholic Doctor*, 2nd ed., p. xiii.

[19]*Ibid.*, p. xiv.

[20]*Ibid.*, p. xiv.

outstandingly well informed person might disagree with a
non-infallible decree. He would then be bound to avoid any
public (external) dissent. But he considers this last case
"an almost impossible hypothesis,"[21] because the teaching of
the ordinary (non-infallible) magisterium is that of a lawful, divinely guaranteed authority. Bonnar then discusses
Canon Law, the Church as sanctifier, and the Church and
science.

     In his third chapter, Bonnar presents the traditional
distinction between natural law, "the sum-total of all that
our unaided reason prescribes as necessary for the proper
moral ordering of our lives,"[22] and divine positive law, as
it is found in the Judaeo-Christian tradition. The former
"obliges all men, everywhere, at all times."[23] The latter
obliges those who are Jews or Christians.[24]

     Bonnar explains the relationship between Church author-
ity and the natural law.

> To digress for a moment. These matters [abortion,
> scandal, cooperation in evil] are all matters of *natu-*
> *ral* morality. We must not envisage them as being wrong
> because the Church forbids them, but remember that the
> Church forbids them because they are wrong: and the
> Church (as we have already pointed out) has the right
> and duty to define or interpret natural morality. When,
> therefore, I speak here of a Catholic not being allowed
> to do certain things, I do not imply that a non-Catholic
> is allowed to do them, but merely that the non-Catholic
> often does not know his duty in these things. . . . If
> there is opposition between common medical teaching and
> the morality defined by the Church, one or the other
> must be wrong: and we know that the Church is right and
> must be obeyed. It is for medical teaching to bring

---

[21]*Ibid.*, p. 7.

[22]*Ibid.*, p. 30.

[23]*Ibid.*, p. 32.

[24]*Ibid.*, p. 33.

itself into line with morality.[25]
Thus we can see that Bonnar is not theoretically a theonomous moral positivist. Natural morality ought to be known
by all men. But since it is not, and since the Church alone
has the divinely guaranteed authority to define and interpret
that law, it is in fact the pronouncements of the Church
which are definitive in distinguishing right from wrong actions. Thus practical ecclesiastical positivism is a dominant methodological modality in Bonnar's work. An explicit
defense of the teaching authority of the Catholic hierarchy
is a part of his medical ethics. This explicit emphasis
typifies the theological methodology of the works of the
later period.

In his analysis of individual medical ethical issues,
Bonnar uses both physicalist and positivist modalities. The
teaching of Church authorities is frequently cited. He distinguishes direct and indirect abortion, and allows the removal of a tubal pregnancy as an indirect abortion, though
he gives little detail here concerning the specifications
developed by other moralists we have studied.[26] His treatment of sterilization is likewise brief, and contains little
detailed analysis. Bonnar is content here to condemn the
practice, and to insist that the Church opposes sterilization
on the basis of the natural law, not on the basis of any
purely ecclesiastical promulgation.[27]

Bonnar's emphasis is thus on presenting the authoritative teaching of the Church in medico-moral matters, and in
defending that authority. He avoids any detailed analysis of
the double effect principle with its physicalist specifica-

---

[25]*Ibid.*, p. 39, italics his.

[26]*Ibid.*, pp. 72-88.

[27]*Ibid.*, pp. 116-117.

tions, though he does present it briefly[28] and does make use
of the direct-indirect distinction. In Bonnar's work the
basic operative modality is that of ecclesiastical positivism.[29]

2. Some Works of the Early 1940's

Both methodological modalities are operative in the
pocket-sized *Handbook of Medical Ethics* by Canadian scholars
La Rochelle and Fink. This work gives less emphasis to
Church authority than did Bonnar, and provides somewhat more
detail concerning the double effect distinctions. The authors name as the two sources of morality the natural law
and "the positive laws of God which have been revealed."[30]
They claim that "the *teaching* of morals belongs to the
Church, since our Lord Himself entrusted to it the mission
to teach all nations."[31] A nurse must follow her conscience
faithfully, "above all when it is supported by an authentic
interpretation by the Church."[32] The authors continue:

> It is therefore necessary to understand why certain
> operations and manipulations are forbidden. In the
> first place they are not explicitly so forbidden by

---

[28]*Ibid.*, p. 42.

[29]This emphasis is also found in some of the reviews
written of the work. "They [Catholic physicians] should
firmly unite to uphold the teaching of the Church, which appears in this day to be the only authority which stands
squarely on the bedrock of sane reason" (*Sign*, 17 [1938],
569). "In a word, it is only the doctor with the complete
Catholic mind, informed by Catholic doctrine and morals, who
can fully appreciate the reasons for which certain things
are said to be unlawful" (*Irish Ecclesiastical Record*, 51
[1938], 332).

[30]La Rochelle and Fink, *Handbook*, 8th ed., p. 24.

[31]*Ibid.*, p. 24, italics his.

[32]*Ibid.*, p. 62.

priests, bishops or the Pope and not even by the Catholic Church as such, but they are declared to be forbidden by these authorities because they are contrary
to the laws of nature and to God Who is the author of
these laws. The Church which is the guardian of inte-
gral truth is charged with the mission of making it
known to us in a more concise and authentic manner than
profane science which is not concerned with morality.[33]

An entire chapter is devoted to the double effect principle, which is applied to a wide variety of cases, including
abortion, sterilization, the professional secret, and scandal. The authors list the four conditions of the principle,
and are careful to distinguish effect from intention, thus
differentiating the first two conditions from the third.[34]

In their section on contraception, La Rochelle and Fink
give a number of reasons against the practice, among which
are spiritual and physical harm to both man and woman (a
long list of diseases is presented which are said to result
from contraception, and the woman is warned that the more
she has sexual intercourse, "the more she herself must endure as a result"[35]), as well as a general demoralization of
the family and society. God's punishment of Onan in the Old
Testament is cited.[36] The central argument is that contraception *directly* prevents procreation, and is thus contrary
to God's will.[37] Periodic continence is allowed as morally
indifferent in itself, but the authors insist that it is
often sinful because selfish. They suggest as most conform-

---

[33]*Ibid.*, pp. 62-63.

[34]*Ibid.*, p. 54. For the problem, see above, pp. 255-256.

[35]*Ibid.*, p. 73. The authors do not explain what it is
that she must endure, but the implication is that she must
endure more sex. She is urged not to be "a slave to a de-
generate" (*Ibid.*, p. 74).

[36]*Ibid.*, pp. 66-67.

[37]*Ibid.*, p. 72.

able to the marriage ideal the limitation of intercourse to
periods of fertility, in order that a couple may have a
large family and still "concede as little as possible to
their fleshly appetite."[38]   Thus a clear anti-sexual dualism
is present in the argument along with the proscription of
direct frustration of the physical end of the sexual faculty.

Artificial insemination is forbidden when it involves
masturbation, allowed when it consists of pushing sperm
further into the vaginal tract after normal intercourse.[39]
Decrees of the Holy Office are cited.

When considering abortion, the authors make the traditional distinction between direct and indirect abortion.
They cite the fifth commandment as forbidding abortions
which are directly induced.   They are quite clear that the
key issue is the means involved, regardless of the reason
which motivates the action.[40]   A physical evil (the death of
the mother) must be preferred to a moral evil (direct abortion).[41]   The unjust aggressor theory is rejected.[42]   The
authors show that indirect abortion in the case of a diseased
uterus is permitted to save the life of the mother.[43]   With
respect to ectopic operations, they present the various arguments we have already discussed, and conclude that it is not
necessary to wait until tubal rupture has occurred before
removing the tube and, indirectly, the fetus.   Any operation
which would remove the fetus from the tube is forbidden as a

---

[38] *Ibid.*, p. 81.

[39] *Ibid.*, p. 90.

[40] *Ibid.*, pp. 95-98.

[41] *Ibid.*, p. 105b.

[42] *Ibid.*, p. 107.

[43] *Ibid.*, pp. 115-119.

direct abortion. The authors state that since some of
these conclusions are still controverted (we have noted the
debate between Finney and Bouscaren), the procedures are
authorized "until competent authorities explicitly express a
contrary opinion."[44] Thus the physicalist natural law arguments are subordinated to the pronouncements of the magisterium.

The theological principle of God's dominion over human
life is explicitly cited in the section on sterilization and
mutilation. "To understand more fully what follows," say the
authors, "let us remember that *God alone is the absolute*
master of our bodies and of all their parts, while we are
simply the custodians. We have over our own members only
that power which is given them for their natural ends."[45]
Direct mutilations are allowed for the good of the whole
body, but only indirect sterilizations are permitted. This
is because direct sterilization "frustrates nature's plan,
and thus opposes the will of the Creator; because it refuses
to acknowledge the sovereign right of God over our bodies;
because it opens the door to all sorts of abuses . . . because it is contrary to the chief end of marriage, procreation . . . because it robs marriage of its moral side, of occasions of practicing virtue and the graces which follow the
Christian acceptance of suffering."[46] The theological principles of God's dominion over life and of the redemptive
value of suffering are thus incorporated into the argument,
the main basis of which is to distinguish right from wrong
acts according to the direct and indirect specifications of
the double effect principle. A sterilization is permitted

---

[44]*Ibid.*, p. 127.

[45]*Ibid.*, p. 132, italics his.

[46]*Ibid.*, p. 135.

if indirect, that is, if the organ removed is diseased and
the sterilizing effects are not directly intended. If the
sterilization is done in order to prevent future pregnancies,
it is immoral regardless of the reason which militates
against such pregnancy. The authors also argue against punitive sterilization, while conceding that other, non-sterilizing punitive mutilations are licit. The difference is
that in sterilization "we enter the *sacred domain of the be-
getting of children*."[47] While it is licit to kill a criminal, it is illicit to sterilize him. The authors seem unsure as to the ultimate reason for this, and simply appeal
to the authoritative condemnation by the Church.[48]

Concerning euthanasia and the prolongation of life, the
authors again make use of the theological principles of God's
dominion and of redemptive suffering. The patient must be
given the chance to bear sufferings as a means of sanctifica-
tion and purification. The final argument is that "*God* alone
has full dominion over human lives."[49] The authors make explicit use here of the double effect principle, proscribing
the deliberate hastening of death, while allowing the use of
sedatives in the degree necessary to alleviate pain, even if
the dose necessary "will *send him to sleep* and make him slip
out quietly when his time comes, *without wakening . . . provided the patient has been made ready*."[50] The authors also
insist on non-physicalist theological arguments against the
use of such sedatives when there is a chance of the dying
patient making good use of his consciousness or of his sufferings to prepare for death. On the other hand, if it is

---

[47]*Ibid.*, pp. 153-154, italics his.

[48]*Ibid.*, p. 155.

[49]*Ibid.*, p. 169, italics his.

[50]*Ibid.*, p. 180, italics his.

feared that a conscious patient might commit a mortal sin,
sedatives may be given in order to render him unconscious,
provided he has been prepared for death.[51]   This opinion is
at variance with the more general theory that loss of consciousness may not be directly induced, but only indirectly
allowed when pain is relieved.

La Rochelle and Fink thus utilize both the physicalist
and the positivist modalities. Generally the theological
principles of God's dominion and of redemptive suffering are
applied within these frameworks. An exception is the question of the spiritual preparation of a dying patient.[52]

The importance of ecclesiastical decrees is noted in
the 1940 fourth edition by Perrier of Trudel's *Éléments de
morale médicale*. In explaining why he believes a revision
to be necessary, Perrier states that "changing circumstances,
the progress of medical science, and above all the official
declarations of the ecclesiastical magisterium touching on
these matters have imposed themselves on those whose vocation
is the care of the sick."[53]   In this work, as well as in the
similar text of Dufort,[54] both physicalist and positivist
modalities are operative.

In an article written in 1943, the Redemptorist moralist
Francis J. Connell lists five basic principles of Catholic

---

[51]*Ibid.*, pp. 179-180.

[52]This exception has already been noted. See above, pp.
276-277, n. 42.

[53]Trudel and Perrier, *Éléments de morale médicale,* introduction to the fourth edition, [p. 1], translation mine.
"le changement des circomstances, les progrès de la science
médicale et surtout les déclarations officielles du magistère
Ecclésiastique touchant ces mattières imposaient à la
conscience de ceux dont le devoir d'état est le soin des
malades."

[54]Dufort, *Application de l'éthique professionelle.*

medical ethics.[55] Of the five, four are physicalist: first,
the end does not justify the means (the second condition of
double effect); second, the double effect principle itself;
third, the distinction of formal and material cooperation in
an evil operation (another way of stating double effect, in
that an action not evil in itself [material cooperation] may
be performed even though an indirect evil effect may be foreseen to result); and fourth, the end of the marriage act is
procreation. We have already given a detailed discussion of
the physicalist implications and specifications of these
principles as they operate in the double effect framework.
Connell's fifth principle is the "principle of relative
values." By this he means that *the welfare of a patient's
soul is always to be preferred to the welfare of his body.*"[56]
This principle is to be applied in preparing a patient for
death. He must be informed of his condition even if this
knowledge should cause some anxiety. Fetuses should be baptized.

     The principles Connell enumerates are thus the tradi-
tional physicalist ones we have come to recognize as central
in Catholic medical ethics (with the exception of the specifically spiritual principle concerned with the patient's
preparation for death). Connell's article, an address delivered to a largely non-Catholic audience, is not especially polemical, and presents the Catholic teaching "in a purely academic manner, free from any spirit of antagonism toward those who do not agree with the Catholic position."[57]
His emphasis throughout the article on the *Catholic* position,
however, typifies the subtle shift which we have suggested to

---

[55]Connell, "Catholic Moral Principles," pp. 287-291.

[56]*Ibid.*, p. 290, italics his.

[57]*Ibid.*, p. 287.

be characteristic of the forties and fifties. Whereas many
earlier authors emphasized the purely natural basis of Catholic ethics,[58] Connell, without denying that position, presents the Catholic teaching as specifically Catholic, a co-
herent system which can be explained to others. Connell's
article demonstrates the growing dialogue and confrontation
between Catholic medical ethics and non-Catholic approaches
to medicine which occurred in the forties and fifties.

The growing importance of specifically Catholic structures in medical ethics can be seen in an article written by
a Catholic physician in 1943. Dr. Edgar Hull's article in
The Linacre Quarterly addresses the problem of "Medical Education and Catholic Doctrine." Hull suggests that much of
medical ethical teaching has no "doctrinal implications,"
and thus is the same for Catholics and for non-Catholics.[59]
However, some ethical judgments do have such doctrinal implications, and Catholic medical students in non-Catholic
schools are urged to join religious organizations so that
they may know the correct Catholic teaching.[60] Hull lists
three types of problems as the only ones in which doctrinal
implications are relevant: "The first relates to the preven-

---

[58]An excellent example is a parallel article, written
twenty years earlier, also in *Hospital Progress*, by the
Jesuit moralist William F. Robison. Robison's article, entitled "The Catholic Code Based on Natural Law," intends to
demonstrate how the proscriptions against abortion and sterilization contained in the new surgical code of the Catholic
Hospital Association are based entirely on the natural law
principle of double effect, and not at all on specifically
Catholic teaching. The shift from Robison's article to
Connell's is a subtle one, but demonstrates the growing
recognition of a specifically Catholic approach in dialogue
with other approaches. See Robison, "The Catholic Code,"
esp. p. 1.

[59]Hull, "Medical Education and Catholic Doctrine," p. 31.

[60]*Ibid.*, p. 31.

tion of pregnancy, the second to sterilization, and the
third to the interruption of pregnancy."[61] Clearly Hull's
opinion is not that held theoretically by the trained moralists of his time. These maintain the belief that issues
such as abortion, sterilization, and contraception do not
depend for their solution upon specifically Catholic teaching, but are derived rather from the natural law. We have
seen numerous instances of this insistence. Nonetheless,
Hull's article is of interest in that it demonstrates how an
educated Catholic physician in the early forties *perceives*
such teaching in his practice. For him it is clear that
these ethical judgments *are indeed* specifically Catholic, *do*
have "doctrinal implications," *are* connected with Church
teaching. Hull's article is thus another example of the
growing awareness of a specifically Catholic system of medical ethics.

3. Bert Cunningham: An Early Challenge to Physicalism

Thus far in our survey of authors we have noted the more
or less consistent use of both physicalist and positivist
modalities. We have begun to see a shift in emphasis from
the former to the latter, but we have discovered no real
challenge to either approach. Nor will such a challenge occur in any widespread way until the 1960's and the Second
Vatican Council. The one important exception was the publication in 1944 of the doctoral thesis of Bert Cunningham,
entitled *The Morality of Organic Transplantation.*[62] While

---

[61]*Ibid.*, p. 31.

[62]Bert Cunningham was born in 1914 in Chicago, entered
the Congregation of the Missions, and was ordained in 1939.
His doctoral thesis was written at Catholic University in
1943 and published as one of that University's *Studies in
Sacred Theology* in 1944.

not challenging the adequacy of physicalism in *all* medical
ethical applications, Cunningham clearly breaks through the
physicalist approach in presenting his judgment on the question of organ transplants. On the other hand, Cunningham remains completely faithful to the teaching authority of the
Church magisterium. His thesis is an excellent example of
the growing operative importance in the forties of ecclesiastical positivism as the central modality of application of
theological principles in medical ethics.

Though Bouscaren had developed precise specifications
for the application of physicalism to the question of abortion,[63] this same precision had not yet been attained with
respect to the question of mutilation and sterilization. We
have noted the confusion present in the analyses of some authors of the early period.[64] Nonetheless, a general consensus had developed that mutilations were licit, even though
they might be "direct," provided they were done for the physical welfare of the individual body upon which they were performed. This judgment was grounded in the principle of totality, whose physicalist limitations we have already described.[65] Sterilizations had to be indirect, never intended

---

[63]See above, pp. 305-308.

[64]Especially O'Malley and Finney. See above, pp. 295-
296; 304. The confusion concerned the precise specification
of the act-in-itself and the failure to differentiate between
the physical effect of the act (to be applied in the second
condition of the double effect principle) and the intention
of the agent (to be applied in the third condition). If the
act-in-itself were specified as one of simple cutting, then
all licit mutilations might be considered indirect. And if
the intention of the agent were used instead of the effect of
the act, then the agent's intention might be said to make a
mutilation indirect. In addition to the sections on Finney
and O'Malley, see above, pp. 267-270.

[65]See above, pp. 261-262. The consensus is clear even
from the works of O'Malley and Finney, despite their confusion.

as a means or an end, but allowed only as an indirect effect
of a mutilation permitted by the principle of totality.[66]

The question of organ transplants, a procedure only recently tried by physicians, added a new dimension to the
question of mutilation. This was the topic Cunningham chose
for his doctoral dissertation. His central thesis was that
such direct mutilations are indeed licit according to the
principle of totality, if this principle is extended to include not only the particular physical body from which the
organ is removed, but the entire Mystical Body of Christ.
In this way Cunningham broke through the physicalist limitations associated with the traditional principle of totality.

After giving various definitions of mutilation, Cunningham describes the debate concerning whether mutilation should
be considered direct or indirect. "*Direct mutilation*," he
says, "is present when the mutilative action is chosen as a
means to an end [the second condition of double effect would
be violated], or is chosen for its own sake as an end in itself [the third condition would be violated]. For example,
to cut off a foot as an act of vengeance would constitute
direct mutilation. Also, to cut off one's hand as a means
to escape being burned to death . . . would be a direct mutilation. This point, however, is questioned by some authors."[67] Cunningham shows how some authors define the latter as a case of indirect mutilation, but opts himself,
along with most authors, to consider it a case of direct mutilation, where mutilation is directly intended as a means
to a further end. We have already noted the subtleties involved here, as the option depends on how precisely the act-

---

[66]For example, see La Rochelle and Fink, *Handbook*, pp.
131-140, discussed above, pp. 325-328.

[67]Cunningham, *The Morality of Organic Transplantation*,
p. 15, italics his.

in-itself is specified.[68]

The first principle Cunningham uses in his analysis is
the theological principle of God's dominion over the human
body.

> Mutilation is forbidden by the formal, negative element
> of the Fifth Commandment. Now the Fifth Precept forbids
> man to take his own life as well as the life of another
> because man does not have absolute dominion over his own
> body, nor over the body of his neighbor. . . . Theolo-
> gians in general will constantly appeal to the basic
> principle of man's relative dominion over his own body,
> a dominion which renders him only the guardian of his
> body and of its welfare, and which prevents him from
> taking away life, since life came from God alone.[69]

The author then goes on to cite a number of the fathers and
later theologians on the question of God's dominion over
life. He then quotes Thomas Aquinas citing his formulation
of the principle of totality, and shows how some other theologians approached the issue of mutilation.

After a chapter describing the current medical aspects
and possibilities of transplant surgery, particularly of
ovarian graft and corneal transplant, Cunningham proceeds to
his main thesis. He describes the negative judgment of some
authors on transplant surgery.[70] Their main objection lies
in the fact that the physicalist restrictions of the principle of totality are not met in mutilation for transplantation, since it is not the health of the same physical body

---

[68]See above, pp. 267-268.

[69]*Ibid.*, p. 18.

[70]The moralists whom Cunningham cites are not the North
American medical ethicists we have been studying, but European moralists whose general moral manuals include, as we
have noted, sections on medical ethical issues. North American works in medical ethics prior to the 1940's do not include any detailed analysis of organ transplantation. Cunningham cites the late 1930's manuals of Noldin-Schmitt and
Iorio. Ovarian graft and corneal transplant were first performed in the 1930's (Cunningham, pp. 49-59).

which demands the surgery. Nor can the mutilation be seen
as indirect, since the second condition of the double effect
principle is violated, and since most authors define the act-
in-itself of mutilation in such a way as to define all mutilation, licit as well as illicit, as direct. With this latter judgment Cunningham agrees:

> Well, for that matter, every operation is a direct muti-
> lation. And, as such, it is permitted when it is neces-
> sary for the well-being of the entire body or for the
> saving of life. While it is true that I may not kill
> myself to save another, that is, I may not directly kill
> myself, yet I may directly mutilate myself in order to
> save my own life. The person who kills himself does not
> act justly because he does not exercise correctly his
> relative dominion over his own body. He usurps dominion
> which he does not have. But the man who mutilates him-
> self or allows his body to be mutilated in order to
> safeguard the whole body, or his life, does act prudent-
> ly and as a wise custodian of the body and life given to
> him. In such cases, it has been stated, the permission
> of God is presumed.[71]

Thus far in his analysis, Cunningham has remained within the physicalist approach. The theological principle of
God's dominion over life is applied to the question of mutilation within the physicalistically limited principle of totality. A mutilation is allowed if for the physical good of
the body, and not otherwise. But Cunningham then proceeds
to challenge these limitations in the question of organ
transplants. It is this challenge which marks the first radical break with the physicalist modality. He continues:

> Now, if a man may mutilate himself to save his own life,
> and, in so acting, fulfill the role of a wise custodian
> of his own body, why can he not do the same thing when
> there is a question of saving the life of another, or
> even of notably improving the bodily health of the
> other party? . . . In the course of this chapter, an at-
> tempt will be made to show that because of the unity of
> men in species, their unity in the Mystical Body of
> Christ (actual or potential), there exists an ordination

---

[71]*Ibid.*, p. 62.

> of men to one another, and, as a consequence, an order
> of their members to one another. . . . We contend that
> men are ordinated to society as parts to the whole,
> and, as such, are in some way ordinated to one another,
> because of these unities mentioned above.[72]

Of course Cunningham continues to respect physicalist limitations and direct-indirect distinctions in areas other than
transplant surgery. It is never allowed to kill oneself directly for another, though it is permitted to allow oneself
(indirectly) to be killed.[73] But since all mutilations are
considered direct anyhow, Cunningham sees no reason for restricting these mutilations to those which are for the physical good of the person's own body. It is in this narrow
area that Cunningham breaks with physicalism, but it is a
radical break nonetheless.

The author then goes on to describe the Scriptural and
theological bases for the unity of mankind, as a race created by God and as a Body redeemed by Christ. Thus unity
serves in turn as a basis for arguing that a man may licitly
mutilate himself directly for the good of his neighbor.

In his final chapter, Cunningham gives some examples of
his thesis. These demonstrate the (highly problematic) extent to which Cunningham was willing to go in allowing transplant surgery. They also give clear witness to the special
set of controls Cunningham accepted in regard to sterilization, and demonstrate how he insisted on the importance of
magisterial decisions as ultimately definitive in moral judgments.

Cunningham recognizes that some limits must be imposed
by the principle of proportionality.[74] He suggests that "it

---

[72]*Ibid.*, p. 63.

[73]*Ibid.*, p. 67.

[74]We have discussed this principle above as the fourth

would hardly seem permissible for an individual to surrender
one of his eyes for the purpose of a corneal transplant for
a convict about to be executed. Nor could a child do the
same for an aged parent. There would hardly be a just proportion."[75] These restrictions, however, are without the
clean precision offered by physicalist specifications and
positivist applications. Like today's moralists, Cunningham
here suggests some general probabilities of right and wrong
operations, without being able to draw any clean lines of demarcation. Among organ transplants which he considers licit
are the transplantation of one ovary, the corneal transplant
of one eye from a living donor, and the corneal transplant
of one eye *from a one-eyed donor*, thus resulting in total
blindness. In this last case, the donor is presented as a
convict sentenced to life in prison, and thus "not needed by
anyone."[76] It is clear that Cunningham is willing to allow
transplant operations which are directly and seriously harmful to the donor, and in doing so has broken with all physicalist restrictions to the principle of totality.

There are nonetheless two clear and precise exceptions.
These exceptions are dictated by the official pronouncements
of the Church.

> Two exceptions must be maintained, exceptions which find
> their justification in traditional moral teaching and in
> the Church's interpretation of the natural law. First of
> all, if a person's being a donor . . . would certainly
> or very probably cause his own death, then it would not
> be licit for him to allow such a mutilation. . . . The
> second exception is this: if the result of such an oper-

---

condition of the double effect principle. Cunningham here
uses it as do today's personalist moralists, without physicalist restrictions. See above, pp. 256-257. See also the
final chapter for a brief review of contemporary approaches.

[75]*Ibid.*, p. 104.

[76]*Ibid.*, p. 106.

ation would be sterility for the donor, then it would
be illicit to permit or perform such a mutilation.[77]
Both physicalist and positivist principles are used to defend
these exceptions. In the former case, it would seem that the
operation would be not only a direct mutilation, but also a
direct suicide, forbidden by the double effect principle. In
the latter case, the similar distinction between direct and
indirect sterilization is cited. But when Cunningham goes on
to discuss the reasons for this distinction, his basic argument is an appeal to the pronouncements of the magisterium.
Cunningham has argued that a mutilation, even one which totally blinds the donor, is justified as an act of charity.
Yet a sterilizing mutilation is not so justified.

> Since . . . such a donation would be obtained by direct
> mutilation, it would likewise be a direct steriliza-
> tion.[78] Now the Holy Office, in reply to the question,
> "whether the direct sterilization of a man or a woman,
> whether perpetual or temporary, is licit?" responded in
> the negative and classified such a mutilation as con-
> trary to the law of nature. . . . From the arguments

---

[77]*Ibid.*, p. 101.

[78]Cunningham seems to get his "directs" and "indirects"
confused. A direct mutilation can be an indirect sterilization, if the act-in-itself is specified as a mutilating
act-in-itself which effects a sterilization but which is not
itself a sterilization. We have discussed this already (see
above, pp. 268-269). Cunningham thinks that the magisterium
allows direct sterilizations for the good of the whole body
(p. 102), whereas such operations were generally defined as
indirect sterilizations. Likewise he allows direct punitive
sterilizations (p. 102), an opinion contrary to that of other
authors (see, for example, La Rochelle and Fink, *Handbook,*
pp. 153-157). Cunningham's confusion is understandable in
view of the different kinds of act-specifications used to arrive at the distinctions. Though the distinctions themselves
had become by now traditional enough, and were used without
much hesitation, the specifications of the act-in-itself,
still highly problematic, were generally passed over with
little critical analysis. Nonetheless, Cunningham's confusion here does represent a deficiency in his thesis, one
which he ought to have corrected.

previously enunciated it might seem to follow that a
man could allow the direct mutilation of his sex organs
to the extent of sterilization for the good of his
neighbor . . . However, in view of the pronouncement of
the Holy Office, one cannot state this as an absolute
conclusion. Because the Church, authentically inter-
preting the Natural Law, determines that direct sterilization is illicit, it would seem safer to maintain that
a donation . . . which effectively renders the donor
sterile is entirely illicit. Again it is a question of
the powers involved, of their sacredness, and the danger
to the common good in abuses which might find place.[79]

It is clear that the ultimate reason for this absolute proscription of sterilizing transplants is the operative role of
magisterial decrees in Cunningham's medical ethical methodology.

Cunningham's thesis set off a debate within Catholic
medical ethics. Authors tried to decide whether or not organ
transplants were moral. On the one hand were the traditional
physicalist limitations of the principle of totality, as well
as some Roman decrees which seemed to forbid direct mutilations except for the good of the same physical body.[80] On the
other hand were the specifically Christian arguments based
on self-sacrifice, charity, the unity of mankind, and the
Mystical Body of Christ.

In this one area Cunningham had rejected physicalism.

---

[79]*Ibid.*, pp. 101-103.

[80]Gerald Kelly considered the thesis in his "Notes on
Moral Theology" for 1946. He states: "Undoubtedly the most
serious objection against Cunningham's thesis is not drawn
from any theological manual, but from these strong words of
Casti Connubii [which present the physicalist interpretation
of the principle of totality]: . . . [people] 'are not free
to destroy or mutilate their members, or in any other way
render themselves unfit for their natural functions, except
when no other provision can be made for the good of the
whole body'" (Kelly, "Notes," 1947, p. 99). Kelly's statement itself reflects the importance of ecclesiastical
positivism in medical ethics.

The result was a lack of any totally clean line between
right and wrong actions. Though Cunningham himself remained
faithful to traditional physicalist conclusions in other
areas of medical ethics, and faithful to the decrees of the
Church in all areas, the questions he raised and the thesis
he proposed concerning transplant surgery afforded a preview
of what would happen when Catholic moral thought in general
began to question both physicalism and ecclesiastical positivism in the revisionist critique of the sixties and seventies. For his own time, Cunningham remained more or less
alone. Though some other authors would cite his conclusions
approvingly, or at least admit that the subject was an open
question, the methodological impact of Cunningham's work was
limited. There was no attempt until the sixties to extend
his breakthrough to other areas of medical ethics.

4. Physicalism and Positivism in Charles McFadden

Both modalities are operative in Charles McFadden's *Medical Ethics*, whose popularity we have already noted. While
presenting the traditional distinction between natural law
ethics and supernatural moral theology, and insisting that
his work is based principally on the natural law, McFadden
nonetheless gives a good deal of emphasis to the teachings of
the Church. In his analysis of individual medical ethical
issues, both physicalist and positivist approaches are evident. The theological principles of God's dominion over life
and of redemptive suffering are generally subordinate, in
their actual operation, to these two modalities.

The difficulties we have already noted concerning the
tension between a theoretical rejection of moral positivism
and a *de facto* use of it are found in McFadden's introductory
material. He clearly wishes to present his work as primarily
one of natural ethics. His first two chapters deal almost
exclusively with principles of "natural" ethics, and do not

present any detailed arguments of apologetics in defense of
magisterial inerrancy. Yet McFadden adds that the infallible Church is often the best source for assuring correct interpretation of the natural law. He states:

> Ethics . . . is a natural science in the sense that
> it uses a purely natural means, the power of human rea-
> son, to arrive at its conclusions. It is based neither
> on the revealed word of God nor on the traditional
> teachings of Christ's infallible Church. Ethics is a
> branch of philosophy, a science which derives its
> truths from the accurate use of unaided human reason.
> It is admittedly true that the infallible teaching
> of Christ's Church is of indirect value to the student
> of Ethics. Such teachings serve as an excellent guide
> and constant "check-up" on the accuracy of our reason-
> ing processes. But, in itself, Ethics depends solely
> on the natural power of human reason to discover the
> morality of any specific action. For this reason,
> Ethics is properly called a purely natural science.[81]

And again:

> The Natural Law is universal because, being based on hu-
> man nature, it binds all men. . . . There are, however,
> some moral truths which are so abstract and complex that
> it is most difficult for even the best intellects to ar-
> rive at complete accuracy regarding them. Many men,
> moreover, are not blessed with fine intellects . . . All
> men should have at their disposal from the beginning of
> their rational life all those truths which will help
> them develop themselves spiritually . . . It is for
> these good reasons that God in His Mercy and Wisdom has
> seen fit to reveal to man in a complete and accurate
> manner all of the moral truths which he must observe.
> The Moral Law possessed by the Christian is therefore
> most perfect. It is to be found in tradition, in Sacred
> Scripture, and in the teaching of Christ's infallible
> Church. It is this law known both by reason and Divine
> Revelation which should be cherished by doctor and nurse
> alike as the source and basis of their moral ideals.[82]

And finally:

---

[81]McFadden, *Medical Ethics for Nurses*, p. 2; *Medical
Ethics*, 2nd, 3rd, 4th, 5th eds., p. 2.

[82]*Ibid.*, 3rd and 4th eds., p. 18; 5th ed., pp. 15-16.
The first two editions contain nearly identical statements
on p. 18.

        The foregoing explanation of the nature of Ethics
    should be understood, but it must not be allowed to
    create a false impression. There is no intention to
    restrict the various topics in this book to the purely
    ethical and natural level. The nature of Ethics has
    been explained in detail because our approach is to be
    primarily, but by no means exclusively, a rational one.
        God has raised man to a higher level than the
    natural . . .
        The moral ideals of the Christian doctor and nurse
    should certainly be molded on the revealed word of God
    and the teachings of Christ's Church, as well as on the
    dictates of reason. Both reason and revelation will,
    therefore, be utilized in this work. But no doctor or
    nurse, regardless of his or her religious background,
    may ever forget that all men are bound by the Natural
    Law--and practically all of the moral conclusions in
    this work, save those that are expressly related to the
    sacraments, are simply expressions of Natural Law.[83]

McFadden thus insists that his conclusions are binding

on all because they are derived by unaided human reason from

the natural law, and do not depend on specifically Christian

or Catholic sources of revelation. Yet he also states his

intention to use these sources when necessary, and, as we

will discover, the pronouncements of the magisterium do in-

deed exert significant influence on McFadden's work.

    In line with his desire to emphasize the universality

of his conclusions, McFadden states in the introduction to

his third edition that he intends to eliminate the constant

use of the word "Catholic" in his work. This, he says,

"created the false impression on many that no . . . obliga-

tion rested on those who are not members of the Church. . . .

Actually, of course, almost all of the moral principles

treated in this book are principles of Natural Law or Divine

Positive Law which bind *all* men."[84] This elimination might

---

        [83]*Ibid.*, 3rd ed., p. 6. Similar passages in all edi-
tions. His italics deleted.

        [84]*Ibid.*, 3rd ed., p. xiii, italics his. McFadden's in-
clusion of divine positive law in this context is proble-

be seen as a movement away from an emphasis on ecclesiastical positivism. And, indeed, McFadden's work emphasizes
this methodological modality less than some other books we
have seen and will see later. Nonetheless, it seems a more
accurate interpretation, in light of McFadden's significant
use of magisterial decrees, to see this more as an attempt
to insist on the universal applicability of his conclusions
than as a rejection of practical positivism. He continues,
in fact, in the same introduction, to note that among the
more significant changes in the new edition are lengthy
treatments of "the Holy Father's addresses on the Safe Period Method and Artificial Insemination."[85]

McFadden's repeated attempts to emphasize both the universalist nature of natural law ethics and the role of
"Christ's infallible Church" demonstrate the subtle shift in
emphasis which is occurring in the 1940's. It is becoming
more important to stress the specific role of Church authorities while at the same time maintaining that this "Catholic"
system of ethics is binding on all. Roman Catholic medical
ethics is coming more and more into dialogue with other ethical approaches. No longer is it possible merely to assume
the assent of one's readers. McFadden finds it necessary to
remove the word "Catholic" precisely in order to convince
his non-Catholic readers that they, too, are bound by his
conclusions. At the same time he continues to make use of
specifically Catholic magisterial pronouncements in his

---

matic. He states that such revelation binds all men. Yet
in the other passages we have cited, the implication is that
this universality comes from the fact that it is a natural
law and not dependent on revelation. This must be seen as
an inconsistency in McFadden's thought, due no doubt to the
generally problematic context of the relationship of theoretical natural law to practical ecclesiastical positivism which
we have been describing.

[85] *Ibid.*, 3rd ed., p. xiii.

approach to the various medical procedures he examines.
Thus McFadden's work provides an example of the growing importance of visible Church structures in the discipline's
methodology.

Physicalism plays a central role in McFadden's method.
In the second of his introductory chapters he describes the
double effect principle with its four conditions, and is
careful to distinguish the effect of the act (second condition) from the intention of the agent (third condition), as
well as to insist that the second condition ("The good effect must precede the evil effect or at least be simultaneous with it.") refers to primacy of causality rather than
temporality. He applies the principle to various cases of
indirect abortion.[86]

In his treatment of abortion, McFadden uses four chapters to discuss, respectively, direct abortion, therapeutic
abortion (morally the equivalent of direct abortion, but
done for some "therapeutic" reason), indirect abortion, and
cases of ectopic gestation. The distinction between direct
and indirect abortion is based on the double effect principle. Among reasons given for the immorality of direct abortion is the theological principle of God's dominion over
life[87] and the principle that the end (some temporal good)
cannot justify the means (a moral evil).[88] Regardless of
the reasons given for a direct abortion, such an action constitutes a direct and immoral killing. Passages from Church
law and from Pius XII are quoted.[89] McFadden includes abortions performed in order to safeguard the mother's health as

---

[86]*Ibid.,* 3rd ed., pp. 31-38. Other editions are similar.

[87]*Ibid.,* 3rd ed., p. 165.

[88]*Ibid.,* p. 166.

[89]*Ibid.,* pp. 173-176, 200.

direct abortions, among them the sometimes controverted procedure of amniotic rupture in cases of hydramnion.[90] Indirect abortions are permitted according to the double effect
principle, which McFadden cites explicitly on several occasions. Thus removal of a cancerous, and, in some cases, a
fibroid uterus is permitted as the abortion is indirect.
Drugs may be given for the treatment of diseases during
pregnancy if they are needed and if the risk to the fetus is
only indirect.[91] McFadden's treatment of ectopic gestation
is presented explicitly along the lines of the four conditions of double effect, which he considers to be met. He
announces his agreement with Bouscaren, whose detailed study
we have already described.[92]

Physicalist and positivist modalities are also evident
in McFadden's treatment of mutilation and sterilization.

---

[90]*Ibid.*, pp. 194-199. Some moralists had defined this
procedure as an indirect abortion, since the act-in-itself
(perforating the amniotic sac to allow release of the fluid)
indirectly caused the subsequent abortion. McFadden cites
Antonelli and Capellmann. He argues, with most moralists,
that this constitutes a direct attack on the fetus, since
the removal of the fluid is equivalent to suffocation (p.
197). It is interesting to point out, however, that McFadden, along with most scholars, permits the removal of a
pregnant cancerous uterus as an indirect abortion. One might
validly argue that the latter is more necessary to the mother's health than the former, at least in many cases, but it
seems doubtful that the acts-in-themselves differ all that
substantially in their physical specificity. For treatment
of the topic by Klarmann, see above, pp. 287-288.

[91]*Ibid.*, pp. 218-222.

[92]*Ibid.*, pp. 236-248. McFadden's 1st, 2nd, and 3rd
editions are the same. In his fourth he eliminates all historical detail concerning the controversy and Bouscaren's
conclusions, perhaps because the issue was by this time
(1956) largely settled. His fifth edition (1961) eliminates
the chapter altogether, for that specific reason (see the
5th edition, p. xiv). In any case, his conclusions are in
each edition those of Bouscaren.

McFadden's first three editions evidence some confusion in
his use of terms to be applied to such procedures, a confusion not his alone.[93] He seems to use the term "mutilation" only for immoral mutilations. Thus operations allowed by the principle of totality for the good of the whole
physical body are specifically removed from the category
"mutilation."[94] Lobotomy is allowed in cases of necessity,
since, in McFadden's opinion, "it does not seem that the
operation has, or can have, any *direct* effect on the inherent powers of man's rational faculties. . . . The effect of
lobotomy upon the specifically rational powers of man is,
therefore, an *indirect* one."[95] Despite the work of Cunningham, which he cites, McFadden rejects corneal transplants on
the basis of an encyclical of Pius XI.[96]

Sterilizations are allowed when they are for the "personal health or life of an individual,"[97] and not allowed
when the purpose is to prevent pregnancy. This applies even
when previous births by Caesarian section might render future
pregnancies inadvisable. Only if the condition of the uterus
itself and its very "presence in the body" endanger the woman's life is its removal justified.[98] Allowable "therapeutic" sterilization "is permitted because it is neither an
act of mutilation nor an invasion of the supreme dominion of
the Creator, but an act done in the interests of preserving

---

[93]For examples, see above, p. 333, n. 64.

[94]*Ibid.*, 3rd ed., pp. 282-284.

[95]*Ibid.*, p. 286, italics his.

[96]*Ibid.*, p. 291.

[97]*Ibid.*, p. 294.

[98]*Ibid.*, p. 295.

the body as a whole."[99] Forbidden "eugenic" sterilization,
on the other hand, performed in order to prevent pregnancy,
is proscribed as a grave mutilation which "ignores completely the supreme dominion of God over His creatures and the
inherent dignity of a human being."[100] McFadden goes on to
give other practical reasons against eugenic sterilization,
but states that "even if none of these criticisms were true,
eugenic sterilization could not be permitted. It is an unnecessary mutilation, since the conservation of the whole
body of the defective person is not dependent upon the sacri-
fice of this part. It is immoral because it is a deliberate
and serious invasion of the supreme rights of the Creator
over one of His creatures."[101] McFadden quotes lengthy sections from papal statements.[102]

In his fourth edition (1956) McFadden changes his terminology to bring it more in accordance with the generally accepted terms for distinguishing types of mutilations and
sterilizations.[103] Mutilations are now included in a new

---

[99]*Ibid.*, p. 294.

[100]*Ibid.*, p. 313.

[101]*Ibid.*, p. 313.

[102]*Ibid.*, pp. 310-312.

[103]Though not completely. McFadden still does not use
the technical term "indirect sterilization." His conclusions
are identical to those of scholars who do use this word, however, and his reasoning process, as we are noting, uses the
same physicalist criteria. Of some interest is a criticism
by Gerald Kelly to the first edition of McFadden's work.
Kelly argues that McFadden should style all permissible sterilizations as "indirect" in order to accord with the language
of the official statements of the Holy See (Kelly, "Review:
McFadden," p. 618). Kelly's own reliance on such decrees is
evident from this critique. McFadden did not take Kelly's
advice on this particular point, but did change some of his
terminology in the fourth edition.

chapter on man's duty to preserve life, and the section is
preceded with descriptions both of the principles of totality and of double effect.[104] Allowable operations which
were previously called not mutilations, are now recognized
as mutilations, but allowed according to the principle of
totality. McFadden specifically rejects Cunningham's thesis,
and states that "the author [McFadden] regards as immoral
the mutilation of a person which is not done in the interests of that person's own body."[105] This change in language
brings about no change in McFadden's conclusions, but puts
his physicalist methodology more in terminological harmony
with his contemporaries. Throughout the section on mutilation and sterilization, McFadden cites statements of the
magisterium pertaining to the issue.[106]

McFadden's treatment of these issues indicates clearly
his reliance on physicalist and positivist methodologies.
He does cite the theological principle of God's dominion
over human life, but this dominion is said to be violated by
some acts and respected by others. The criteria by which
the former are distinguished from the latter are physicalist
ones. It is the violation of the physical end of the sexual
faculty as well as the actual physical causal chain of acts
and effects which form the core of McFadden's reasoning.
Statements of ecclesiastical authorities are used to defend
this reasoning process.

Similar modalities of reasoning can be found in other
areas of McFadden's work. We have noted that his fourth edition makes more explicit use of physicalist terminology in
the area of mutilation than earlier editions. The same is

---

[104]*Ibid.*, 4th ed., pp. 297-305.

[105]*Ibid.*, p. 317.

[106]*Ibid.*, pp. 304-305; 355-357.

true in his treatment of euthanasia and the preservation of
life. The earlier editions of the book include these issues
in a chapter entitled "The Christian Philosophy of Suffering." Here McFadden explicitly cites the theological principle of God's dominion over life: "Almighty God, as the
Creator of the universe, is its one supreme Lord and Master.
In the most absolute sense all things belong to Him. . . .
If, perchance, certain individuals are born with physical or
mental deficiencies, who is man to pass judgment on the creative act of God? Is the creature to say that the Almighty
has erred . . . For man is merely the custodian of life, not
its Master."[107] For McFadden, "The fundamental immorality
of euthanasia, therefore, lies in its *direct* violation of
the supreme dominion of God over His creation."[108]

Similarly, McFadden uses the theological principle of
the Christian meaning of suffering. He states:

> The advocates of euthanasia moreover disregard the su-
> pernatural destiny of man and the rôle which suffering
> can play in the achievement of sanctity. They do not
> realize the ability of man, aided by God's grace, to
> bear sufferings patiently. They do not know how resig-
> nation to pain can serve as penance and temporal punish-
> ment for personal moral failings. Lacking a true be-
> lief in the supernatural, they have no respect for the
> power of faith and prayer to produce miracles in even
> the most hopeless cases. Neither do they understand
> how the Communion of Saints makes possible vicarious
> suffering, that is, the ability of man to endure pain
> for the spiritual good of fellow-man. The proponents
> of "mercy-killing," steeped as they are in a material-
> istic philosophy of life, cannot grasp the significance
> of these profound vital truths of Christianity.[109]

McFadden speaks of the theological problem of reconciling the
existence of pain and evil with a good God, and, while

---

[107]*Ibid.*, 3rd ed., pp. 146-147; also 4th ed., p. 251.

[108]*Ibid.*, p. 147; also 4th ed., p. 251, italics mine.

[109]*Ibid.*, pp. 147-148; also 4th ed., p. 252.

admitting the mystery of this reality, points to Christ as a
model for finding meaning in human pain. He suggests resignation to God's will, and argues that suffering borne in
this context is profitable to the spiritual growth of the
patient.[110] In this context he forbids the giving of pain-
relieving drugs which cause unconsciousness to those "dying
in great pain *without being spiritually prepared for death*,"
while allowing it for those "known to be spiritually at
peace with God."[111] The latter practice, however, while
licit, is "not to be recommended. It is often difficult to
be certain that a person is spiritually prepared to die, and
the loss of consciousness deprives the dying person of the
spiritual merit which might be derived from resignation to
suffering."[112] As we have noted already on several occasions, this particular ethical application of the theological
principle of the meaning of suffering is not subordinated to
the physicalist modality. The spiritual good of the person's
soul is the direct criterion used in distinguishing right
from wrong use of pain-killing drugs.

Apart from this one exception, however, McFadden does
subordinate the theological principles to physicalist criteria when he arrives at actual ethical applications, distinguishing right from wrong procedures. This is clearest in
the fourth edition, though his conclusions here are identical
to those of earlier versions. In the fourth edition, McFadden distinguishes the Negative Natural Law from the Affirma-
tive Natural Law. The former "prohibits the commission of
morally evil acts," while the latter "orders us to perform

---

[110]*Ibid.*, pp. 153-158; also 4th ed., pp. 257-263.

[111]*Ibid.*, p. 151, italics his; also 4th ed., p. 255.

[112]*Ibid.*, also 4th ed., p. 255.

certain morally good acts."[113] The notion of negative natural law is merely another way of stating the absoluteness of
the first condition of the double effect principle.[114]
McFadden goes on to explain:

> The fundamental reason for the absolute inflexibility
> of Negative Natural Law is that it concerns actions
> which are substantially evil (such as blasphemy) or
> evil in their attendant circumstances (such as theft),--
> and acts which are immoral may never be committed in
> order to avoid thereby any kind of hardship or incon-
> venience. It was this principle which was utilized in
> the previous chapter to establish the invariably grave
> immorality of "mercy-killing." Thus we saw that no
> reason whatsoever--such as the severity of pain, the
> hopelessness of the case, the magnitude of expense--
> would ever justify a doctor or nurse in adopting any
> procedure which is *directly intended and aimed* at the
> destruction of the life of the patient.[115]

All direct acts of euthanasia are thus forbidden. On
the other hand, it is not necessary to use "extraordinary
means" to preserve the life of a dying patient. This distinction between ordinary and extraordinary means is not at
all in itself physicalistically limited. Criteria for determining which means are which include questions of spiritual good, readiness for death, reasonable hope of success,
possibility of scandal, excessive pain, expense, and other
explicitly subjective elements.[116] If one can judge from

---

[113]*Ibid.*, 4th ed., p. 265.

[114]See Knauer, "The Hermeneutic Function," pp. 139-140.
Knauer argues that this negative-positive distinction can
also be used in a more modern formulation of double effect
where the accent is on the principle of commensurate reason
(the fourth condition of the traditional principle).
McFadden's use is clearly within the physicalist four-
condition framework. In either case, however, the negative-
positive distinction is merely another way of stating the
double effect framework.

[115]*Ibid.*, 4th ed., p. 265, italics mine.

[116]*Ibid.*, pp. 267-293.

the presence of such criteria that a particular medical procedure is morally "extraordinary," then one is not obliged to
use it. However, it is never permitted *directly* to inter-
vene with a procedure whose direct intention and effect is
to end suffering by killing the patient. It is in this aspect of the reasoning process, which presents the general
governing principle for forbidding all direct euthanasia,
that physicalist criteria are paramount. If a procedure has
as its direct effect the killing of the patient, then it is
forbidden by the first and second condition of double effect. If, on the other hand, it is an action which merely
indirectly hastens the dying process, such as the avoidance
of a means for preserving life, then its liceity is to be
judged by the third and fourth (non-physicalist) conditions,
especially the principle of due proportion. McFadden does
not explicitly use the term "indirect" to apply to such procedures. Other authors do. Nor does he apply double effect
explicitly to the case. But his argument from negative and
positive natural law, his use of the term "direct," and his
inclusion of the ordinary-extraordinary distinction within
this framework make it clear that physicalist criteria are
of central operative importance.

Physicalist and positivist criteria are evident in
McFadden's discussion of artificial insemination and contraception. He insists that "it is a principle of Natural Law
that a woman has no right to receive into her vagina the
semen of any man except her husband."[117] This physical act-
in-itself is intrinsically immoral regardless of the reason.
McFadden also forbids any kind of artificial insemination
from the husband where there is a tampering with the sexual
act and its immediate physical goal: the procreation of children. Thus he states as illicit the injection of semem

---

[117]*Ibid.*, 3rd ed., p. 68; 4th ed., p. 68.

obtained from the husband by masturbation or by syringe from
his testicles. In this latter instance specific statements
of Pope Pius XII are cited as definitive. Earlier moralists
who allowed the syringe technique are exhonerated, since
"they expressed this opinion previous to the . . . address of
Pope Pius XII on artificial insemination. It is now clear
that the foregoing opinion is no longer tenable. The Holy
Father has sanctioned only such artificial aid to producing
conception between husband and wife as could be construed as
assistance to a completed act of natural sex relationship."[118]
Here both physicalist and positivist criteria are evident.
The latter can be said to dominate, however, since McFadden's
own opinion has been changed by it. In the first and second
editions, McFadden merely cites the opinion of the authors,
and implies his agreement with it.[119] As long as all sexual
pleasure is avoided (masturbation is forbidden, since here
the sexual faculty is used while its concomitant physical
end, procreation, is not in direct physical connection to the
act), artificial insemination from the husband is permitted.
But the statement of Pius XII caused McFadden to change his
opinion in the later editions. The only method of "artificial insemination" now permitted is the use of a syringe to
move semen already deposited in the wife's vagina further into the genital tract. This procedure is seen to have a "firm
basis" in the writings of Pius XII.[120]

McFadden forbids all forms of contraception, since these
are "aimed at preventing the conjugal act from achieving its
natural end"[121] which is procreation, the primary purpose of

---

[118]*Ibid.*, 3rd ed., p. 72; 4th ed., p. 71.

[119]*Ibid.*, 1st ed., p. 67; 2nd ed., p. 69.

[120]*Ibid.*, 3rd ed., pp. 72-73; 4th ed., p. 72.

[121]*Ibid.*, 3rd ed., p. 93.

the sexual faculty. The specifically biological purpose of
sexual intercourse must be present in each and every act.
The use of the safe period method (rhythm) is permitted,
however, since there is no unnatural act involved.[122] Again
it is evident that McFadden's basic criteria are limited to
the physical and biological aspects of sexuality. Similarly
masturbation for obtaining semen for sterility testing is
forbidden since the "act is intrinsically evil."[123] Withdrawal and the use of a condom are likewise intrinsically
immoral methods of obtaining semen for analysis. In his
third edition, McFadden discusses the possibility of using a
condom with holes in it. This would allow some semen to be
collected for testing, while allowing the rest to be deposited in the vagina. He merely states that moralists disagree
concerning the liceity of this method.[124] In his fourth
edition he again presents both sides of the argument, but
himself argues for the immorality of such a procedure. His
basic reasoning is that "there is the direct intention to
deposit and retain semen in an unnatural place . . . [and]
there is the direct intention to restrict the volume of semen deposited in the vagina."[125] He then proceeds in two
pages to describe in detail the size and number of holes in
a condom required to allow the deposit of a sufficient amount
of semen to ensure the possibility that the end of the sexual
faculty will not be directly thwarted. He states that one
"*tiny* hole" or "a few pin-point perforations" are not sufficient.[126] At least two and one half cubic centimeters of

---

[122]*Ibid.*, pp. 123-124.

[123]*Ibid.*, p. 97.

[124]*Ibid.*, pp. 97-98.

[125]*Ibid.*, 4th ed., p. 95.

[126]*Ibid.*, p. 96.

ejaculate is required, and, since this is unlikely with a
perforated condom, the method is probably immoral.[127]   McFadden's emphasis on this kind of detail demonstrates the importance of physicalist criteria in his method.

   In our description of physicalism in chapter four, we
noted that one possible application of physicalist criteria
to medical ethics concerned the question of the physician's
obligation to tell the truth to his patient. According to
double effect physicalism, a direct lie is always immoral.
That is, the actual words used may never be directly untruthful. They must have some possibility of meaning a strictly
true communication as they stand, even though the hearer will
doubtless understand the words in a different sense.[128]   Thus
moralists distinguish between a lie (always intrinsically immoral regardless of reason) and a "mental reservation," where
the physical words themselves have two possible meanings and
the speaker reserves or withholds the correct meanings, presumably hoping that the listener will understand them in
their more common, and, in the case, inaccurate sense. McFadden specifically applies the notion of mental reservation to
the physician. Recognizing that there will be cases where
the physician and nurse "cannot tell the truth, because the
revealing of actual facts would constitute a violation of
professional secrecy,"[129] the author nonetheless insists that
they must not tell a lie, either. If silence is impossible,
since it would imply the answer which they cannot give, they
may make use of mental reservation. "The careful use of
mental reservation will provide the solution to such

---

[127]*Ibid.*, pp. 96-97.

[128]See above, pp. 271-272.

[129]McFadden, 3rd ed., p. 371.

difficulties."[130] The example he gives is that of a doctor or nurse whose patient asks about his temperature. The
doctor or nurse has reason, supposedly, to feel that the
correct answer (102 degrees) should not be given. Yet he
cannot remain silent nor can he lie by giving an incorrect
number of degrees. Thus he says, "Your temperature is normal today."[131] The phrase has two meanings: the technical
one which the patient will not grasp (that he has a temperature which is normal for his condition, since he is sick),
and the common one (that his temperature is normal for normal people). In this way the physician or nurse may avoid
both a direct lie and the doing of harm to the patient.
Again, the solution depends on the actual physical action
(here, the speaking of specific words). The personal context of human communication is secondary to the distinction
between an act-in-itself which is immoral and an act-in-
itself which is morally neutral. Only after the act-in-
itself has been determined as morally neutral (the first two
conditions of double effect) can the question of proportionate good (the fourth condition) be considered. McFadden goes
on to insist that a proportionate reason is necessary even
for the use of a mental reservation. In addition, the device may not be used if the listener has a right to the information which he seeks.[132] These latter criteria are not
physicalist. But they may be applied only after the act-in-
itself has been so posited as to avoid being qualified as a
direct lie.

We have studied McFadden's work in detail, not because
it was of importance in developing a new methodology, nor

---

[130]*Ibid.*, p. 371, italics deleted.

[131]*Ibid.*, p. 372.

[132]*Ibid.*, p. 373.

even because his book is sufficiently precise in its terminology to allow an exact specification of the physicalist
method. Rather it is because his work served for almost two
decades as the standard medical ethics text in use in Roman
Catholic schools in North America.[133] We have seen a clear
emphasis on both physicalist and positivist methodological
modalities. The theological principles of God's dominion
over life and of redemptive suffering are used explicitly
and frequently. They are, however, with few exceptions,
used within the physicalist and positivist frameworks.
McFadden's work is an excellent example of the theological
methodology of North American Roman Catholic medical ethics
of the forties and fifties.

Brief mention is in order here of a doctoral dissertation on artificial insemination written in 1948 by William
Glover, an Australian priest, and published in the United
States.[134] The thesis breaks no new ground in the field,
but is an excellent example of the strictest sort of physicalism. Various methods of obtaining semen are rejected regardless of the intention (here fertility), since the nature
of the act is thwarted. He states in one place:

> The person's intention is immaterial. The nature of
> the act is the important point from which comes the
> intrinsic morality of the act. By using a condom
> during intercourse, even though the condom has been
> previously pierced, some of the semen will be deliber-
> ately prevented from entering the vagina--that is the
> very purpose for which the condom is used! Consequently
> the ordination of that semen which is prevented from
> entering the vagina is destroyed, a thing which has just
> been proved to be intrinsically evil and unlawful.[135]

---

[133]See above, pp. 161-162.

[134]Glover, *Artificial Insemination*. Glover, an Australian Marist priest, presented his thesis at Catholic University.

[135]*Ibid.*, pp. 73-74.

That is, despite the fact that the semen involved is to be
used precisely for procreation, its "ordination" has been
destroyed since, "in order that the semen be physically
ordained to generation it must remain within the generative
organs of either the male or the female."[136] A physical
separation of the semen from the generative organs is itself
immoral, "*per se*, apart from any action which may follow."[137]
Glover's strict physicalism leads him to insist that if a
syringe is used to push semen deposited lawfully in the
vagina further up the vaginal tract, the filled syringe may
not leave the vaginal area. Even then, however, he is not
entirely satisfied, and holds as his personal opinion that
such a procedure, allowed by most moralists, is illicit since
physical contact of the semen with the genital tract cannot
be maintained.[138]

Glover's opinion is stricter in some ways than those of
most of his contemporaries. Nonetheless his conclusions
concerning *most* of the issues involved are identical to
others which we have studied. His emphasis on actual physical presence of semen to the vaginal tract may be a new
wording, but it is substantially identical to the equally
physicalist criteria used by other moralists in deciding
this and similar issues.

5. Gerald Kelly and the Problem of Ecclesiastical Positivism

Gerald Kelly's *Medico-Moral Problems* was, as we have
seen in the previous chapter, a series of articles written
in connection with the new "Ethical and Religious Directives"

---

[136]*Ibid.*, p. 79.

[137]*Ibid.*, p. 80.

[138]*Ibid.*, p. 135.

of the Catholic Hospital Association. Both the directives,
of which Kelly was the primary author, and Kelly's articles
demonstrate the importance of physicalist and positivist
methodologies. In the directives frequent reference is made
to the direct-indirect distinction.[139] Direct killing
(abortion, euthanasia) is always forbidden, whereas indirect
killing (ectopic gestation operations for the removal of the
pathological tube, hysterectomies of a cancerous uterus, and
the withholding of extraordinary means of preserving life)
is permitted "for proportionate reasons."[140] Periodic continence (rhythm) is allowed whereas all other methods of
contraception are forbidden. The very fact that the directives were issued by an official Catholic agency and became
the accepted code for Catholic hospitals is indicative of
the importance of visible Roman Catholic structures in the
discipline.

The articles which comprise Kelly's work likewise demonstrate the importance of physicalist and ecclesiastical positivist criteria. We have noted Kelly's insistence that
McFadden use the correct physicalist terms in order to maintain terminological harmony with Rome.[141] Kelly's ability
to maintain a consistent and relatively clear methodology
contributed to the acceptance of these criteria in Catholic
medical ethics of the period.

We have had frequent occasion to mention the tension
arising from insistance on natural law universalism as theoretical basis for medical ethics on the one hand together
with practical ecclesiastical positivism and the insistence

---

[139]See above, p. 174.

[140]Catholic Hospital Association, "Ethical and Religious
Directives," *Linacre Quarterly,* p. 3.

[141]See above, p. 348, n. 103.

on the role of the Church as interpreter of the natural law
on the other. We have seen instances of this in individual
authors.[142] We have not yet found any explicit attempt to
deal with the problem as a problem. Authors have simply
stated both that their conclusions are binding on all since
they are derived from the natural law, which is discoverable
by unaided right reason, and that the natural law requires
interpretation by the Church which alone is given supernatural guarantee that such interpretation is accurate. Gerald
Kelly attempts to examine this issue. The context of his
presentation is the question often posed by non-Catholics as
to why the Catholic codes can be said to apply also to them.
There are three sections in Kelly's work where he deals explicitly with this question.

The first is an article entitled "Non-Catholics and Our
Code" which appears in the 1949 booklet which is Part I of
Kelly's first edition.[143] In it, Kelly insists mainly on
the specifically natural scientific expertise of Catholic
moralists. He states that

> the answer to the question really touches two spheres,
> the *religious* and the *scientific* . . . I could hardly
> expect non-Catholics to accept the religious authority
> of moralists, because this would imply acceptance of
> the teaching authority of the Church; hence I will
> stress the explanation of scientific competence and
> will later add merely for information a few words con-
> cerning the religious aspect.[144]

He then goes on to show that "aside from any question of religion, the Catholic moralists represent by far the world's

---

[142]See above, on Bonnar, pp. 321-323; on La Rochelle
and Fink, pp. 324-325; on McFadden, pp. 341-345; also part
one of this chapter.

[143]Kelly, *Medico-Moral Problems,* Part I, 1949, pp. 5-9.
For an explanation of the various editions, see above, pp.
169-170.

[144]*Ibid.*, p. 7, italics his.

largest group of specialists in the science of ethics. . . .
When such men agree . . . their unanimity is worthy of . . .
intellectual respect."[145] Thus Kelly's basic argument is
that Catholic moralists should be respected *not* because they
are supernaturally guaranteed interpreters of God's will but
because they are scientifically competent in their field.
He goes on to admit that Catholic moralists accept the official declarations of the Church on account of the Church's
religious authority, but emphasizes that non-Catholics will
accept their conclusions not on this basis but on the basis
of their scientific competence. In any case, Kelly adds
that "as regards medical questions, the study and united
teaching of the moralists has usually preceded the official
declarations . . . Moreover, official declarations on moral
questions have been comparatively infrequent."[146] This is
Kelly's opinion in 1949.

Regarding the *religious* issue, Kelly states that Catholics believe from a religious perspective that the Church
has authority in moral matters, but this is added as "merely
informative; I have no intention of turning this article into a one-sided debate."[147] Thus he avoids any attempt to
convince non-Catholics of the religious authority of the
Roman Catholic Church. Like other moralists of the time,
Kelly insists that there be no double standard in morality,
with one set of principles binding Catholics and another
non-Catholics. He suggests that the natural law is like a

---

[145]*Ibid.*, p. 8. This argument clearly fails to come to
grips with the questions raised by the sociology of knowledge. Unanimity demands intellectual respect if it is based
on independent research and investigation. But such inde-
pendence is problematic at best, and in this instance is
largely lacking.

[146]*Ibid.*, p. 9.

[147]*Ibid.*, p. 9.

set of instructions for a machine which any expert mechanic
could derive from an examination of the machine itself. The
divine positive law (Ten Commandments, for example) is merely a set of instructions *also* given, in direct revelation
from God, but "any man with sufficiently developed reason
and with sufficient opportunity could arrive at the same
conclusions, and even more detailed ones, by an intense
study of his own nature."[148] Kelly's emphasis, then, in the
1949 article, is on natural law universalism and the scientific expertise of Catholic moralists.

Evidently this proved insufficient in Kelly's mind, and
the 1958 version of the same article shows a definite change
in emphasis. Here the specifically *religious* authority of
the Church is given a greater explicit role. Kelly no longer
claims that official declarations on medical moral matters
are infrequent. Though this was the case until the time of
Pius XII, "official pronouncements have multiplied" during
his reign, as "he has had frequent requests from medical societies to speak on various moral topics."[149] Kelly no
longer organizes his answer to the problem by distinguishing
between scientific and religious spheres. He repeats his
description of the natural law as a set of instructions
which a talented mechanic might derive from examining the
machine, and states again that the Ten Commandments are
instructions *also* given, not added arbitrarily to the natural law. Again he states that a man with sufficiently developed reasoning powers could arrive at these truths, but this
time he adds an important corrective: "As I have already
noted and shall explain more fully, this kind of divine help
[the ten commandments and, as clear from the larger context,
the teachings of the Catholic Church] is a practical neces-

---

[148]*Ibid.*, p. 7.

[149]Kelly, *Medico-Moral Problems,* 1958 edition, p. 33.

sity for most men."[150]   Instead of emphasizing the scientific competence of Catholic moralists, Kelly then proceeds
to describe the competence of the Church as a teaching
authority. He continues to insist, of course, that the
Church does not *make* the natural law. Yet it is now clear
that for Kelly the role of Church authorities must be seen
as central. In contrast to the statements of the 1949 version, Kelly now states: "Rather frequently, circumstances
have made it necessary for the Holy See to explain the natural law as it applies to medical problems. Many examples of
this teaching, especially as given by Pius XI and Pius XII,
are given in this book."[151]   The role of the Church is thus
extended. "It should be added here," he says, "that the
Church not only claims divine authorization to interpret the
moral law; it also claims that its teachings are a practical
necessity for a clear and adequate knowledge of this law."[152]
In his next section, Kelly describes the various kinds of
Church teaching, those of the extraordinary (infallible) and
ordinary magisteria. Finally, with less emphasis than in
the 1949 version, Kelly describes the natural scientific
competence of Catholic moralists.

It is clear from the changes Kelly makes in his later
version that his earlier explanation no longer satisfies
him. The role of visible Church authority has been too
strong to allow a solution basing the competence of Catholic
moralists primarily on their natural expertise as ethicists.
Kelly has shifted his emphasis toward an explicit practical
ecclesiastical positivism as necessary in medical ethics,
though he is not, in the strictest sense, a theonomous moral

---

[150]*Ibid.*, p. 29.

[151]*Ibid.*, p. 31.

[152]*Ibid.*, pp. 31-32.

positivist or a theoretical ecclesiastical positivist. That
is, he maintains that the decrees of the Church do not create the moral law. Yet, since such decrees are now seen as
de facto necessary for an understanding of the (supposedly
natural) moral law, the natural law becomes natural only
theoretically. In practice, it is derived from the (supernaturally guaranteed) teachings of the Roman Catholic Church.

The third location where Kelly addresses the problem is
Chapter 19 of the 1958 version, concerning contraception and
sterilization. Kelly is aware that in this area more than
in many others there appears to be a difficulty in finding
natural reasons for the Church's teachings. He recognizes
that many competent physicians with a wholesome general attitude to procreation find at least "*some* cases in which
artificial birth-prevention is the only reasonable solution
to an acute problem."[153] He goes on to suggest that, although the natural law is not *absolutely* beyond the power of
unaided human reason, in practice it cannot be known apart
from supernatural revelation. This revelation, in turn,
"has been entrusted to the Church to be preserved and explained."[154]   He continues:

> It follows, therefore, that the teaching of the Church
> is a practical necessity for an adequate knowledge of
> the natural law; and we should not be surprised or
> shocked when those who lack the benefit of this teach-
> ing are in error as to the existence or extent of some
> obligations. It follows also that the complete truth
> is not expressed by the statement that there is no
> such thing as "Catholic ethics." This is certainly
> true in the sense that the duties studied in ethics
> are duties of *human beings*, regardless of the religion
> they profess; and, for this reason, we cannot admit two
> objective standards in matters of medical ethics: one
> for Catholics, the other for non-Catholics. The state-
> ment is true, also, in the sense that men can learn

---

[153]*Ibid.*, p. 149, italics his.

[154]*Ibid.*, p. 153.

much about the natural law without the guidance of the
Church. But it is definitely not true if it means
that the generality of men can get a clear and adequate knowledge of the natural law, especially as regards its finer points, without the guidance of the
Church. In our age, this guidance seems to be particularly necessary in the matter of artificial birth prevention; and it has been given repeatedly and solemnly,
especially by two Popes, Pius XI and Pius XII.[155]

Kelly's explanation fails to satisfy completely. He is unable to suggest who might be the specialists capable of
understanding the natural law naturally, if supernatural
guidance is needed for "the generality of men." In the absence of such, it is hard to see how the natural law is
natural in any meaningful sense.

In any case, for our purposes it is clear that practical ecclesiastical positivism is explicitly recognized by
Kelly as a central methodological modality in medical ethics.
In his treatment of the various individual ethical issues,
he quotes, often at length, from papal documents. An appendix added to the 1958 edition lists references to statements of the Holy See on medical ethics.[156]

Physicalism is also an important operative modality in
Kelly's work, though here the criteria are assumed, and
there is less attempt made to speak to the problematic issues. In a *Linacre Quarterly* article written in 1953, Kelly
lists briefly eight basic principles of medical ethics.
Many are physicalist. First is the principle of patient
consent. This, of course, is not at all physicalist, but it
is clear that the patient may never consent to a procedure
which is itself immoral. Second is the inviolability of innocent human life. Kelly describes the principle: "This
principle recognizes the fact that God is the Author of life

---

[155]*Ibid.*, p. 153, italics his.

[156]*Ibid.*, pp. 336-339.

and that no one may take it without His permission. By reason of this principle, we exclude direct killing (e.g. by
destructive craniotomy), direct abortion, and 'mercy killing."[157] This is the theological principle of God's dominion, set explicitly within the vocabulary of the direct-
indirect distinctions of the double effect principle.

Third is the principle of totality, which Kelly sees in
its physicalist limitations. Thus, in another place, he
specifically states that the principle cannot be used to
justify organic transplantation or sterilization, since in
neither case is there a direct subordination of the part to
the whole of the same individual.[158] Fourth is the "intrinsic finality of the sex faculties," which principle insists
that the biological effect of the sexual faculties never be
thwarted. From this principle comes opposition to contraception, direct sterilization, masturbation in sterility
testing, and artificial insemination.[159]

The next three principles are merely restatements of
the principle of double effect or of its four conditions.
Thus the fifth principle is that "the end never justifies
the means,"[160] another way of stating the first two conditions of double effect. Sixth is the distinction between
doing good, not always required, and avoiding evil, always
demanded. Again, as we have seen, this is a restatement of
the first two conditions of double effect.[161] Seventh is

---

[157]Kelly, "Medico-Moral Notes," 1953, p. 112. The
same eight principles are also reviewed in Finucane, "Fundamental Principles."

[158]Kelly *Medico-Moral Problems,* 1958 edition, p. 11.

[159]Kelly, "Medico-Moral Notes," 1953, p. 112.

[160]*Ibid.*, p. 113.

[161]See above, p. 352.

the double effect principle itself.

The eighth and last principle is one based on the modality of ecclesiastical positivism. Kelly refers to the
"principle of liberty," by which he means that in any case
where there is not a unanimous opinion among theologians nor
an official Church decision, the individual may follow his
own conscience.

The principles and modalities of application which
Kelly describes in the introductory passages we have examined are applied to the various individual medical ethical
questions treated in his book. He makes consistent use both
of the direct-indirect distinction based on criteria which
we have described as physicalist, and of official pronouncements of the magisterium.

Kelly's treatment of abortion is based on these modalities. Direct abortions are always forbidden, whereas indirect abortions are sometimes permitted.[162] Kelly cites the
various opinions of earlier moralists as well as numerous
decrees of the magisterium which have settled the disputes.[163]
He accepts the opinion (of Bouscaren) that ectopic tubal
pregnancies may be licitly removed by indirect methods, and
insists that no direct removal of ectopic fetuses is allowed.[164] Again, decrees of the Church are cited.

The section on euthanasia is basically identical to
many we have already seen. Euthanasia in the sense of
murder of a person is not permitted, whereas it is allowed
to give pain-killing drugs and to withhold extraordinary
means of preserving life. Kelly does not use the direct-

---

[162]Kelly, *Medico-Moral Problems*, 1958 edition, p. 65
and elsewhere.

[163]*Ibid.*, pp. 69-75.

[164]*Ibid.*, pp. 105-114.

indirect distinction explicitly here, but his judgment dividing right from wrong acts is clearly made along these
lines. The theological principle of redemptive suffering is
cited in this context. Kelly states that "through suffering
a man can beautify his character, atone for his sins, take a
special part in the sublime work of Redemption, and win for
himself an eternity of glory."[165] He goes on to say, however, that it is also Christlike to alleviate pain, and that
the Christian does not "deify pain and sit idly by while men
suffer."[166] Clearly the difference is determined not by the
theological principle of suffering itself but by the ethical
judgment made on the procedure whereby pain is relieved.
Official documents on euthanasia are cited.

The various questions of mutilation and sterilization,
including contraception, are examined according to the direct-indirect distinction. We have already seen the importance of ecclesiastical decrees in deciding on contraception.
In distinguishing evil contraception from allowable rhythm,
Kelly uses the distinction between doing something evil and
not doing something good, that is, not having sexual intercourse during fertile periods.[167] The difference is thus
specified along physicalist lines. The former is evil in
itself whereas the latter is not, even though the two methods have the same results and are used for the same motives.
The moral quality of the procedure is determined according
to the physical structure of the act. Other forms of direct
sterilization are also prohibited, whereas indirect sterilization is allowed. On the question of hysterectomy after
repeated Caesarian sections, however, Kelly takes the more

---

[165] *Ibid.*, p. 118.

[166] *Ibid.*, p. 118.

[167] *Ibid.*, pp. 157-182, esp. pp. 168-169.

permissive view that the procedure is allowed since the
uterus is presently dangerous to the woman. This is disputed by moralists who adhere more strictly to the second
condition of double effect. Kelly insists that at the least
this is an "open question" (moralists disagree) and that the
laxer opinion may be followed.[168] All direct sterilization
is in any case forbidden. Non-sterilizing mutilations are
allowed according to the principle of totality. Concerning
organ transplants Kelly says only that it is an open question. The principle of totality itself cannot justify
them.[169]

When obtaining sperm for sterility testing, masturbation and the use of a non-perforated condom are immoral.
The use of a perforated condom is probably moral, that is,
some authors at least approve it and the question is still
under debate.[170] Thus Kelly combines physicalist criteria
(some semen must reach the vaginal tract so that this physical act can possibly reach its biological end) with positivist ones (no official position has yet been taken by the
magisterium, so the individual is free to choose). Similar
criteria are applied to the question of artificial insemination.[171] Frequent citations are made from official documents.

We have already noted Kelly's influence in North American medical ethics. His work provided, more clearly than
many others, statements as to the rightness and wrongness of
medical procedures. By combining physicalist and positivist

---

[168]*Ibid.*, pp. 213-217. We have already spoken of this
question (see above, pp. 268-269.)

[169]*Ibid.*, pp. 245-252, esp. 252; also pp. 8-11.

[170]*Ibid.*, pp. 218-227.

[171]*Ibid.*, pp. 228-244.

criteria, Kelly was able to offer medical practitioners concise analyses of the practical questions they were asking.
They could find easily and quickly whether an action was definitely forbidden, definitely allowed, or under dispute.
Kelly represented, more than any other single moralist, the
official voice of Roman Catholic medical ethics. In his
work the importance of both physicalist and positivist modalities is evident. He also gives clear evidence of the
shift in the 1940's and 1950's towards a greater emphasis
than before on the role of the official Church in making
medical ethical decisions.

6. Some Works of the Early 1950's

Other authors of the early 1950's, less influential
than McFadden and Kelly, also demonstrate the operative importance of physicalist and positivist criteria.

Physicalism is the primary methodological modality in
both editions (1952 and 1962) of John Kenny's text, *Princi-*
ples of Medical Ethics. Kenny exhibits a consistent application of physicalist specifications to medical ethical issues. Ecclesiastical positivism, while of secondary importance, is nonetheless significant. The growing role of this
modality in Kenny's work can best be seen by comparing the
two editions.

In his chapter on fundamental principles, Kenny describes the principle of double effect. He names the three
traditional determinants of morality as "*the object, the cir-*
cumstances, and the end of the agent."[172] Of these three the
object is the primary determinant. Though Kenny insists
that the object is not the physical, but the moral object
(not the amount stolen for example, but the moral act of

---

[172]Kenny, *Principles,* 1st ed., p. 15; 2nd ed., p. 14,
italics his.

stealing) it is clear that for him the "object" is what we
have described as the physical act-in-itself with its proper
physical or biological goal. "The moral object," he says,
"refers to the action stripped of all its circumstances. As
such it may be good, bad, or indifferent. If the act is indifferent, considered in the abstract, then it receives all
of its morality from the circumstances. If the act is good,
it may still become evil by reason of the circumstances."[173]
Thus Kenny states the first and second conditions of the
double effect principle. Only if they are met, and the act-
in-itself is determined not to be immoral, can the principle
of proportion (the circumstances) be applied. Only then are
the motive, the human effects, and other moral factors of
significance in judging the act.

Like McFadden, Kenny applies the physicalist criteria
of mental reservation to the question of truth-telling.[174]
He insists that a "mental reservation may not be used if the
person can in no way suspect or perceive the less obvious
sense. For example, if the professor announces that there
will be no examination next class and then gives a quiz,
making the distinction in his mind, such a procedure would
be a lie."[175] He continues:

> However, if a statement with a double meaning is made
> and both meanings can be understood, either through the
> words or the circumstances, such a reservation may be
> used. The reply, "The doctor is not in," may mean that
> he is not in his office or that he is not in to you.
> If the hearer does not understand the less obvious
> meaning, the reservation is still permissible by reason
> of the principle of the double effect. It is an evil
> effect (indirectly willed) of an action licit in it-

---

[173]*Ibid.*, 1st ed., p. 16; 2nd ed., p. 14.

[174]For McFadden, see above, pp. 356-357. For an introduction to the question, see above, pp. 271-272.

[175]Kenny, *Principles,* 1st ed., p. 21.

self, and done for a proportionately grave cause.
Since a person may never lie, even to secure a good
effect [the first and second condition would then be
violated], mental reservation has a very practical
aspect for all professional people.[176]

Kenny thus makes explicit the precise way in which mental
reservation fits into double effect. Some other authors we
have seen use the same or similar methodologies without the
same precision as to exact specifications. But the same
physicalist criteria are at work.

Kenny uses similar distinctions in dealing with scandal
and cooperation in an evil procedure, differentiating between direct and indirect scandal, formal and material cooperation. Material cooperation is justified by the double
effect principle, provided the four conditions are met.[177]

In his treatment of marriage, Kenny emphasizes that the
primary purpose of marriage and of sexual intercourse is
procreation.[178] Papal statements are cited.[179] The morality of intercourse is determined primarily by the "object,"
the action itself, which must be able to achieve its primary
biological purpose.[180] Thus the use of masturbation to obtain sperm for sterility testing is immoral, as it is contrary to the direct physical purpose of the sexual act, despite the fact that in this circumstance the reason for it
is precisely procreation.[181] Likewise, the only moral method of artificial insemination is that of pushing the

---

[176]*Ibid.*, p. 21.

[177]*Ibid.*, pp. 25-28.

[178]*Ibid.*, pp. 58, 67.

[179]*Ibid.*, pp. 58, 61, 67-68.

[180]*Ibid.*, p. 68.

[181]*Ibid.*, p. 78.

husband's sperm further into his wife's vagina. All other
methods, including the gathering of sperm from the husband
without venereal activity, are forbidden. Kenny notes that
this last was for a time admitted, but that the recent papal
statement on the question has decided it in the negative.[182]
Thus ecclesiastical positivism is seen as also operative in
Kenny's thought. His opinions on contraception, are the same
as those of other authors we have studied. "Contraception,
in any form, is intrinsically immoral because it frustrates
both the primary and the secondary ends of the act of intercourse."[183] It is interesting to note that Kenny holds that
the secondary ends of sexual intercourse (mutual love and
assistance) are also frustrated by contraception "since mutual love cannot be perfectly expressed except in the manner
ordained by nature. Carnal intercourse should be a complete
surrender of each person to the other spouse. This is both
physically and psychologically impossible with most contraceptive techniques."[184] Periodic continence (rhythm) is
permitted. Again papal statements are cited.[185]

Kenny cites briefly the theological principle of God's
dominion over life.[186] The actual judgment concerning medical procedures of euthanasia, mutilation, sterilization,

---

[182]*Ibid.*, pp. 79-83.

[183]*Ibid.*, p. 87.

[184]*Ibid.*, pp. 87-88. It is interesting to note that in
the 1960's at least one moralist allowed the pill while forbidding other techniques precisely on these grounds, that
while the others made a total act of love impossible, the
pill did not (Janssens, "Conjugal Morality," pp. 65-82).
Janssens, however, no longer held that the primary end of
procreation had to be respected directly in each act. In
this sense he had rejected physicalism.

[185]*Ibid.*, pp. 90-96.

[186]*Ibid.*, pp. 97, 101.

etc., however, are decided according to physicalist criteria. Direct suicide is forbidden, while indirect suicide
may be lawful.[187] Euthanasia (direct killing) is forbidden,
while drugs may be given to alleviate pain, even though they
may induce unconsciousness.[188] In his second edition, Kenny
makes the distinction between ordinary and extraordinary
means of preserving life.[189] Mutilation is allowed by the
physicalistically limited principle of totality. Concerning
organ transplants Kenny is not totally clear. He implies in
the first edition that these are forbidden since the principle of totality cannot be extended to include them.[190] He
cites a statement of Pius XI. In the second edition, he
states that this is an open question, and either opinion may
be held.[191] Direct sterilization is forbidden, indirect
sterilization is allowed. Kenny implies that he includes
hysterectomy after Caesarian section as a direct sterilization.[192]

Direct abortions are forbidden, indirect ones sometimes
allowed. Kenny makes it clear that the distinction between
them is determined primarily by the means used: "Abortion is
indirect when means are used which immediately and directly
are ordained to some end other than the expulsion of the
fetus, but which may unintentionally and indirectly cause an
abortion."[193] Official ecclesiastical statements are in-

---

[187]*Ibid.*, p. 101.

[188]*Ibid.*, pp. 119-127.

[189]*Ibid.*, 2nd ed., pp. 116-126.

[190]*Ibid.*, 1st ed., pp. 108-110.

[191]*Ibid.*, 2nd ed., pp. 162-163.

[192]*Ibid.*, 1st ed., pp. 113-118.

[193]*Ibid.*, p. 182, italics deleted.

cluded in the section. The double effect principle is explicitly applied to cases of indirect abortion, including
cases of tubal ectopic gestation.[194]

Physicalism is thus Kenny's primary methodological modality. Yet we have also seen that the author makes use of
official Church decrees in his method. In his preface to
the second edition, Kenny states:

> The late Pope Pius XII led the way in the development
> of medical ethics and is primarily responsible for its
> astonishing growth. During his pontificate, he de-
> livered approximately seventy-five allocutions on the
> moral aspects of medical procedures. He discussed
> practically every conceivable topic in his addresses
> to various associations of physicians, dentists, nurses,
> psychiatrists, anesthetists, and hospital administra-
> tors. These moral teachings of the Pontiff possess
> doctrinal value insofar as they belong to the ordinary
> magisterium of the Church. For this reason, the second
> edition contains numerous quotations from the allocu-
> tions of Pius XII who will go down in history as the
> "Pope of Medical Ethics."[195]

Kenny does not develop in any detail the question of the
Church's authority in moral matters. He merely states that
"the Church tells us that certain things are right or wrong
precisely because in reality they are either in accord with
or against the sound judgment of reason. In other words,
an action is good if it is reasonable, and it is evil if it
is unreasonable. Moral principles are not the heritage of
any particular religion; they belong to the whole human race,
and should be known and practiced by every human being."[196]
It is nonetheless evident from Kenny's use of Church statements that practical ecclesiastical positivism is operative
in his reasoning process. His primary criteria are physicalist ones, which he shows to be consistent with the official

---

[194]*Ibid.,* pp. 149-161.

[195]*Ibid.,* 2nd ed., pp. vii-viii.

[196]*Ibid.,* both editions, p. 1.

teachings of the Church.

One of the papers presented at the 1954 Workshop of the
Catholic Hospital Association of Canada concerns the role of
the Church in medicine. Léon Loranger describes the importance of adhering to the official teaching of the Church.
He insists that all hospital administrators develop the
"professional competency, that tact and judgment and charity
we need to do our work in perfect accord with the directives
of the Church in matters of medical ethics."[197] He regrets
"that too often some of our Catholic doctors do not have a
Catholic morality and a Catholic professional attitude."[198]
"The doctrinal authority of the Church," he states, "is a
religious authority instituted by Christ for the preservation and interpretation of the revealed divine truths and of
the natural law. . . . If it intervenes in matters concerning medicine, it does not do so for any medical reasons, and
on the basis of medical knowledge, but solely on the basis
of faith and morals and for religious and moral reason."[199]
Loranger goes on to describe the important role of Pope Pius
XII in medicine: "This attitude of the Pope should not, cannot, be explained solely by his turn of mind so open to all
scientific developments, by his Christian humanism . . . No.
His attitude finds its roots in his historical supernatural
role."[200] Loranger's article is a further example of the
importance attributed during the 1950's to the role of the
magisterium, especially to that of Pius XII, in deciding on
medical ethical issues. The author clearly cites the
Church's specific supernatural role in guaranteeing correct
medical morality.

---

[197]Loranger, "The Church and Medicine," p. 42.

[198]*Ibid.*, p. 44.

[199]*Ibid.*, p. 44.

[200]*Ibid.*, p. 49.

The year 1954 also saw the appearance of the first important Protestant work in medical ethics: *Morals and Medi-*
cine by Joseph Fletcher. The book received universally bad
reviews from Catholic moralists, who criticized it as lacking in principles and full of serious errors. In defending
their position against Fletcher's opposition, Catholic
moralists stressed the role of the Roman Catholic Church in
medical ethics. Thus one reviewer, Joseph Farraher, states
that Fletcher "opposes Catholic teaching, and hence his book
clearly comes under the prohibition of canon 1399 [the law
prohibiting Catholics from reading certain books]."[201] He
goes on to note that the book has been called a challenge to
Catholic moralists, "not that there is any doubt about the
correctness of the Catholic position, thanks to the advantage of the infallible teaching authority of the Church; but
it can be considered, perhaps, a challenge to state more
clearly and forcefully the reasons behind the Catholic position."[202] Gerald Kelly likewise insists that the book
comes under canon 1399, and that Catholics may not read it
without permission.[203]

In his major work, *Morale et médecine* (1955), French-
Canadian Jules Paquin makes use both of positivist and physicalist approaches. Throughout his work he cites texts of
official documents, and devotes a section to the teaching of
the Church concerning most of the issues he treats. In all
cases he remains explicitly faithful to the official teaching of the magisterium, especially to that of Pius XII.
Physicalist criteria are essential in most of the major traditional issues, such as abortion, euthanasia, mutilation,

---

[201]Farraher, "Notes," 1955, p. 239.

[202]*Ibid.*, p. 239.

[203]Kelly, "Medico-Moral Notes," 1955, p. 60.

sterilization, birth control, etc. On the other hand,
Paquin includes in his text many issues which do not involve
operations or other kinds of directly physical medical intervention.[204] In his treatment of these issues, Paquin's
method is not physicalistically limited. In at least one
case, that of truth-telling, he specifically rejects a
strictly physicalist approach. In addition, he emphasizes
more than many other moralists those psychological and subjective elements which, while not relevant to the ethical
questions themselves (these judgments are still made according to the analysis of the act-in-itself, double effect,
etc.), must be considered when dealing pastorally with people and when judging the moral disposition of persons in the
sacrament of penance.

The direct-indirect distinction is central to Paquin's
methodology. He differentiates formal from material cooperation, direct from indirect homicide in cases of euthanasia
and abortion, and preventative (direct) from curative (indirect) sterilization. In each case the "direct" procedure
is forbidden while the "indirect" one may be allowed according to double effect. In his section on euthanasia he refers to the theological principle of redemptive suffering,
and emphasizes the role of the Christian in relieving suffering, whenever possible. But if the suffering cannot
licitly be alleviated, then it becomes redemptive when cou-
rageously accepted.[205] Paquin thus makes use of the tradition of redemptive suffering as an ancillary argument
against active euthanasia. Because this procedure is contrary to the natural law (physicalist criteria) and to the
teachings of the Church (positivist criteria), the Christian

---

[204]See above, pp. 193-199.

[205]Paquin, *Morale et médecine*, p. 198.

ought to accept the sufferings which his illness brings.
The theological principle of God's dominion over life is
used in a similar manner. Direct homicide is forbidden:
"The basic principle which regulates this entire question of
respect for life can be stated in these terms: we are not
masters of life; even though God has given each of us the
administration of this good, he keeps the ownership of it
for himself; human life, in each and every instant, belongs
to God and to God alone. . . . For this reason, direct homicide (and suicide) is always forbidden."[206] Indirect homicide, on the other hand, is justified because, "if we are
not the owners of our life, we are nonetheless its administrators; the care of our life is given immediately to us,
by the natural law itself."[207] Thus the principle of God's
dominion is used both to proscribe direct homicide and to
permit indirect homicide, but the criteria for the distinction are the physicalist ones of double effect rather than
the more directly theological ones of the tradition concerning God's creating and conserving action.

In his section on mutilation and sterilization, Paquin
makes use of the principle of totality. Concerning organ
transplants he states simply that there is controversy, and
the question is an open one. Because the pope has not explicitly ruled in the issue, organ transplantation may be

---

[206]*Ibid.*, p. 191, translation mine. "Le principe de
base qui régit toute cette question du respect de la vie
peut s'énoncer en ces termes: nous ne sommes pas les maîtres
de la vie; même si Dieu a confié à chacun de nous l'administration de ce bien, il en garde la propriété; en chacun de
ses instants, la vie humaine appartient à Dieu et à Dieu
seul. . . . A ce titre, l'homicide (et le suicide) direct est
toujours défendu."

[207]*Ibid.*, p. 192, translation mine. "Si nous ne sommes
pas les propriétaires de notre vie, nous en sommes cependant
les administrateurs; la vie est un bien dont le soin nous
est confié immédiatement, par la loi naturelle elle-même."

performed, provided there is no danger of death for the
donor (direct suicide is forbidden) and provided the donor
is not made sterile (direct sterilization is forbidden).[208]
Thus both physicalist and positivist criteria are introduced.
In his treatment of hysterectomy after a series of Caesarian
sections, he implies that his own opinion is negative, that
this is a preventative (direct) sterilization, and thus prohibited. Nonetheless, he cites the approval of other moralists, among them Gerald Kelly, and thus allows it as a probable opinion: "we would not dare blame the physician who performed a hysterectomy in an extreme case of this kind. But
let it be always well understood: the hysterectomy would be
permitted on account of the present pathological condition
of the uterus, and not only because of the danger which a
future pregnancy would cause."[209]

We have noted the use in some authors of strict physicalist criteria in their treatment of lying and mental reservation. Paquin explicitly rejects this approach. He presents the theory of mental reservation, but adds: "However,
we do not like this theory of mental reservation very much,
since it seems to restrict more or less the possibility of
avoiding a lie only to sophisticated intellects."[210]

---

[208]*Ibid.*, p. 247.

[209]*Ibid.*, p. 260, translation mine. "nous n'oserions
pas blâmer le médecin qui pratiquerait une hystérectomie
dans un cas extrême de ce genre. Qu'on le comprenne bien,
toutefois: l'hystérectomie serait permise alors à cause de
l'état délabré où se trouve actuellement l'utérus, et non
pas uniquement à cause du danger causé par une grossesse
future."

[210]*Ibid.*, p. 408, translation mine. "Pourtant, nous
n'aimons pas beaucoup cette théorie de la restriction
mentale, qui semble réserver plus ou moins aux seuls esprits
vifs la possibilité de toujours éviter le mensonge."

The theory which Paquin espouses emphasizes the wholistic
personal meaning of truth in a social context, and allows a
"direct" falsehood when this is required in the service of
truth humanly defined. In this instance Paquin breaks with
physicalism. Indeed, much of the total volume deals with
issues not generally included (or at least not included in
this great detail) in North American medical ethics texts.
We have described these in chapter two. Concerning these
issues there are fewer direct applications of physicalist
criteria.

Throughout his work Paquin insists on the significance
of the official teachings of the Church. Though he does not
include any detailed theoretical treatment of the Church's
authority, he includes a section on the doctrine of the
Church in most of his discussions. Quotations from papal
statements, especially those of Pius XII, are numerous. His
bibliography includes a lengthy section devoted solely to
statements of Pope Pius XII on medicine.[211] Reviews of his
book emphasized the value of this approach.[212]

7. The Manuals of Edwin Healy and Thomas O'Donnell

Edwin Healy's *Medical Ethics* (1956) places heavy emphasis on physicalism. Drawing on the terminological development of his predecessors, Healy is able to present his specifications and conclusions in a consistent fashion. Positivism is of less significance.

Healy applies physicalist criteria to many different issues. He distinguishes between direct lies and mental reser-

---

[211]*Ibid.*, pp. 465-467.

[212]*Homiletic and Pastoral Review*, 55 (1955), 1062;
American Ecclesiastical Review, 133 (1955), 216.

vations.[213] He explains the principle of double effect and
applies it to cases of erotic stimulation during therapy,
cooperation in evil, and scandal.[214] These are immoral if
direct, allowed under certain circumstances if indirect.
Mutilation is allowed according to the criteria of the (physicalist) principle of totality, though the principle itself
is not explicitly mentioned; and the theological principle
of God's dominion over life is set in this context.[215]
Healy's treatment of transplantation from living donors is
scant, and he implies his approval without any real analysis.[216] Certain methods of obtaining sperm for sterility
testing are proscribed because they directly thwart the purpose of the generative faculties.[217] Artificial birth control thwarts the natural effect (physical effect) of the
(physical) act.[218]

Direct sterilization is forbidden, indirect sterilization sometimes allowed. Here Healy is consistent with the
strict interpretation of the first and second conditions of
double effect. He explicitly declares hysterectomy after
Caesarean sections to be an immoral direct sterilization.
His reasoning here is an excellent example of the physicalist modality:

> Hence he [the physician] intends to excise the uterus
> as a means of preventing a danger which would sub-
> stantially arise from pregnancy alone. His intention,
> then, is evil, for he directly seeks sterilization, and

---

[213]Healy, *Medical Ethics,* pp. 38-45.

[214]*Ibid.,* pp. 94-120.

[215]*Ibid.,* pp. 121-139.

[216]*Ibid.,* pp. 139-143.

[217]*Ibid.,* p. 147.

[218]*Ibid.,* pp. 156-162.

direct sterilization is gravely illicit. But could not
the surgeon "purify" his intention? Could he not intend merely the removal from the woman's body of a useless organ? The answer is that here there is no other
reason for the operation except that of a future pregnancy. The surgeon cannot claim that the purpose of
the excision is to rid the body of what he considers
to be an obstruction, for actually the uterus when not
pregnant is not a source of inconvenience, of pain, or
of any other physical disturbance. The operation does
not tend to promote the health of the patient's body
except insofar as it is contraceptive. The chief reason for condemning this operation is that it appears to
be one of direct sterilization.[219]

Since the good effect (the future health of the woman) is
achieved through the causality of the evil effect (the prevention of future pregnancy), the second condition of double
effect is violated, and the operation is forbidden as a direct sterilization.[220]

Healy distinguishes direct and indirect abortions, differentiating cases consistently according to physicalist
criteria. Again the theological principle of God's dominion
over life is subordinated to these criteria:

Directly to kill an innocent person constitutes the
crime of murder. . . . Such an action would be evil,
even though one were directly to hasten another's death
by only an hour or even by only a few minutes. The
reason for this assertion is that God has supreme and
exclusive ownership over the lives of all human beings.
He and He alone has supreme dominion over every moment
of their lives . . . Quite different, however, from
the *direct* hastening of death is the act of *indirectly*
shortening life. . . . For a proportionately grave reason this is justified according to the teaching explained in the application of the principle of the two-
fold effect.[221]

Operations for removal of tubal pregnancies are permitted as

---

[219]*Ibid.*, p. 175.

[220]The reader is again referred to pp. 268-269 above.
for further discussion of this issue.

[221]*Ibid.*, pp. 209-210, italics his.

indirect abortions. Healy's analysis of non-tubal ectopic
gestations consistently allows the removal of any organ
which the fetus has caused to be dangerous to the mother's
health, and along with the removal of that organ, the indirect abortion of the fetus. If the fetus should attach itself to a vital organ, however, which could not be removed,
the fetus itself could never be directly aborted. Healy implies that in such a theoretical case, both fetus and mother
must be allowed to die.[222]

Healy's section on euthanasia is brief, probably because
he has already considered the question of direct killing.
Euthanasia, by which he means direct killing, is forbidden
because "God alone has the ownership of human life."[223] Healy
also refers to the redemptive meaning of suffering in this
context, argues that the practice would lessen confidence in
physicians, and cites a decree of the Holy Office.[224] His
primary argument, however, is that the action is in itself
a moral evil: "Murder, or the unjust killing of an innocent
person, is of its very nature evil and will remain evil in
every set of circumstances."[225]

Ecclesiastical positivism is less prominent in Healy's
work than in many other works of the forties and fifties.
It is nonetheless clear that Healy's conclusions and methodology are intended to be faithful to the Church's official
teaching. He intends his book to be "an application to the
practice of medicine of the principles of the natural law.
The Catholic looks to his Church for guidance in his interpretation of the natural law . . . Because of confused notions . . . the Church has issued clarifying and authoritative pronouncements which serve to protect her subjects from

---

[222]*Ibid.*, pp. 226-227.

[223]*Ibid.*, p. 267.

[224]*Ibid.*, pp. 268-270.

[225]*Ibid.*, p. 267.

error."[226]   Healy appeals to such pronouncements in his discussion of various topics.   Reviewers of his work praise him
for agreeing with papal decisions, and criticize him when
they judge that he has departed from them.[227]

Thomas O'Donnell's *Morals in Medicine* (1956 and 1959)
emphasizes both physicalism and ecclesiastical positivism.
It is his treatment of natural law and divine positive law
which is of most interest for our study.

It is difficult to determine with any precision the exact relationship O'Donnell proposes between the natural law
and the authoritative teaching of the magisterium.   It is
clear that ecclesiastical positivism is an important practical methodological modality.   It is also clear that O'Donnell does not argue that the teachings of the Church take on
their universally binding force from their relationship to
the universally binding natural law.   We have noted that
some authors insist that the conclusions of Catholic ethicists are binding on all because they are based on the natural law, which is discoverable by unaided reason.   This
natural law is supplemented by the direct revelation of the
divine positive law (generally described as including all of
God's supernatural revelation, as found in Scripture and in
the authentic teaching of the Catholic Church), which *as
such* binds only those who accept it, that is, Catholics in
the case of the pronouncements of the magisterium, and

---

[226]*Ibid.*, p. 8.

[227]*Clergy Review*, 42 (1957), 115; *Irish Ecclesiastical
Record*, 87 (1957), 473.   This latter reviewer criticizes
Healy for not mentioning the principle of totality explicitly, since its use has been "canonized" by its appearance in
so many papal allocutions.   Thus we have another example of
how official pronouncements are seen to be authoritative not
only with respect to the ethical conclusions reached but
also as to the terminology used in the discussion.

Christians (and Jews) in the case of the Bible.[228] Inasmuch
as supernatural revelation (the divine positive law) explains and interprets the natural law, it takes on a universally binding force. That force, however, comes not from
supernatural revelation itself, but from the natural law
which it interprets. We have discussed at length the problematic nature of this position.

O'Donnell's position, on the other hand, is that the
divine positive law obliges all men. He makes no attempt to
explain this by appealing to any relationship the divine
positive law might have with the natural law. Both the natural law and the divine positive law are binding on all.[229]
It is difficult to know exactly what empirical elements
O'Donnell includes in the divine positive law. He explicitly includes "the moral precepts of the Old Testament, insofar as they have been confirmed *and supplemented* and fulfilled in the New Testament by the direct revelation of
Jesus Christ, true God and true man."[230] He then develops
his idea of this messianic revelation, defending the his-
toricity of the New Testament and the authority of

---

[228]We have seen this in Bonnar (see above, pp. 321-323),
McFadden (see above, pp. 341-345), and Kelly (see above, pp.
360-366). Our study of each has disclosed inconsistencies
and/or changes of position, but this is the basic approach
taken by these authors.

[229]O'Donnell, *Morals in Medicine,* both eds., pp. 12, 18.
He makes the theoretical distinction that the divine positive
law can oblige only those who have reached the use of reason,
but this is of no concern to us, and, indeed, since those
who have not reached the age of reason can hardly be asked
to obey *morally* the natural law either, this distinction
seems of little importance. It should be noted that McFadden also states that the divine positive law obliges all,
but in his case, as we have pointed out, there is reason to
believe that the implications are different (see above, pp.
343-344, n. 84).

[230]*Ibid.,* both eds., p. 12, emphasis added.

Christ.[231] From this basis he goes on to argue for the divine origin of the Roman Catholic Church and specifically for papal infallibility. He distinguishes between infallible and non-infallible, yet authoritative decrees. The latter, which are of most concern for medical ethics, "although not enjoying the infallibility of the Chair of Peter, merit and demand total acceptance by all of the faithful."[232] Are these decrees also binding for non-Catholics? Inasmuch as O'Donnell implies their inclusion in divine positive law, it would seem that they are. The context suggests that these authoritative pronouncements are among the supplements and fulfillments which the revelation of Christ adds to the Old Testament precepts. Yet O'Donnell is never explicit.

Though the question as to the exact extension of the divine positive law is never precisely answered, it is clear that O'Donnell's theoretical position concerning the relationship of this law to natural law, and concerning its universally binding force, differs somewhat from other authors we have studied. O'Donnell avoids any complex discussion of the relationship of natural and divine positive laws. The universal force of divine positive law comes from itself, and not from any supposed relationship to the natural law. In this sense O'Donnell is closer to being a theonomous moral positivist than most Roman Catholic authors of the period. That is not to suggest that he would consider God's supernaturally revealed laws to be totally arbitrary, the mere result of divine whim. It is the same God who creates human nature with its natural law and who reveals supernaturally his will for man. Yet in giving to supernaturally revealed and ecclesiastically interpreted divine positive law

---

[231] *Ibid.*, both eds., pp. 12-14.

[232] *Ibid.*, 2nd ed. only, p. 18.

a status of universal force independent of its role as interpreter of the natural law, O'Donnell gives it greater *theoretical* importance than do most of his contemporaries.

The extent of O'Donnell's treatment of the role of divine positive law and the authoritative decrees of the Roman Catholic magisterium demonstrates the importance of ecclesiastical positivism in his methodology. Physicalism is also operative. The author describes the principle of double effect with its four conditions, and distinguishes immediate and mediate cooperation in an evil action.[233]

O'Donnell's discussion of euthanasia is brief. He appeals directly to the theological principle of God's dominion over human life as sufficient reason for forbidding suicide and euthanasia.[234] He does not make the physicalist distinctions between direct and indirect euthanasia. These can be presumed from the context, however, since he goes on to a lengthy discussion concerning the obligation of using various means to preserve life.[235] In this section he cites the opinions of many authors as to which means are ordinary and thus obligatory, and which are extraordinary and thus optional. We have already noted that this distinction as such is not at all physicalist. Yet it falls within the general context of the distinction between direct or active euthanasia, always forbidden, and indirect or passive euthanasia, sometimes permitted. Though O'Donnell does not make the distinction clear, his general arguments presuppose it.

Physicalist criteria are invoked in the lengthy section on mutilation. Direct non-sterilizing mutilation is justi-

---

[233]*Ibid.*, both eds., pp. 39-50.

[234]*Ibid.*, 1st ed., pp. 51-54; 2nd ed., pp. 53-56, 60.

[235]*Ibid.*, 1st ed., pp. 55-68; 2nd ed., pp. 61-74.

fied according to the principle of totality.[236]   O'Donnell
discusses various kinds of mutilating operations, including
psychosurgery, human experimentation, and organ transplantation, and generally argues for their liceity. The justification for organic transplantation does not come from the
principle of totality, however, which is limited to the good
of the one physical body. O'Donnell cites a pronouncement
of Pius XII to that effect.[237] Organ transplantation is
justified by the law of charity. In this case, therefore,
O'Donnell breaks with physicalism. The result is a lack of
clarity concerning exactly which operations are justified
and which are not.[238] As we have seen in our study of
Cunningham's thesis on the same topic, once strict physicalist limits are removed, no clear line of separation remains
between right and wrong actions.[239]

The section on sterilization emphasizes the distinction
we have noted many times between sterilizing and non-sterilizing mutilations. Whereas direct non-sterilizing mutilations
are justified according to the principle of totality, sterilizing mutilations "must not only conform with the principle
of totality, but must also be judged in the light of the principle of double effect."[240] O'Donnell explains that the reason for this is that the organs of generation exist not "for
the good of the body, but for the good of the species. Therefore, according to right order, precisely in so far as they

---

[236]*Ibid.*, 1st ed., pp. 70-73; 2nd ed., pp. 76-79.

[237]*Ibid.*, 2nd ed., p. 128.

[238]*Ibid.*, pp. 129-130.

[239]See above, pp. 337-338.

[240]O'Donnell, 1st ed., p. 104; 2nd ed., p. 131.

are generative they are not to be considered as subordinated
to the good of the individual."[241] Accordingly, direct or
"contraceptive" sterilization is forbidden: "If this contraceptive effect were directly intended, that is, if the mutilation were undertaken precisely as a contraceptive measure,
even though in the interests of the whole body, this would
be a violation of right order and immoral."[242] Hence sterilization in the presence of a cardiac disease which would
render pregnancy inadvisable is forbidden.[243] On the other
hand, O'Donnell takes the more liberal position in the case
of hysterectomy after multiple Caesarean sections, arguing
that the condition of the uterus renders it functionally
pathological in its present state, and hence its removal is
justified as an indirect sterilization.[244] He cites his
opinion as at least "solidly probable."[245] Throughout the
entire section on mutilation, O'Donnell cites decrees of the
magisterium.

O'Donnell distinguishes direct and indirect abortion
according to physicalist criteria. He forbids abortion in
cases of pre-eclampsia "because the evil effect (the removal

---

[241]*Ibid.*, 1st ed., p. 72; 2nd ed., p. 78.

[242]*Ibid.*, 1st ed., pp. 104-105; 2nd ed., p. 131.

[243]*Ibid.*, 1st ed., p. 73; 2nd ed., p. 79.

[244]*Ibid.*, 1st ed., pp. 108-110; 2nd ed., pp. 146-150.
For an expression of the contrary opinion, see above, pp.
383-384, on Healy. Healy's argument is more accurate from
a strictly physicalist perspective. O'Donnell also remains
within a physicalist framework, as his analysis of other
cases demonstrates. In this case, his physicalist criteria
are broadened a bit to allow the notion of functional pathology which would allow the sterilization to be considered
indirect.

[245]*Ibid.*, 1st ed., p. 109; 2nd ed., p. 148. That is,
since no definitive pronouncement has ruled otherwise, and
since at least some approved Catholic moralists hold it, it
may safely be followed.

of the fetus from its vital environment) is necessarily directly willed since it is a necessary means to producing
the good effect (the health of the mother) [second condi-
tion]."[246]   In cases of hydramnios, on the other hand, a
case disputed by moralists, O'Donnell argues that the removal of the fluid from the womb constitutes an act which is
only an indirect abortion, resulting with equal causal immediacy in both the good effect (the health of the mother)
and the evil effect (the death of the fetus).[247]   He compares the case to that of hysterectomy of a pregnant cancerous uterus, traditionally allowed as an indirect abortion. He allows the removal of a pathological fallopian
tube in cases of ectopic pregnancy as indirect abortion,
insisting with Bouscaren that to remove the fetus and leave
the tube would be a direct abortion. On the other hand,
O'Donnell argues that the exact timing of the series of
physical interventions could be altered, so that the physician might first clamp off the blood supply to the tube,
then remove the fetus, then remove the tube. This is at
slight variance with the more traditional position of
Bouscaren and others.[248]

In his condemnation of contraception, O'Donnell quotes
at length from Pius XI, citing the argument that contraception thwarts the (physical) purpose of intercourse. Pius
XII is cited as approving the practice of periodic continence (rhythm).[249]   While forbidding masturbation and condomistic intercourse as methods of obtaining sperm for

---

[246]*Ibid.*, 1st ed., p. 133; 2nd ed., p. 179.

[247]*Ibid.*, 1st ed., pp. 137-144; 2nd ed., pp. 183-190.

[248]*Ibid.*, 1st ed., pp. 154-159; 2nd ed., pp. 199-206.
One reviewer notes this variation with surprise (*Priest,* 13
[1957], 222).

[249]*Ibid.*, 1st ed., pp. 203-208; 2nd ed., pp. 271-279.

analysis, O'Donnell favors the more liberal opinion that a
condom with holes in it may be used for the purpose.[250]
Artificial insemination of all types is forbidden. The previous opinion of some moralists allowing insemination with
the semen of a husband obtained by syringe (thus avoiding
masturbation) is no longer acceptable, since the practice
has been forbidden by Pius XII.[251]

In his work O'Donnell thus makes use of both physicalist and positivist modalities. The theological principle of
God's dominion over life is used in the context of euthanasia, and that of redemptive suffering is not explicitly
mentioned. Of the two modalities, O'Donnell emphasizes that
of positivism, both theoretically and practically. He consistently cites papal decrees as definitive in his ethical
argumentation. Though he generally argues for the more
liberal opinion in disputed issues, it is clear that dispute
is possible only until an authoritative decision settles the
matter.

8. Some Other Works

Before concluding the present section, we will add
brief methodological summaries of several remaining works,
pointing out only their most important features.

Patrick O'Brien's revised edition of Patrick Finney's
Moral Problems in Medical Practice (1956), like the original, emphasizes physicalist criteria. O'Brien devotes much
of his work to a defense of Finney's opinion concerning the
immorality of the removal of a fallopian tube containing a
pre-viable fetus until it is morally certain that the physical life of the mother is in "serious and immediate dan-

---

[250]*Ibid.*, 1st ed., pp. 118-228; 2nd ed., pp. 294-302.

[251]*Ibid.*, 2nd ed. only, p. 306.

ger."[252]   Finney's application of the principle of double
effect is maintained throughout the work. O'Brien argues
merely that too easy an application of Bouscaren's theory
(we have noted moralists who hold that the tube is pathological by the very fact of the ectopic pregnancy, and hence
may be removed as dangerous) leads to abortions where none
are necessary. The physician must wait until more serious
degeneration has taken place. The high probability of
saving the mother's life, together with the virtual certainty of the eventual natural death of the fetus, is not sufficient for O'Brien. Instead of high probability he requires the certainty of saving the mother's life, that is,
that the tubal degeneration has reached an immediately and
seriously dangerous point. As long as there is a chance
that the mother will not die, regardless of the eventual
outcome for the fetus, the operation is not warranted, since
the good to be gained (health of the mother) is not proportionate to the evil effect (death of the fetus) caused by
the act. For O'Brien, the fact that the fetus will die in
any case is irrelevant.[253] *This* surgical procedure cannot
morally *cause* the death of the fetus in the absence of immediate and serious danger to the life of the mother.[254]

     O'Brien clarifies some of the terminological con-
fusion present in Finney's original work concerning mutilation. He argues for the stricter opinion in the case
of hysterectomy following Caesarean section, since "such
good effect as may materialize in the future (the avoidance of a possible future danger) is produced by means

---

[252]Finney and O'Brien, *Moral Problems,* p. 188.

[253]*Ibid.,* pp. 167, 171.

[254]For a response to an earlier article by O'Brien
making the same basic points, see Davis, "Ectopic Gestation."

of this evil effect."[255]   Thus the second condition of
the double effect principle is violated.[256]   On the other
hand, he allows Cunningham's thesis permitting organ transplantation for charitable reasons, thus breaking with physicalism in this one case. He gives no analysis, merely
stating that "the opinion has been debated but has not been
conclusively disproved."[257]

Ecclesiastical positivism is not a dominant modality
for O'Brien, though he does cite papal statements at times,
and avows that the "work of interpretation and recognition
[of the natural law] is the proper work of the Catholic
Church."[258]

Nicholas Lohkamp's 1956 doctoral dissertation examines
the problem of hysterectomy operations.[259]   His basic approach is that of double effect physicalism. He argues
that all mutilations are direct, since "the physical evil
[supposed evil effect] is the *means whereby* the good effect
is accomplished."[260]   These direct mutilations are justified
by the principle of totality. Direct sterilizations, on the
other hand, are never allowed, since here "the mutilation is
such that it effects directly only sterility, or benefits
the whole body through a bad means, sterility [the second
condition of double effect is violated]."[261]   Direct sterilization is a usurpation of God's authority, since the

---

[255]*Ibid.*, p. 223.

[256]*Ibid.*, p. 215.

[257]*Ibid.*, p. 232.

[258]*Ibid.*, p. 8.

[259]Lohkamp, *The Morality of Hysterectomy Operations*.

[260]*Ibid.*, p. 19, italics his.

[261]*Ibid.*, p. 22.

Creator intended this power for the good of the species.[262]
Thus the theological principle of God's dominion is used
within the context of physicalist distinctions. Lohkamp
describes in detail the problem of hysterectomy after repeated Caesarean sections, presents the arguments of many
moralists, and concludes to the immorality of the procedure.[263] His arguments are in accord with the stricter application of double effect physicalism.

In their brief work, *Moral Handbook of Nursing* (1956),
Hayes, Hayes, and Kelly distinguish between ethics, which is
a natural science based only on natural reason and "not
based on the teachings of the Catholic Church, nor . . . on
the Bible,"[264] and moral theology, which deals with "the
morality of human acts in relation to man's supernatural
end. . . . The sources which moral theology utilizes are
these: I. Divine revelation as interpreted by the Catholic
Church II. Human reason III. Experience. . . . Medical
ethics is [a] particular aspect of the science of ethics."[265]
The authors continue:

> Although ethics uses as its only tool the light of hu-
> man reason, nevertheless the student of nursing ethics
> can find great help in the moral teachings of Almighty
> God as revealed in the Written Word of God and in
> Tradition as interpreted and explained in the living
> teaching Authority of God's Church. . . . Medical eth-
> ics *in practice,* as Catholics understand it, is not
> merely a philosophical science but a supernatural moral
> science, and as such subject to the authority of the
> Church.[266]

---

[262]*Ibid.*, p. 23.

[263]*Ibid.*, pp. 119-142.

[264]Hayes, Hayes, and Kelly, *Moral Handbook,* p. 3.

[265]*Ibid.*, p. 5.

[266]*Ibid.*, p. 7, emphasis added.

This statement shows quite clearly the practical operative
significance of ecclesiastical positivism. Both physicalist
and positivist criteria are used in the work.

John Shinners' 1958 dissertation studies the question
of medical experimentation. From his title, *The Morality of
Medical Experimentation on Living Human Subjects in the
Light of Recent Papal Pronouncements,* the importance of the
ecclesiastical positivist modality is clear. Shinners argues that papal decrees have allowed a certain amount of
medical experimentation. He suggests three possible lines
of analysis according to which this could be justified.
Some authors permit it according to the principle of the
double effect, but Shinners, like Cunningham on the more
limited yet quite similar question of organ transplantation,
argues that this is not valid for those experiments in which
the physical evil effect is the means for achieving the good
effect (here the medical knowledge to be gained for others).
"In experiments in which injury of some kind or risk of injury is the means to the end, the principle of the double
effect is not applicable."[267] The second possible approach
is that of Cunningham, who extends the principle of totality
to include not only the one physical body of the subject of
experimentation (the organ donor), but also the entire human
brotherhood as Mystical Body of Christ.[268] Against this approach Shinners cites papal documents and arguments that the
individual person is not merely a part of society to the
same degree that an organ is part of the whole body. If
this kind of subordination were true, then society would
have the right to demand involuntary compliance with such
experiments. "The principle of totality is not applicable

---

[267]Shinners, *The Morality,* p. 65.

[268]See above, pp. 332-341.

here," Shinners says, "since society is a moral unity--a
unity of finality and action, and thus only a man's *actions*
are subordinated to the common good and can be used directly
for the good of others by society."[269] Papal decrees are
cited in support of this. Shinners opts for a third approach, that "the licitness of experimentation is to be determined according to the limits of man's dominion over his
body."[270] God is the "substantial owner" of a man's body
and its organs. Man has only "imperfect administrative dominion."[271] He can directly mutilate himself to the extent
of a substantial tampering only if that mutilation is necessary for the physical good of the same body (principle of
totality physicalistically limited).[272] Mutilations for the
good of others are permitted only as long as the person
"does not change the nature of the property" over which he
has only imperfect dominion.[273] Thus, "man can use his
physical and psychic *esse* but he can do nothing which will
materially and permanently change the nature of it, so as to
render it impossible for him to return to God, substantially
the same at the end of life."[274]

     The practical consequence of Shinners' reasoning is a
reduction in the degree of severity of licit experiments.
Some restrictions are thus placed on Cunningham's conclusions, restrictions which do seem morally warranted. Like
Cunningham, Shinners remains entirely and explicitly faith-

---

[269]Shinners, p. 71, italics his.

[270]*Ibid.*, p. 78.

[271]*Ibid.*, p. 29.

[272]*Ibid.*, p. 37.

[273]*Ibid.*, p. 38.

[274]*Ibid.*, p. 39.

ful to the pronouncements of the magisterium. Like him, he
rejects a strict physicalist analysis in terms of double effect or physicalistically limited principle of totality. He
makes use of the theological principle of God's dominion
over human life to restore some restrictions to the broad
range of licit mutilating experiments which might be permitted under Cunningham's theory.

Conclusion

We have now completed our methodological survey of the
literature of the later period in the emergence of Roman
Catholic medical ethics in North America. We have seen how
the explicit use of the authoritative decrees of the magisterium has taken on more and more importance. We have noted
and described efforts by various authors, especially McFadden, Kelly, and O'Donnell, to analyze the importance of
Church decrees and to relate them to the natural law.
Whereas the early period (1900-1940) gave greatest emphasis
to working out the precise specifications of physicalist
criteria for application to medical ethical issues, the
later period (1940-1960) emphasized a defense of these specifications and conclusions, based largely on the authority
of the Church, especially on the decrees of Pope Pius XII.
His numerous statements on medical ethical issues were cited,
explained, defended, and interpreted in the literature.
Physicalist criteria remained important, of course. But we
have discovered a subtle yet nonetheless significant shift
in emphasis toward the modality of ecclesiastical positivism
as a central operative approach in medical ethics. Even in
those cases where a break with explicitly physicalist criteria occurred, as in the question of organ transplantation
and medical experimentation, authors were clear that the official pronouncements of the magisterium were definitive,

and subjected their reasonings and conclusions to them.

We have seen how, with some exceptions, the theological
principles of God's dominion over human life and of redemptive suffering found ethical application to the rightness
and wrongness of medical procedures as subordinate or ancillary principles to the two dominant methodological modalities: physicalism and ecclesiastical positivism. Though
the principles were cited frequently, the actual judgment as
to which acts were licit and which illicit were made according to physicalist and positivist criteria. We have noted
exceptions, such as the question of spiritual care of the
dying, but have discovered that most often these theological
principles were not suggested as mystery-filled hermeneutic
instruments for approaching the question of the meaning of
life. Rather they were used as supportive principles for
the clear answers reached by physicalist or positivist criteria.

In chapter two, when we described the definition of our
discipline, we noted the central importance of the influence
of professional scientific medicine. Roman Catholic medical
ethics stressed the procedures central to modern technological medicine: direct physical interventions for the cure of
physical disease. The methodological modalities described
in chapters three, four, and five can also be seen as harmonious with modern medical method. Physicalism, like scientific technological medicine, operated by arriving at solutions on the basis of physical, cause-and-effect criteria.
It enabled the moralist, like the scientific physician, to
reach conclusions applicable in each instance where the physical details were the same. It enabled correct scientific
answers of a universally applicable nature to be deduced
from the data. Like scientific, technological medicine, it
evolved out of an Aristotelian-Thomistic thought system
where nature, secondary causality, and rationality were

emphasized. Ecclesiastical positivism acted, as we have
seen, as an authoritative defense of this approach and of
the conclusions reached in accordance with it. Thus it
paralleled the authoritative defense by the medical profession of the scientific conclusions reached in the development of their profession.

Pius XII died on October 9, 1958. With his death and
the preparation for the Second Vatican Council, the period
of emergence of our discipline ended. The writers of the
sixties and seventies would begin a radical methodological
critique which would seriously challenge the established modalities, and ultimately the conclusions derived from them.
In the next chapter we will present a survey of the broadest
outlines of this challenge, in order to offer an evaluation
and critique of the discipline in its emergent phase, the
analysis and description of which we have now completed.

CHAPTER SIX

CRITIQUE: SOME RECENT DEVELOPMENTS

The purpose of this final chapter is to note briefly
some developments in medical ethics of the last two decades,
in order to offer a critique of the definition and theological methodology of Roman Catholic medical ethics in its
emergent (pre-Vatican II) phase. No detailed analysis of
recent biomedical ethics similar to the one we have just
completed of the emergent phase will be attempted. Such a
study would require an entire volume by itself, and even
then, given the truly vast amount of medical ethical literature currently appearing,[1] the task would be problematic at
best. No easily defineable *terminus ad quem* could be chosen. No historical perspective would be possible. Nonetheless, some attempt at a brief overview is desirable in order

---

[1]As can be readily seen by glancing at any of the bibliographies of medical ethics currently available. Among
them must be listed in first place the Hastings Center's
Bibliography of Society, Ethics and the Life Sciences, which
was first compiled in 1973 and has appeared annually or bi-
annually since then. Equally important and comprehensive is
the annual *Bibliography of Bioethics,* edited by LeRoy Walters
of the Kennedy Institute in Georgetown, the first volume of
which appeared in 1975. Other less comprehensive works,
which may include items on specific topics not found in the
above annual or biannual bibliographies, include: Hall and
Swenson, *Psychological and Social Aspects of Human Tissue
Transplantation;* Geijerstam, *An Annotated Bibl. of Induced
Abortion;* Carmody, *Ethical Issues in Health Services;* Dollen,
Abortion in Context; Adams, *Therapeutic Abortion;* Gothie, *A
Select Bibl. of Applied Ethics in the Professions;* Wojcichowsky, *Ethical-Social-Legal Annotated Bibl. of English Language
Studies on Abortion;* Sorenson, *Social and Psychological As-
pects of Applied Human Genetics;* Clouser and Zucker, *Abortion
and Euthanasia;* Muldoon, *Abortion: An Annotated Bibl.*

to set the definition and methodology of our discipline into the perspective of current thinking in medical ethics.

Perhaps the most obvious characteristic of Roman Catholic medical ethics of the last ten or fifteen years is that it is no longer the only source or even by itself the most important source of medical ethical scholarship.[2] Indeed, with the exception of certain methodological discussions, where some literature continues to investigate and criticize specifically Catholic approaches to the theological methodology of medical ethics, it is no longer possible to locate Catholic medical ethics as in any sense distinct. The field is now essentially ecumenical. Though some few texts have

---

[2]We discussed earlier two specifically Roman Catholic groups which contributed to the field: The Catholic Hospital Association of the United States and Canada, with its journal *Hospital Progress*, and the National Federation of Catholic Physicians' Guilds, which publishes *Linacre Quarterly*. Numerous research centers and professional groups have recently been established. A partial list includes the Hastings Center Institute of Society, Ethics, and the Life Sciences, which publishes the important *Hastings Center Report* (incorporating the *Hastings Center Studies,* originally published separately) and the annual bibliography already noted; the Kennedy Center for Bioethics of the Kennedy Institute for the Study of Reproduction and Bioethics connected with Georgetown University in Washington, which is currently completing work on a new *Encyclopedia of Bioethics;* the Institute of Religion and Human Development of the Texas Medical Center in Houston; the Society for Health and Human Values, which publishes *The Journal of Medicine and Philosophy* out of the University of Chicago; the Harvard Program on Science, Technology, and Public Policy of Harvard University; the Institute for the Study of Humanistic Medicine in San Francisco; the Centre for Bioethics in Montreal; and the Society for the Study of Medical Ethics in England, which publishes *The Journal of Medical Ethics*. Other periodicals include *The Journal of Health Politics, Policy and Law* of the Duke University Department of Health Administration; *The Journal of Values and Ethics in Health Care* of the Columbia University College of Physicians and Surgeons; *Ethics in Medicine and Science,* published in London, England; and *Ethics in Medicine and Society.*

been written since Vatican II by Catholic authors,[3] an

---

[3]We have already mentioned the texts of McFadden, *The Dignity of Life,* and O'Donnell, *Medicine and Christian Morality,* both published in 1976. O'Donnell's work is basically a third revised edition of his *Morals in Medicine,* which we have already studied at length. McFadden's is largely a new work, but his approach resembles that of his previous *Medical Ethics* more than that of many contemporary Catholic authors. His conclusions are generally the same as those of his basic text, and, though the language is sometimes different, are based on the same modalities as found in his previous work. The German moralist Bernard Häring's book is as much North American as European: the author has studied and traveled in America and the work is not a translation but a direct English edition. Häring's *Ethics of Manipulation* appeared in 1975, the result of work done at Georgetown's Kennedy Institute, and covers some of the topics of today's bioethics. John Dedek's text *Contemporary Medical Ethics,* is indeed a *new* general text in the field, though it often, perhaps unavoidably, becomes a comparative survey of other authors and fails to be analytically consistent. Similar to this, if somewhat less ambitious, is William Jacobs' *The Pastor and the Patient* (1973), subtitled *An Informal Guide to New Directions in Medical Ethics.* Like Dedek, Jacobs describes the difficulties in arriving at solutions to medical ethical dilemmas. His work is more an attempt at challenging pastors than at actual ethical analysis (pp. 2-3). Dedek's *Human Life: Some Moral Issues* speaks of the medical ethical issues of abortion, euthanasia, and genetic engineering along with the question of modern war. An English language publication by a Jesuit moralist in India, George Lobo, entitled *Current Problems in Medical Ethics,* was published in 1974, and is generally unknown in North America. Both in definition and in methodology Lobo's book belongs to the literature written before Vatican II. Charles Curran's *Medicine and Morals* is not a general work, but an article on methodology. His *Politics, Medicine, and Christian Ethics* is what the subtitle suggests: *A Dialogue with Paul Ramsey,* again a largely methodological analysis.
    In addition to these few general texts there are, of course, works written by Catholics on individual medical ethical issues. A selected list, by no means complete, and including some English language non-North American works of influence in the American discipline, follows.
    On contraception: Rock, *The Time Has Come* (the beginning of the "pill" controversy, 1963); Dupré, *Contraception and Catholics;* Grisez, *Contraception and the Natural Law;* Roberts, *Contraception and Holiness;* Noonan, *Contraception:*

investigation of these similar to the study we have done in
the previous chapters would no longer be appropriate as a
valid attempt at defining the discipline. Catholic authors
are also contributing to the numerous collections of articles which have become one of the primary genres of medical
ethical literature of recent years,[4] and these articles discuss the various topics proposed for inclusion in contemporary interdisciplinary medical ethics. Attempts by Catholics
at formal definitions of the discipline appear in dialogue
with those of scholars writing from specifically non-Catholic religious (largely, but not exclusively Christian) perspectives,[5] as well as scholars writing from perspectives

---

A History; Noonan, *The Church and Contraception;* Egner, *Con-
traception vs. Tradition;* Hoyt, *The Birth Control Debate;*
Valsecchi, *Controversy: The Birth Control Debate 1958-1968;*
Callahan, *The Catholic Case for Contraception;* Curran, *Con-
traception: Authority and Dissent;* Shannon, *The Lively De-
bate: Response to Humanae Vitae.*
    On abortion: Shaw, *Abortion on Trial;* Ransil, *Abortion;*
Granfield, *The Abortion Decision;* Callahan, *Abortion: Law,
Choice, and Morality* (the "definitive" work so far); Grisez,
Abortion: The Myths, the Realities, and the Arguments;
Noonan, *The Morality of Abortion;* Connery, *Abortion: The De-
velopment of the Roman Catholic Perspective* (a detailed his-
torical analysis of the Catholic position).
    On other issues: Lyons, *Organ Transplants;* Maguire,
Death by Choice.

[4]A *preliminary* search of bibliographical sources uncovered nearly one-hundred such works in English written
since the mid-1960's. Most are published as separate volumes collecting essays and articles written either for the
volume or gathered from previous periodical appearances.
Some are issues of periodicals devoted to medical ethics in
general or to one bioethical topic. The large number of
such works shows the impossibility of limiting the definition of medical ethics any longer to Roman Catholic sources,
or of separating Roman Catholic contributions from the wider
spectrum. Many of the collections include articles by Catholics, many do not. The distinction is no longer crucial.
Some are listed in the bibliography.

[5]Included in this group are some important works.

not directly religious.[6]

In this chapter, therefore, our overview of the discipline's definition, which constitutes part one of the chapter, applies to contemporary medical ethics as a whole, including Roman Catholic contributions, but not limited to them. Our overview of recent methodological developments as a critique of the theological methodology of the discipline, which makes up the second part of the chapter, is limited to a greater degree to specifically Roman Catholic approaches. Here there has been an ongoing process of critique and development related explicitly to Catholic methodologies, which permits such a limitation. Even here, of course, the process has not been isolated from developments in non-Catholic religious and in secular approaches.

Recent Protestant texts in medical ethics include Nelson, *Human Medicine;* Ramsey, *The Patient as Person;* Smith, *Ethics and the New Medicine;* and Vaux, *Biomedical Ethics.* Other works which deal with medical ethics from a Protestant perspective, but which are not as such general texts, include Augenstein, *Come, Let Us Play God;* Fletcher, *The Ethics of Genetic Control;* Frazier, *Should Doctors Play God?;* Nelson, *Rediscovering the Person; On Dying Well: An Anglican Contribution;* and Ramsey, *Fabricated Man.* A Buddhist perspective is explored in Swyhart, *Bioethical Decision-Making.* In addition, of course, many of the collections of essays noted in the previous footnote approach their topics from a religious perspective, and most include at least some articles which do so. One such book concerns specifically the relationship of medicine and theology: White, *Dialogue in Medicine and Theology.* A short essay published as a monograph explores the role of theology in medical ethics: Gustafson, *The Contributions of Theology to Medical Ethics.*

[6]A *preliminary* search of bibliographical sources uncovered more than fifty such works. Some approach the topic from a purely secular perspective. Others include religious dimensions in a general way, but do not claim any directly theological or religious methodology. Some are listed in the bibliography.

<u>Part</u> <u>One</u>

<u>Name</u> <u>and</u> <u>Definition</u>

In chapter two we discovered that Roman Catholic medical ethics in North America came to define itself as the
moral theological investigation of the ethical issues
arising from the actual daily professional activity of the
medical doctor and nurse. Emphasis was given, we concluded,
to those explicitly medical procedures, such as surgery and
other types of physical intervention, which had come to occupy the central portion of a physician's daily practice.

In contrast to this individual professional approach,
today's medical ethics has extended its topical array to include the entire sphere of individual and social, microethi-
cal and macroethical problems connected directly or indirectly to the areas of medicine and biology. Political, social,
psychological, national, and international concerns now make
up much of the material definition of medical ethics.

In recent years a new name for the discipline has come
into general acceptance, appearing with growing frequency
along with "medical ethics." This new rubric, "bioethics"
or "biomedical ethics," suggests the newer emphasis found in
the discipline's definition. It has appeared as rubric for
the discipline in the titles of some of the newer books.[7]
The emphasis it offers, as distinguished from the more restricted sort of medical ethics we have investigated, is on
the implications of biological research and techniques for

---

[7]The term "bioethics" was coined by Van R. Potter, who
wrote *Bioethics: Bridge to the Future* in 1971 (the attribu-
tion is made by Marty and Peerman in *New Theology No. 10,* p.
vii, p. xx). In addition to this book, examples include:
Restak, *Premeditated Man: Bioethics;* Swyhart, *Bioethical Decision-Making;* Vaux, *Biomedical Ethics;* Shannon, *Bioethics;*
and many articles, etc.

the nature and future of humankind. "Bioethics" suggests a
widened scope for the discipline, no longer limited to the
professional practice of the medical doctor, but including
as well the social and futurological consequences of medicine and biology.[8] This is not to say, however, that the
older term has become obsolete. It continues in constant
use. Nor has there been a formal split between medical ethics and bioethics, such that the former would continue to
study actual medical practice and the latter the implications of biology in a wider sense. The discipline itself
has shifted to the wider definition. Medical ethics, bioethics, and biomedical ethics are three rubrics for what is
basically the same general field.[9]

Suggestions for the material definition of contemporary
medical ethics are numerous. Their common characteristic is
an insistence that the discipline be extended beyond individualistic concerns of doctor and patient to include social
factors. Roman Catholic moralist Richard McCormick offers a
typical set of topics to be studied by medical ethics. He
divides them into four general areas. First are topics con-

---

[8]Numerous examples could be cited. Among them Marty
and Peerman, *New Theology No. 10,* pp. vii–xviii; Callahan,
"Bioethics as a Discipline," p. 68; the book jacket to
Häring's *Ethics of Manipulation,* which describes the shift
from medical ethics to bioethics as entering an "almost sci-
fi world"; the Foreword to Gorovitz, *Moral Problems in
Medicine;* and others.

[9]The terms are used interchangeably in much of the contemporary literature, e.g. Shannon, *Bioethics,* pp. 3–5.
More significantly, works which use the older term in fact
approach the discipline from the same widened perspective as
do those which use the newer rubric. For example, the Preface to Reiser, Dyck, and Curran, *Ethics in Medicine,* uses
the term "medical ethics," and the general approach is the
same as that suggested in Shannon, *Bioethics.* No separation
is apparent.

cerning the sanctity and quality of life, including "keeping
alive, allowing to die, hastening death, abortion, radical
surgery, definition of death, allocation of scarce medical
resources, treatment of retardation, drug use and abuse,
alcoholism, care of the elderly."[10]   Second are issues concerning sexuality and the family, such as "sterilization,
contraception, donor and husband insemination, genetic counseling, *in vitro* fertilization, and eventually the exotic
matter of cloning."[11]   The third heading includes questions
concerning the "value of the personal physician-patient relationship," such as "the patient's right to be informed,
confidentiality, the physician as counselor, the canon of
informed consent, the 'closing ranks syndrome' where protection of the physician is concerned, malpractice problems,
and medical treatment of minors and dependents."[12]   Fourth
are topics involved in questions of individual and social
justice concerned with health care delivery, including
"group practice, volunteer medical work for the poor, fee
structures, racial discrimination in physician training and
hospital care, hospital fees, national health plans, conscience rights of physicians and so on."[13]   McCormick continues:

> We have been accustomed to think of "medico-moral" prob-
> lems in terms of decisions about procedures touching the
> health and life of individual patients. In this sense
> medical ethics has suffered from the individualism which
> has infected ethics in general. It has equivalently
> excluded a whole crucial domain from the area of ethical
> concern, or at least it has not given proportionate

---

[10]McCormick, "Issue Areas," p. 106.

[11]*Ibid.*, p. 108.

[12]*Ibid.*, pp. 110-111.

[13]*Ibid.*, p. 112.

                    attention to this area.[14]

When this last area is extended beyond national policy to
global policy, and beyond directly "medical" treatment to
questions of food and wealth distribution and of ecology and
pollution (the allocation of those resources needed for
"health" in its broadest sense), the scope of contemporary
medical ethics is extensive indeed.[15]

        In chapter two we described in detail how the defini-
tion of pre-Vatican II Roman Catholic medical ethics emerged
in response to the growing professionalization and secularization of modern Western medicine. It came to emphasize
those procedures which medical practitioners were actually
doing, and thus stressed physical interventions for physical
ailments. Though the moralists were not formally content
with a materialistic definition of health (their purpose
was explicitly to bring moral guidance to these questions),
from a material perspective, that is, from the perspective
of the topics which were included, Catholic moralists of the
period emphasized most the directly physical procedures
utilized by the medical doctor.

        Contemporary medical ethics has changed this approach.
Neither formally nor materially are today's "bioethicists"
content with a materialistic emphasis. They are aware that
human health involves more than physical interventions.
Psychological and social concerns are thus stressed along

---

        [14]*Ibid.*, p. 112.

        [15]Articles on such issues appear in medical ethics
collections and periodicals. Thus a section of articles
on pollution and health is found in Hamilton, *The New
Genetics;* numerous articles on international social justice
appear in the *Hastings Center Report* (Levine, "Ethics,
Justice, and International Health"; Ratcliffe, "Poverty,
Politics, and Fertility"; Callahan, "Doing Well by Doing
Good: Garrett Hardin's 'Lifeboat Ethic'"; and many
more).

with the more traditional analyses of medical procedures.
Whereas, as we have discovered, earlier moralists tended to
pass over questions of psychotherapy, except inasmuch as
they involved more or less directly physical interventions
such as psychosurgery, today's medical ethicists include all
areas of behavior control as directly pertaining to their
discipline.[16] Whereas earlier moralists tended to limit
their discussion of sexual issues to necessary background
for more immediately medical questions, or to brief discussion needed to help the physician as counsellor, today's
scholars include these questions as part of their investigation of the medical model, of labelling, of psychiatric
treatment, of the social issues of bioethics, in short, as
part of the discipline which studies the ethical implications of all processes concerning total human health.[17]
Whereas the pre-Vatican II literature tended to limit its
analysis of the relationship of religion and medicine to
those directly practical ethical questions which a doctor or
nurse might encounter (how to baptize a dying person, e.g.),
contemporary ethicists are apt to include in some of their
studies the basic question of *kinds* of healing, to investigate the interrelationships of faith and health, to question

---

[16]Again, examples abound. A section on behavior modi-
fication is part of Shannon, *Bioethics*; Häring treats the
question in his *Ethics of Manipulation,* and also in some detail in *Medical Ethics*; articles appear often in *Hastings
Center Report* and other journals of medical ethics.

[17]Dedek includes a chapter on transsexualism and homosexuality in his *Contemporary Medical Ethics*; Häring does
likewise in *Medical Ethics*; articles and books on psychiatric treatment, considered a part of medical ethics, include
reference to sexual questions (see, for example, Macklin,
"Ethics, Sex Research, and Sex Therapy"); an article on consecrated virginity is included in Marty and Peerman, *New
Theology No. 10,* pp. 140-153.

the very premises of modern scientific medicine.[18]

This process is best seen as a reversal of the trend we
have described earlier. We noted that North American medical ethicists continued the direction already begun within
pastoral medicine, but never carried out to as great a degree within the European pastoral medicine literature: a
trend toward emphasis on specifically moral questions with
directly practical import for the physician. The contemporary attempt at a widened scope for bioethics is in some re-
spects a return to the earlier approach of pastoral medicine,
which we described as the discipline investigating all aspects
of the interface of religion and medicine. Though many of
today's medical ethicists do not approach the field from any
specific denominational or systematic religious or theological perspective, in a wider sense today's field is indeed
quite similar to pastoral medicine. It is interested in the
entire interface of human values and medicine, in all questions pertaining to total human health, physical, social,
psychological, and spiritual. In this it resembles pastoral
medicine more than pre-Vatican II Roman Catholic medical
ethics.

When compared with this contemporary attempt at "holism,"
our discipline, in its emergent pre-Vatican II phase, must be
seen as unduly restricted. In its emphasis on individual

---

[18]Many monographs and articles include these kinds of
questions. Some are radical critiques. Many deal with the
largest types of philosophical and theological questions.
Examples include Illich, *Medical Nemesis;* Callahan, *The
Tyranny of Survival;* Cassell, "Illness and Disease"; a section of essays in Marty and Peerman, *New Theology No. 10;*
sections in Häring, *Medical Ethics;* a critique of the critics
by Starr, "The Politics of Therapeutic Nihilism"; Holton,
"Scientific Optimism and Societal Concerns"; Steinfels, "The
Concept of Health"; Steinfels, "The Future of Individualism."
These are "religious" questions connected with healing, in
the broadest sense of the term.

procedures of medical personnel it neglected wider social and
political concerns, areas which demand attention of ethicists. In its emphasis on strictly physical medical techniques it neglected other kinds of processes which affect,
less visibly but no less critically, the health of humankind.
To this extent the newer developments are to be welcomed,
and serve as a valid criticism of pre-Vatican II Catholic
medical ethics.

The change in approach brings its own difficulties,
however. With its emphasis on "holism" and its critique of
specialization, contemporary medical ethics often lacks all
definition, and, as a result, all definitional limitations.
Bioethics becomes materially, if not formally, identical to
ethics as such. If all ethical topics are bioethical, then
ethics and bioethics are synonymous and the latter discipline
loses its meaning. We have already noted the relative formlessness of much of pastoral medicine literature. With the
developments of modern biology and the growing social interdependence of global populations, even the minimal limitations of that discipline are unavailable to modern bioethics
when it chooses to include everything connected to total human health.

There is an additional danger, beyond the obvious logical problem of how bioethics can be a subdivision of ethics
if it speaks of any and all ethical issues. The danger
arises from the fact that, despite the relative formlessness
of the discipline both definitionally and, as we will see in
the next section, methodologically, it is commonly assumed
that bioethics or medical ethics is a specialized discipline
with its own form of expertise.[19] The supposed expertise of

---

[19]See for example Gorovitz, "Bioethics and Social Responsibility," p. 3. Universities and medical schools advertise for scholars with specialization in bioethics.

a specialization is thus attributed to the bioethicist, who
becomes strangely recognized as competent in a discipline
without definitional limits. Bioethicists could appropriate
to themselves the entire spectrum of ethics. If this hap-
pens, and to the extent that it is already beginning, it
presents a danger which may well eclipse the dangers of
specialization that holistic bioethics is intended to correct. As bioethicists come more and more to play an advo-
cacy role as regulators of medicine and biology, working for
governments, paid by government grants, advancing professionally as a result of publications which are exposés of medical and biological evils, they fall more and more prey to
the very danger they claim to oppose: a kind of "generalization of expertise"[20] whereby they become experts on everything. This danger is inherent in any professional endeavor.
Theoretically a relatively formless discipline might be im-
mune. But in practice the lack of limitation is more apt to
allow bioethicists to play the expert role in virtually
every area of human life.

To what extent, then, should limits be placed on the
topical array of biomedical ethics? At present the only answer which can be given must be generic. Bioethics must not
be so strictly limited in its topical array that it becomes
merely a consulting discipline to the medical profession,
limiting its scope to those questions which concern individual physicians in their individual practices.[21] In its most
extreme form, this would reduce bioethics to the kind of
"medical ethics" of the intraprofessional variety described

---

[20]See Veatch, "Generalization of Expertise." Veatch
argues convincingly that scientists are not automatically
qualified as experts in non-scientific (ethical) matters.

[21]The case is made strongly in Branson, "Bioethics as
Individual *and* Social."

in the first chapter. Even with less radical intraprofessional limitation, bioethics would still suffer from an
overly strict limitation were it to be restricted to the
kinds of topics we have found in the pre-Vatican II Roman
Catholic discipline. Yet the fear of such a reduction cannot remove the need for limits altogether. Bioethics ought
to restrict itself to the individual and social ethical implications of medicine and biology, with the latter disciplines defined in a relatively strict way. Medical ethics
should exclude from its material definition topics which ex-
plore non-medical and non-biological aspects of social justice, for example, such as international economics, monetary
policy, distribution of food and money, general theories of
social justice and political ethics. Clearly the latter
cannot be rigidly excluded as having nothing to do with the
social implications of medicine and biology. But bioethicists *as such* would do better to recognize their own limitations, and the limitations of their discipline, than to attempt an extension of their claim to expertise to so many
different areas.

When compared with contemporary biomedical ethics, then,
our discipline (Roman Catholic medical ethics in its emergent, pre-Vatican II phase) must be criticized as overly restricted. Its goal was to apply moral principles to the
medical procedures utilized by physicians in their professional practice. It was thus limited to individual actions
and was apt to ignore to a large extent the wider personal,
social, and political implications of medical and biological
policy. Both in its definition, and, as we have noted and
will see again in the next section, in its methodology, it
was too closely wedded to a reductionist individualistic
cause-and-effect analbsis. It tried too hard to identify
with the restricted scope and analytic methodology of modern
scientific medicine, to give universally normative answers

to clearly defined questions. To the extent that contemporary biomedical ethics has freed itself from these restrictions, its development is a welcome one.

Part Two

Theological Methodology

In chapters three, four, and five we described at
length the theological methodology of our discipline. We
concluded to the operative influence of two dominant methodological frameworks within which medical ethical decisions
were made: physicalism and ecclesiastical positivism. We
described each in detail. We noted their development, and
saw how ecclesiastical positivism became predominant during
the forties and fifties. We analyzed the use of two "other
theological principles," namely the principle of God's dominion over life and that of redemptive suffering, and found
that they were generally not used as mystery-filled hermeneutic devices in medical ethics, but rather operated as
secondary norms, subordinated to the two methodological modalities of physicalism and ecclesiastical positivism. We
saw how actual conclusions as to the rightness or wrongness
of individual procedures were arrived at according to physicalist and/or positivist criteria.

In this final section of our study we will attempt a
critique of the methodological approach of pre-Vatican II
medical ethics by reviewing briefly the reaction against it
which has occurred since the mid-1960's. It is not our purpose here to argue that this reaction has resulted in the
development of a definitive adequate methodology for medical
ethics, or to defend it against its critics. We will suggest, however, that these recent developments point out
grave inadequacies in the previous methodology.

When we discussed the methodological modalities of

medical ethics in chapter three, we introduced the term
"personalism" as the name of the modality which arose after
Vatican II in reaction against physicalism and ecclesiastical positivism. The word itself is problematic, but is
probably the best rubric for describing this general approach. Other terms have also been suggested. Authors
speak of the "new morality," either as advocates or as critics, or use other terms which imply the same idea of revision or change in a traditional methodology.[22]

   Personalism defies exact definition or even adequate
description. The general approach which is suggested by the
term is probably best defined in a negative way, as a reaction against the previous methodological modalities of physicalism and ecclesiastical positivism as they operated within Roman Catholic sexual and medical ethics.[23] It is not
itself a systematic approach to moral theological theory.

---

   [22]This rubric is not precisely coined as a technical
term, but, like personalism, represents a general sort of
approach, suggested by words like "revision," "renewal," etc.
Among works which can be mentioned favoring some such approach are Van der Marck, *Toward a Christian Ethic: Renewal
in Moral Theology;* Wassmer, *Christian Ethics for Today;*
Häring, *Christian Renewal in a Changing World: A New Approach to Moral Theology;* his *The Law of Christ;* and other
works by Häring; and the various books by Curran, including
*New Perspectives in Moral Theology; Ongoing Revision; Chris-
tian Morality Today: The Renewal of Moral Theology; Contemporary Problems in Moral Theology;* and others. Opposed are
Lunn and Lean, *The New Morality;* Grisez and Shaw, *Beyond the
New Morality;* and others.

   [23]Curran points this out in an article in which he attempts to distinguish the newer approach from utilitarianism.
He describes the newer emphasis on proportionate reason
(which, as we shall see, is an important part of the personalist method) as a reaction against physicalism (Curran,
"Utilitarianism," p. 249), and continues: "Notice that early
in the discussion within Roman Catholicism the debate centered almost exclusively on problems present in the Catholic
theological tradition such as contraception and sterilization" (p. 250).

Whether or not it can become such is debatable, and, in any
case, beyond our present task. Much of the present literature is devoted to assessing whether or not personalism (the
"new approach" by whatever name it is to be called) is utilitarian, individualistic or privatistic, hedonistic, relativistic, situationalist, and so on.[24] That is, its precise

---

[24]The best analysis of these questions in English is
done, in my judgment, by Louis Janssens, Charles Curran, and
Richard McCormick. McCormick's "Notes on Moral Theology"
for 1975, 1976, and 1977 each contain excellent analyses
and references to other sources. See also Curran, "Utilitarianism," and Janssens, "Ontic Evil." By no means is the
debate settled, however. For example, Curran's (and McCormick's) recent attempts to distinguish their approach from
utilitarianism seem often to be based on a wish to distance
themselves from that term, with the often unsavory implications associated with it by religious ethicists, more than
on actual distinguishing criteria. Curran and McCormick
argue that they include *also* certain non-teleological (thus
non-utilitarian) criteria in their method. I have found it
difficult to identify these as having any significant role
in the actual argument. Though they may be theoretically
present, in practice the newer modality is highly teleological or consequentialist. Janssens, whose approach is among
the most balanced of contemporary moralists, is less afraid
of the word, and applies it to his ethic in some cases
(Janssens, "Norms and Priorities," pp. 220, 225). Eike-
Henner Kluge attacks the third and fourth conditions of the
double effect principle (that is, the principle of intention
of the agent and that of proportionality, the conditions
maintained and stressed by the personalist approach, as we
will note) as utilitarian (Kluge, *The Practice of Death,* pp.
63-65). Whether or not the charge of "individualism" is applicable is also problematic. To some extent, any approach
which argues against an *a priori* ethic or an authoritarian
ethic can be charged with individualism. Personalism is
certainly not intended to be privatistic, in the sense of
arguing for the morality of doing anything that feels good
for the individual, regardless of social consequences. Nonetheless, respect for individual creativity and uniqueness is
an essential part of the approach (again see Janssens, "Norms
and Priorities," pp. 221, 224; yet Janssens argues against
19th century individualism, p. 223). The relativism and
situationalism debate often results from poorly defined use
of these terms, from the inability to distinguish metaethical

positive characteristics and its exact relationship to other
methodologies in theological and philosophical ethical theory are not yet fixed. What is clear is that personalism
represents an important reaction against and criticism of
the physicalist and ecclesiastical positivist methods used
in pre-Vatican II Catholic medical ethics.

In general, personalism refers to that modality of application of theological principles whereby an emphasis is
placed on the entire personal complexus of the act in its
human dimensions, circumstances, and consequences. In con-
tradistinction to the modalities which preceded it, personalism does not limit its scope to the physical or biological
qualities of the action, but rather extends its purview to
psychological, social, and spiritual dimensions. It does
not emphasize one or several specifically defineable sources
of revelation, but rather insists on a wider (theoretically
on the "total") spectrum of human experience, which includes,
but is not limited to and often does not emphasize, either
Scriptural or magisterial ethical judgments.

In the broadest sense, personalism is offered as an
alternative to what preceded it. One moralist describes the
alternatives as follows:

> Broadly speaking, there are two approaches to morality:
> 1. The modern, personalist school approaches morality
> from the point of view of persons and personal rela-
> tionships, which begins with man's relationships with

---

from normative ethical issues (see Veatch, "Does Ethics Have
an Empirical Basis?"). Nonetheless, the newer approach,
with its consequentialist *a posteriori* emphasis, is more
akin to an ethic which takes relativity and situation into
account than was the deontological *a priori* ethic which it
reacts against (McCormick's "Notes" for 1975, 1976, 1977 argue these issues; see also Janssens, "Norms and Priorities,"
pp. 216-218; Janssens argues for the relativity of concrete
material norms, which is, in different words, exactly what
McCormick is saying in his "Notes on Moral Theology" of the
last three years).

> God in Christ and the Spirit. 2. The traditional
> norm-centered school approaches morality from the
> point of view of abstract principles and applies a
> deductive method to reach moral conclusions.[25]

However the trend is defined, it includes the notion that
the total good of the person (this is not intended to mean
the good of the individual as opposed to that of people in
general) is the central criterion in moral analysis. Thus
Curran describes personalism as holding that "all things are
to be integrated into the good of the person."[26] And Warren
Reich describes it as the "trend in contemporary medical
ethics . . . toward seeing the total good of the person as
the overriding ethical criterion."[27]

This essential characteristic of personalism is best
seen in its proper historical context as a reaction against
the physicalism and ecclesiastical positivism which together
formed the framework for medical ethics, and which enabled
medical moralists to arrive at precise, "scientifically accurate," universally applicable norms. In a manner similar
to the shift we have seen in the discipline's definition,
the discipline's methodology has changed from one of scientific clarity and precision to a more "holistic" approach.

Our critique of the methodology of pre-Vatican II Catholic medical ethics, based on this new personalist develop-

---

[25]Sean O'Riordan, in McManus, O'Riordan, and Stratton,
"The Declaration," pp. 231-232. The context of the statement is the author's reaction to the 1976 Vatican "Declaration of Certain Questions Concerning Sexual Ethics." It is
clear that the "traditional" approach is what we have described as the methodology operative in our discipline. The
declaration, according to O'Riordan, "follows the old method-
ology--principles are stated, and conclusions are drawn more
or less independently of human persons and the complexities
of human existence" (*Ibid.*, p. 232).

[26]Curran, *Ongoing Revisions,* p. 98.

[27]Reich, "Medical Ethics," p. 183.

ment, will be divided into three sections. First, we will
note the reaction against physicalism. Second, we will
speak of the critique made against ecclesiastical positivism.
Third, we will suggest the way in which the theological
principles of God's dominion over life and of redemptive
suffering can be applied within a personalist modality.

1.   The Critique of Physicalism

The central characteristic of personalism is that it
stands in direct opposition to physicalism as we have described this modality in medical ethics. Its basic tenet
is that the whole person must be considered, and not merely
the physical criteria of the act-in-itself or of the biological faculty (reproductive faculty, for example) under
analysis. It properly insists on the inadequacy of limiting
criteria for ethical analysis to physical cause-and-effect
relationships, and insists that these criteria not be made
determinative in moral judgment.

This reaction against physicalism which typifies personalism arose primarily in the context of the birth control debate during the 1960's.[28] Catholic moralists began to ask
whether or not the traditional condemnation[29] of artificial
contraception was valid. The earliest controversy surround-
ed the use of the contraceptive pill, and the issue quickly
spread to contraception in general. Typical of the newer

---

[28]For the history of this controversy, see especially
Valsecchi, *Controversy;* Hoyt, *The Birth Control Debate;*
Shannon, *The Lively Debate;* and Noonan, *Contraception.*

[29]The traditional opinion on this and other issues has
already been analyzed at length. The reader is advised that
the present section requires, for a complete understanding,
a knowledge of the analysis of physicalism in the double effect framework given above, which will not be repeated here.
See part one of chapter four.

approach is this argument by Louis Dupré against the traditional opinion:

> Such a way of reasoning about nature contains, I feel,
> two basic flaws. It confuses man's biological struc-
> ture with his human nature. And it takes human nature
> as a static, unchangeable thing, rather than as a prin-
> ciple of development. Man's biological life and its
> intrinsic laws are but one aspect of human existence.[30]

In a similar context, Ambrogio Valsecchi insists that

> we must give primacy to the human person and to man's
> more characteristically spiritual values, rather than
> to biological mechanisms and processes which in them-
> selves can never have any absolute value--and this
> means that the notion of the necessity of the physical
> integrity of copulation must be abandoned (as no longer
> sacrosanct) when it is impossible otherwise to procure
> a proportionate personal good, of authentic value, for
> the married couple. We must assign to a man a more
> active and extended control over his natural functions
> in order that he may promote his personal development
> in a more ordered evolution of society. Therefore, for
> the sake of an adequate control of births, it is more
> 'unnatural' to submit to the determinism of biological
> processes than to control them and direct them in a
> responsible manner to that end.[31]

Personalism as a methodological reaction against physicalism was not long limited to the question of contraception.
It was logically extended to the similar issues of sterilization and abortion, to sexual ethics, and to general methodological debates involving not only medical and sexual ethics but including social ethics as well. The controversy
extended to the theoretical question of how ethics should be
done. Proponents of personalism consistently criticize the
physicalist limitations of the older methodology.

In his analysis of sterilization, Curran argues that

> the discussion should not be confined to the organs in
> question and their relationship to the organism, but

---

[30]Dupré, *Contraception and Catholics*, pp. 43-44.

[31]Valsecchi, *Controversy*, p. 211.

rather the good of the whole man and his relationship
to his family, community and the larger society must be
taken into account. Such an approach echoes the often
heard complaint that an older Catholic theology emphasized too much the finality of particular organs and
did not give enough attention to the *person* and to his
relationships with others.[32]

In another place he states:

The danger that arises if we identify the moral action
simply with the biological and physical structure of
the human act is evident in the controversy over contraception and sterilization. The notion of "direct" in
the principle of double effect also seems to be too
closely tied both to the physical structure of the human
act and the sole immediate physical effect of that action.[33]

In his book, *Human Life,* which discusses various medical
and social ethical questions, John Dedek states:

The physical structure of an act is not enough to determine its moral significance. The immediate intersubjec-
tive implications also must be taken into account. The
means-ends categories expose one to the risk of ignoring
this aspect since the end frequently specifies and determines the human meaning of a concrete piece of behavior. This understanding of moral reality helps one
to avoid a unilateral physicalism in assessing the moral significance of human actions, but it does not do
our practical casuistry for us.[34]

In his analysis of the principle of double effect, Peter
Knauer uses the question of direct and indirect abortion as
his example:

When the categories direct and indirect are confused
with purely physical categories, a blind hairsplitting
is introduced into ethics. Removal of a cancerous
uterus is permitted even though as a consequence the
fetus within the uterus loses its life. But to remove

---

[32]Curran, *New Perspectives,* pp. 205-206, italics mine.

[33]Curran, *Medicine and Morals,* p. 8. Similar statements
are found in "Absolute Norms and Medical Ethics," "Natural
Law and Moral Theology," "Natural Law and Contemporary Moral
Theology," and elsewhere.

[34]Dedek, *Human Life,* p. 28.

only the fetus, because the uterus may still be healed,
is said by some theologians to be murder; they think
the death of the fetus is used as a means and so is directly willed. In other words, a solution which includes both the death of the fetus and the removal of
the entire uterus with consequent sterility is said to
be better than that the fetus alone lose its life. Who
can understand this?[35]

In his criticism of physicalism in the traditional
double effect principle, Cornelius Van der Poel states:

A second major difficulty with the traditional application of the principle of double effect is that the
present understanding of the principle seems to over-
emphasize the importance of the *physical* effect in the
judgment about the *moral* value of the human action.
Some theologians determine what is direct merely by
considering the physical structure of the act itself
[the first condition of double effect], or the immediate physical causality of the act itself [the second
condition].[36]

He goes on to present some of the more absurd casuistry
which results from this overemphasis on physicalist specifications.[37]

In our analysis of physicalism we described the importance of the double effect principle as framework for the
application of physicalist criteria to medical ethical problems. We noted that the first two conditions of the double
effect principle were the ones most directly involved in
this process, since, as the double effect principle actually
operated in medical ethical application, the act-in-itself
(first condition) and the cause-and-effect chain (second
condition) were physically specified. Many of the more complex and analytical criticisms of physicalism made by today's

---

[35]Knauer, "The Hermeneutic Function," p. 149.

[36]Van der Poel, "The Principle of Double Effect," p.
194, italics his.

[37]*Ibid.*, pp. 194-195. We have already noted examples
of this kind in our analysis of double effect physicalism.

moralists are attempts to reformulate the principle of
double effect in a non-physicalist way.[38] The human act is
defined as more than a mere physical act-in-itself, and the
cause-and-effect chain is not accepted as a central moral
determinant. The emphasis is thus placed on the third and
fourth conditions of the principle. The agent must not have
evil as the intended end of the action; there must be a due
proportion or commensurate reason for placing an act which
will unavoidably have some ontic or premoral evil effects.

Janssens puts it this way:

> We can establish as a principle that it is impossible
> to pronounce a moral judgment on an exterior action
> which contains ontic evil--e.g., to kill somebody, to
> utter a falsehood--if this action is viewed only as a
> factual and actual event (*secundum speciem naturae*) and
> without paying attention to the end of the inner act of
> the will. We can further establish that, in order to
> be able to make a moral evaluation, we must consider:
> 1) if the end of the agent, the object of the inner act
> of the will, is morally good; 2) if the exterior action
> has a *debita proportio* [due proportion] to this end or
> if, on the contrary, it contains the negation of the
> value or principle which is affirmed in the end.[39]

Knauer distinguishes his version of double effect from
the traditional one (what we have described as four-condition
double effect). He states concerning the traditional version:

> If the evil permitted or caused accompanies the good to
> be achieved only as a consequence or a concomitant, the
> act is permitted [second condition, which, as we have
> seen is but another way of stating the first condi-
> tion];[40] otherwise not. But if the evil physically

---

[38]These include Peter Knauer, "The Hermeneutic Function
of the Principle of Double Effect"; Janssens, "Ontic Evil and
Moral Evil"; Curran, "The Principle of Double Effect"; Curran, "Utilitarianism and Contemporary Moral Theology"; Van
der Poel, "The Principle of Double Effect."

[39]Janssens, "Ontic Evil," pp. 148-149.

[40]See above, pp. 251-253.

precedes the willed good and so is "the means" to its
achievement, then it is directly willed and makes the
entire act evil, just as if the evil was intended by
the act. In this case, the principle of double effect
is replaced by another principle: A good end does not
justify a bad means.[41]

Then he goes on to criticize this approach, and to offer his

own formulation:

Such a contrast between these two principles involves
a logical error. In the principle that the good end
does not justify a bad means it is already assumed that
the means are morally bad [this would apply both to the
first and the second condition, though Knauer seems to
speak only of the second condition]. The principle is
only applicable if the moral judgment has already been
formed; in the moral evil of the means something new is
not discovered; the evil was already established. In
the principle of double effect, in contrast, a moral
judgment of this kind is in process of being determined.
The two principles are not parallel in their applicability. *That a means is morally bad signifies in our
sense that the reason for the application of the means
is not commensurate.*[42]

Knauer thus formulates his central criterion as "commensurate

reason." The evil effects of the act are permitted if a com-

mensurate reason is present which makes the whole action mor-

ally good. In the examples he uses, it seems that such a

reason is present if the good achieved by the action is pro-

portionate to the evil effected, in other words, the fourth

condition of the double effect principle.

Similar is this statement by Van der Poel:

However, not *any* material effect can be used to obtain
a good result; there needs to be a proportionate reason
which makes the occurrence of the physical evil acceptable in view of the total human experience.[43]

---

[41]Knauer, "The Hermeneutic Function," p. 148.

[42]*Ibid.*, italics mine.

[43]Van der Poel, "The Principle of Double Effect," p.
198, italics his.

Daniel Maguire, in his book *Death by Choice,* which defends euthanasia in certain cases, proposes in some detail
a similar approach to the "doing" of ethics. He applauds
the newer insistence on commensurate reason,[44] and develops
his own theory accordingly. One of his key notions is that
exceptions to a general principle, such as the norm "Thou
shalt not kill," "can only be justified if they proceed from
the primal experience of the value of human life and *if they*
express in exception form what the principle expresses in
rule form."[45] It is clear from Maguire's subsequent analysis
of euthanasia, as well as from his explicit acceptance of the
notion of proportionate reason, that this criterion for the
justification of exceptions depends on a weighing of the
various goods and evils which the action will bring about
within the specific context and circumstances of this moral
event, that is, on the fourth condition of double effect.

Contemporary moralists who attempt in this fashion a
non-physicalist revision of the double effect principle are
not agreed on exactly how the new principle ought to be
phrased. Nor are they clear on what exact importance should
be given to consequences in ethical analysis, on how non-
consequentialist criteria can be significant in establishing
concrete behavior norms, on whether or not their theory differs from strict consequentialism or utilitarianism and if
so, how, or on the extent to which the notion of "intrinsic
evil" is or ought to be maintained within the newer non-
physicalist approach. In their formulations of the principle
of due proportion or commensurate reason they tend to avoid

---

[44]Maguire, *Death by Choice,* pp. 67-71. Maguire correctly points out how some moralists who adopt the "new" approach
hesitate to draw the conclusions which their methodology
would seem to indicate, and argues himself for those conclusions.

[45]*Ibid.,* pp. 96-97, italics his.

extrinsic phrases which suggest a purely consequentialist or
utilitarian ethic.[46] The debate continues as to how these
formulations differ from consequentialism, and it is indeed
difficult to locate any *practically* significant way in which
they do.[47]

What is clear is that Roman Catholic medical ethical
methodology has freed itself from the kinds of physicalist
restrictions which once offered it clear and universally applicable norms and criteria for the solution of nearly all
of its medical ethical questions. The recent revisionist
critique has correctly pointed out the inconsistencies and
inadequacies, indeed the absurdities in certain cases, of
the physicalist method and of some of the conclusions reached
by it. The present methodological debate has not reached a
consensus concerning the correct moral theological method.
Now that the methodology is no longer dominated by physicalist criteria, no easy consensus is possible.

---

[46]Janssens puts it this way: "Consequently, in Thomas'
view [which Janssens here accepts] due proportion is an *intrinsic* requisite in the one but composed action; it is a
due proportion between means and end, between the material
and the formal element of the action, while the principles
of the acts with more effects [double effect] require a due
proportion between the direct and indirect effect [in our
analysis, between the good effects intended and the evil effects tolerated but not intended]" ("Ontic Evil," p. 140).
Yet in determining this intrinsic "debita proportio" it is
the proportion between good and evil ontic effects which is
determinative, since a disproportion of ontic evil effects
is what makes the means (the material element) disproportion-
ate to the end (the formal element).

[47]Curran argues that the newer approach is a mixed consequentialism, that other, non-consequentialist factors are
also included ("Utilitarianism"). But though his position,
and that of the other Catholic moralists of the non-physicalist variety, includes *theoretically* certain deontological
(duty-based, or *a priori*) factors, in practice these are applied in individual cases in ways which subordinate them to
consequences. See above, pp. 418-419, n. 24.

This represents an advance for Catholic moral theology. Now
its criteria may include and give due importance to individual and social personal factors which make moral judgment
more difficult and closer to human experience. And, as we
will note in a few pages, its newer methodology allows Christian theological principles to be applied in a manner which
better preserves their character of mystery and their proper
role as hermeneutic themes for approaching the question of
the meaning of human life.

2. The Critique of Ecclesiastical Positivism

The personalist approach has included a critique of the
practical ecclesiastical positivism which we saw to be a
dominant modality in pre-Vatican II literature.[48] The question as to whether or not this opposition was theoretically
inevitable is highly problematic. To some extent, just as
practical ecclesiastical positivism (as distinguished from
theoretical moral positivism in the strict sense) coexisted
with natural law physicalism despite the ambiguities and implicit contradictions which this combination presented, so
a practical ecclesiastical positivism might have coexisted
with personalism. That is, the personalist approach might
have been adopted and defended by magisterial authority in a
way similar to that in which physicalism was adopted and defended. Official ecclesiastical decrees might have switched
their language from the one to the other, and prescribed
authoritatively the "newer" kind of approach typified by appeal to proportionate reason.

---

[48]Our description of this modality is given above, in
part one of chapter five, and generally in part two of that
chapter. The reader is again advised that the present section presupposes an understanding of the issues presented
already.

For various reasons this has not occurred. The newer
approach, in its *a posteriori* consequentialist emphasis and
its insistence on circumstances, is less compatible with ecclesiastical positivism than was the deductive and universally applicable physicalist modality. Perhaps more important
is the fact that personalist medical moralists arrive at conclusions which are at variance with previous official pronouncements.[49] Thus to change from physicalism and physicalist conclusions would be to admit previous error and thus
weaken the case for magisterial inerrancy in moral matters.[50]

Like the critique of physicalism, opposition to ecclesiastical positivism arose largely in the context of the
birth control controversy. Though some of the early critics
of the traditional position on contraception explicitly
stated their intention to submit to final magisterial judgment, many others included a critique of this approach in
their works.

Louis Dupré's early revisionist appraisal of contraception typifies the attempt made by some to remain loyal to
magisterial decisions while questioning the birth control issue. Though his book includes a chapter which suggests

---

[49]No attempt will be made to list these in detail. In
the previous description of the critique on physicalism we
have noted some: birth control by the "pill" and by other
"artificial" means, sterilization, and positive euthanasia.
Other changes include abortion in some limited cases (Häring,
Medical Ethics, pp. 75-119; Callahan, *Abortion,* esp. pp.
495-501; Curran, *New Perspectives,* pp. 163-193, esp. pp.
188-193; Dedek, *Contemporary Medical Ethics,* pp. 120-131;
and others), artificial insemination (Dedek, *Contemporary
Medical Ethics,* p. 101; Häring, *Medical Ethics,* pp. 91-94;
and others), and other questions as well.

[50]For a brief sociological analysis of the problem besetting the pope in this kind of dilemma, see Imse, "Spiritual Leadership."

nuances for the positivist modality,[51] Dupré explicitly recognizes the role which magisterial decisions play and ought
to play in medical ethics. He thus remains within the tradition of ecclesiastical positivism. In his preface he
states: "For a Roman Catholic, the Church has a teaching
authority in morals as well as in matters of faith. It is
this authority that will give the ultimate answer . . . As a
Catholic, I wish to state explicitly that whatever the
magisterium's final word on the question will be, it will
also be mine."[52]

Such a position has been rejected, however, by most
contemporary revisionist moralists. Personalism has come to
oppose ecclesiastical positivism. The event which served as
catalyst for this opposition was the publication on July 29,
1968, of the papal encyclical *Humanae Vitae (On Human Life)*,
which reaffirmed the traditional condemnation of all methods
of contraception except periodic continence (rhythm).[53] Per-
sonalists had been rejecting precisely this universal proscription, and now found themselves in direct opposition to
an official decree of the magisterium. Their reaction took
different forms. One argument was that this particular docu-
ment was not strictly infallible, and thus dissent in this
case was possible. The statement published by a number of
Catholic theologians in August, 1968, stresses this:

> It is common teaching in the church that Catholics may
> dissent from authoritative, non-infallible teachings
> of the magisterium when sufficient reasons for doing so

---

[51]Dupré, *Contraception and Catholics*, pp. 29-36.

[52]*Ibid.*, pp. 5-6.

[53]The importance of this event for the authority question is well known. In addition to the works on the controversy already cited (see above, p. 421, n. 28), see Milhaven,
Toward a New Catholic Morality, pp. 181-197; McCormick,
"Notes," 1969, p. 644.

exist. Therefore, as Roman Catholic theologians, conscious of our duty and our limitations, we conclude
that spouses may responsibly decide according to their
consciences that artificial contraception in some circumstances is permissible and indeed necessary to preserve and foster the values and sacredness of marriage.[54]

But if a papal encyclical, delivered personally by Paul
VI after years of publicized debate, is not considered
strictly binding on the consciences of Catholics, then the
operative importance of practical ecclesiastical positivism
as we have described it in medical ethics is seriously weak-
ened, and the entire process challenged. Indeed, contemporary personalist theologians have continued to question and
to restrict the role which the magisterium ought to play in
moral matters.

Gregory Baum points up the ambiguity we have already
described which results when ecclesiastical positivism is
used to defend a natural law physicalism which theoretically
is derived from "nature" and not from supernatural authority.[55]

By what argument does Pope Paul establish his position?
The argument, we note, is not drawn from divine revelation. The argument is based on rational reflection:
It [sic] belongs to the order of reason. . . . It is
difficult to explain how a rule of life that is based
on natural law and hence corresponds to the universal
moral experience of man, is advocated in the present
culture only by the Catholic Church, unless one wants
to suggest that the consciences of other men and even
other churches are so corrupt that they are no longer
in touch with the foundation of human morality.[56]

A somewhat similar analysis is made by Curran.[57]

---

[54] "Theologians' Statement," pp. 69-70.

[55] See above, pp. 316-320, esp. pp. 319-320, n. 16.

[56] Baum, "The Right to Dissent," pp. 72-73.

[57] Curran, *Christian Morality Today*, pp. 82-83; *A New
Look*, pp. 128-129.

The use of *epikeia* as a positive virtue which ought to
be used when positive law is insufficient is stressed by
Curran. He states:

> The individual Catholic must respect and follow the
> laws of the Church, but a true understanding recognizes
> the provisional and imperfect nature of Church law.
> The virtue of *epikeia* moderates the literalness and in-
> applicability of the law in the face of the very real
> Christian demands in a concrete situation.[58]

Daniel Maguire calls for a reappraisal of practical ecclesiastical positivism, pointing out three difficulties
with the approach:

> Three critical problem areas seem to call for special
> attention: (1) the concept of handing down a deposit
> of wisdom in which the "natural law" is somehow con-
> tained; (2) the notion of "assistance of the Holy
> Spirit" which somehow guarantees even the fallible ut-
> terances of Church officers; (3) the juridical paradigm
> by which official teaching is conceived and explained.[59]

He concludes that the moral magisterium is never infallible except when it speaks tautologously, that is, when it
affirms the immorality of a formal concept such as "murder."
This is to do no more than affirm that an unjust killing is
unjust and urge its avoidance in practice. No infallible
statements can be made on what kinds of killing are inevitably, in every case, unjust, that is, on what kind of killing
inevitable constitutes murder. No infallible statements can
be made which set a particular kind of killing, apart from
its own situation and circumstances, into the category
"murder."[60] He goes on to argue that non-infallible statements are prone to error, and therefore dissent is possible.[61]

---

[58]Curran, *A New Look,* p. 143.

[59]Maguire, "Moral Inquiry and Religious Assent," p. 129.

[60]Maguire, "Moral Absolutes," p. 80, pp. 85-87.

[61]*Ibid.*, pp. 98-99.

In *Medical Ethics* Bernard Häring argues in a similar
manner:

> On questions of morality, the *rôle* of infallibility
> is limited to the enunciation of the most basic princi-
> ples, to declaring, for instance, the fundamental right
> of man to life and prohibiting unjust killing. . . . In
> the realm of purely natural morality, that is, natural
> law, the believer is bound to the extent that the di-
> rectives manifest rational insights and reflect man's
> shared experience and co-reflection. . . . If an utter-
> ance of the magisterium is no longer in tune with new
> insights and the modern context, physicians and theo-
> logians have a joint obligation to look for better so-
> lutions and, if need be, to inform the magisterium of
> this. . . . The final court is the conscience of the
> physician and/or that of the patient.[62]

In his book he criticizes some of the traditional answers
given to medical ethical dilemmas, and argues that where "a
new common opinion is taking shape" it may be followed in
practice despite previous official pronouncements to the
contrary.[63]

John Dedek likewise insists on the right of practical
dissent from magisterial teaching:

> Contemporary ecclesiology affirms the right of any per-
> son to dissent from noninfallible decisions of the
> Church when he has sufficient reason for doing so.
> There can be many good reasons why people should prac-
> tice birth control.[64]

A group of Catholic medical moralists reacted critically

---

[62]Häring, *Medical Ethics*, p. 37.

[63]*Ibid.*, p. 104. The context is the question of very
early abortions. Häring also arrives at conclusions different from previous teaching in other matters: contraception
(pp. 87-90), sterilization (pp. 90-91), and artificial insemination (pp. 91-94).

[64]Dedek, *Contemporary Medical Ethics*, p. 59. Dedek also
departs from official teaching concerning sterilization (pp.
72-76), artificial insemination (p. 101), transsexual surgery (pp. 77-80), homosexual lovemaking (p. 86), and abortion
(pp. 120-131).

to the latest revision of the "Ethical and Religious Directives for Catholic Health Facilities." Included were criticisms of the ecclesiastical positivist modality which it
utilized.[65]

From this sampling of recent personalist opposition to
ecclesiastical positivism in medical ethics it is clear that
the approach is no longer acceptable in its traditional form
to many Catholic moralists. Difficulties remain as authors
try to determine what exactly the role of the magisterium
should be.[66] Some authors defend the older position.[67] No
consensus has been reached.

The critique of ecclesiastical positivism in medical
ethics, together with that of physicalism, has freed Catholic medical ethics from its former restrictive methodology.

---

[65]Reich, et al., "Catholic Hospital Ethics," esp. pp.
193-199. The 1971 version of the "Directives" is published
by the United States Catholic Conference, and is included in
Dedek, Contemporary Medical Ethics, pp. 206-214. Dedek also
has the text of the reaction against them, pp. 173-200.

[66]An addition to the articles cited elsewhere in this
section, see Hughes, "Infallibility in Morals"; and Tierney,
"Infallibility in Morals: A Response."

[67]For example, Dubay, "The State of Moral Theology";
Rice, Authority and Rebellion. Other examples are reviewed
by McCormick, "Notes," esp. for the years 1974 through 1977.
In addition, three recent manuals, as we have already noted
(p. 404, n. 3), remain within the physicalist and positivist
tradition: Lobo, Current Problems in Medical Ethics; O'Don-
nel, Medicine and Christian Morality; and McFadden, The Dignity of Life. McFadden's close adherence to papal decisions
is clear from the sixth edition of Medical Ethics as contrasted with his most recent volume. The sixth edition was
written in 1967, just before the appearance of Humanae Vitae.
In it McFadden agrees to silence concerning certain aspects
of birth control, especially the pill, until the pope makes
his decision, despite his own earlier rejection of all artificial birth control (Medical Ethics, 6th ed., p. 87).
After Humanae Vitae he again condemns all artificial contraception (The Dignity of Life, pp. 83-94).

Individual consciences and differences of situation are better recognized. The human aspects of the moral dilemma can
achieve their proper place in ethical analysis and judgment.
Principles derived from Christian tradition can be properly
significant in medical ethics as hermeneutic themes concerned with the meaning of human life.

3.   Theological Principles as Hermeneutic Themes

Personalism has freed theological principles from their
subordination in medical ethical application to the restrictive framework modalities of physicalism and ecclesiastical
positivism. In chapter three we argued that two central theological themes or "other theological principles" (as distinguished from the general framework modalities of application within which they were applied) are of central importance to medical ethics.[68] The first principle or set of
principles concerns God's dominion over human life, and purports to judge concerning the obligation of women and men,
faced with various ethical dilemmas, to respect God's sovereignty. The second principles or set of principles concerns
the redemptive meaning of suffering, and purports to judge
concerning one's obligation to join one's own suffering love
to the redemptive sacrificial love of Jesus. We noted that
these two theological principles are not in fact separate,
but are rather two aspects of one central theological axis:
what is one's relationship to the creator? To what extent is
one a creature; to what extent a co-creator, or at least a
co-agent with God? Is it God's will that we try to "create
a better world," that we join with our creator in eliminating
suffering to the extent that we can? Or is it God's will
that we respect the sovereignty of God alone, and of the

---

[68]The description, which is only briefly summarized
here, is found in chapter three, pp. 232-234.

"nature" that he has created, that we accept our position in resignation to God's will, realizing that our suffering is redemptive when joined in active resignation to the redemptive suffering of Jesus?

In our descriptive analysis of pre-Vatican II medical ethics we saw how, with some exceptions, such as the question of spiritual care of the dying, these theological principles were applied to medical ethical questions as subordinate or ancillary principles to the dominant methodological modalities of the period: physicalism and ecclesiastical positivism. The ethical judgment as to the rightness or wrongness of a specific procedure was first made according to the framework modality and the theological themes of divine dominion and redemptive suffering, if they were used at all, were added as supportive ethical arguments or motivations for doing what had already been judged good. We noted many examples of this in our description of the literature.

The recent personalist critique is characterized basically by a rejection of both physicalism and ecclesiastical positivism. Personalism itself is not sufficiently systematic or rigid to dominate the use of theological themes in ways similar to those effected by the previous modalities. As a modality of application of theological principles in medical ethics, personalism frees the theological themes from their subordinate role, and allows them to find their proper place in theological medical ethics: to act as hermeneutic themes in the context of the central question of Christian anthropology, the question which is central to all of medical ethics, which, if a neologism is warranted, could be called the "biosignificance question": what is the meaning of human life?

Examples of this kind of application of theological themes are found not only in contemporary Roman Catholic literature, but in that of other religious traditions as well.

Whereas physicalism and ecclesiastical positivism were mainly Roman Catholic approaches, the theological themes of
God's dominion and of redemptive suffering, in the general
context of the theological-philosophical creature and co-
creator axis, are common to all traditions.[69]

The precise manner in which theological principles as
hermeneutic themes in a personalist framework are and ought
to be applied to medical ethical questions is problematic.
Often moralists use such principles as part of their argument
for or against a specific procedure. Moralists tend to position themselves more or less at one point on the axis, and
to reason for their conclusions from that perspective, emphasizing either human co-agency or the need for resignation.
Seldom is such a stance univocally consistent, however, and
each ethicist finds at least some variation in the way she
or he applies these hermeneutic themes to particular issues
of individual procedure or social medical policy. What is
clear is that these themes, once freed from the restriction
of the physicalist and positivist modalities, no longer operate unidirectionally across the entire spectrum of Roman
Catholic medical ethics. To this extent they have been freed
to approach more nearly their proper role in medical ethical
application.

One example of this can be seen in the different conclusions arrived at by personalist moralists concerning euthanasia, and in the different ways in which they apply theological principles to this issue.

It is within the personalist framework that Charles

---

[69]Dialogue with non-Roman Catholic approaches has played
a significant role in the emergence of the personalist critique. We have already seen that Catholic medical ethics has
disappeared as a self-contained discipline. Medical ethics
is now essentially ecumenical. That fact has both led to and
been aided by the changing Catholic approach. See Curran,
Medicine and Morals, pp. 43-44.

Curran makes use of the principle of God's dominion over human life in his treatment of euthanasia. His application of
the principle is no longer dominated by physicalist-positiv-
ist methodology, and he arrives at a conclusion which differs significantly from the traditional one. "The question,"
says Curran, "centers on the dominion which man has over the
dying process."[70] He goes on to make various distinctions
in the way this theme should be applied to this and other
issues:

> I distinguish this [the dying process] from life itself
> and from other processes. I agree with the traditional
> argument against euthanasia, that man does not have
> full dominion over his life and therefore, cannot posi-
> tively interfere to take his life. Man does have do-
> minion over his bodily processes so that he can inter-
> fere, for example, in the generative process through
> contraception and sterilization. Man does have some
> dominion over the dying process because of which he
> can as a matter of fact shorten the time of his dying
> by not using or discontinuing even readily available
> means to prolong life.[71]

It is clear from this passage that Curran accepts no clearly
unilateral manner in which the theological theme of God's
dominion is to be applied. He argues for one emphasis when
the question is positive euthanasia before the dying process
has begun (God's dominion forbids this), and for another
when the question is contraception or sterilization (God
gives man dominion here). And, he continues, once the dying
process has begun, man's positive intervention is in keeping
with a true understanding of the principle:

> Is there that great difference to accept a shortening
> that one can readily avoid and to positively interfere
> to shorten the dying process? I do not accept as great
> a distinction between the acts of commission and acts
> of omission in this case as Ramsey does. Precisely
> because the dying process has now begun, man's positive

---

[70]Curran, *Politics, Medicine,* p. 161.

[71]*Ibid.*

intervention is not an arrogant usurping of the role of
God but rather in keeping with the process of dying
which now encompasses the person. . . . in theory I
propose the dying process as the time in which the distinction between omission and commission no longer involves a meaningful moral difference.[72]

Thus the theological principal of God's dominion over human
life no longer leads to an absolute proscription of interventions of this kind, interventions which physicalism would
have condemned on the basis of the first two conditions of
the double effect principle.

A different conclusion is reached by Bernard Häring in
his analysis of positive euthanasia. Though Häring rejects
traditional conclusions in areas of contraception, sterilization, artificial insemination, and even early abortion
(some human intervention is possible in these matters), he
argues against positive euthanasia at any point in the dying
process. His argument is explicitly theological. He recognizes "the difficulty of providing convincing motives for
those who do not believe in the death-passion-resurrection
of Christ, and who have been unable to grasp the full value
of suffering and of selfless service to suffering mankind."[73] He calls this issue "a touchstone of the medical
ethos and ethics at large."[74]

Häring recognizes the inadequacy of a facile argument
based on a simplistic application of the principle of God's
dominion over human life:

In earlier times, the general argument, 'You may not
choose when to fall into the arms of God who alone is
Lord over life and death' seemed sufficient. Today,
however, it is not as simple as that because Christian
Scientists and the Witnesses of Jehovah invoke this

---

[72]*Ibid.*, pp. 161-162.

[73]Häring, *Medical Ethics,* p. 150.

[74]*Ibid.*

argument equally in proscribing blood transfusions.
Neither can our argument be the old slogan, 'Let nature
run its own course,' for the problem of artificial prolongation of life . . . arises chiefly from the fact
that modern medicine controls the course of nature.[75]

Yet Häring insists that the exercise of human freedom in our
creaturely status differs when applied to the two different
contexts of living and dying. His argument against positive
euthanasia is based on this distinction:

I think that, for the believer, the strongest argument
against [positive] euthanasia is in the perspective of
freedom. The so-called 'free choice' of death, that is,
forcing death to take us at the moment and under the
conditions we stipulate, would 'not increase but dimin-
ish the fullness of the free acceptance of death, which
is the course we have chosen. To exercise freedom's
choice in life according to our own power, and in death
according to our own powerlessness, is the most truthful admission of our creaturely human existence in
these two realities. This choice is the only acceptable foundation on which we have to build day after
day.'[76]

Häring's conclusion thus differs from Curran's. Like
Curran, he distinguishes between the processes of living and
of dying, and allows a wide degree of human intervention
over bodily processes during life. Like Curran, he argues
against full human dominion over the dying process, over
life itself. But unlike Curran, he rejects positive euthanasia even after the dying process has begun. Whereas Curran thinks that human intervention at this point is not a
usurpation of God's dominion, Häring argues that it is, that
our existence as creatures of God demands our admission of
powerlessness in the face of death.

---

[75]*Ibid.*, pp. 148-149.

[76]*Ibid.*, p. 149, italics his. Häring refers in a footnote to R. Kautuzky, 'Der Arzt,' p. 138. Presumably the
material in single quotes (which Häring uses) is from
Kautuzky.

A similar application of theological themes to the
euthanasia question is made by John Dedek. He cites the
Protestant ethicist Joseph Fletcher, who "argues that man
need not leave this decision to chance or fate or the will
of God. He should make a rational decision, and it would
be reasonable for him to prefer a painless release from a
useless and excruciating process of physical and personal
disintegration."[77] Dedek goes on to offer a counterpoint
based on the value of human suffering for the Christian believer:

> Christians of course understand that suffering and pain
> are physical evils. It is not without precedent for a
> man faced with a miserable death to wish that cup to
> pass from him. But it is the New Testament, not some
> perverse masochism, that invites us to see a trans-
> cendent meaning and redemptive purpose in physical suf-
> fering. This does not mean that the Christian does not
> recognize physical suffering as evil, does nothing to
> relieve it, or chases after it with the fanaticism of
> some of his religious ascendants. It does mean that he
> does not interpret the inevitable presence of suffering
> and death in God's creation as empty of all possible
> purpose and meaning as long as he continues to believe
> in the meaning of the cross and his union with the
> Crucified.[78]

But an ambivalence remains. On the one hand, suffering
is redemptive, and should be accepted. On the other, it is
evil, and should be eliminated. Traditional analysis had
decided that the distinction between active and passive interference was the crucial one. For Dedek this distinction
lacks perfect clarity.[79] He cites Curran's arguments, and

---

[77]Dedek, *Contemporary Medical Ethics,* pp. 151-152.
Fletcher generally emphasizes man as co-agent with God (*Mor-
als and Medicine,* pp. 8-33, and elsewhere generally in
Fletcher's writings).

[78]Dedek, *Contemporary Medical Ethics,* p. 152.

[79]*Ibid.,* pp. 153-154.

then opts himself for a position similar to Häring's, mainly because of the possible negative social consequences of
active euthanasia.

These examples demonstrate how contemporary moralists
use theological principles, freed from dependence on physicalist and positivist frameworks, in analyzing medical ethical issues. There is no longer any universally accepted set
of conclusions common to all Catholic moralists. The theological principles of God's dominion and of redemptive suffering cannot of themselves produce the precise and universally applicable kinds of solutions which were possible
under the cause-and-effect analysis, defended by authority,
which was dominant in the pre-Vatican II stage of the discipline.

This change in the use of theological principles is a
valid corrective. The theological themes we have been discussing ought not to be seen as giving in themselves clear
solutions to individual problems. They are not properly
used to replace the systematically rigid framework modalities within which they were formerly bound. Indeed, they
more closely approach their proper role in medical ethics
when they function within the context of the more general
and central question of Christian anthropology, the question
of the meaning of human life, than when they are used to
deal specifically with an individual medical procedure. The
theological principles of God's dominion over human life and
of redemptive suffering are best used as hermeneutic themes
to approach the meaning of human life and human action as
God intends it to be.

In this context, theological principles are applied to
medical ethical problems in a manner which is both more and
less direct than was the case within physicalist and positivist modalities. Inasmuch as they are no longer subordinated to these frameworks they can be of more "direct"

influence. They are not mediated by distorting modalities.
On the other hand, their use is a less direct one in that
their context is more properly that of the meaning of human
life than that of precise distinctions between medical procedures. It is in this wider context that the mystery-
filled aspect of theological themes becomes most compelling.
Here, in the context of human life as a whole, it is more
immediately apparent that women and men are of necessity, as
created by God and redeemed by Christ in the Spirit, both
creatures and co-agents, both called to accept suffering and
to fight against it. The dimensions of paradox, mystery,
and myth inherent in these central truths find a more force-
ful expression in this context than when the principles are
dichotomized into their separate poles and one emphasis is
used in isolation from the other to demand or forbid a specific procedure. When the proper stress is given to the
creative tension inherent in the theological principles, as
hermeneutic themes, a wider latitude is granted to the range
of human actions which are recognized as licit in at least
some cases. It becomes less easy to arrive at universally
applicable concrete behavior (material) norms, while formal
exhortations toward moral excellence can be retained and
emphasized.

It is true, of course, that not all moralists remain
consistently aware of the dialectic inherent in the
themes.[80] Often only one pole of the axis is stressed to
to the neglect of the other. This can result in the kind of

----

[80]No attempt can be made here to categorize contemporary medical ethicists. Indeed, as we have already pointed
out, seldom is a rigorous categorization possible or helpful. For some examples of the role theological principles
as hermeneutic themes play when used in the context of the
meaning of human life, see Fletcher, *Morals and Medicine,*
esp. pp. 8-33 (emphasizes man's co-agency and active intervention); Augenstein, *Come, Let Us Play God,* p. ix (similar
generally to Fletcher); Ramsey, *Patient as Person,* pp. xii-

legalism common to physicalism and positivism. Some contemporary
tend to emphasize only the evil found in human activity, and
to see human progress, especially if it is related to technology, as contrary to God's will and to his sovereignty
over nature and human life.[81] They thus forbid many kinds

---

xiii (emphasizes man's creatureliness and the need to avoid
trespass against human nature); Miller and Bloom, "Keeping
People Alive" (Miller upholds a secular humanist position,
Bloom the need for resignation); Vaux, *Who Shall Live?* p. 3
(a "balanced" approach); Vaux, *Biomedical Ethics,* pp. 43-45
(similar); Thieliche, "Ethics in Modern Medicine," pp. 155,
181-182 (recognizing the ambiguity in creativity and arguing
against any attempt by man to transcend himself); Janssens,
"Norms and Priorities," and "De Jure" (showing the creative
tension present in human activity, and stressing generally
the beneficial possibilities of intervention); Häring, *Medical Ethics,* esp. pp. 11-14, 120-131, 152-166 (stressing the
ambiguity in co-agency and in suffering, and discussing the
question of suffering and Christian sanctity); Nelson, *Human
Medicine,* esp. pp. 13-15, 119-122 (both poles need to be
heard from, neither is enough in itself); Callahan, *The
Tyranny of Survival,* and "Health and Society" (stresses the
dangers of technology and argues against technological optimism); Illich, *Medical Nemesis* (a radical critique of scientific medicine); Gustafson, *The Contributions of Theology to
Medical Ethics* (perhaps the best analysis of the issue to
date--Gustafson explicitly discusses the issues we have been
describing, and argues, as I have done, for maintaining the
creative balance of the creature and co-actor poles;
Gustafson's work is highly recommended to the reader who
wishes further discussion of this question); Gustafson,
"Basic Ethical Issues in the Bio-Medical Fields" (a brief
statement of similar opinions).

[81]The theological principles as hermeneutic themes offer a perspective for dialogue with non-religious medical
ethicists. These often emphasize the questions of technology, progress, environmental hazards, scientific optimism,
etc. Many among the contemporary ethicists have, in my
judgment, reacted in a far too extreme manner against science and technology. A stress on the inherently dialectic
creative tension of the theological themes in their religious history would tend to correct such a one-sided reaction. Often the concept "holistic" is given this too-narrow
denotation. Holism, which reacts properly against any reductionist rational positivism or mechanism as definitional

of human interventions which might be judged licit if proper
weight were also given to humanity's created co-agency with God
Other ethicists, together with many scientists, tend on the
other hand to see technological development only in its
beneficial aspects. They believe in automatic progress.
They thus command activities which may be destructive of
the sanctity and dignity of human life and the future of humankind.

The theological themes of God's dominion over life and
of redemptive suffering, when properly applied to the context of the "biosignificance question," the question of the
meaning of life, serve to better unfold the mystery which is
within the ethical dilemma in medical ethics. Theological
principles cannot *solve* the question as an equation solves
for the value of a function. Instead they make their con-

---

approach to human life, becomes indeed quite dualistic in
its rejection of the scientific method or of technology altogether as "dehumanizing." For a discussion of these issues, see Frankel, "The Nature and Sources of Irrationalism,"
and "The Specter of Eugenics," esp. pp. 25-33.
The principle of double effect in its modern form
(stress on the third and fourth conditions, on the principle
of commensurate reason), which we have described in the
previous section, offers an excellent framework for cor-
recting this extreme reaction. Anti-technologists are
united in seeing evil in everything humans do, and in arguing from this observation to conclusions which oppose
technological development because of the evil inherent in
it. Double effect likewise recognizes the human condition.
Human actions cause ontic (pre-moral) evil because they
are of necessity finite. Double effect provides a model
for allowing such ontic evil when the physical action which
inevitably includes these evil consequences can be determined to be commensurate with the good to be achieved which
is formally intended. Double effect in its modern form thus
counters the pervasive pessimism and apocalypticism of much
of today's medical and social ethics. Human action is not
paralyzed in an impossible attempt to avoid any and all
evil results. In this sense double effect provides an excellent framework for "doing" ethics.

tribution precisely by denying to us the escape of an ethical short-cut. By refusing to allow facile judgments, theological principles as mystery-filled hermeneutic themes recall the creative tension inherent in humankind, and help us
to avoid destructively rigid policies.

Conclusion

Roman Catholic medical ethics has undergone a radical
critique in recent years. In its emergent, pre-Vatican II
phase, Catholic medical ethics was too closely bound, both
in its definition and in its methodology, to the restricted
scope and analytic approach of modern scientific medicine.
Its formal and material definition neglected social aspects
of medical policy and emphasized exclusively the actual
daily professional practice of medical personnel. To the
physical interventions which made up the core of modern
medical practice it purported to bring a clear and precise.
set of directives, based on physical cause-and-effect analysis and supported by authoritative statements, which could
provide accurate and universally applicable answers to the
ethical dilemmas connected with individual medical procedures. The theological principles of God's dominion over
human life and of redemptive suffering were subordinated in
actual application to the dominant framework modalities of
physicalism and ecclesiastical positivism. They were shorn
of mystery.

Contemporary medical ethics is not without its problems and, indeed, its dangers. In its reaction against the
definitional limitations of its predecessor, it threatens
in the name of "holism" to claim an all-inclusive status
and an unrestricted expertise. In its reaction against
scientific rationalism and double effect physicalism, it
threatens, again in the name of "holism," to adopt an anti-

rational, anti-scientific, anti-technological dualism which
will ill serve the future of humankind.

The answer cannot be, however, a return to the restrictive definition and methodology of the pre-Vatican II
discipline. While recognizing the contributions made by
Roman Catholic medical ethics in its period of emergence,
contemporary theological medical ethics will properly reject
its restrictive definition and its physicalist and positivist methodologies. In using theological principles, medical
ethics will remain more faithful to Catholic and Christian
tradition if it recalls the dimension of mystery. Thus
freed from distortion, Christian tradition is better able to
approach the mystery of human life. It can better contri-
bute to the endeavor of medical ethics, an endeavor which
will help in creating the future to which God, in a shrouded
and indefineable, yet enticing way, beckons us.

APPENDIX

THE STRUCTURAL RELATIONSHIP OF
THE THREE METHODOLOGICAL MODALITIES

In our methodological study of the discipline we emphasize three modalities: physicalism, ecclesiastical positivism, and personalism. They are the dominant aspects of
the discipline's theological methodology in its three periods of development. They serve as the best hermeneutic
devices for a valid exposition and critique. They best
typify each period. A more complex analysis of the *structural* and *theoretical* relationship among the modalities
themselves, and, in light of this, a more precise theoretical description of the stages of development is presented
in this appendix.

Our analysis here will suggest that the three modalities consist of approaches on two different levels of ethical theory: that of normative theory and that of metaethics. That is, they are not structurally parallel or independent solutions posed to the *same* question or set of
questions, but rather they interact on two different theoretical levels. The structural result is four, not three
stages, resulting from combinations of *two* different approaches on each of the two different levels.

The distinction between metaethics and normative theory
generally proposed is that normative theory deals with the
kinds of norms which are applied to moral issues while metaethics deals with the problem of verification of these norms
and of the conclusions drawn from them. Thus, for our purposes we can describe the normative problem as asking whether one ought to use physicalist or personalist criteria in

deciding medical ethical questions. That is, does one look
at the physical and biological structures of the act, or
does one look at the personal and social context of the act?
This corresponds to some extent, though not exactly, with
the widely known central division of normative theory between deontological and consequentialist approaches.[1]

Metaethical theory, on the other hand, is interested in
the possibility of *verification* of these norms. How can physicalist and personalist norms, and the conclusions derived from
them, be verified? The two answers to this question which
concern us here are those proposed by Catholic medical ethicists during the development of our discipline: empirical metaethical absolutism and supernatural metaethical absolutism.
Thus, as we have noted, physicalist norms and conclusions were
verified by appeal to the natural law discovered by human reason (empirical metaethical absolutism) and by appeal to the
teachings of the supernaturally guaranteed magisterium of the
Church (a species of supernatural metaethical absolutism--the
supernatural source for verification might also be direct individual revelation, Scripture, an inspired body of elders,
etc.). Similarly, if personalist norms are to be used, how
can they and their conclusions be verified: from empirical
data (the natural law in the metaethical though not in the
physicalist essentialist sense),[2] or from some supernatural source such as Scripture or the infallible Church?[3]

---

[1]This brief description of normative theory is enough
for the specific questions raised in this appendix. For a
discussion of the relationship between physicalism and personalism on the one hand with the more widely used deonto-
logical-consequentialist (utilitarian) distinction on the
other, see Curran, "Utilitarianism," esp. pp. 249-251.

[2]See above, pp. 245-246, n. 4.

[3]We have noted that personalism in fact rejected ecclesiastical positivism and quickly adopted a metaethical

There are, of course, other possible answers to the metaethical question of verification,[4] but they were not generally given by Roman Catholic moralists.

The structural interrelationship of the three methodological modalities is illustrated in the diagram. The
three modalities result from combinations of two metaethical theories: empirical metaethical absolutism (natural law
theory in the metaethical sense) and supernatural metaethical absolutism (ecclesiastical positivism), with two different approaches to normative theory, two different kinds of
criteria which can be applied to medical ethical issues:
physicalism and personalism. The results are four combina-

---

natural law stance (pp. 429-435). We also saw, however,
that this was not inevitable (pp. 429-430). In fact, as we
will suggest in this appendix, there was a brief period
during which some personalist authors seemed committed to
the practical ecclesiastical positivism which had operated
previously.

[4] Perhaps verification is possible from common intui-
tion or from some universally accepted system of reasoning
(intuitional and rational metaethical absolutism). Some
elements of these approaches are found in Catholic ethics,
but they are subordinate to the governing approaches of
natural law theory and ecclesiastical positivism. Or perhaps no meaning at all can be found in ethical statements,
and all verification is impossible (non-cognitivism). Or
perhaps all ethical judgments are totally relative, so that
even granting identical circumstances, consequences, and
situations, no universally verifiable ethical judgment can
be made, since people will differ in their conclusions and
approaches, and since each person or culture is equally
right (individual and cultural metaethical relativism).
It is important to distinguish metaethical relativism from
ethical situationalism. The former refuses to allow verification of ethical judgment even granting exactly identical situations. The latter argues that situations are not
exactly repeatable. Situationalists are often accused of
being relativists, though they may well not be. For more
detail on metaethics, see especially Veatch, "Does Ethics
Have an Empirical Basis?" His typology is used here. See
also Kelly, "Clyde Kluckhohn's Ethical Theory." See also
above, p. 315, n. 9.

METAETHICAL THEORY / BASIC NORMATIVE THEORY	SUPERNATURAL METAETHICAL ABSOLUTISM ECCLESIASTICAL POSITIVISM	EMPIRICAL METAETHICAL ABSOLUTISM NATURAL LAW THEORY
PHYSICALISM	MODALITY II: ECCLESIASTICAL POSITIVISM STAGE II (1940-1960) Ecclesiastical Positivism with Physicalism	MODALITY I: PHYSICALISM STAGE I (1900-1940) Natural Law Physicalism
PERSONALISM	MODALITY III: PERSONALISM STAGE III (1960-1970) Ecclesiastical Positivism with Personalism	STAGE IV (1965- Empirical (Natural Law) Personalism

tions: 1) natural law physicalism; 2) ecclesiastical positivism with physicalism; 3) ecclesiastical positivism with personalism; and 4) natural law personalism or empirical personalism.

These combinations resulted in four stages in the methodological development of the discipline. First, from 1900-1940, which we have characterized as the period of physicalism, the natural law as a metaethical theory was used to verify physicalist criteria for application to medical ethical issues. Second,

from 1940-1960, which we have characterized as the period of
ecclesiastical positivism, since this became the dominant modality, physicalist criteria were kept as the normative ethical approach, but empirical metaethical theory (natural law
based on unaided human reason), though retained theoretically, was more and more abandoned in practice. Appeal for verification of physicalist norms and conclusions was now made
more and more to the magisterium of the Church, whose authority was based on supernatural revelation.

Third, beginning around the time of Vatican II, a radical shift occurred when physicalist norms were replaced with
personalist ones. This shift occurred not so much on the
metaethical level as on the level of normative theory. Indeed, for a time some authors used personalist criteria while
maintaining a strong allegiance to magisterial authority.[5]
Few actual conclusions were changed.[6] Personalism was combined with a continuing ecclesiastical positivism to characterize this transitional period in Catholic moral theology.

Fourth, as we have seen, due largely to *Humanae Vitae* and
to the reaction against it, a *metaethical* shift *back to* the
natural law (revisionist natural law theory, critical natural
law theory) and away from ecclesiastical positivism has taken
place.[7] In this contemporary phase, not only is the norma-

---

[5]For an example, see Dupré, *Contraception and Catholics,*
pp. 5-6, 43-44, discussed above, pp. 422, 430-431.

[6]An excellent example of this is found in Louis Janssens'
course notes and in his first articles on birth control.
Though Janssens had changed from physicalist to personalist
criteria, only in the one issue of the pill had he varied
from traditional conclusions. Other methods of "artificial"
contraception, as well as all sterilization, were still forbidden. Janssens has since changed his opinion. See Janssens, "Conjugal Morality," and "Morale Conjugale et
Progestogènes."

[7]See above, pp. 429-435.

tive methodology changed, but conclusions reached have
changed, since they need no longer conform in every instance to those of the ordinary, non-infallible magisterium. These changes in methods and conclusions which
have occurred in the third and fourth stages are still
being debated. By no means have moralists arrived at
consensus.

BIBLIOGRAPHY AND INDICES

This section contains five instruments: first, an index to "bibliographical footnotes" found in the text; second, an alphabetical index of works discussed in the text (a chronological listing is found on pages 7-12); third, a general bibliography of works consulted in preparation of the study; fourth, an index of names; and fifth, an analytical index.

Index to Bibliographical Footnotes

Certain footnotes in the text may be of help in locating sources. These group together sources of a specific genre. They do *not* include the primary sources for the study, which are listed chronologically on pages 7-12, and indexed alphabetically on pages 456-459.

Associations and research centers of medical ethics, p. 403, n. 2.

Bibliographies, p. 402, n. 1.

Cases of conscience collections, p. 39, n. 87.

Codes of intraprofessional "medical ethics," p. 88, n. 185.

Double effect principle, histories, p. 247, n. 5.

Ethics, "natural," general texts, p. 40, n. 89.

"Medical ethics" (intraprofessional) histories, p. 88, n. 182.

Moral theology histories, p. 15, n. 3; p. 18, n. 6; p. 18, n. 7.

Moral theology manuals, commandment organization, p. 30, n. 41.

Moral theology manuals, virtue organization, p. 38, n. 86.

Non-Christian works, pre-1960, p. 2, n. 2.

Non-Christian works, post-1960, p. 405, n. 5.

"Nursing ethics" (intraprofessional) works, p. 94, n. 199.

Papal pronouncements, p. 314, n. 8.

Pastoral counselling works, p. 203, n. 215.

Pastoral medicine histories, p. 43, n. 92.

Pastoral medicine twentieth century European works, p. 81,
     n. 174.

Patristic period studies, p. 18, n. 7.

Philosophical ethics texts, *see* ethics, "natural."

Protestant works, pre-1960, p. 2, n. 2.

Protestant works, post-1960, p. 405, n. 5.

Question and answer collections, p. 40, n. 88.

Roman Catholic monographs on specific topics, 1900-1940,
     p. 149, n. 99.

Roman Catholic monographs on specific topics, 1940-1960,
     p. 219, n. 256.

Roman Catholic texts, post-Vatican II, p. 404, n. 3.

Rural medicine works, p. 64, n. 134.

Scripture and morality studies, p. 18, n. 6.

Alphabetical Index of Works Discussed

     This index includes North American Roman Catholic works
together with other literature studied in the text. For a
chronological listing of North American Roman Catholic works
from 1900-1960, including each edition and length in pages,
see pages 7-12. Full publication data can be found in the
general bibliography. Only important passages are indexed
here. Further references may be found in the index of names.

Antonelli, Giuseppe. *Medicina pastoralis*. 78-80.

Bonnar, Alphonsus. *The Catholic Doctor*. 149-153, 321-324.

Boudewyns, Michael. *Ventilabrum medico-theologicum*. 57-59.

Bourke, Michael P. *Some Medical Ethical Problems Solved*.
     130-132.

Glover, William K. *Artificial Insemination among Human Be-*
    ings. 358-359.

Godin, Edgar, and J. P. E. O'Hanley. *Hospital Ethics: A*
    Commentary on the Moral Code of Catholic Hospitals.
    212.

Good, Frederick L., and Otis F. Kelly. *Marriage, Morals*
    and Medical Ethics. 181-183.

Hayes, Edward J., Paul J. Hayes, and Dorothy Ellen Kelly.
    Moral Handbook of Nursing. 208-209, 396-397.

Healy, Edwin F. *Medical Ethics.* 200-204, 382-386.

Kelly, Gerald. *Medico-Moral Problems.* 170-180, 359-371.

Kenny, John P. *Principles of Medical Ethics.* 185-189, 371-
    377.

Klarmann, Andrew. *The Crux of Pastoral Medicine.* 120-123,
    286-291.

La Rochelle, Stanislaus A., and Charles T. Fink. *Handbook*
    of Medical Ethics for Nurses, Physicians, and Priests.
    153-158, 324-329.

Lohkamp, Nicholas. *The Morality of Hysterectomy Operations.*
    395-396.

Loranger, Léon. "The Church and Medicine." 377.

McAllister, Joseph B. *Ethics: With Special Application to*
    the Medical and Nursing Professions. 168-169.

McFadden, Charles J. *Medical Ethics.* 161-168, 211, 216-
    218, 341-358.

Marshall, John. *Medicine and Morals.* 214.

Medicus (pseud.). *Medical Essays.* 136-137.

Moore, Thomas Verner. *Principles of Ethics.* 138-140.

--------, and Gregory Stevens. *Principles of Ethics.* 5th
    ed. 212-213.

Murphy, Richard J. *The Catholic Nurse.* 138.

Niedermeyer, Albert. *Compendium of Pastoral Medicine.* 215-
    216.

--------. *Compendium of Pastoral Hygiene.* 215-216.

O'Connell, Timothy P. *Morality in Medicine.* 170.

O'Donnell, Thomas J. *Morals in Medicine.* 204-208, 386-
    393.

O'Malley, Austin. *The Ethics of Medical Homicide and Muti-*
    lation. 127-128, 291-298.

BIBLIOGRAPHY

List of Works Consulted[1]

Ackerknecht, Erwin Heinz. *A Short History of Medicine*. New York: Ronald Press, 1955.

Adams, David W. *Therapeutic Abortion: An Annotated Bibliography*. [Hamilton, Ontario]: McMaster Univ. Medical Center, 1973.

Aertnys, J[oseph], and C[ornelio] A. Damen. *Theologia moralis secundum doctrinam S. Alfonsi de Ligorio*. 15th ed. 2 vols. Turin: Marietti, 1947.

Agnew, L[eslie] R[obert] C[orbet]. "Medicine (History of)." *New Catholic Encyclopedia*. Vol. 9. 1967.

Aikens, Charlotte A[lbina]. *Studies in Ethics for Nurses*. 4th ed. Philadelphia: W. B. Saunders, 1939.

Albertus, Josephus. *Compendium theologiae moralis*. 3 vols. in 1. Rome: S. Joseph, 1905.

Allaire, J.-B.-A. *Dictionnaire biographique de clergé Canadien-Français*. 6 vols. Montreal: École Catholique des Sourds-Muets, 1910-1934.

American Dental Association. "Code of Ethics" (1866), in John E. Gurley, *The Evolution of Professional Ethics in Dentistry: Report of the Historian*. St. Louis, Mo.: American College of Dentists, 1961, pp. 78-91.

American Dental Hygienists' Association. "Code of Professional Ethics for the Dental Hygienist" (1969), in Wilma E. Motley, *Ethics, Jurisprudence and History for the Dental Hygienist*. Philadelphia: Lea and Febiger, 1972, pp. 20-21.

American Federation for Clinical Research. "Toward a Definition of Fetal Life: Ethical and Legal Options and Their Implications for Biologists and Physicians." *Clinical Research*, 23 (1975), 210-237.

American Medical Association. "Code of Ethics of the American Medical Association" (1847), in Chauncey D. Leake, ed., *Percival's Medical Ethics*. Baltimore: Williams

---

[1]All works are included in this general listing except book reviews, which are listed separately at the end.

and Wilkins, 1927, pp. 218-238.

--------. "Principles of Medical Ethics of the American Medical Association" (1903), in Chauncey D. Leake, ed., *Percival's Medical Ethics*. Baltimore: Williams and Wilkins, 1927, pp. 239-256.

--------. "Principles of Medical Ethics of the American Medical Association" (1912). *Annals of the American Academy of Political and Social Sciences,* 101 (1922), 260-265.

American Medical Association Judicial Council. *Opinions and Reports, Abstracted and Annotated to the Principles of Medical Ethics*. American Medical Association, 1960.

--------. *Opinions and Reports of the Judicial Council, Including the Principles of Medical Ethics and Rules of the Judicial Council*. Chicago: American Medical Association, 1971.

--------. *Principles of Medical Ethics: Opinions and Reports of the Judicial Council*. Chicago: American Medical Association, 1958.

American Nurses' Association. "Code for Professional Nurses" (1950), in Joseph B. McAllister, *Ethics: With Special Application to the Medical and Nursing Professions*. 2nd ed. Philadelphia: W. B. Saunders, 1955, pp. 390-391.

--------. "Code for Professional Nurses" (1960), in Cordelia W. Kelly, *Professional Dimensions of Nursing*. New York: Macmillan, 1962, p. 24.

American Pharmaceutical Association. "Code of Ethics" (1852). *Annals of the American Academy of Political and Social Sciences,* 101 (1922), 267-268.

--------. "Principles of Pharmaceutical Ethics." *Annals of the American Academy of Political and Social Sciences,* 101 (1922), 268-271.

American Psychiatric Association. "The Principles of Medical Ethics with Annotations Especially Applicable to Psychiatry." *American Journal of Psychiatry,* 130 (1973), 1057-1064.

American Registry of Radiologic Technologists. "Code of Ethics," in James Ohnysty, *Aids to Ethics and Professional Conduct for Student Radiologic Technologists*. Springfield, Ill.: Charles C. Thomas, 1964, p. 123.

Anderson, C. G. "Priest versus Physician." *Westminster Review,* 170 (1908), 330-332.

Anderson, Odin W. *Health Care: Can There Be Equity? The United States, Sweden, and England.* New York: John Wiley and Sons, 1972.

Annas, George J., Leonard H. Glantz, and Barbara F. Katz. *Informed Consent to Human Experimentation: The Subject's*

Dilemma. Cambridge, Mass.: Ballinger, 1977.

Antonelli, Giuseppe. *Medicina pastoralis in usum confessar-*
    iorum et curiarum ecclesiasticarum. 4th ed. 3 vols.
    New York: F. Pustet, 1920.

--------. *Medicina pastoralis in usum confessariorum,*
    professorum theologiae moralis, et curiarum ecclesias-
    ticarum. 5th ed. 4 vols. Rome: F. Pustet, 1932.

Antoninus of Florence. *Repertorium literale summe* (1477)
    cui et folia et columne . . . accesserunt. 4 vols. in
    2. [Lyons, 1529].

Applegarth, J. J. "Materialism and Modern Medicine." *Cath-*
    olic World, 170 (1949), 98-103.

Atti del IV Congresso Internazzionale dei Medici Cattolici.
    Rome: Orizzonte Medico, 1950.

Augenstein, Leroy. *Come, Let Us Play God.* New York: Harper
    and Row, 1969.

Ayd, Frank J., Jr., ed. *Medical, Moral, and Legal Issues in*
    Mental Health Care. Baltimore: Williams and Wilkins,
    1974.

Azor, Juan. *Institutionum moralium in quibus universae*
    quaestionibus ad conscientiam recte, aut prave factorum
    pertinentes, breviter tractantur pars prima [-*tertia*].
    3 vols. Rome: Aloysius Zannettum, Carolus Vulliettum,
    and Aegidij Spadae, 1600-1611.

Azpilcueta, Martín de. *Enchiridion sive manuale confessar-*
    iorum et poenitentium. Cologne, 1579.

Babbie, Earl R. *Science and Morality in Medicine: A Survey*
    of Medical Educators. Berkeley: Univ. of California
    Press, 1970.

Back, Kurt W., and James T. Fawcett, eds. "Population Policy
    and the Person: Congruence or Conflict?" *Journal of*
    Social Issues, 30, No. 4 (1974), 1-324.

Ballerini, Antonio, and Domenico Palmieri. *Opus theologicum*
    morale in Busembaum medullam. 7 vols. Prati: Gia-
    chetti and Sons, 1889-1893.

Barber, Bernard, et al. *Research on Human Subjects: Problems*
    of Social Control in Medical Experimentation. New York:
    Russell Sage Foundation, 1973.

Barnesby, Norman. *Medical Chaos and Crime.* New York: M.
    Kennerley, 1910.

Barry, [Sister] M. J[ustin]. "Aspilcueta, Martin (Doctor
    Navarrus)." *New Catholic Encyclopedia.* Vol. 1. 1967.

Barton, Richard Thomas. *Religious Doctrine and Medical*

Practice. Springfield, Ill.: Charles C. Thomas, 1958.

Baum, Gregory. "The Right to Dissent." *Commonweal,* Aug. 23, 1968; rpt. in Daniel Callahan, ed., *The Catholic Case for Contraception.* New York: Macmillan, 1969, pp. 71-76.

Behnke, John A., and Sissela Bok, eds. *The Dilemmas of Euthanasia.* Garden City, N.Y.: Doubleday, 1975.

Beregoff-Gillow, Pauline. *A Doctor Dares to Tell: The Inside Story of Medicine.* New York: Comet, 1959.

Berens, Anthony. "Moral Problems in the Hospital." *Hospital Progress,* 16 (1935), 389-392.

Berg, Joseph F., ed. *A Synopsis of the Moral Theology of Peter Dens, as Prepared for the Use of Romish Seminaries and Students of Theology.* Trans. from the Latin of the Mechlin Edition of 1838 by J. F. Berg. 4th ed. Philadelphia: Lippincott, 1856.

Bernard, Claude. *An Introduction to the Study of Experimental Medicine* (1865). Trans. Henry Copley Greene, 1927. New York: Dover, 1957.

Bibliography of Bioethcs. Ed. LeRoy Walters. Detroit: Gale Research Company, 1975+.

Bibliography of Society, Ethics and the Life Sciences. Compiled Sharman Sollitto and Robert M. Veatch. Hastings-on-Hudson, N.Y.: Hastings Center, 1973+.

Bieler, L[udwig]. "Penitentials." *New Catholic Encyclopedia.* Vol. 11. 1967.

Bier, W[illiam] C. "Pastoral Psychology." *New Catholic Encyclopedia.* Vol. 10. 1967.

Biltz, Joseph Henri. *The Obligation to Preserve Life.* Diss., Catholic Univ. of America Studies in Sacred Theology, 2nd ser., No. 129. Washington: Catholic Univ. of America Press, 1962.

"Bioethics and Social Responsibility." *The Monist,* 60 (1977), 3-146.

Blishen, Bernard R. *Doctors and Doctrines: The Ideology of Medical Care in Canada.* Toronto: Univ. of Toronto Press, 1969.

Bliss, Brian P., and Alan G. Johnson. *Aims and Motives in Clinical Medicine: A Practical Approach to Medical Ethics.* London: Pitman Medical Publishing Company, 1975.

Bogomolny, Robert L., ed. *Human Experimentation.* Dallas: Southern Methodist Univ. Press, 1976.

Bon, Henri. *Précis de médecine Catholique.* Paris: Felix
    Alcan, 1936.

Bonnar, A[lphonsus]. *The Catholic Doctor.* London: Burns,
    Oates, and Washbourne, 1937.

--------. *The Catholic Doctor.* 2nd ed. New York: P. J.
    Kenedy and Sons, 1939.

--------. *The Catholic Doctor.* 6th ed. London: Burns,
    Oates, and Washbourne, 1952.

--------. *Medicine and Men.* London: Burns and Oates, 1962.

Boston Medical Association. *The Medical Police and Rules
    and Regulations of the Boston Medical Association, with
    a Catalogue of the Officers and Members.* Boston: David
    Clapp, 1864.

Boudewyns, Michael. *Ventilabrum medico-theologicum quo
    omnes casus, tum medicos, cum aegros, aliosque con-
    cernentes eventilantur, et quod S.S. P.P. conformius,
    scholasticis probabilius, et in conscientia tutius est,
    fecernitur: Opus cum theologis et confessariis, tum
    maxime medicis perquam necessarium.* Antwerp: Cornelius
    Woons, 1666.

Bourke, Michael P. *Some Medical Ethical Problems Solved.*
    Milwaukee: Bruce, 1921; rpt. in Leo Gregory Fink, ed.,
    Graduate Nurses: Symposium of Ethical Inspiration.
    New York: Paulist Press, 1938, pp. 198-220.

--------. "Talks to Nurses on Ethics and Jurisprudence."
    Hospital Progress, 1 (1920), 47-50.

Bouscaren, T[imothy] Lincoln. *Ethics of Ectopic Operations.*
    Chicago: Loyola Univ. Press, 1933.

--------. *Ethics of Ectopic Operations.* 2nd ed. Milwaukee:
    Bruce, 1944.

Branson, Roy. "Bioethics as Individual *and* Social: The Scope
    of a Consulting Profession *and* Academic Discipline."
    Journal of Religious Ethics, 3 (1975), 111-139.

Brennan, J[ames] H[enry]. "Pastoral Theology." *New Catho-
    lic Encyclopedia.* Vol. 10. 1967.

Brody, Howard. *Ethical Decisions in Medicine.* Boston:
    Little, Brown and Company, 1976.

--------. "The Systems View of Man: Implications for Medi-
    cine, Science, and Ethics." *Perspectives in Biology
    and Medicine,* 17 (Autumn, 1973), 71-92.

--------. "Teaching Medical Ethics: Future Challenges."
    Journal of the American Medical Association, 229 (1974),
    177-179.

Browne, Thomas. *Religio Medici* (1642). Ed. James Winny. Cambridge: Univ. Press, 1963.

Bucceroni, Gennaro. *Casus conscientiae propositi a Card. de Lugo, a P. Benjamino Elbel, a P. Joanne Petro Gury, aliisque auctoribus resoluti.* 6th ed. 2 vols. Rome: Institutum Pii IX, 1913.

Bulger, Roger J., ed. *Hippocrates Revisited: A Search for Meaning.* New York: Medcom, 1973.

Bunker, John P., Benjamin A. Barnes, and Frederick Mostellar, eds. *Costs, Risks, and Benefits of Surgery.* New York: Oxford Univ. Press, 1977.

Burke, Edward F. *Acute Cases in Moral Medicine.* New York: Macmillan, 1922.

Burns, Chester R., and H. Tristram Engelhardt, Jr., eds. "The Humanities and Medicine." *Texas Reports on Biology and Medicine,* 32 (1974), 1-368.

Busenbaum, Hermann. *Medulla theologiae moralis* (1652) . . . *Accedunt propositiones . . . epistolae encyclicae, atque decreta apostolica Benedicti Papae XIV . . . materiam morum respicientes.* Rome: Remondini, 1746.

Butler, J[ohn J.], and H[arold] Jeghers. "Medicine, Catholic Schools of." *New Catholic Encyclopedia.* Vol. 9. 1967.

Cabot, Richard C. "Ethics and the Medical Profession." *Survey,* 55 (1926), 618-621, 641-643.

Callahan, Daniel. *Abortion: Law, Choice, and Morality.* New York: Macmillan, 1970; rpt. Macmillan Paperbacks, 1972.

--------. "Bioethics as a Discipline." *Hastings Center Studies,* 1, No. 1 (1973), 66-73.

--------. "Doing Well by Doing Good: Garrett Hardin's 'Lifeboat Ethic'." *Hastings Center Report,* 4, No. 4 (Dec., 1974), 1-4.

--------. "Health and Society: Some Ethical Implications." *Daedalus,* 106 (Winter, 1977), 23-33.

--------. *The Tyranny of Survival: And Other Pathologies of Civilized Life.* New York: Macmillan, 1973.

--------, ed. *The Catholic Case for Contraception.* New York: Macmillan, 1969.

--------, et al. *Recent Activities: 1973; Institute of Society, Ethics, and the Life Sciences.* Hastings-on-Hudson, N. Y.: Institute of Society, Ethics, and the Life Sciences, 1973.

Campbell, Alastair V. *Moral Dilemmas in Medicine.* 2nd ed.

Edinburgh: Churchill Livingstone, 1975.

Cangiamila, Francesco Emanuello. *Sacra embryologia sive de officio sacerdotum, medicorum, et aliorum circa aeternam parvulorum in utero existentium salutem* (1745). Ieper: Thomas F. Walwein, 1775.

Capellmann, C[arl Franz Nicolaus]. *Medicina pastoralis*. 11th ed. Aix-la-Chapelle: Rudolph Barth, 1896.

--------. *Pastoral Medicine* (1877). Trans. William Dassel (1878). New York: F. Pustet, 1882.

--------, and W. Bergmann. *Pastoralmedizin*. 19th ed. Paderborn: Bonifacius, 1923.

Carmody, James. *Ethical Issues in Health Services: A Report and Annotated Bibliography*. Rockville, Md.: National Center for Health Services Research and Development, 1970.

Cartwright, Ann, Lisbeth Hockey, and John L. Anderson. *Life Before Death*. London: Routledge and Kegan Paul, 1973.

Cassell, Eric J. "Illness and Disease." *Hastings Center Report*, 6, No. 2 (April, 1976), 27-37.

Cathell, Daniel Webster. *Book on the Physician Himself and Things that Concern His Reputation and Success*. 10th ed. Philadelphia: F. A. Davis, 1898.

"Catholic Church and Medicine." *America*, 78 (1948), 618.

The Catholic Encyclopedia and Its Makers. New York: The Encyclopedia Press, 1917.

Catholic Hospital Association of Canada. *Moral Code*. Ottawa: The Catholic Hospital Association of Canada, 1955.

--------. *A Workshop on Medico-Moral Problems*. Proceedings of the Institute on Medico-Moral Problems, March 30-31, April 1-2, 1954. Ottawa: The Catholic Hospital Association of Canada, 1955.

Catholic Hospital Association of the United States and Canada. "Ethical and Religious Directives for Catholic Hospitals." *Linacre Quarterly*, 15, Nos. 3-4 (July-Oct., 1948), 1-9.

--------. *Ethical and Religious Directives for Catholic Hospitals, 1949*. St. Louis, Mo.: The Catholic Hospital Association, 1949.

--------. *Ethical and Religious Directives for Catholic Hospitals*. 2nd ed. St. Louis, Mo.: The Catholic Hospital Association of the United States and Canada, 1955.

--------. *The Formation of Hospital Religious*. [St. Louis Mo.: The Catholic Hospital Association of the United

States and Canada], 1956.

————————. "Surgical Code for Catholic Hospitals (1921)," in Leo Gregory Fink, ed., *Graduate Nurses: Symposium of Ethical Inspiration.* New York: Paulist Press, 1938, pp. 293-295.

"Catholic Nurses in Council." *Month,* 162 (1933), 295-296.

Cattell, Raymond. *A New Morality from Science: Beyondism.* New York: Pergamon, 1972.

Chamberlain, Edith M. *Orientation to Nursing.* New York: McGraw-Hill, 1962.

Chase, Allan. *The Biological Imperatives: Health, Politics, and Human Survival.* Holt, Rinehart, and Winston, 1971; rpt. Baltimore: Penguin, 1973.

————————. *The Legacy of Malthus: The Social Costs of the New Scientific Racism.* New York: Alfred A. Knopf, 1977.

Chesterton, G[ilbert] K[eith]. *Eugenics and Other Evils.* Brussels: Wm. Collins Sons, 1922.

"Church and Medicine." *America,* 79 (1948), 524.

Church [of England] Assembly Board for Social Responsibility. *Abortion: An Ethical Decision.* Westminster: Church Information Office, 1965.

————————. *Decisions about Life and Death: A Problem in Modern Medicine.* Westminster: Church Information Office, 1965.

————————. *On Dying Well: An Anglican Contribution to the Debate on Euthanasia.* London: Church Information Office, 1975.

Churchill, Larry R. "The 'Territory' of Medical Ethics." *Hastings Center Report,* 4, No. 2 (April, 1974), 13.

Clark-Kennedy, Archibald Edmund. *Man, Medicine, and Morality.* London: Faber and Faber, 1969.

Claxton, Ernest Edward, and H. A. C. McKay, eds. *Medicine, Morals, and Man.* London: Blandford, 1969.

Clouser, K. Danner. "Medical Ethics and Related Disciplines," in Robert M. Veatch et al., eds., *The Teaching of Medical Ethics.* Hastings Center, 1973, pp. 38-46.

————————. "Some Things Medical Ethics Is Not." *Journal of the American Medical Association,* 223 (1973), 787-789.

————————, and Arthur Zucker. *Abortion and Euthanasia: An Annotated Bibliography.* Philadelphia: Society for Health and Human Values [1974].

"Code of Medical Ethics? Editorial Comments." *Month,* 162

(1933), 492.

Codex Juris Canonici Pii X Pontificis Maximi jussu digestus,
   Benedicti Papae XV auctoritate promulgatus, praefatione
   . . . ab Emo. Petro Card. Gasparri auctus. [Vatican
   City]: Polyglottis Vaticanis, 1948.

College of Physicians and Surgeons of the Province of Quebec.
   Code of Medical Ethics: Acts Derogatory to the Honor
   and Dignity of the Profession. Montreal, 1971.

Connell, Francis J. "Catholic Moral Principles in Medical
   and Nursing Practice." *Hospital Progress,* 24 (1943),
   287-291.

--------. "Double Effect, Principle of." *New Catholic En-*
   cyclopedia. Vol. 4. 1967.

--------. *Father Connell Answers Moral Questions.* Ed.
   Eugene L. Weitzel. Washington: Catholic Univ. of
   America Press, 1959.

--------. *Morals in Politics and Professions: A Guide for*
   Catholics in Public Life. Westminster, Md.: Newman,
   1946.

--------. *More Answers to Today's Moral Problems.* Ed.
   Eugene J. Weitzel. Washington: Catholic Univ. of
   America Press, 1965.

--------. *Outlines of Moral Theology.* Milwaukee: Bruce,
   1953.

Connery, John R. *Abortion: The Development of the Roman*
   Catholic Perspective. [Chicago]: Loyola Univ. Press,
   1977.

--------. "Notes on Moral Theology."
   Theological Studies, 15 (1954), 594-626.
                       16 (1955), 558-590.
                       17 (1956), 549-583.
                       18 (1957), 560-595.
                       19 (1958), 533-571.
                       20 (1959), 590-629.

Conway, Bertrand L. *The Question Box.* New ed. New York:
   Paulist Press, 1929.

Conway, J[ohn] D[onald]. *Modern Moral Problems.* Notre Dame,
   Ind.: Fides, 1961.

Coppens, Charles. *Moral Princples and Medical Practice: The*
   Basis of Medical Jurisprudence. New York: Benziger
   Brothers, 1897.

--------. *Moral Principles and Medical Practice: The Basis*
   of Medical Jurisprudence. 4th ed. New York: Benziger
   Brothers, 1905.

--------, and Henry S. Spalding. *Moral Principles and Medi-
    cal Practice: The Basis of Medical Jurisprudence.* New
    ed. New York: Benziger Brothers, 1921.

Cox, Ignatius W. "Catholic Principles in Medical Ethics."
    Catholic Mind, 30 (1932), 469-474.

Craisson, D. [Jean-Étienne-Xavier]. *Notiones theologicae
    circa sextum decalogi praeceptum et usum matrimonii,
    artis medicae recenter inventis adaptae, seu de rebus
    veneriis ad usum confessariorum.* New York: Benziger
    Brothers, 1875.

Cronin, Michael. *The Science of Ethics.* 2 vols. 4th ed.
    Dublin: M. H. Gill and Sons, 1939.

Cunningham, Bert Joseph. *The Morality of Organic Transplan-
    tation.* Diss., Catholic Univ. of America Studies in
    Sacred Theology, No. 86. Washington: Catholic Univ. of
    America Press, 1944.

Curran, Charles E. "Absolute Norms and Medical Ethics," in
    Charles E. Curran, ed., *Absolutes in Moral Theology?*
    Washington: Corpus, 1968, pp. 108-153.

--------. "Absolute Norms in Moral Theology," in his *A New
    Look at Christian Morality.* Notre Dame, Ind.: Fides,
    1970, pp. 73-123.

--------. "Afterword: Moral Theology Today," in his *Con-
    temporary Problems in Moral Theology.* Notre Dame, Ind.:
    Fides, 1970, pp. 242-268.

--------. *Catholic Moral Theology in Dialogue.* Notre Dame,
    Ind.: Fides, 1972.

--------. *Christian Morality Today: The Renewal of Moral
    Theology.* Notre Dame, Ind.: Fides, 1966.

--------. *Contemporary Problems in Moral Theology.* Notre
    Dame, Ind.: Fides, 1970.

--------. *Medicine and Morals.* Washington: Corpus, 1970.

--------. "Moral Theology and Genetics: A Dialogue," in his
    Contemporary Problems in Moral Theology. Notre Dame,
    Ind.: Fides, 1970, pp. 189-224.

--------. "Natural Law and Contemporary Moral Theology,"
    in his *Contemporary Problems in Moral Theology.* Notre
    Dame, Ind.: Fides, 1970, pp. 97-158.

--------. "Natural Law and Moral Theology," in Charles E.
    Curran, ed., *Contraception: Authority and Dissent.* New
    York: Herder and Herder, 1969, pp. 151-175.

--------. "Natural Law and the Teaching Authority of the
    Church," in his *Christian Morality Today: The Renewal*

of Moral Theology. Notre Dame, Ind.: Fides, 1966, pp. 79-91.

--------. *A New Look at Christian Morality.* Notre Dame, Ind.: Fides, 1970.

--------. *Ongoing Revision: Studies in Moral Theology.* Notre Dame, Ind.: Fides, 1975.

--------. *Politics, Medicine, and Christian Ethics: A Dialogue with Paul Ramsey.* Philadelphia: Fortress, 1973.

--------. "The Principle of Double Effect," in his *Ongoing Revision: Studies in Moral Theology.* Notre Dame, Ind.: Fides, 1975, pp. 173-209.

--------. "Utilitarianism and Contemporary Moral Theology: Situating the Debates." *Louvain Studies,* 6 (1977), 239-255.

--------, ed. *Absolutes in Moral Theology?* Washington: Corpus, 1968.

--------, ed. *Contraception: Authority and Dissent.* New York: Herder and Herder, 1969.

Cutler, Donald R., ed. *Updating Life and Death: Essays in Ethics and Medicine.* Boston: Beacon, 1968.

Daly, Cahal B. *Morals, Law, and Life.* Chicago: Scepter, 1966.

D'Annibale, Josephus. *Summula theologiae moralis.* 5th ed. 3 vols. Rome: Desclée, Lefebvre, 1908.

Davidson, Maurice, ed. *Medical Ethics: A Guide to Students and Practitioners.* London: Lloyd-Luke, 1957.

Davis, Henry. *Birth Control: The Fallacies of Dr. M. Stopes.* New York: Benziger Brothers, 1928.

--------. "Ectopic Gestation—A Rejoinder." *Linacre Quarterly,* 10 (1942), 60-63.

--------. *Eugenics: Aims and Methods.* London: Burns, Oates, and Washbourne, 1930.

--------. *Moral and Pastoral Theology.* 6th ed. 4 vols. London: Sheed and Ward, 1949.

--------. *Moral and Pastoral Theology: A Summary.* London: Sheed and Ward, 1952.

--------. *State Sterilization of the Unfit.* London: Burns, Oates, and Washbourne, 1931.

Davis, Nathan Smith. *History of Medicine: With the Code of Medical Ethics.* Chicago: Cleveland Press, 1903.

Day, Stacey B[iswas], ed. *Proceedings: Ethics in Medicine in a Changing Society.* Minneapolis: Bell Museum of

Pathobiology, 1973.

Debreyne, P[ierre] J[ean] C[orneille]. *Thérapeutique appliquée ou traitements spéciaux de la plupart des maladies chroniques.* New ed. Brussels: J. B. Tircher, 1845.

————, and A[nge Ernest] Ferrand. *La Théologie morale et les sciences médicales.* 6th ed. Paris: Poussielgue Frères, 1884.

Decker, Barry, and Paul Bonner, eds. *PSRO: Organization for Regional Peer Review.* Cambridge, Mass.: Ballinger, 1973.

Dedek, John F. *Contemporary Medical Ethics.* New York: Sheed and Ward, 1975.

————. *Human Life: Some Moral Issues.* New York: Sheed and Ward, 1972.

————. *Titius and Bertha Ride Again: Contemporary Moral Cases.* New York: Sheed and Ward [1974].

DeGuchteneere, Raoul. *Judgment on Birth Control.* New York: Macmillan, 1931.

D[e] L[etter], P. "The Pope on Medical Questions." *Clergy Monthly,* 20 (1956), 380-386.

Desjardins, Édouard. *Initiation au devoir: Leçons de déontologie médicale.* Montreal: Déom, 1933.

Dietz, Lena Dixon. *Professional Adjustments.* 2 vols. 3rd ed. Philadelphia: F. A. Davis, 1948-1950.

"Doctors in Print." *Newsweek,* 34 (Sept. 5, 1949), 50.

"The Doctors Talk: The Heart, Nutrition, Smoking, Ethics." *Newsweek,* 49 (June 17, 1957), 96-99.

Dolan, Jerome A. "Catholic Writers and Doctors." *Commonweal,* 47 (1948), 592-595.

Dollen, Charles. *Abortion in Context: A Select Bibliography.* Metuchen, N.J.: Scarecrow, 1970.

Donohue, J[ohn] W[aldron]. "Ratio Studiorum." *New Catholic Encyclopedia.* Vol. 12. 1967.

Dubay, Thomas. "The State of Moral Theology: A Critical Appraisal." *Theological Studies,* 35 (1974), 482-506.

Dublanchy, E. "Morale." *Dictionnaire de Théologie Catholique.* Vol. 10. 1928.

Dubos, René [Jules]. *Man Adapting.* New Haven: Yale Univ. Press, 1965.

————. *Man, Medicine, and Environment.* New York: Frederick A. Praeger, 1968.

Dufort, Josaphat-Z[éphirin]. *Application de l'éthique professionnelle.* 3rd ed. Cartierville, Quebec: Hôpital du Sacre-Coéur [1944]: rpt. 1951.

Dunne, George H. "The Blanshard Charges." *Commonweal,* 47 (1948), 536-542.

--------. "Paul Blanshard and the Catholic Church, V: The Church and Medicine." *America,* 81 (1949), 438-440.

Dupré, Louis. *Contraception and Catholics: A New Appraisal.* Baltimore: Helicon, 1964.

Ebling, F[rancis] J[ohn], ed. *Biology and Ethics: Proceedings of a Symposium Held at the Royal Geographical Society, London, on 26 and 27 September, 1968.* New York: Academic Press, 1969.

Edelstein, Ludwig. *The Hippocratic Oath, Text, Translation, and Interpretation.* Baltimore: Johns Hopkins Press, 1943.

Edmunds, Vincent, and C[harles] Gordon Scorer, eds. *Ethical Responsibility in Medicine: A Christian Approach.* Edinburgh: E. and S. Livingstone, 1967.

--------, eds. *Ideals in Medicine: A Christian Approach to Medical Practice.* London: Tyndale, 1958.

--------, eds. *Medical Ethics: A Christian View.* London: Tyndale, 1966.

Egan, W[illiam] J[oseph]. "National Federation of Catholic Physicians' Guilds." *New Catholic Encyclopedia.* Vol. 10. 1967.

Egner, G. (pseud.). *Contraception vs. Tradition: A Catholic Critique.* New York: Herder and Herder, 1967.

Ehrenreich, Barbara and John, eds. *The American Health Empire: Power, Profits, and Politics: A Report from the Health Policy Advisory Center.* New York: Random House, 1970; rpt. Vintage, 1971.

Ehrlich, Paul R., ed. "Ecologists, Ethics, and the Environment." *Bioscience,* 27 (1977), 239-278.

Ellis, John Tracy. *American Catholicism.* 2nd ed. Chicago: Univ. of Chicago Press, 1969.

Engelhardt, H. Tristram, Jr., and Daniel Callahan, eds. *Science, Ethics, and Medicine.* Hastings-on-Hudson, N.Y.: Hastings Center, 1976.

Ennis, Bruce, and Loren Siegel. *The Rights of Mental Patients: The Basic ACLU Guide to a Mental Patient's Rights.* New York: Avon, 1973.

Enos, Darryl D., and Paul Sultan. *The Sociology of Health*

      Care: Social, Economic, and Political Perspectives.
      New York: Praeger, 1977.

Entralgo, P[edro] Lain. *Doctor and Patient.* Trans. Frances
      Partridge. New York: McGraw-Hill, 1969.

E[schbach], A[lphons]. *Disputationes physiologico-theologicae
      de humanae generationis oeconomia, de embryologia sacra,
      de abortu medicali et de embryotomia, de colenda
      castitate.* Paris: Vict. Palmé, 1884.

--------. *Disputationes physiologico-theologicae, tum
      chirurgis tum theologis et canonistis utiles.* 3rd ed.
      3 vols. in 1. Rome: Desclée [c. 1915].

Étienne, Jacques. "Fundamental Moral Theology." Mimeographed
      student notes. [Louvain: American College, 1962-1963].

Etzioni, Amitai. *Genetic Fix.* New York: Macmillan, 1973.

Etziony, M. B. *The Physician's Creed: An Anthology of Medi-
      cal Prayers, Oaths, and Codes of Medical Ethics Written
      and Recited by Medical Practitioners through the Ages.*
      Springfield, Ill.: Thomas, 1973.

Fabrega, Horacio, Jr. *Disease and Social Behavior: An Inter-
      disciplinary Perspective.* Cambridge, Mass.: MIT Press,
      1974.

Fagothey, Austin. *Right and Reason: Ethics in Theory and
      Practice.* 2nd ed. St. Louis, Mo.: C. V. Mosby, 1959.

--------. *Right and Reason: Ethics in Theory and Practice.*
      3rd ed. St. Louis, Mo.: C. V. Mosby, 1963.

--------. *Right and Reason: Ethics in Theory and Practice.*
      4th ed. St. Louis, Mo.: C. V. Mosby, 1967.

Fanfani, Lodovico G[iuseppe]. *Manuale theorico-practicum
      theologiae moralis ad mentem D. Thomae.* 4 vols. Rome:
      Ferrari, 1950-1951.

Farraher, J[oseph] J[ames]. "Moral Theology, History of
      (Contemporary Trends)." *New Catholic Encyclopedia.*
      Vol. 9. 1967.

--------. "Notes on Moral Theology."
      Theological Studies, 16 (1955), 233-269.
                          21 (1960), 581-625.
                          22 (1961), 610-651.
                          24 (1963), 53-105.

Farrell, Allan P., ed. *The Jesuit Ratio Studiorum of 1599.*
      Trans. Allan P. Farrell. Washington: Conference of
      Major Superiors of Jesuits, 1970.

Feldman, David M. *Birth Control in Jewish Law: Marital Rela-
      tions, Contraception, and Abortion as Set Forth in the
      Classic Texts of Jewish Law.* New York: New York Univ.
      Press, 1968.

Ferreres, Juan B[autista]. *Compendium theologiae moralis ad normam codicis canonici*. 13th ed. 2 vols. in 4. Barcelona: Subirana, 1925.

--------. *Death, Real and Apparent in Relation to the Sacraments*. Trans. from the Spanish. St. Louis, Mo.: B. Herder, 1906.

Ficarra, Bernard J[oseph]. *Newer Ethical Problems in Medicine and Surgery*. Westminster, Md.: Newman, 1951.

"Finding a Place for Medical Ethics." *Canadian Medical Association Journal*, 107 (1972), 1159.

Fink, Leo Gregory, ed. *Graduate Nurses: Symposium of Ethical Inspiration*. New York: Paulist Press, 1938.

Finney, Patrick A. *Moral Problems in Hospital Practice: A Practical Handbook*. St. Louis, Mo.: B. Herder, 1922.

--------, and Patrick O'Brien. *Moral Problems in Hospital Practice: A Practical Handbook*. St. Louis, Mo.: B. Herder, 1956.

Finucane, Thomas. "Fundamental Principles of Morality," in Catholic Hospital Association of Canada, *A Workshop on Medico-Moral Problems*. Ottawa: The Catholic Hospital Association of Canada, 1955, pp. 3-20.

Fishlock, David. *Man Modified: An Exploration of the Man-Machine Relationship*. London: Paladin, 1969.

Flanagan, J[ohn Joseph]. "Hospitals, Modern." *New Catholic Encyclopedia*. Vol. 7. 1967.

Fleckenstein, H[einz]. "Pastoralmedizin." *Lexikon für Theologie und Kirche*. Vol. 8. 1963.

Fleetwood, John F., ed. *Transactions of Congress: Sixth International Congress of Catholic Doctors, Dublin, June 30th to July 4th, 1954*. Dublin: Irish and Overseas Publishing Co., 1954.

Fletcher, John [C]. "Who Should Teach Medical Ethics?" in Robert M. Veatch et al., eds., *The Teaching of Medical Ethics*. Hastings Center, 1973, pp. 166-172.

Fletcher, John [Rory]. *Notes for Catholic Nurses*. London: Catholic Truth Society [1912]; 4th impression, 1919.

Fletcher, Joseph [Francis]. *The Ethics of Genetic Control: Ending Reproductive Roulette*. Garden City, N.Y.: Doubleday, 1974.

--------. "Medicine and the Nature of Man," in Robert M. Veatch et al., eds., *The Teaching of Medical Ethics*. Hastings Center, 1973, pp. 47-58.

--------. "Medicine, Morals, and Religion." *Theology Today*,

31 (1974), 39-46.

————. *Morals and Medicine*. Princeton Univ. Press, 1954; rpt. Boston: Beacon, 1960.

Flood, Peter, ed. *The Ethics of Brain Surgery*. Trans. from *Cahiers Laënnec* by Malachy Gerard Carroll. Cork: Mercier, 1955.

————, ed. *Medical Experimentation on Man*. Trans. from *Cahiers Laënnec* by Malachy Gerard Carroll. Cork: Mercier, 1955.

————, ed. *New Problems in Medical Ethics*. Trans. from *Cahiers Laënnec* by Malachy Gerard Carroll. 4 vols. Cork: Mercier, and Westminster, Md.: Newman, 1953-1960.

Ford, John C. "Notes on Moral Theology."
Theological Studies, 1 (1940), 412-443.
2 (1941), 527-556.
3 (1942), 579-607.
4 (1943), 561-600.
5 (1944), 495-538.
6 (1945), 524-546.
15 (1954), 51-102.

Frankel, Charles. "The Nature and Sources of Irrationalism." *Science,* 180 (1973), 927-931.

————. "The Specter of Eugenics." *Commentary,* 57 (March, 1974), 25-33; rpt. in Nancy C. and John M. Ostheimer, eds., *Life or Death—Who Controls?* New York: Springer, 1976, pp. 16-34.

Frazier, Claude A[lbee], ed. *Is It Moral to Modify Man?* Springfield, Ill.: Charles C. Thomas, 1973.

————, ed. *Should Doctors Play God?* Nashville, Tenn.: Broadman, 1971.

Freund, Paul A[braham], ed. *Experimentation with Human Subjects*. New York: Braziller, 1969.

Gabriele de Guarcino (or de Varceno). *Compendium theologiae moralis ex opere morali Scavini, Gury, et Charmes*. 7th ed. 2 vols. Turin: Marietti, 1884.

Gagnier, Léglius A. *Droits et devoirs de la médecine et des médecins canadiens-français*. Montreal: Devoir, 1926.

Garceau, Oliver. "Morals of Medicine." *Annals of the American Academy of Political and Social Science,* 363 (1966), 60-69.

Garesché, Edward F[rancis]. "The Catholic Hospital Association of the United States and Canada." *Month,* 145 (1925), 341-351.

--------. *Ethics and the Art of Conduct for Nurses.*
    Philadelphia: W. B. Saunders, 1929.

--------. *Ethics and the Art of Conduct for Nurses.* 2nd ed.
    Philadelphia: W. B. Saunders, 1944.

Gauvreau, Joseph. *Les Médecins au Canada français: Vademecum
    de l'étudiant en médecine et du jeune médecin.*
    Montreal: G. Ducharme, 1933.

Gaylin, Willard [M.]. "Medical Ethics: The Issues at Stake,"
    in Robert M. Veatch et al., eds., *The Teaching of Medical
    Ethics.* Hastings Center, 1973, pp. 1-13.

--------, Joel S. Meister, and Robert C. Neville, eds. *Oper-
    ating on the Mind: The Psychosurgery Conflict.* New
    York: Basic Books, 1975.

Geijerstam, Gunnar K. af. *An Annotated Bibliography of In-
    duced Abortion.* Ann Arbor, Mich.: Center for Popula-
    tion Planning, Univ. of Michigan, 1969.

Gelfand, Michael. *Philosophy and Ethics of Medicine.* Lon-
    don: E. and S. Livingstone, 1968.

Génicot, Eduard. *Theologiae moralis institutiones.* 3rd. ed.
    2 vols. Louvain: Polleunis and Ceuterick, 1900.

--------, and Jos[eph] Salsmans. *Casus conscientiae pro-
    positi ac soluti.* 8th ed. Brussels: L'Édition
    Universelle, 1947.

--------. *Institutiones theologiae moralis.* 10th ed. 2
    vols. Brussels: Alb. Dewit, 1922.

Ghoos, J. "L'Acte à double effet: Étude de théologie
    positive." *Ephemerides Theologicae Lovanienses,* 27
    (1951), 30-52.

Gilleman, Gérard. *The Primacy of Charity in Moral Theology.*
    Trans. William F. Ryan and André Vachon. Westminster,
    Md.: Newman, 1959.

Gladwin, Mary E[lizabeth]. *Ethics: Talks to Nurses.* Phila-
    delphia: W. B. Saunders, 1930.

Glover, William Kevin. *Artificial Insemination among Human
    Beings: Medical, Legal, and Moral Aspects.* Catholic
    Univ. of America Studies in Sacred Theology, 2nd ser.,
    No. 15. Washington: Catholic Univ. of America Press,
    1948.

Godin, Edgar, and J[ohn] P[eter] E[mmett] O'Hanley. *Hos-
    pital Ethics: A Commentary on the Moral Code of Catho-
    lic Hospitals.* Bathurst, N.B.: Hotel Dieu Hospital,
    1957.

Goldman, Louis. *When Doctors Disagree: Controversies in*

Medicine. London: Hamish Hamilton, 1973.

González, Ireneo. "Positivism, Moral," in Karl Rahner, ed., *Encyclopedia of Theology: The Concise Sacramentum Mundi.* New York: Seabury, 1975, pp. 1257-1258.

Good, Frederick L., and Otis F. Kelly. *Marriage, Morals and Medical Ethics.* New York: P. J. Kenedy and Sons, 1951.

Goodfield, June. "Reflections on the Hippocratic Oaths." *Hastings Center Studies,* 1, No. 2 (1973), 79-92.

Goodrich, Annie Warburton. *The Social and Ethical Significance of Nursing: A Series of Addresses.* New York: Macmillan, 1932.

Gorovitz, Samuel. "Bioethics and Social Responsibility." *Monist,* 60 (1977), 3-15.

--------, et al. *Teaching Medical Ethics: A Report on One Approach.* Cleveland: Case Western Reserve Univ., 1973.

--------, eds. *Moral Problems in Medicine.* Englewood Cliffs, N.J.: Prentice-Hall, 1976.

Gothie, Daniel L. *A Selected Bibliography of Applied Ethics in the Professions, 1950-1970.* Charlottesville, Va.: Univ. Press of Virginia, 1973.

Gousset, [Thomas Marie Joseph]. *Théologie morale à l'usage des curés et des confesseurs* (1866). 16th ed. 2 vols. Paris: Jacques Lecoffre, 1874.

Gove, Walter R., ed. *The Labelling of Deviance: Evaluating a Perspective.* New York: John Wiley and Sons, 1975.

Graduate Nurses' Association of the State of Pennsylvania. "Code of Ethics" (1904). *Annals of the American Academy of Political and Social Sciences,* 101 (1922), 265.

Granfield, David. *The Abortion Decision.* 2nd ed. Garden City, N.Y.: Doubleday, 1969; rpt. Doubleday Image, 1971.

Gray, Bradford H. *Human Subjects in Medical Experimentation: A Sociological Study of the Conduct and Regulation of Clinical Research.* New York: John Wiley and Sons, 1975.

Grisez, Germain G. *Abortion: The Myths, the Realities, and the Arguments.* New York: Corpus, 1970.

--------. *Contraception and the Natural Law.* Milwaukee: Bruce, 1964.

--------, and Russell Shaw. *Beyond the New Morality: The Responsibilities of Freedom.* Notre Dame, Ind.: Univ. of Notre Dame Press, 1974.

Group for the Advancement of Psychiatry. *The Right to Die: Decisions and Decision Makers.* New York: Jason

Aronson, 1973.

Gurley, John E. *The Evolution of Professional Ethics in Dentistry: Report of the Historian.* St. Louis, Mo.: American College of Dentists, 1961.

Gury, Jean Pierre. *Casus conscientiae in praecipuas questiones theologiae moralis* (1866). 6th ed. 2 vols. Lyons: Briday, 1881.

--------. *Compendium theologiae moralis.* 18th ed. 2 vols. Paris: H. Pelaguad, 1869.

--------, and Antonio Ballerini. *Compendium theologiae moralis.* 2nd ed. 2 vols. Rome: Civilitas Catholica, 1869.

Gustafson, James M. "Basic Ethical Issues in the Bio-Medical Fields." *Soundings,* 53 (1970), 151-180.

--------. *The Contributions of Theology to Medical Ethics.* [Milwaukee, Wis.]: Marquette Univ. Theology Department, 1975.

Häring, Bernard. *Christian Renewal in a Changing World: A New Approach to Moral Theology.* New York: Desclee, 1964.

--------. *Ethics of Manipulation: Issues in Medicine, Behavior Control and Genetics.* New York: Seabury, 1975.

--------. *The Law of Christ: Moral Theology for Priests and Laity* (1959). Trans. Edwin G. Kaiser. 3 vols. Westminster, Md.: Newman, 1961-1966.

--------. *Medical Ethics.* Ed. Gabrielle L. Jean. Notre Dame, Ind.: Fides, 1973.

Hagmaier, George, and Robert Gleason. *Counselling the Catholic: Modern Techniques and Emotional Conflicts.* New York: Sheed and Ward, 1959.

Hall, Jacquelyn H., and David D. Swenson. *Psychological and Social Aspects of Human Tissue Transplantation: An Annotated Bibliography.* Chevy Chase, Md.: DHEW, Public Health Service, Health Services and Mental Health Administration, 1968.

Hamilton, Frank Hastings. *Conversations between Drs. Warren and Putnam on the Subject of Medical Ethics, with an Account of the Medical Empiricisms of Europe and America.* New York: Bermingham, 1884.

Hamilton, Michael P., ed. *The New Genetics and the Future of Man.* Grand Rapids, Mich.: William B. Eerdmans, 1972.

Handler, Philip, ed. *Biology and the Future of Man.* New York: Oxford University Press, 1970.

Hardin, Garrett. *Exploring New Ethics for Survival: The Voyage of the Spaceship Beagle*. Viking, 1972; rpt. Baltimore: Penguin, 1973.

Hastings Center. *Bibliography of Society, Ethics and the Life Sciences*. Compiled Sharman Sollitto and Robert M. Veatch. Hastings-on-Hudson, N.Y.: Hastings Center, 1973+.

Hatfield, Charles, ed. *The Scientist and Ethical Decision*. Downers Grove, Ill.: InterVarsity Press, 1973.

H[avard], J[ohn] D[avid] J[ayne]. "Medical Jurisprudence." *New Encyclopaedia Britannica*. Micropaedia, Vol. 11. 1974.

Hayes, Edward J[ames], Paul J[ames] Hayes, and Dorothy Ellen Kelly. *Moral Handbook of Nursing: A Compendium of Principles, Spiritual Aids, and Concise Answers Regarding Catholic Personnel, Patients, and Problems*. New York: Macmillan, 1956.

--------. *Moral Principles of Nursing*. New York: Macmillan, 1964.

Healy, Edwin F[rancis]. *Medical Ethics*. Chicago: Loyola Univ. Press, 1956.

Hendrick, Burton J. "How Should a Doctor Behave?" *World's Work,* 33 (1916), 208-216.

--------. "New Medical Ethics." *McClure,* 42 (Jan., 1914), 117-125.

Higgins, Thomas J. *Man as Man: The Science and Art of Ethics*. Milwaukee: Bruce, 1949.

Hilgers, Thomas W., and Dennis J. Horan, eds. *Abortion and Social Justice*. New York: Sheed and Ward, 1972.

Hilton, Bruce, et al., eds. *Ethical Issues in Human Genetics: Genetic Counseling and the Use of Genetic Knowledge*. New York: Plenum, 1973.

Hoehn, Matthew, ed. *Catholic Authors: Contemporary Biographical Sketches, 1930-1947*. Newark, N.J.: St. Mary's Abbey, 1948.

Hofmann, Rudolf. *Moraltheologische Erkenntnis- und Methodenlehre*. Vol. VII of *Handbuch der Moraltheologie*. Munich: Max Hueber, 1963.

Holden, Constance. "Ethics: Biomedical Advances Confront Public, Politicians, as well as Professionals with New Issues." *Science,* 175 (1972), 40-41.

Holder, Angela Roddey. *Legal Issues in Pediatrics and Adolescent Medicine*. New York: John Wiley and Sons, 1977.

Holton, Gerald. "Scientific Optimism and Societal Concerns."
    Hastings Center Report, 5, No. 6 (Dec., 1975), 39-47.

Hooker, Worthington. *Physician and Patient: Or, A Practical
    View of the Mutual Duties, Relations, and Interests of
    the Medical Profession and the Community.* New York:
    Baker and Scribner, 1849.

Houssiau, Albert. "Penance and the Anointing of the Sick: A
    Course in Sacramental Theology." Mimeographed student
    notes. Louvain: American College, 1965-1966.

Hoyt, Robert G., ed. *The Birth Control Debate.* Kansas City,
    Mo.: National Catholic Reporter, 1968.

[Hrrdesty, Gilbert]. *Medical Ethics: Principles and Cases.*
    Oklahoma City, Okla.: St. Anthony Hospital, n.d. (post
    1960).

Huant, Ernest. *Le Péché contre la chair: Étude des problèmes
    scientifiques et humains de l'intervention de l'homme
    sur l'homme.* Paris: Beauchesne, 1961.

Hughes, Charles M. *A Moral Judgment Concerning the Trans-
    plantation of Organs.* Diss. Angelicum. Rome: Poliglotta
    Vaticana, 1959.

Hughes, Gerard J. "Infallibility in Morals." *Theological
    Studies,* 34 (1973), 415-428.

Hull, Edgar. "Medical Education and Catholic Doctrine."
    Linacre Quarterly, 11 (1943), 31-35.

"The Human Population." *Scientific American,* 231, No. 3
    (Sept., 1974), 31-182.

Illich, Ivan. *Medical Nemesis: The Expropriation of Health.*
    London: Calber and Boxars, 1975.

"Improving Health Care in America." *Current History,* 73, No.
    428 (July/Aug., 1977), 1-38.

Imse, Th[omas] P. "Spiritual Leadership and Organizational
    Leadership: The Dilemma of Being Pope." *Social Compass,*
    16 (1969), 275-280.

Ingle, Dwight. *Who Should Have Children? An Environmental
    and Genetic Approach.* New York: Bobbs-Merrill, 1973.

Institute on Human Values in Medicine. *Reports of the Insti-
    tute Fellows, 1973-74.* Philadelphia: Society for Health
    and Human Values, 1974.

International Council of Nurses. "Code of Ethics as Applied
    to Nursing" (1965), in Cordelia W. Kelly, *Professional
    Dimensions of Nursing.* 2nd ed. New York: Macmillan,
    1968, p. 23.

--------. "International Code of Nursing Ethics" (1953), in

Cordelia W. Kelly, *Professional Dimensions of Nursing*.
New York: Macmillan, 1962, p. 26.

Iorio, Thomaso A[ngelo]. *Theologia moralis*. 3rd ed. 3
vols. Naples: M. d'Auria, 1946-1947.

Jacobs, William. *The Pastor and the Patient: An Informal
Guide to New Directives in Medical Ethics*. New York:
Paulist Press, 1973.

Jakobovits, Immanuel. *Jewish Medical Ethics: A Comparative
and Historical Study of the Jewish Religious Attitude
to Medicine and Its Practice*. [2nd ed.] New York:
Bloch, 1975.

Janssens, Louis. "Conjugal Morality." Mimeographed student
notes. Louvain: American College, 1963-1964.

--------. "De Jure et Justitia: Student Notes for the Course
in Special Moral Theology." Mimeographed student notes.
Louvain: American College, 1964-1965.

--------. "Morale Conjugale et Progestogènes." *Ephemerides
Theologicae Lovanienses,* 39 (1963), 787-826.

--------. "Norms and Priorities in a Love Ethics." *Louvain
Studies,* 6 (1977), 207-238.

--------. "Ontic Evil and Moral Evil." Trans. Peter Ver-
gauwen. *Louvain Studies,* 4 (1972), 115-156.

Johnson, Brian. *The Catholic Nurse*. London: Burns, Oates,
and Washbourne, 1950.

Jone, Heribert. *Moral Theology*. Trans. and adapted from
the 13th German ed. (1949) by Urban Adelman. Westminster, Md.: Newman, 1953.

Jones, Alun, and Walter F. Bodmer. *Our Future Inheritance:
Choice or Chance?* London: Oxford Univ. Press, 1974.

Jones, Harold Wellington. "Medical Jurisprudence." *Encyclopedia Americana*. Canadian Edition. Vol. 18. 1962.

Jones, W[illiam] H[enry] S[amuel]. *Hippocrates and the
Corpus Hippocratum*. London: G. Cumberledge, 1945.

--------. *Philosophy and Medicine in Ancient Greece*. Sup-
plement to the *Bulletin of the History of Medicine,* No.
8. Baltimore: The Johns Hopkins Press, 1946.

Katz, Jay. *Experimentation with Human Beings: The Authority
of the Investigator, Subject, Professions, and State
in the Human Experimentation Process*. New York: Russell Sage Foundation, 1972.

Kelly, Cordelia W. *Dimensions of Professional Nursing*. New
York: Macmillan, 1962.

--------. *Dimensions of Professional Nursing*. 2nd ed. New

York: Macmillan, 1968.

Kelly, David [F.]. "Clyde Kluckhohn's Ethical Theory: Cultural Relativism and Empirical Absolutism." *Ohio Journal of Religious Studies,* 5 (1977), 17-34.

Kelly, Gerald [Andrew]. "Medico-Moral Notes." *Linacre Quarterly,* 20 (1953), 106-117.

--------. "Medico-Moral Notes." *Linacre Quarterly,* 22 (1955), 55-61.

--------. *Medico-Moral Problems.* 5 parts. St. Louis, Mo.: The Catholic Hospital Association of the United States and Canada, 1949-1954.

--------. *Medico-Moral Problems.* 1958 ed. St. Louis, Mo.: The Catholic Hospital Association of the United States and Canada, 1958.

--------. "Notes on Moral Theology."
Theological Studies, 8 (1947), 97-117.
9 (1948), 85-120.
10 (1949), 67-117.
11 (1950), 34-77.
12 (1951), 52-92.
13 (1952), 59-100.
14 (1953), 31-72.
15 (1954), 51-102.
24 (1963), 626-651.

--------. "Review: McFadden, *Medical Ethics for Nurses,*" *Theological Studies,* 7 (1946), 616-618.

--------. "Review of Existing Codes: An Analysis of Their Background, Differences, and Significance." *Hospital Progress,* 37, No. 3 (March, 1956), 53, 80.

--------. "The Teaching of Pope Pius XII on Artificial Insemination." *Linacre Quarterly,* 23 (1956), 5-17.

Kelly, Jerome A. "The Mystery of Suffering." *Linacre Quarterly,* 24 (1957), 27-30.

Kempf, Florence C. *The Person as a Nurse: Professional Adjustments.* 2nd ed. New York: Macmillan, 1957.

Kenny, John P[aulinus]. *Principles of Medical Ethics.* Westminster, Md.: Newman, 1952.

--------. *Principles of Medical Ethics.* 2nd ed. Westminster, Md.: Newman, 1962.

Kenrick, Francis Patrick. *Theologia moralis.* 2 vols. in 1. Mechlin: H. Dessain, 1860-1861.

--------. *Theologiae moralis volumen I* [-III]. 3 vols. Philadelphia: Eugene Cummiskey, 1841-1843.

Klarmann, Andrew [Francis]. *The Crux of Pastoral Medicine:*
    The Perils of Embryonic Man. 4th ed. New York: F.
    Pustet, 1912.

————————. *The Crux of Pastoral Medicine: The Perils of Em-*
    bryonic Man. 5th ed. New York: F. Pustet, 1915.

Kluge, Eike-Henner W. *The Practice of Death.* New Haven:
    Yale Univ. Press, 1975.

Knauer, Peter. "The Hermeneutic Function of the Principle
    of Double Effect." *Natural Law Forum* (now *American*
    Journal of Jurisprudence), 12 (1967), 132-162.

Knowles, John H. [ed.]. "Doing Better and Feeling Worse:
    Health in the United States." *Daedalus,* 106 (Winter,
    1977), 1-278.

Koch, Antony, and Arthur Preuss. *A Handbook of Moral Theol-*
    ogy. 5 vols. St. Louis, Mo.: B. Herder, 1918-1924.

Kohl, Marvin, ed. *Beneficent Euthanasia.* Buffalo, N.Y.:
    Prometheus, 1975.

Konings, A[ntony]. *Theologia moralis novissimi ecclesiae*
    doctoris S. Alphonsi, in compendium redacta, et usui
    venerabilis cleri americana accomodata. 4th ed. 2 vols.
    New York: Benziger Brothers, 1880.

Konold, Donald Enloe. *A History of American Medical Ethics,*
    1847-1912. Madison: State Historical Society of Wis-
    consin for the Department of History, Univ. of Wiscon-
    sin, 1962.

Kothen, Robert. *Directives récentes de l'Église concernant*
    l'exercice de la médecine. Louvain: E. Warny, 1952.

Kramer, Herbert G. *The Indirect Voluntary or Voluntarium in*
    Causa. Diss., Catholic Univ. of America Studies in
    Sacred Theology, No. 42. Washington: Catholic Univ. of
    America Press, 1935.

Krause, Elliot A. *Power and Illness: The Political Sociology*
    of Health and Medical Care. New York: Elsevier, 1977.

Kremer, E[lmer] J., and E[dward] A. Synan, eds. *Death Before*
    Birth: Canada and the Abortion Question. Toronto:
    Griffin House, 1974.

Kunz, Robert M., and Hans Fehr, eds. *The Challenge of Life:*
    Biomedical Progress and Human Values. Roche Anniversary
    Symposium, Basel, 1971. Basel: Binnhaüser, 1972.

Labby, Daniel H., et al. *Life or Death: Ethics and Options.*
    Portland, Oregon: Reed College, and Seattle: Univ. of
    Washington Press, 1968.

Labrecque, Cyrille. *Consultations théologiques.* 2nd ed.
    Quebec: Action Catholique, 1946.

La Croix, Claude. *Theologia moralis . . . R. P. Herman.*
    Busembaum . . . nunc pluribus aucta. 8 vols.
    Cologne: Servatium Noethen, 1707-1714.

————————. *Theologia moralis: Seu eiusdem in H. Busembaum*
    medullam commentaria (1707-1714). Ed. A[ntony]
    Zacharias (1755). New ed., annotated by P. Dion. 4
    vols. Paris: L. Vivès, 1866-1867.

Ladimer, Irving, and Roger W. Newman, eds. *Clinical Investi-*
    gation in Medicine: Legal, Ethical, and Moral Aspects;
    An Anthology and Bibliography. Boston: Law-Medicine
    Research Institute, Boston Univ., 1963.

Lambert, A. "Azpilcueta (Martin de)." *Dictionnaire d'his-*
    toire et de géographie ecclésiastiques. Vol. 5. 1931.

Landis, Leonard Lincoln. *The Physician and the People.* New
    York: American Association of Independent Physicians,
    1924.

Lanza, Antonio. *Theologia moralis.* 2 vols. plus appendix.
    Turin: Marietti, 1949-1953.

————————, and Pietro Palazzini. *General Moral Theology*
    (1952). Trans. W. J. Collins. Vol. I of *Principles of*
    Moral Theology. Boston: St. Paul Editions, 1961.

La Rochelle, S[tanislaus] A., and C[harles T[élesphore] Fink.
    Handbook of Medical Ethics for Nurses, Physicians, and
    Priests. Trans. M. E. Poupore (1941). 2nd ed. West-
    minster, Md.: Newman, 1943.

————————. *Handbook of Medical Ethics for Nurses, Physicians,*
    and Priests. Trans. M. E. Poupore (1941). 8th ed.
    Westminster, Md.: Newman, 1948.

————————. *Précis de morale médicale pour infirmières,*
    médecins et prêtres. Montreal: Beauchemin, 1940.

Lasagna, Louis. *The Doctors' Dilemmas.* New York: Harper
    and Brothers, 1962.

————————. *Life, Death, and the Doctor.* New York: Alfred A.
    Knopf, 1968.

Laska, Eugene M., and Rheta Bank, eds. *Safeguarding Psychi-*
    atric Privacy: Computer Systems and Their Uses. New
    York: John Wiley and Sons, 1975.

Laycock, Thomas. *Religio medicorum: A Critical Essay on*
    Medical Ethics. New York: Coultas, 1855.

Laymann, Paul. *Theologiae moralis in quinque libros partitae*
    . . . tomus primus [-tertius] (c. 1610). *Accedunt*
    quaestiones canonicae . . . additis de apostasia a
    religione Fr. Caroli Tirelli. 2 vols. in 1. Venice:
    Blasius Meldura, 1719.

Leach, Gerald. *The Biocrats: Implications of Medical Pro-
     gress.* Rev. ed. Harmondsworth, Middlesex, England:
     Penguin, 1972.

Leake, Chauncey D., ed. *Percival's Medical Ethics* (1803).
     Baltimore: Williams and Wilkins, 1927.

Leavenworth, May. "A Suggestion for an Interdisciplinary
     Approach to Ethics." *Zygon,* 8 (1973), 135-147.

Lehmkuhl, Augustin. *Casus conscientiae ad usum confessar-
     iorum compositi et soluti.* 3rd ed. 2 vols. Fribourg
     in Germany: Herder, 1907.

--------. *Theologia moralis.* 10th ed. 2 vols. Fribourg
     in Germany: Herder, 1902.

Lennon, Mary Isidore, Sr. *Professional Adjustments.* 2nd
     ed. St. Louis, Mo.: C. V. Mosby, 1950.

Levey, Martin. *Medical Ethics of Medieval Islam, with
     Special Reference to al-Ruhāwī's "Practical Ethics of
     the Physician."* Transactions of the American Philo-
     sophical Society, n.s., 57, pt. 3. Philadelphia:
     American Philosophical Society, 1967.

Levine, Carol. "Ethics, Justice, and International Health."
     Hastings Center Report, 7, No. 2 (April, 1977), 5-7.

Levine, Maurice. *Psychiatry and Ethics.* New York: George
     Braziller, 1972.

"Life, Death, and Medicine." *Scientific American,* 229, No.
     3 (Sept., 1973), 22-175.

Liguori, Alfonso Maria de'. *R. P. Hermanni Busembaum,
     Societatis Jesu, theologia moralis, nunc pluribus
     partibus aucta a R. P. D. Alphonso de Ligorio.* Editio
     post duas Neapolitanas prima Veneta . . . Adcedit etiam
     nunc primum R. P. Francisci Antonii Zachariae . . .
     dissertatio. 3 vols. in 1. Rome: Remondini, 1757.

--------. *Theologia moralis* (1748-1785). Ed. Michael
     Heilig. Editio novissima. 10 vols. in 5. Malines:
     P. J. Hanicq, 1852.

--------. *Theologia moralis* (1748-1785). Editio nova. Ed.
     Léonard Gaudé. 4 vols. Rome: Vaticana, 1905-1912.

Lilly, Linus A. "The Surgical Code." *Hospital Progress,* 13
     (1932), 283-284.

Lindsay, J. A. "Ethics of Medical Practice." *Nineteenth
     Century and After,* 70 (Sept., 1911), 513-523.

Linsenmann, Karl W., ed. *Colloquium on Christian Medical
     Ethics.* 2nd Colloquium, Concordia Senior College, 1964.
     St. Louis, Mo.: Lutheran Academy for Scholarship, 1965.

--------, et al. *Colloquium on Medical Ethics, Concordia
Senior College, 1961.* St. Louis, Mo.: Lutheran Academy
for Scholarship, 1962.

Littlewood, Thomas B. *The Politics of Population Control.*
Notre Dame, Ind.: Univ. of Notre Dame Press, 1977.

Lobo, George V. *Current Problems in Medical Ethics: A Comprehensive Guide to Ethical Problems in Medical Practice.* Allahabad, India: St. Paul Publications, 1974.

Lohkamp, Nicholas. *The Morality of Hysterectomy Operations.*
Diss., Catholic Univ. of America Studies in Sacred The-
ology, 2nd ser., No. 92. Washington: Catholic Univ. of
America Press, 1956.

--------. "Self-Defense." *New Catholic Encyclopedia.* Vol.
13. 1967.

Loranger, Léon. "The Church and Medicine," in Catholic Hos-
pital Association of Canada, *A Workshop on Medico-Moral
Problems.* Ottawa: The Catholic Hospital Association of
Canada, 1955, pp. 41-70.

Lottin, Odon. *Morale fondamentale.* Vol. I in Series II
(Théologie Morale) of *Bibliothèque de Théologie.*
Tournai: Desclée, 1954.

Lugo, Juan de. *Tractatus de justitia et jure* (1642), in
Disputationes scholasticae et morales. Ed. nova. Ed.
J. B. Fournials. Paris: L. Vivès, 1868-1869, V, 437-
VII.

Lunn, Arnold, and Garth Lean. *The New Morality.* London:
Blandford, 1964.

Lupo, Tiburzio. *La pietas materna di fronte all'isterectomia
e operazioni affini.* Turin: Società editrice inter-
nazionale, 1953.

Lynch, John J. "Medico-Moral Notes." *Linacre Quarterly,* 23
(1956), 23-27.

--------. "Notes on Moral Theology."
Theological Studies, 17 (1956), 167-196.
                   18 (1957), 216-248.
                   19 (1958), 165-198.
                   20 (1959), 231-263.
                   21 (1960), 221-249.
                   22 (1961), 228-269.
                   23 (1962), 233-265.
                   24 (1963), 213-249.
                   25 (1964), 232-253.
                   26 (1965), 242-279.

--------. "Pain and Anesthesia: A Papal Allocution."
Linacre Quarterly, 24 (1957), 123-129.

--------. "Religion and Medicine." *Linacre Quarterly,* 24
    (1957), 21-26.

--------. "A Topical Index to Moral Problems of Medicine."
    Linacre Quarterly, 21 (1954), 87-104.

Lyons, Catherine. *Organ Transplants: The Moral Issues.*
    Philadelphia: Westminster, 1970.

Maas, F[erdinand]. "Josephinism." *New Catholic Encyclo-
    pedia.* Vol. 7. 1967.

--------. "Josephinismus." *Lexikon für Theologie und
    Kirche.* Vol. 5. 1960.

Mabe, Alan R., ed. "New Technologies and Strategies for So-
    cial Control: Ethical and Practical Limits." *American
    Behavioral Scientist,* 18 (1975), 595-722.

McAllister, Joseph B[ernard]. *Ethics: With Special Applica-
    tion to the Nursing Profession.* Philadelphia: W. B.
    Saunders, 1947.

--------. *Ethics: With Special Application to the Medical
    and Nursing Professions.* 2nd ed. Philadelphia: W. B.
    Saunders, 1955.

McAuliffe, C[larence Richard]. "Kelly, Gerald Andrew." *New
    Catholic Encyclopedia.* Vol. 8. 1967.

McCarthy, John. *Problems in Theology.* 2 vols. Dublin:
    Browne and Nolan, 1956-1960.

McCarthy, Raphael C. *Safeguarding Mental Health.* New York:
    Bruce, 1937.

McCormick, Richard A. "Genetic Medicine: Notes on the Moral
    Literature." *Theological Studies,* 33 (1972), 531-552.

--------. "Issue Areas for a Medical Ethics Program," in
    Robert M. Veatch et al., eds., *The Teaching of Medical
    Ethics.* Hastings Center, 1973, pp. 103-121.

--------. "The New Medicine and Morality." *Theology Digest,*
    21 (1973), 308-321.

--------. "Notes on Moral Theology."
    Theological Studies, 26 (1965), 596-662.
                        27 (1966), 607-654.
                        28 (1967), 749-800.
                        29 (1968), 679-741.
                        30 (1969), 635-692.
                        32 (1971),   66-122.
                        33 (1972),   68-119.
                        34 (1973),   53-102.
                        35 (1974), 312-359.
                        36 (1975),   77-129.
                        37 (1976),   70-119.

38 (1977), 57-114.
39 (1978), 76-138.

McDonald, James F. "Why Catholic Physicians' Guilds?" *Cath-olic Mind,* 36 (1938), 58-60.

McFadden, Charles J[oseph]. *The Dignity of Life: Moral Values in a Changing Society.* Huntington, Ind.: Our Sunday Visitor, 1976.

--------. *Medical Ethics.* 2nd ed. Philadelphia: F. A. Davis, 1949.

--------. *Medical Ethics.* 3rd ed. Philadelphia: F. A. Davis, 1953.

--------. *Medical Ethics.* 4th ed. Philadelphia: F. A. Davis, 1956.

--------. *Medical Ethics.* 5th ed. Philadelphia: F. A. Davis, 1961.

--------. *Medical Ethics.* 6th ed. Philadelphia: F. A. Davis, 1967.

--------. *Medical Ethics for Nurses.* Philadelphia: F. A. Davis, 1946.

--------. *Reference Manual for Medical Ethics.* Philadelphia: F. A. Davis, 1949.

McGoldrick, Joseph L. "Mr. Blanshard in Medicine." *Homiletic and Pastoral Review,* 48 (1948), 358-364.

McGovern, John P., and Chester R. Burns, eds. *Humanism in Medicine.* Springfield, Ill.: Charles C. Thomas, 1973.

[McHugh, John Ambrose, ed.]. *The Casuist: A Collection of Cases in Moral and Pastoral Theology.* 5 vols. New York: Joseph F. Wagner, 1906-1917.

--------, and Charles J. Callan. *Moral Theology: A Complete Course Based on St. Thomas Aquinas and the Best Modern Authorities* (1929). Ed. Edward P. Farrell. 2 vols. New York: Joseph F. Wagner, 1960.

Mackness, James, ed. and trans. *The Moral Aspects of Medical Life, Consisting of the "Akesios" of Prof. K. F. H. Marx.* London: J. Churchill, 1846.

McManus, James, Sean O'Riordan, and Henry Stratton. "The 'Declaration on Certain Questions concerning Sexual Ethics': A Discussion." *Clergy Review,* 61 (1976), 231-237.

McNeill, John Thomas, and Helene M. Gamer, eds. and trans. *Medieval Handbooks of Penance.* New York: Columbia Univ. Press, 1938.

Maguire, Daniel C. *Death by Choice.* Garden City, N.Y.:

Doubleday, 1974.

--------. "Moral Absolutes and the Magisterium," in Charles
E. Curran, ed., *Absolutes in Moral Theology?* Washington: Corpus, 1968, pp. 57-107.

Mahoney, Edward J. "The Morality of Terminating Life vs.
Allowing to Die." *Louvain Studies,* 6 (1977), 256-272.

Mahoney, E[dward] J. *Questions and Answers.* 2 vols. London: Burns, Oates, and Washbourne, 1946-1949.

Mangan, Joseph T. "An Historical Analysis of the Principle
of Double Effect." *Theological Studies,* 10 (1949), 41-
61.

Mann, Kenneth W[alker]. *Deadline for Survival: A Survey of
Moral Issues in Science and Medicine.* New York: Seabury, 1970.

Mannheim, Karl. "The Problem of a Sociology of Knowledge"
(1925), in Kurt H. Wolff, ed., *From Karl Mannheim.* New
York: Oxford Univ. Press, 1971, pp. 59-115.

Marc, Clement. *Institutiones morales alphonsianae seu . . .
S. Alphonsi . . . doctrina moralis ad usum scholarum
accomodata.* 6th ed. 2 vols. Rome: P. Cuggiani, 1891.

Marshall, John. *Medicine and Morals.* Twentieth Century Encyclopedia of Catholicism, Vol. 129. New York: Hawthorn, 1960.

--------. "Review: McFadden, *Medical Ethics,* 5th ed."
Month, 214 (n.s. 28) (1962), 314-315.

Martin, Étienne. *Précis de déontologie et médecine professionnelle.* Paris: Masson, 1914.

Marty, Martin E., and Dean G. Peerman, eds. *New Theology No.
10: The Ethical and Theological Issues Raised by Recent
Developments in the Life Sciences.* New York: Macmillan,
1973.

Mazzolini, Silvestro da Prierio. *Summae Sylvestrinae, quae
summa summarum merito nuncupatur pars prima* [-secunda]
(c. 1516). Ed. Petro Vendrameno. 2 vols. Venice:
Francisco Zilettus, 1587.

Mead, Margaret. "The Cultural Shaping of the Ethical Situation," in Kenneth Vaux, ed., *Who Shall Live?* Philadelphia: Fortress, 1970, pp. 3-24.

"Medical Ethics." *America,* 90 (1953), 64.

"Medical Ethics." *New Encyclopaedia Britannica.* Micropaedia,
Vol. 6. 1974.

"Medico-Moral Problems." *Theological Studies,* 15 (1954),
600-609.

Medicus (pseud.). *Medical Essays: Compiled from Various
Sources.* "Printed for the Author," 1926.

Mendelsohn, Everett, Judith P. Swazey, and Irene Travis, eds.
Human Aspects of Biomedical Innovation. Cambridge,
Mass.: Harvard Univ. Press, 1971.

Merkelbach, Ben[oît] H[enri]. *Quaestiones de castitate et
luxuria quas in utilitatem cleri proposuit . . . .* 3rd
ed. Vol. I of his *Quaestiones pastorales.* Liége: La
Pensée Catholique, 1929.

————————. *Quaestiones de embryologia et de ministratione
baptismatis quas in utilitatem cleri resolvit . . . .*
2nd ed. Vol. II of his *Quaestiones pastorales.* Liége:
La Pensée Catholique, 1928.

————————. *Quaestiones de embryologia et de sterilisatione
quas in utilitatem cleri resolvit . . . .* Liége: La
Pensée Catholique, 1937.

————————. *Quaestiones de variis peccatis in sacramentali
confessione medendis quas in utilitatem cleri collegit
. . . .* Vol. VI of his *Quaestiones pastorales.* Liége:
La Pensée Catholique, 1935.

————————. *Summa theologiae moralis ad mentem D. Thomae et
ad normam juris novi . . . in usum scholarum.* 3rd ed.
3 vols. Paris: Desclée de Brouwer, 1938.

————————. *Summa theologiae moralis ad mentem D. Thomae et
ad normam juris novi . . . in usum scholarum.* 8th ed.
3 vols. [Paris]: Desclée de Brouwer, [c. 1946].

Mertens, Thomas R., ed. *Human Genetics: Readings on the Implications of Genetic Engineering.* New York: John Wiley
and Sons, 1975.

Mesthene, Emmanuel G. "Technology and Values," in Kenneth
Vaux, ed., *Who Shall Live?* Philadelphia: Fortress,
1970, pp. 24-48.

Michaud-Quantin, Pierre. *Sommes de casuistique et manuels
de confession au moyen âge (XII-XVI siècles).* *Analecta
Mediaevalia Namurcensia,* No. 13. Louvain: Nauwelaerts,
1962.

Michael, A. "Volontaire." *Dictionnaire de Théologie
Catholique.* Vol. 15. 1946.

Milhaven, John Giles. *Toward a New Catholic Morality.* Garden City, N.Y.: Doubleday, 1970.

Miller, George W[illiam]. *Moral and Ethical Implications of
Human Organ Transplants.* Springfield, Ill.: Charles C.
Thomas, 1971.

Miller, Henry, and Anthony Bloom. "Keeping People Alive,"

in *Morals and Medicine*. London: British Broadcasting
Corporation, 1970, pp. 9-28.

Miller, Josef. *Am Krankenbett: Gewissenfragen und Aposto-
latsaufgaben*. 2nd ed. Innsbruck: Feliciani-Rauch,
1958.

Milunsky, Aubrey, and George J. Annas, eds. *Genetics and
the Law*. New York: Plenum, 1976.

Mintz, Morton. *By Prescription Only: A Report on the Roles
of the United States Food and Drug Administration, the
American Medical Association, Pharmaceutical Manufactur-
ers, and Others in Connection with the Irrational and
Massive Use of Prescription Drugs that May Be Worthless,
Injurious, or Even Lethal*. Rev. ed. Boston: Beacon,
1967.

Moll, Albert. *Ärztliche Ethik: Die Pflichten des Arztes in
allen Beziehungen seiner Thätigkeit*. Stuttgart: F.
Ekke, 1902.

Montgomery, D. Wayne, ed. *Healing and Wholeness*. Richmond,
Va.: John Knox Press, 1971.

Moore, Charles B. "This Is Medical Ethics? What Is the Field
and How Should It Be Defined?" *Hastings Center Report*,
4, No. 5 (Nov., 1974), 1-3.

Moore, Edward Roberts. *The Case Against Birth Control*. New
York: Century, 1931.

Moore, Thomas Verner. *Heroic Sanctity and Insanity: An Introduction to the Spiritual Life and Mental Hygiene*.
New York: Grune and Stratton, 1959.

--------. *The Nature and Treatment of Mental Disorders*. 2nd
ed. New York: Grune and Stratton, 1951.

--------. *Personal and Mental Hygiene*. New York: Grune and
Stratton, 1944.

--------. *Principles of Ethics*. Philadelphia: J. B. Lippincott, 1935.

--------. *Principles of Ethics*. 4th ed. Philadelphia: J.
B. Lippincott, 1943.

--------, and Gregory Stevens. *Principles of Ethics*. 5th
ed. Philadelphia: J. B. Lippincott, 1959.

*Morals and Medicine: Discussions from the B.B.C. Third Pro-
gramme*. London: British Broadcasting Corporation, 1970.

"Morals for Surgeons: Question Put to Pope Pius XII." *America*, 90 (1953), 86.

Motley, Wilma E. *Ethics, Jurisprudence, and History for the
Dental Hygienist*. Philadelphia: Lea and Febiger, 1972.

Muldoon, Maureen H. *Abortion: An Annotated Bibliography*
    (1967-1977). New York: Edwin Mellen Press, 1978.

Murphy, F[rancis] X. "Moral Theology, History of (to 700)."
    New Catholic Encyclopedia. Vol. 9. 1967.

Murphy, Richard J. *The Catholic Nurse: Her Spirit and Her*
    Duties. Milwaukee: Bruce, 1923.

National Association of Catholic Chaplains. *The Apostolate*
    to the Sick: A Guide for the Catholic Chaplain in Health
    Care Facilities. St. Louis, Mo.: The Catholic Hospital
    Association, 1967.

--------, ed. *Pastoral Care of the Sick: A Practical Guide*
    for the Catholic Chaplain in Health Care Facilities.
    Washington: United States Catholic Conference, 1974.

National Dental Association. "Code of Ethics." *Annals of*
    the American Academy of Political and Social Sciences,
    101 (1922), 266-267.

Navarro, Vicente. *Medicine under Capitalism*. New York:
    Prodist, 1976.

Nelson, J. Robert. "New Dimension: The Teaching of Bio-
    ethics." *Christian Century,* 89 (1972), 817-819.

Nelson, James B. *Human Medicine: Ethical Perspectives on New*
    Medical Issues. Minneapolis: Augsburg, 1973.

--------. *Rediscovering the Person in Medical Care: Patient,*
    Family, Physician, Nurse, Chaplain, Pastor. Minneapolis:
    Augsburg, 1976.

New York Academy of Medicine Committee on Medicine and the
    Changing Order. *Medicine in the Changing Order*. New
    York: The Commonwealth Fund, 1947.

Neyraguet, D[éod.]. *Compendium t[h]eologiae moralis S.*
    Alphonsi Mariae de Ligorio. 3rd ed. Palermo:
    Pedoniana, 1846.

Niedermeyer, Albert. *Allgemeine Pastoralmedizin*. 2 vols.
    Vienna: Herder, 1955.

--------. *Compendium of Pastoral Hygiene* (1956). Trans.
    Fulgence Buonanno. New York: Joseph F. Wagner, 1963.

--------. *Compendium of Pastoral Medicine* (1953). Trans.
    Fulgence Buonanno. New York: Joseph F. Wagner, 1961.

--------. *Handbuch der speziellen Pastoralmedizin*. 6 vols.
    Vienna: Herder, 1948-1952.

--------. *Wahn, Wissenschaft und Wahrheit: Lebenserinnerungen*
    eines Arztes. Innsbruck: Tyrolia-Verlag, 1956.

Noldin, H[ieronymus]. *Summa theologiae moralis scholarum*
    usui. Innsbruck: Feliciani-Rauch, 1904-1906.

--------, and A[lbert] Schmitt. *Summa theologiae moralis scholarum usui*. 30th, 31st eds. Ed. Godfrey Heinzel. 3 vols. Innsbruck: Feliciani-Rauch, and Westminster, Md.: Newman, 1953-1954.

Noonan, John P. *General and Special Ethics*. Chicago: Loyola Univ. Press, 1947.

Noonan, John T., Jr. "An Almost Absolute Value in History," in John T. Noonan, Jr., ed., *The Morality of Abortion: Legal and Historical Perspectives*. Cambridge: Harvard Univ. Press, 1970.

--------. *The Church and Contraception: The Issues at Stake*. New York: Paulist Press, 1967.

--------. *Contraception: A History of Its Treatment by the Catholic Theologians and Canonists*. Cambridge: Harvard Univ. Press, 1965; rpt. New York: New American Library Mentor, 1967.

--------. "Responding to Persons: Methods of Moral Argument in Debate over Abortion." *Theology Digest*, 21 (1973), 291-307.

--------, ed. *The Morality of Abortion: Legal and Historical Perspectives*. Cambridge: Harvard Univ. Press, 1970.

"Notes on Moral Theology." *Theological Studies*. See the individual authors: Ford, John C.; Kelly, Gerald A.; Connery, John R.; Farraher, Joseph J.; Lynch, John J.; McCormick, Richard A.

Noyes, Edmund. *Ethics and Jurisprudence for Dentists*. Chicago: Tucker-Kenworthy, 1915.

O'Brien, Patrick. *A Handbook for Hospital Chaplains*. St. Louis, Mo.: B. Herder, 1959.

O'Connell, Timothy P. *Morality in Medicine*. Paterson, N.J.: St. Anthony Guild Press, 1949.

--------. *Morality in Medicine*. 3rd ed. Paterson, N.J.: St. Anthony Guild Press, 1959.

O'Connor, J. A. "Sociological Aspects of Medico-Moral Problems." *Dublin Review*, 191 (Oct., 1932), 200-218.

Oden, Thomas C. *Should Treatment Be Terminated? Moral Guidelines for Christian Families and Pastors*. New York: Harper and Row, 1976.

O'Donnell, Thomas J. *Medicine and Christian Morality*. New York: Alba House, 1976.

--------. *Morals in Medicine*. Westminster, Md.: Newman, 1956.

--------. *Morals in Medicine*. 2nd ed. Westminster, Md.:

Newman, 1959.

————————. "Review: McFadden, *Medical Ethics*, 5th ed." *Theological Studies*, 22 (1961), 722.

Ogletree, Thomas W. "Values, Obligations, and Virtues: Approaches to Bio-Medical Ethics." *Journal of Religious
Ethics*, 4 (1976), 105-130.

Ohnysty, James. *Aids to Ethics and Professional Conduct for
Student Radiologic Technologists*. Springfield, Ill.:
Charles C. Thomas, 1964.

Okinczyc, Joseph. *Humanisme et médecine*. Paris: Labergerie
[1936].

Oliver, John Rathbone. *Psychiatry and Mental Health*. New
York: C. Scribner's Sons, 1932.

O'Malley, Austin. *The Ethics of Medical Homicide and Mutilation*. New York: Devin-Adair, 1919.

————————. *The Ethics of Medical Homicide and Mutilation*.
2nd ed. 3rd printing. New York: Devin-Adair, 1922.

————————. "The Works of Dr. James J. Walsh." *America*, 23
(1920), 401-402.

————————, and James J. Walsh. *Essays in Pastoral Medicine*.
New York: Longmans, Green, and Co., 1906.

Ostheimer, Nancy C., and John M. Ostheimer, eds. *Life or
Death—Who Controls?* New York: Springer, 1976.

Ott, Karen J., and Philip W. Ott. "Moral Dilemmas in Biomedicine: An Interdisciplinary Approach." Mimeographed
paper delivered at the American Academy of Religion
Convention, St. Louis, Mo., Oct. 30, 1972.

Page, Irvine H. "The Ethics of Heart Transplantation."
Journal of the American Medical Association, 207 (1969),
109-113.

————————. "Medical Ethics." *Science*, 153 (1966), 371.

Palazzini, P[ietro]. *Casus conscientiae: De praecipuis pro-
fessionibus*. Vol. IV of *Casus conscientiae*. Rome:
Catholic Book Agency, 1961.

Palmieri, Vincenzo Mario. *Medicina legale canonistica*.
Città di Castello: L. Macri, 1946.

Papal Teachings: Matrimony. Selected and arranged by the
monks of Solesmes. Trans. Michael J. Byrnes. Boston:
St. Paul Editions, 1963.

Papal Teachings: The Human Body. Selected and arranged by
the monks of Solesmes. Boston: St. Paul Editions, 1960.

Pappworth, M[aurice] H[enry]. *Human Guinea Pigs: Experimen-

tation on Man. Routledge and Kegan Paul, 1967; rpt. Harmondsworth, Middlesex, England: Penguin, 1969.

Paquin, Jules. "Course in Medical Ethics: Three Conditions Must Be Fulfilled for Course to Be Effective—Part One." *Hospital Progress*, 35, No. 4 (April, 1954), 68-71.

--------. "Course in Medical Ethics: Practical Suggestions for a Course Outline (Part Two)." *Hospital Progress*, 35, No. 5 (May, 1954), 84-88.

--------. *Morale et médecine*. Montreal: Comité des Hôpitaux du Québec, 1955.

Parsons, Sara E. *Nursing Problems and Obligations*. Boston: M. Barrows, 1919.

Pattison, E. Mansell, et al. *The Experience of Dying*. Englewood Cliffs, N.J.: Prentice-Hall, 1977.

Payen, G. *Déontologie médicale d'après le droit naturel: Devoirs d'état et droits de tout médecin*. 2nd ed. T'ou-sé-wè, China: Mission Catholique, 1935.

Pearce, Evelyn C[lare]. *Nurse and Patient: An Ethical Consideration of Human Relations*. Philadelphia: J. B. Lippincott, 1953.

Pellegrino, Edmund D. "Reform and Innovation in Medical Education: The Role of Ethics," in Robert M. Veatch et al., eds, *The Teaching of Medical Ethics*. Hastings Center, 1973, pp. 150-165.

--------. "Toward an Expanded Medical Ethics: The Hippocratic Oath Revisited," in Roger J. Bulger, ed., *Hippocrates Revisited: A Search for Meaning*. New York: Medcom, 1973, pp. 133-147.

Percival, Thomas. *Percival's Medical Ethics* (1803). Ed. Chauncey D. Leake. Baltimore: Williams and Wilkins, 1927.

Perico, Giacomo. *Difendiamo la vita*. Milan: Centro Studi Sociali, 1960.

Pius XII, Pope. *Discorsi ai medici*. Rome: Orizzonte Medico, 1954.

Placzek, S[iegfried]. *Berufsgeheimnis des Arztes*. 2nd ed. Leipzig: Georg Thieme, 1898.

Plater, Charles. "Why a Catholic Medical Guild?" *The Catholic Mind*, 29 (1931), 309-316.

"The Political Economy of Health." *Review of Radical Political Economics*, 9, No. 1 (Spring, 1977), 1-140.

Pompey, Heinrich. *Die Bedeutung der Medizin für die kirchliche Seelsorge im Selbstverständnis der sogenannten*

Pastoralmedizin: Eine bibliographisch-historische
Untersuchung bis zur Mitte des 19. Jahrhunderts.
Fribourg in Germany: Herder, 1968.

"Pope Pius XII and Medicine: List of Discourses on Medical
Topics." *Guild of Catholic Psychiatrists Bulletin,* 8
(Jan., 1961), 27-29.

Portes, Louis. *A la recherche d'une éthique médicale.*
Paris: Masson, Presses Universitaires de France, 1954.

Porzio, Ralph. *The Transplant Age: Reflections on the Legal*
and Moral Aspects of Organ Transplants. New York:
Vantage, 1969.

Post, Alfred C., et al. *An Ethical Symposium: Being a Series*
of Papers Concerning Medical Ethics and Etiquette from
the Liberal Standpoint. New York: C. P. Putnam's Sons,
1883.

Potter, Van Rensselaer. *Bioethics: Bridge to the Future.*
Englewood Cliffs, N.J.: Prentice-Hall, 1971.

Price, Alice L[ouise]. *Professional Adjustments I.* Philadelphia: W. B. Saunders, 1946.

Pringle, Henry F. "Aesculapius in Manhattan." *American*
Mercury, 10 (1927), 364-369.

Pringle, J[ohn] W[illiam] S[utton], ed. *Biology and the Hu-*
man Sciences. Oxford: Clarendon, 1972.

Prosperini, Ferdinando. *L'Ostrica e la sua missione.*
Rome: Editrice Studium, 1954.

Prümmer, Dominic M. *Handbook of Moral Theology* (1923).
Trans. Gerald W. Shelton. Ed. John Gavin Nolan. New
York: P. J. Kenedy and Sons, 1957.

--------. *Manuale theologiae moralis secundum principia S.*
Thomae Aquinatis in usum scholarum. 3 vols. Fribourg
in Germany: Herder, 1915.

Pujiula, Jaime. *De medicina pastorali: Recentiores quaes-*
tiones quaedam exponuntur. 2nd ed. Turin: Marietti,
1953.

"Quality of Death." *Month,* 236 (1975), 35-59.

Ramirez, J[acobus] M. "Moral Theology." *New Catholic Ency-*
clopedia. Vol. 9. 1967.

Ramsey, I[an] T., and Ruth Porter, eds. *Personality and*
Science: An Interdisciplinary Discussion. Edinburgh:
C. Livingstone, 1971.

Ramsey, Paul. *Fabricated Man: The Ethics of Genetic Control.*
New Haven: Yale Univ. Press, 1970.

--------. "The Nature of Medical Ethics," in Robert M.

Veatch et al., eds., *The Teaching of Medical Ethics*. Hastings Center, 1973, pp. 14-28.

--------. *The Patient as Person: Explorations in Medical Ethics*. New Haven: Yale Univ. Press, 1970.

Ransil, Bernard J. *Abortion*. New York: Paulist Press, 1969.

Ratcliffe, John W. "Poverty, Politics, and Fertility: The Anomaly of Kerala." *Hastings Center Report,* 7, No. 1 (Feb., 1977), 34-42.

Ravà Anna. *I trapianti di organi da individuo a individuo nel diritto canonico*. Milan: A. Giuffrè, 1956.

Raymond of Peñafort. *Summa de poenitentia et matrimonio* (1235). Rome: Joannis Tallini, 1603.

Regan, George M. *New Trends in Moral Theology: A Survey of Fundamental Moral Themes*. New York: Newman, 1971.

Reich, Warren T. "Medical Ethics in a Catholic Perspective: Some Present-Day Trends," in National Association of Catholic Chaplains, ed., *Pastoral Care of the Sick: A Practical Guide for the Catholic Chaplain in Health Care Facilities*. Washington: United States Catholic Conference, 1974, pp. 171-184.

--------, et al. "Catholic Hospital Ethics: The Report of the Commission on Ethical and Religious Directives for Catholic Hospitals Commissioned by the Board of Directors of the Catholic Theological Society of America." *Linacre Quarterly,* 39 (1972), 246-268; rpt. in Dedek, *Contemporary Medical Ethics*. New York: Sheed and Ward, 1975, pp. 173-200.

Reiser, Stanley Joel, Arthur J. Dyck, and William J. Curran, eds. *Ethics in Medicine: Historical Perspectives and Contemporary Concerns*. Cambridge, Mass.: MIT Press, 1977.

Restak, Richard M. *Premeditated Man: Bioethics and the Control of Future Human Life*. New York: Penguin, 1973.

[Reynolds, Charles, ed.]. "Editorial." *Journal of Religious Ethics,* 2 (1974), 3-9.

Ricaud, M[aria]-A[nge]. *La Vie est sacrée*. [Bruges: Desclée de Brouwer], 1945.

Rice, Charles E. *Authority and Rebellion: The Case for Orthodoxy in the Catholic Church*. Garden City, N.Y.: Doubleday, 1971.

Rice, Frederick W. "Ethics of Ectopic Pregnancy." *Homiletic and Pastoral Review,* 35 (1935), 1150-1162.

Riese, Walther. *La Pensée morale en médecine: Premiers*

principes d'une éthique médicale. Paris: Presses
Universitaires de France, 1954.

Rivlin, Alice M., and P. Michael Timpane, eds. *Ethical and
Legal Issues of Social Experimentation*. Washington:
The Brookings Institution, 1975.

Robb, Isabel Hampton. *Nursing Ethics: For Hospital and Private Use*. Cleveland: E. C. Koeckert, 1912 (original
printing 1900).

Roberts, Harry. "Medical Ethics." *Fortnightly*, 146 (n.s.
140) (1936), 472-479.

--------. *Medical Modes and Morals: With Chapters on Doctors
and Patients in the Past by Margaret Jackson*. London:
M. Joseph, 1937.

Roberts, Thomas D., et al. *Contraception and Holiness: The
Catholic Predicament*. New York: Herder and Herder,
1964; rpt. London: Collins Fontana, 1965.

Robinson, William J. *Birth Control: The Limitation of Off-
spring by Prevention*. New York: Eugenics Publishing
Co., 1928.

Robison, William F. "The Catholic Code Based on Natural
Law." *Hospital Progress*, 4 (1923), 1-5.

Robitscher, J[onas] D., ed. *Eugenic Sterilization*. Springfield, Ill.: Charles C. Thomas, 1973.

Rock, John. *The Time Has Come: A Catholic Doctor's Proposal
to End the Battle over Birth Control*. New York: Alfred
A. Knopf, 1963; rpt. London: Longmans, 1963.

Romanell, Patrick. "A Philosophic Preface to Morals in
Medicine." *Bulletin of the New York Academy of Medicine*,
50 (1974), 3-27.

Rosenthal, Robert, and Ralph L. Rosnow. *The Volunteer Subject*. New York: John Wiley and Sons, 1975.

Rostand, Jean. *Can Man Be Modified?* (1956). Trans. Jonathan
Griffin. London: Secker and Warburg, 1959.

Ruland, Ludwig, and T[arcisius] A[nthony] Rattler. *Pastoral
Medicine*. St. Louis, Mo.: B. Herder, 1934.

Rumble, Leslie. *Ethical Guide for Nurses*. Kensington,
N.S.W.: Sacred Heart Monastery, 1947.

--------. *Quizzes on Hospital Ethics for Nurses, Doctors,
Priests, and Sisters*. Ed. Charles Mortimer Carty. St.
Paul, Minn.: Radio Replies, 1946.

--------. *Radio Replies in Defense of Religion*. Ed. Charles
Mortimer Carty. 3 vols. St. Paul, Minn.: Cathedral
Press Radio Replies, 1938-1942.

Ryan, Mary Ann (Sister John Gabriel). *Professional Problems: A Text-Book for Nurses.* Philadelphia: W. B. Saunders, 1932.

Sabetti, Aloysius. *Compendium theologiae moralis a Joanne Gury, S.J. primo exaratum et deinde ab Antonio Ballerini . . . auctum nunc vero ad breviorem formam redactum atque ad usum seminariorum hujus regionis accomodatum.* 4th ed. New York: F. Pustet, 1889.

————, and Timothy Barrett. *Compendium theologiae moralis a Joanne Petro Gury, S.J. conscriptum et ab Antonio Ballerini . . . auctum, deinde vero ad breviorem formam exaratum atque ad usum seminariorum hujus regionis accomodatum.* 19th ed. New York: F. Pustet, 1920.

Sagan, Leonard A., and Albert Jonsen. "Medical Ethics and Torture." *New England Journal of Medicine,* 294 (1976), 1427–1430.

St. John-Stevas, Norman. *Law and Morals.* Twentieth Century Encyclopedia of Catholicism, Vol. 128. New York: Hawthorn, 1964.

————. *Life, Death and the Law.* Cleveland: World Publishing Company, 1961. Also published with varying subtitles by the Indiana Univ. Press and in London by Eyre and Spottiswoode, both 1961.

Salmanticensis Collegium. *Cursus theologiae moralis.* 6 vols. in 3. Venice: Nicolaus Pezzana, 1728.

Sanford, Alexander E. *Pastoral Medicine: A Handbook for the Catholic Clergy.* New York: Joseph F. Wagner, 1904.

————. *Pastoral Medicine: A Handbook for the Catholic Clergy.* New ed., rev. and enl. Walter M. Drum. New York: Joseph F. Wagner, 1905.

Sanner, Margaret C. *Trends and Professional Adjustments in Nursing.* Philadelphia: W. B. Saunders, 1962.

Scavini, Pietro. *Theologia moralis universa ad mentem S. Alphonsi M. de Ligorio.* 8th ed. 3 vols. Milan: Ernesto Oliva, 1860.

————. *Theologia moralis universa ad mentem S. Alphonsi M. de Ligorio.* 12th ed. Ed. J. A. Del Vecchio. 4 vols. Milan: Ernesto Oliva, 1874.

Scheff, Thomas J., ed. *Labeling Madness.* Englewood Cliffs, N.J.: Prentice-Hall, 1975.

Scheffel, Carl, and Eleanor McGarvah. *Jurisprudence for Nurses: Legal Knowledge Bearing upon Acts and Relationships Involved in the Practice of Nursing.* 3rd ed. New York: Lakeside, 1945.

Schnackenburg, Rudolf. *The Moral Teaching of the New Testament* (1962). Trans. J. Holland-Smith and W. J. O'Hara. 2nd ed. New York: Herder and Herder, 1967.

Schöllgen, Werner. *Moral Problems Today* (1955). Trans. Edward Quinn. New York: Herder and Herder, 1963.

Schrag, Peter, and Diane Divoky. *The Myth of the Hyperactive Child: And Other Means of Child Control.* New York: Pantheon, 1975.

Schuster, Heinz. "Pastoral Theology." *Encyclopedia of Theology: The Concise Sacramentum Mundi.* Ed. Karl Rahner. New York: Seabury, 1975.

S[chwitalla], A[lphonse] M. "Code of Ethics of Nursing Profession." *Hospital Progress,* 14 (1933), 17.

--------. "Ethics of the Medical Profession." *Hospital Progress,* 19 (1938), 189-195.

Scotti, Angelo Antonio. *Catechismo medico ossio suiluppo delle dottrine cotta che conciliano la religione cotta medicina de piu nuovi capi cresciuto nella presente edizione dal ch. suo autore.* Rome: Facolta, 1836.

Scremin, Luigi. *Dizionario de morale professionale per i medici.* 5th ed. Rome: Editrice Studium, 1954.

Seham, Max. *Blacks and American Medical Care.* Minneapolis: Univ. of Minnesota Press, 1973.

"Selected Issues in Medical Ethics." *Journal of Religious Ethics,* 2 (Spring, 1974), 3-98.

Self, Donnie J. "An Alternative Explication of the Empirical Basis of Medical Ethics." *Ethics in Science and Medicine,* 2 (1975), 151-166.

Shanahan, R[obert John]. "Catholic Hospital Association." *New Catholic Encyclopedia.* Vol. 3. 1967.

Shannon, Thomas A., ed. *Bioethics: Basic Writings on the Key Ethical Questions that Surround the Major, Modern Biological Possibilities and Problems.* New York: Paulist Press, 1976.

Shannon, William H. *The Lively Debate: Response to Humanae Vitae.* New York: Sheed and Ward, 1970.

Shaw, Russell. *Abortion on Trial.* Dayton, Ohio: Pflaum, 1968.

Shea, William R., and John King-Farlow, eds. *Values and the Quality of Life.* New York: Science History Publications, 1976.

Shinners, John Joseph. *The Morality of Medical Experimentation on Living Human Subjects in the Light of Recent*

Papal Pronouncements. Diss., Catholic Univ. of America Studies in Sacred Theology, 2nd ser., No. 106. Washington: Catholic Univ. of America Press, 1958.

Shotter, Edward, ed. *Matters of Life and Death.* London: Darton, Longman and Todd, 1970.

Shryock, Richard Harrison. *The Development of Modern Medicine: An Interpretation of the Social and Scientific Factors Involved.* Philadelphia: Univ. of Pennsylvania Press, 1936.

--------. *Medicine in America: Historical Essays.* Baltimore: The Johns Hopkins Press, 1966.

Sidel, Victor W. "Medical Ethics and Socio-Political Change," in Robert M. Veatch et al., eds., *The Teaching of Medical Ethics.* Hastings Center, 1973, pp. 29-37.

Siegler, Miriam, and Humphrey Osmond. *Models of Madness, Models of Medicine.* New York: Macmillan, 1974.

Sigerist, Henry Ernst. *American Medicine.* Trans. Hildegard Nagel. New York: W. W. Norton, 1934.

Silverman, Milton. "Doctors Who Crack Down on Doctors." *Saturday Evening Post,* 227 (Feb. 12, 1955), 32-33, 82-84.

Singhal, G. D., and Damoda Sharma Gaur. *Surgical Ethics in the Āyurveda.* Varanasi: Chowkhamba Sanskrit Series Office, 1963.

Slater, Thomas. *Cases of Conscience for English-Speaking Countries.* 2 vols. New York: Benziger, 1911-1912.

--------. *A Manual of Moral Theology for English-Speaking Countries.* 4th ed. 2 vols. New York: Benziger Brothers, 1918.

--------. *Questions of Moral Theology.* New York: Benziger, 1915.

Slovenko, Ralph. *Psychotherapy, Confidentiality, and Privileged Communication.* Springfield, Ill.: Charles C. Thomas, 1966.

Smith, Harmon L. *Ethics and the New Medicine.* Nashville: Abingdon, 1970.

Smithies, Frank. "On the Origin and Development of Ethics in Medicine and the Influence of Ethical Formulae upon Medical Practice." *Annals of Clinical Medicine,* 3 (1925), 573-603.

Snoeck, A[ndré]. *Mental Hygiene and Christian Principles.* Ed. Peter Flood. Trans. Malachy Gerard Carroll. Cork: Mercier, 1954.

Sola, Mathilde. *Wissenschaft und Sittlichkeit: Erfahrungen*

und Untersuchungen einer Deutschen Ärztin. Hamburg:
M. Krüger, 1905.

Sorenson, James R. *Social and Psychological Aspects of Applied Human Genetics: A Bibliography.* Washington:
Fogarty International Center, 1973.

Spalding, Eugenia Kennedy. *Professional Nursing: Trends, Responsibilities, and Relationships.* 6th ed. Philadelphia: J. B. Lippincott, 1959.

Spalding, Henry S. *Talks to Nurses: The Ethics of Nursing.*
New York: Benziger Brothers, 1920.

"Special Issue: Professional Ethics and the Human Good."
Soundings, 60 (1977), 1-122.

Sperry, Willard Learoyd. *The Ethical Basis of Medical Practice.* New York: P. B. Hoeber, 1952.

Sprague, James. *Medical Ethics and Cognate Subjects.* Toronto: Charles P. Sparling, 1902.

Springer, Robert H. "Notes on Moral Theology."
Theological Studies, 28 (1967), 308-335.
29 (1968), 277-300.
30 (1969), 249-288.
31 (1970), 476-511.
32 (1971), 465-488.

Starr, Paul. "The Politics of Therapeutic Nihilism."
Hastings Center Report, 6, No. 5 (Oct., 1976), 24-30.

Steinfels, Peter, ed. "The Concept of Health." *Hastings Center Studies,* 1, No. 3 (1973), 1-88.

--------, ed. "The Future of Individualism." *Hastings Center Studies,* 2, No. 3 (Sept., 1974), 1-80.

--------, and Robert M. Veatch, eds. *Death Inside Out.* New
York: Harper and Row, 1974.

Stenger, [Robert] P[ius]. "Raymond of Peñafort, St." *New Catholic Encyclopedia.* Vol. 12. 1967.

"Step Forward in Medical Ethics." *World's Work,* 45 (1923), 352-353.

Strickland, Stephan P. *Politics, Science, and Dread Disease: A Short History of United States Medical Research Policy.*
Cambridge, Mass.: Harvard Univ. Press, 1972.

Stringer, Paul. *Ethics and Judgment in Surgery and Medicine.*
London: Heinemann Medical Books, 1970.

Sullivan, Joseph F. *Special Ethics.* Worcester, Mass.: Holy
Cross College Press, 1929.

Sullivan, Joseph V. *The Morality of Mercy Killing.* Westminster, Md.: Newman, 1950.

Surbled, Georges. *Catholic Moral Teaching in Its Relations to Medicine and Hygiene.* Trans. Hubert J. Eggemann. St. Louis, Mo.: Herder, 1930.

————. *La Morale dans ses rapports avec la médecine et l'hygiène.* 2nd ed. 4 vols. Paris: Victor Retaux, 1892-1898.

Sutherland, Halliday G. *Birth Control: A Statement of Christian Doctrine against the Neo-Malthusians.* New York: P. J. Kenedy and Sons, 1922.

Swyhart, Barbara Ann DeMartino. *Bioethical Decision-Making: Releasing Religion from the Spiritual.* Philadelphia: Fortress, 1975.

Tancredi, Laurence R., ed. *Ethics of Health Care.* Washington: National Academy of Sciences, 1974.

Tanquerey, Adolphe. *Synopsis theologiae moralis et pastoralis ad mentem S. Thomae et S. Alphonsi hodiernis moribus accomodata.* 3 vols. Paris: Desclée, 1936. (The edition numbers of the Tanquerey manual vary by individual volume and are often merely reprints. Specifically the edition numbers of this 1936 edition are 12th, 10th, and 10th respectively for the three volumes.)

Taylor, Carl E. "Ethics for an International Health Profession." *Science,* 153 (1966), 716-720.

Taylor, Gordon Rattray. *The Biological Time Bomb.* New York: New American Library, 1968; rpt. Mentor, 1969.

Tenery, Robert M. "Medical Etiquette." *Journal of the American Medical Association,* 195 (1966), 1137-1138.

"Theologians' Statement," in Daniel Callahan, ed., *The Catholic Case for Contraception.* New York: Macmillan, 1969, pp. 67-70.

Thielicke, Helmut. "Ethics in Modern Medicine," in Kenneth Vaux, ed., *Who Shall Live?* Philadelphia: Fortress, 1970, pp. 145-194.

————. *Wer darf leben? Ethische Probleme der modernen Medizin.* Munich: Goldman, 1970.

Thomas Aquinas. *Summa theologiae* (1266-1273). Ed. Commissio Piana. 5 vols. Ottawa: Commissio Piana, 1953.

————. *Summa theologica* (1266-1273). Trans. by Fathers of the English Dominican Province. 3 vols. New York: Benziger, 1947-1948.

Tiberghien, P[ierre]. *Médecine et morale.* Paris: Desclée, 1952.

Tierney, Brian. "Infallibility in Morals: A Response." *Theological Studies,* 35 (1974), 507-517.

Titus, Harold Hopper. *Ethics for Today*. Boston: American
    Book, 1936.

Torrey, E. Fuller, ed. *Ethical Issues in Medicine: The Role
    of the Physician in Today's Society*. Boston: Little,
    Brown, and Co., 1968.

Treub, Hector, R. van Oppenraay, and Th. M. Vlaming. *The
    Right to Life of the Unborn Child*. Trans. C. Van der
    Donckt. New York: Joseph F. Wagner, 1903.

Trudel, Hervé. *Éléments de morale médicale: À l'usage des
    gardes-malades, praticiens, étudiants en médecine et
    théologie*. 2nd ed. Montreal: Granger Frères, 1928.

————————, and Armand Perrier. *Éléments de morale médicale:
    À l'usage des gardes-malades, praticiens, étudiants en
    médecine et théologie*. 4th ed. [Montreal: Granger
    Frères], 1940.

United States Catholic Conference, Department of Health Af-
    fairs. *Ethical and Religious Directives for Catholic
    Health Facilities*. Washington: United States Catholic
    Conference, 1971.

Valsecchi, Ambrogio. *Controversy: The Birth Control Debate
    1958-1968*. Trans. Dorothy White. Washington: Corpus,
    1968.

Van Der Marck, William H. *Toward a Christian Ethic: A Re-
    newal in Moral Theology*. Trans. Denis J. Barrett.
    Westminster, Md.: Newman, 1967.

Van der Poel, Cornelius. "The Principle of Double Effect,"
    in Charles E. Curran, ed., *Absolutes in Moral Theology?*
    Washington: Corpus, 1968, pp. 186-210.

Vaux, Kenneth. *Biomedical Ethics: Morality for the New Medi-
    cine*. New York: Harper and Row, 1974.

————————, ed. *Who Shall Live? Medicine, Technology, Ethics*.
    Philadelphia: Fortress, 1970.

Veatch, Robert M. *Case Studies in Medical Ethics*. Cambridge:
    Harvard Univ. Press, 1977.

————————. "Codes of Medical Ethics in Medical Education," in
    Robert M. Veatch et al., eds., *The Teaching of Medical
    Ethics*. Hastings Center, 1973, pp. 142-147.

————————. *Death, Dying, and the Biological Revolution*. New
    Haven: Yale Univ. Press, 1976.

————————. "Does Ethics Have an Empirical Basis?" *Hastings
    Center Studies*, 1, No. 1 (1973), 50-65.

————————. "Generalization of Expertise." *Hastings Center
    Studies*, 1, No. 2 (1973), 29-40.

--------. "Medical Ethics: Professional or Universal?" *Harvard Theological Review,* 65 (1972), 531-559.

--------, and Sharmon Sollitto. "Medical Ethics Teaching: Report of a National Medical School Survey." *Journal of the American Medical Association,* 235 (1976), 1030-1033.

--------, Willard Gaylin, and Councilman Morgan, eds. *The Teaching of Medical Ethics.* Proceedings of a Conference Sponsored by the Institute of Society, Ethics, and the Life Sciences and Columbia Univ. College of Physicians and Surgeons, June 1-3, 1972. [Hastings-on-Hudson, N.Y.]: Hastings Center, 1973.

Vereecke, L[ouis Gustav]. "Moral Theology, History of (700 to Vatican Council I)." *New Catholic Encyclopedia.* Vol. 9. 1967.

Vermeersch, Arthur. *Theologiae moralis principia, responsa, consilia.* 4 vols. Bruges: Charles Beyaert, 1922-1924.

V[illada], P[aul]. *Casus conscientiae his praesertim temporibus accomodati, propositi, ac resoluti.* 3 vols. Brussels: Alfred Vromant, 1885-1887.

Visscher, Maurice B. *Ethical Constraints and Imperatives in Medical Research.* Springfield, Ill.: Charles C. Thomas, 1975.

Walbert, David F., and J. Douglas Butler, eds. *Abortion, Society, and the Law.* Cleveland: Press of Case Western Reserve Univ., 1973.

Walker, J[ames] B[ernard]. "Antoninus, St." *New Catholic Encyclopedia.* Vol. 1. 1967.

Walsh, James J. "Dr. Austin O'Malley." *America,* 46 (1932), 550-551.

--------. "Review: Bonnar, *The Catholic Doctor.*" *Commonweal,* 28 (1938), 506.

Walters, LeRoy, ed. *Bibliography of Bioethics.* Detroit: Gale Research Company, 1975+.

Wassmer, Thomas A. *Christian Ethics for Today.* Milwaukee: Bruce, 1969.

Weber, Hans-Ruedi, ed. *Experiments with Man: Report of an Ecumenical Consultation.* World Council of Churches Studies, No. 6. Geneva: World Council of Churches, and New York: Friendship Press, 1969.

Werth, Alvin, and Clement S. Mihanovich. *Papal Pronouncements on Marriage and the Family: From Leo XIII to Pius XII (1878-1954).* Milwaukee: Bruce, 1955.

Wertz, Richard W., ed. *Readings on Ethical and Social Issues in Biomedicine.* Englewood Cliffs, N.J.: Prentice-Hall, 1973.

"What Did the Doctor Say?" *Newsweek,* 26 (Nov. 19, 1945), 109-111.

White, Dale, ed. *Dialogue in Medicine and Theology.* Nashville: Abingdon, 1967.

White, Park J. "Doctor's Ethics." *Hygeia (Today's Health),* 12 (1934), 488-501.

Who Shall Live? Man's Control over Birth and Death. A Report Prepared for the American Friends Service Committee. New York: Hill and Wang, 1970.

Wilder, Alexander. "A Conversation with Alexander Wilder on Medical Freedom." *Arena,* 26 (1901), 631-641.

Williams, Ben Ames. "The Greeks Had a Word for It." *New England Journal of Medicine,* 233 (1945), 427-432.

Williams, Preston, ed. *Ethical Issues in Biology and Medicine: Proceedings of a Symposium on the Identity and Dignity of Man.* Cambridge, Mass.: Schenkman, 1973.

Williams, Robert H., ed. *To Live and To Die: When, Why, and How.* New York: Springer-Verlag, 1973.

Wing, Kenneth R. *The Law and the Public's Health.* St. Louis, Mo.: C. V. Mosby, 1976.

Winslow, Floyd S. "Why Do We Have Medical Ethics?" *Vital Speeches of the Day,* 3 (Dec. 1, 1936), 107-109.

Wogaman, J. Philip, ed. *The Population Crisis and Moral Responsibility.* Washington: Public Affairs Press, 1973.

Wojcichowsky, Stephen. *Ethical-Social-Legal Annotated Bibliography of English Language Studies on Abortion, 1967-1972.* Toronto: Toronto Institute of Public Communications, 1973.

Wolkovich, William L. *Norms of Conduct for Pharmacists.* Clinton, Mass.: Colonial Press, 1962.

Wolstenholme, G. E. W., and Maeve O'Connor, eds. *Ethics in Medical Progress: With Special Reference to Transplantation.* A Ciba Foundation Symposium. London: J. and A. Churchill, 1966.

"Work on Encyclopedia of Medical Ethics Begun." *Christian Century,* 89 (1972), 1003.

Zacchia, Paulo. *Quaestiones medico-legales* (c. 1621). New ed. Ed. Daniel Horst. 3 vols. in 1. Lyons: Anisson and J. Posuel, 1701.

Zalba, Marcellino. *Theologiae moralis summa.* 3 vols. Madrid: Biblioteca de Autores Cristianos, 1952-1954.

Ziegler, J[osef] G[eorg]. "Moraltheologie, Geschichte."
   Lexikon für Theologie und Kirche. Vol. 10. 1962.

Book Reviews

"Bonnar, *The Catholic Doctor.*" *Blackfriars,* 25 (1944), 398.

"_____." *Commonweal,* 27, (1938), 335.

"_____." *Commonweal,* 28 (1938), 506.

"_____." *Irish Ecclesiastical Record,* 51 (1938), 332-333.

"_____." *Month,* 171, No. 884 (Feb., 1938), 176-177.

"_____." *Sign,* 17 (1938), 569-570.

"Bourke, *Some Medical Ethical Problems Solved.*" *America,* 26
   (1922), 452.

"Bouscaren, *Ethics of Ectopic Operations.*" *America,* 50
   (1934), 383.

"_____." *American Ecclesiastical Review,* 90 (1934), 320-
   321.

"_____." *Clergy Review,* 8 (1934), 334-335.

"_____." *Homiletic and Pastoral Review,* 34 (1934), 665-
   666.

"Burke, *Acute Cases in Moral Medicine.*" *America,* 28 (1923),
   500.

"_____." *Catholic World,* 117 (1923), 140-141.

"Coppens, *Moral Principles and Medical Practice: The Basis
   of Medical Jurisprudence.*" *America,* 25 (1921), 406.

"Dufort, *Éthique professionnelle, morale médicale.*" *Relations,* 3 (1943), 336.

"Ficarra, *Newer Ethical Problems in Medicine and Surgery.*"
   Clergy Review, 38 (1953), 126.

"_____." *Dominicana,* 37 (1952), 89.

"_____." *Theological Studies,* 13 (1952), 284-286.

"Fink, *Graduate Nurses: Symposium of Ethical Inspiration.*"
   Sign, 18 (1938), 251.

"Finney, *Moral Problems in Hospital Practice: A Practical
   Handbook.*" *America,* 27 (1922), 596.

"_____." *American Ecclesiastical Review,* 67 (1922), 99.

"_____." *Catholic World,* 115 (1922), 831-832.

"Finney and O'Brien, *Moral Problems in Hospital Practice.*"

Ave Maria, 85 (1957), 23.

"--------." *Homiletic and Pastoral Review*, 57 (1957), 955-958.

"--------." *Social Justice Review*, 50 (1957), 29.

"Flood, ed., *New Problems in Medical Ethics*, Vol. I." *American Ecclesiastical Review*, 131 (1954), 430-431.

"--------." *Clergy Review*, 38 (1953), 632-633.

"--------." *Furrow*, 5 (1954), 58-59.

"--------." *Homiletic and Pastoral Review*, 54 (1953), 276-279.

"--------." *Tablet*, 200 (1953), 38.

"--------." *Theological Studies*, 15 (1954), 159.

"Flood, ed., *New Problems in Medical Ethics*, Vol. II." *Clergy Review*, 40 (1955), 115-116.

"--------." *Homiletic and Pastoral Review*, 55 (1955), 442-444.

"--------." *Irish Ecclesiastical Record*, 83 (1955), 73-74.

"Flood, ed., *New Problems in Medical Ethics*, Vol. III." *America*, 97 (1957), 129-131.

"--------." *Clergy Review*, 42 (1957), 560.

"--------." *Irish Ecclesiastical Record*, 88 (1957), 292.

"Flood, ed., *New Problems in Medical Ethics*, Vol IV." *Theological Studies*, 22 (1961), 141-142.

"Good and Kelly, *Marriage, Morals and Medical Ethics*." *American Ecclesiastical Review*, 128 (1953), 72-76.

"--------." *Blackfriars*, 35 (1953), 247-248.

"--------." *Furrow*, 4 (1953), 357-358.

"--------." *Irish Ecclesiastical Record*, 79 (1953), 78-79.

"--------." *Magnificat*, 89 (1952), 214.

"--------." *Tablet*, 200 (1952), 272.

"--------." *Theological Studies*, 13 (1952), 286-287.

"--------." *Thought*, 27 (1952), 607-608.

"Healy, *Medical Ethics*." *Clergy Review*, 42 (1957), 114-115.

"--------." *Dominicana*, 42 (1957), 53.

"--------." *Irish Ecclesiastical Record*, 87 (1957), 472-474.

"Kelly, *Medico-Moral Problems*," *Clergy Review*, 38 (1953), 126.

"--------." *Clergy Review*, 40 (1955), 298.

"_____." *Irish Ecclesiastical Record,* 77 (1952), 289-290.

"_____." *Irish Ecclesiastical Record,* 85 (1956), 76-77.

"_____." *Theological Studies,* 13 (1952), 287-289.

"Kelly, *Medico-Moral Problems,* 1958 edition." *Theological Studies,* 20 (1959), 145-146.

"Kenny, *Principles of Medical Ethics.*" *Clergy Review,* 39 (1954), 249-250.

"_____." *Dominicana,* 38 (1953), 134.

"_____." *Furrow,* 5 (1954), 58-59.

"_____." *Homiletic and Pastoral Review,* 53 (1953), 853-856.

"_____." *Theological Studies,* 14 (1953), 520-521.

"_____." *Thomist,* 17 (1954), 100-104.

"_____." *Thought,* 28 (1953), 632.

"Kenny, *Principles of Medical Ethics,* 2nd ed." *Blackfriars,* 43 (1962), 443.

"_____." *Theological Studies,* 23 (1962), 515.

"Klarmann, *The Crux of Pastoral Medicine: The Perils of Embryonic Man.*" *Catholic World,* 95 (1912), 258.

"La Rochelle and Fink, *Handbook of Medical Ethics for Nurses, Physicians, and Priests.*" *Revue de l'Université d'Ottawa,* 13 (1943), 261.

"La Rochelle and Fink, *Précis de morale médicale pour infirmières, médecins et prêtres.*" *Revue de l'Université d'Ottawa,* 11 (1941), 127-128.

"McAllister, *Ethics: With Special Application to the Nursing Profession.*" *Sign,* 27, No. 1 (Aug., 1947), 55-56.

"McFadden, *Medical Ethics for Nurses.*" *American Ecclesiastical Review,* 115 (1946), 155-156.

"_____." *Homiletic and Pastoral Review,* 46 (1946), 719.

"_____." *Irish Ecclesiastical Record,* 69 (1947), 170-172.

"_____." *Modern Schoolman,* 24 (1947), 117-119.

"_____." *Sign,* 25 (May, 1946), 56.

"_____." *Theological Studies,* 7 (1946), 616-618.

"McFadden, *Medical Ethics,* 2nd ed." *Ave Maria,* 73 (1951), 154.

"McFadden, *Medical Ethics,* 4th ed." *Irish Ecclesiastical Record,* 88 (1957), 139-140.

"————." *Theological Studies,* 17 (1956), 623.

"McFadden, *Medical Ethics,* 5th ed." *American Ecclesiastical
     Review,* 147 (1962), 70-71.

"————." *Blackfriars,* 43 (1962), 440-443.

"————." *Clergy Review,* 48 (1963), 199-200.

"————." *Furrow,* 14 (1963), 538.

"————." *Month,* 214 (n.s. 28) (1962), 314-315.

"————." *Studies,* 51 (1962), 534.

"————." *Theological Studies,* 22 (1961), 722.

"Marshall, *Medicine and Morals.*" *Downside Review,* 79 (1961),
     272-273.

"Moore, *Principles of Ethics.*" *Catholic World,* 141 (1935),
     382.

"————." *Commonweal,* 22 (1935), 222-223.

"Niedermeyer, *Compendium of Pastoral Medicine.*" *Clergy Re-
     view,* 48 (1963), 200-201.

"————." *Downside Review,* 80 (1962), 191.

"————." *Homiletic and Pastoral Review,* 61 (1961), 1187-
     1190.

"————." *Irish Ecclesiastical Record,* 97 (1962), 128.

"————." *Irish Theological Quarterly,* 29 (1962), 81-82.

"Niedermeyer, *Compendium of Pastoral Hygiene.*" *American
     Ecclesiastical Review,* 151 (1964), 206-207.

"————." *Irish Ecclesiastical Record,* 102 (1964), 412.

"————." *Priest,* 20 (1964), 619-620.

"O'Donnell, *Morals in Medicine.*" *America,* 97 (1957), 129-130.

"————." *Clergy Review,* 42 (1957), 180-181.

"————." *Homiletic and Pastoral Review,* 57 (1957), 958-
     959.

"————." *Priest,* 13 (1957), 221-222.

"O'Donnell, *Morals in Medicine,* 2nd ed." *Downside Review,*
     79 (1961), 271-272.

"O'Malley, *The Ethics of Medical Homicide and Mutilation.*"
     America, 21 (1919), 504.

"————." *Catholic World,* 111 (1920), 690.

"O'Malley and Walsh, *Essays in Pastoral Medicine.*" *American
     Catholic Quarterly,* 31 (1906), 760-763.

"Paquin, *Morale et médecine.*" *American Ecclesiastical Review,*

133 (1955), 214-216.

"————." *Homiletic and Pastoral Review,* 55 (1955), 1062.

"————." *Jurist,* 19 (1959), 270-272.

"————." *Linacre Quarterly,* 22 (1955), 100-102.

"————." *Revue de l'Université d'Ottawa,* 25 (1955), 380-381.

"————." *Theological Studies,* 17 (1956), 120-122.

"Rumble, *Quizzes on Hospital Ethics for Nurses, Doctors, Priests, and Sisters." American Ecclesiastical Review,* 118 (1948), 399.

"St. John-Stevas, *Life, Death and the Law,"* *America,* 105 (1961), 666.

"Spalding, *Talks to Nurses: The Ethics of Nursing."* *America,* 23 (1920), 332-334.

"————." *Catholic World,* 111 (1920), 831-832.

Index of Names[1]

---

[1]See also alphabetical index of works discussed, pp. 456-459, and chronological list of basic works, pp. 7-12. This present index is inclusive of those authors named in previous lists and of other persons mentioned in the text and footnotes. Particularly important passages are in Pica Type.

Analytical Index[1]

---

[1]Does not include passing references to terms indexed. Particularly
important passages are in Pica Type.